"Our Constitution is so simple and practical that it is possible always to meet extraordinary needs by changes in emphasis and arrangement without loss of essential form."
—*Franklin D. Roosevelt*

The U.S. Constitution is the greatest code of law ever written, the culmination of the historic search for individual freedom within a self-governing republic. No other document in history is quite like it. This third revised edition is an important asset in a true understanding of our Constitution. It includes the background story of its creation, character sketches of its signers, and Supreme Court decisions that show changes in its interpretations. An essential section is the full and comprehensive index that contains detailed references and interpretive cross-references to every topic in the Constitution, even to subjects that are implied rather than specifically stated. With this guide the reader can quickly discover what the Constitution says on any given point.

THE LIVING
U.S. CONSTITUTION

HISTORICAL BACKGROUND
LANDMARK SUPREME COURT DECISIONS
WITH INTRODUCTIONS
INDEXED GUIDE
PEN PORTRAITS OF THE SIGNERS

Saul K. Padover

Third Revised Edition by
Jacob W. Landynski
The New School for Social Research

COMPLETELY UPDATED AND ENLARGED

A MERIDIAN BOOK

MERIDIAN
Published by the Penguin Group
Penguin Books USA Inc., 375 Hudson Street,
New York, New York 10014, U.S.A.
Penguin Books Ltd, 27 Wrights Lane,
London W8 5TZ, England
Penguin Books Australia Ltd, Ringwood,
Victoria, Australia
Penguin Books Canada Ltd, 10 Alcorn Avenue,
Toronto, Ontario, Canada M4V 3B2
Penguin Books (N.Z.) Ltd, 182–190 Wairau Road,
Auckland 10, New Zealand

Penguin Books Ltd, Registered Offices:
Harmondsworth, Middlesex, England

Published by Meridian, an imprint of Dutton Signet,
a division of Penguin Books USA Inc.
Previous versions of this book were published in Mentor editions.

First Meridian Printing (Third Revised Edition), May, 1995
5 7 9 10 8 6

 REGISTERED TRADEMARK—MARCA REGISTRADA

LIBRARY OF CONGRESS CATALOGING-IN-PUBLICATION DATA
Padover, Saul Kussiel.
The living U.S. Constitution / Saul K. Padover.—3rd rev. ed. /
by Jacob W. Landynski.
p.   cm.
"Completely updated and enlarged with historical notes."
ISBN 0-452-01147-7
1. United States—Constitutional law.   2. United States—
Constitutional history.   I. Landynski, Jacob W.   II. Title.
III. Title: The living United States Constitution.   IV. Title: The
living US Constitution.
KF4550.U52   1995
342.73'02—dc20
[347.3022]   94-24753
                                                        CIP

Printed in the United States of America
Set in Garamond Condensed and Times Roman
Designed by Julian Hamer

To Miriam
and our children
as always

Acknowledgments

I wish to thank my former graduate research assistant, Mr. Wilbert Quintana, now a student at the Cardozo School of Law, for his extensive and valuable help in the preparation of the manuscript. Professor G. Roger McDonald of John Jay College has once again provided many constructive suggestions, for which I am grateful. Working with Mr. Hugh Rawson of Penguin Books, a thorough professional and perfect gentleman, has been a rewarding experience.

"Our Constitution is so simple and practical that it is possible always to meet extraordinary needs by changes in emphasis and arrangement without loss of essential form."

—Franklin D. Roosevelt

Contents

Foreword

This is a thoroughly revised, up-to-date, and expanded edition of a well-received work on the American Constitution, initially published in 1953. The first chapter contains important background material on the drafting and adoption of the Constitution. The major part of this book focuses on the decisions of the United States Supreme Court, which under our system of government is the final interpreter of the Constitution. Twenty of the cases appear here for the first time. They include decisions on such controversial topics as the legislative veto, stop-and-frisk, ''set asides'' to benefit minorities, and hate speech. I have re-edited the cases and rewritten the case introductions throughout, so as to make this book as informative and concise as possible for teachers and students.

The greater coverage provided by this edition, with selections from all major areas of constitutional law, makes it suitable for use both as a primary text in single-semester courses on the Constitution and as a supplementary text for related courses in political science and the other social sciences.

Saul Padover, my cherished colleague at the New School for Social Research for nearly two decades, asked me to undertake a revision of this book shortly before his death in 1981. My plan for revision met with his complete approval. The march of constitutional law since publication of that revision, in 1983, now necessitates a new edition.

—Jacob W. Landynski
May 1995

Introduction:
The Supreme Court
and the Constitution

Included here are five dozen Supreme Court decisions. They were selected to show the range and complexity of the problems that arise
unavoidably in a federal system based on a written Constitution. Such
a Constitution, containing general propositions stated with brevity, by
its very nature requires interpretation as to meaning, application, and
intent. When legislative or executive acts are challenged by some aggrieved party or person, some institution must adjudicate and decide
what is or is not constitutional. This has been the role of the United
States Supreme Court, notably since the days of Chief Justice John
Marshall, who, in the pioneering decision of *Marbury v. Madison*, asserted: "It is, emphatically, the province and duty of the judicial department, to say what the law is."

The panorama of judicial decisions, ranging from the era of the framers to our own, offers a striking commentary on the soundness of the
original Constitution and the flexibility of its expounders on the Supreme Court. The decisions also show that there is no "last word" in
regard to the Constitution. Times change, new personalities take their
seats on the bench, fresh viewpoints are introduced. In consequence,
Supreme Court opinions, which, by and large, reflect the current of
"sensed or known" ideas of the time, undergo changes in both interpretation and emphasis. On occasion, the Court also reverses itself completely, upsetting previous decisions. A number of such dramatic
reversals are contained in this book.

Each case presented in the following pages elucidates some important aspect of American life—economic, political, social—that called
for interpretation and decision on the part of the highest court in the
land.

Note to the Reader

The conventional categories to which scholars assign constitutional cases are, of course, approximate rather than absolute. Frequently, cases placed in one category by casebook editors can with equal justification be placed in another. This is especially true of cases in which the constitutional issues straddle the categories or in which the significance of the decisions extends beyond the particular issues that were litigated.

For the instructor's convenience I here list the cases that can profitably be read in connection with more than one of the chapters in this book.

In connection with	*Read also*
Ch. II. The Judicial Power	*United States v. Nixon*, p. 119 *Planned Parenthood v. Casey*, p. 251
Ch. III. The Federal System	*Missouri v. Holland*, p. 154
Ch. V. Foreign Affairs and National Security	*Schenck v. United States*, p. 331 *Youngstown Sheet and Tube Co. v. Sawyer*, p. 112 *Dennis v. United States*, p. 333
Ch. VI. The Commerce Power	*West Coast Hotel Co. v. Parrish*, p. 228 *Garcia v. San Antonio Metropolitan Transit Authority*, p. 94

CHAPTER I

The Constitution

The Constitutional Convention

The formation of the Constitution, which British Prime Minister Gladstone once described as "the most wonderful work ever struck off at a given time by the brain and purpose of man," is a story of great historic drama. Its significance transcends the boundaries of the United States, for it offers a lesson and example to peoples throughout the world. The American Constitution has turned out to be perhaps the most successful example in history of a legal instrument that has served both as a safeguard of individual freedom and as a ligament of national unity. Today, generations after it was put into shape, it is still a living document, meeting the needs, as it always has done, of a great, growing, powerful, technologically advanced, self-governing republic.

The Delegates

The gentlemen who met in the State House at Philadelphia in May 1787 to draw up the Constitution represented some of the best talents in America. Fifty-five delegates had been chosen by twelve of the thirteen states, but not all of them attended all the sessions, which continued for nearly four months. In the end only thirty-nine signed the completed document. The aim of the delegates was the construction of a political framework that would both protect property against revolutionary expropriation and secure liberty from a potentially tyrannical government. What they wanted, in other words, was a government that would have power but would not exercise it capriciously or cruelly. How they finally accomplished this is one of the marvels of history.

Among the delegates were men with wide experience in government and business. They were merchants from New England, judges from the middle states, planters from the South. Half of them were lawyers or government officials trained in law. More than two-thirds had served in the Continental Congress. Some were governors. Many were highly educated and were scholars. Half of them were college graduates. The average age was forty-two, the oldest, Benjamin Franklin, being eighty-one, and the youngest, Jonathan Dayton, twenty-seven. Eight of them had signed the Declaration of Independence eleven years before. Their viewpoints ranged all the way from the tough conservatism of Alexander Hamilton, who thought that the best government was an aristocracy, to the warm democracy of James Wilson, who was dedicated to the idea of government by the people. But in spite of the immense diversity of outlook, the delegates shared a common American culture, a common language, and a common respect for law against the whims of personal tyranny. Above all, most of them shared the great eighteenth-century belief in reason and regard for the individual. As reasonable men they could argue vehemently for their particular points of view, and as cultured gentlemen they were bound to come to a working compromise.

WASHINGTON

The fame of some of the delegates was worldwide. Foremost among them, in both reputation and greatness, were the granite-charactered General George Washington and the sage Benjamin Franklin. The sheer presence of General Washington was almost a guarantee of the Convention's success. A silent, big, square-shouldered gentleman with a face molded in chill dignity, Washington had few intimates, but inspired universal respect mixed with awe.

FRANKLIN

Almost opposite in every way was Benjamin Franklin, then eighty-one years old and spry enough to walk to and from the sessions whenever the weather permitted. He was one of the wisest, wittiest, most mellow, humane, and—if the truth be told—most garrulous men of his age, known throughout the civilized world as an inventor, scientist, and philosopher. He was adored by the powerful and humble alike. When he was American minister in Paris, even the haughty Marie Antoinette liked him. He was one of those men who trailed glory and affection. In Paris, when Thomas Jefferson came to succeed him and presented his credentials to the French foreign minister, the latter asked: "It is you who replace Monsieur Franklin?"

Jefferson replied quickly: "No one can replace him, Sir. I am only his successor."

Speaking in support of a proposed one-term limit for the president, Franklin provided the Convention with a delicious sample of his famous wit: "It seems to have been imagined by some that the returning to the mass of the people was degrading the magistrate. This, he thought, was contrary to republican principles. In free governments, the rulers are the servants and the people their superiors and sovereigns. For the former, therefore, to return among the latter was not to degrade, but to promote them. And it would be imposing an unreasonable burden on them to keep them always in a state of servitude and not allow them to become again one of the masters."

Of the other important men at the convention, the men who not only shaped the Constitution of the United States but also the early days of the republic, let us mention only, first, Alexander Hamilton and, second, James Madison.

HAMILTON

Alexander Hamilton is one of the earliest American "success stories." His is a veritable Horatio Alger story with a tragic finish. Foreign-born and of illegitimate birth, he not only married into the American aristocracy, but also occupied high public office. He was one of the most brilliant men in America, a friend of George Washington, and one of the architects of the American republic.

His background helps, perhaps, to explain his personal ambition and drive. Like so many Americans, Hamilton was born abroad (in the British West Indies). He was the son of a Scottish father and a French Huguenot mother. By age eleven he had been orphaned from his mother and abandoned by his father. He was raised by a succession of relatives and friends.

At the ripe age of fifteen he came to New York and attended King's College (now Columbia University). In those days Hamilton was what we would call a "liberal" today. As a political writer he attracted attention with his brilliant polemics against the British crown. When the Revolutionary War broke out, he joined the militia, and a year later General Washington appointed him his aide-de-camp with the rank of lieutenant colonel. He came out of the war a hero and a political conservative. His conservatism—some would call it extreme reaction—was deepened when he married into the bluest of New York's blue-blooded families. Hamilton was twenty-three years old and already a famous man when he married Elizabeth, daughter of General Philip Schuyler. For an immigrant boy this marital alliance was no mean achievement.

He had a powerful mind and he rose to the top rank of the legal profession. In 1787, at the age of thirty, he was already important enough to be one of the delegates to the Constitutional Convention. General Washington was deeply attracted to the swift-minded, brilliant Hamilton, and he made him his secretary of the Treasury in the first American administration. At thirty-two, Alexander Hamilton was to be the youngest member of the cabinet in American history.

Hamilton's later achievements as secretary of the Treasury, though bitterly criticized by the Jeffersonian democrats of the day, must be ranked as epochal. His hard, tough, unsentimental mind gave to the weak young republic the guidance it desperately needed. Hamilton established the national credit, stabilized the currency, encouraged manufactures, and above all he attracted the moneyed and propertied classes to the republic.

Hamilton did this with sharp realism. He reasoned that only the wealthy and well educated—many of whom had only contempt for democracy and entertained doubts as to the efficacy of a republic—could give the young government both prestige and cohesion. To tie them to the unrespected, struggling republic, Hamilton later attracted them with chains of gold. He did this with calculated cynicism, for he had but a low opinion of most of mankind.

Contemporary democrats hated and feared him, for Hamilton was an honest and a blunt man and he did not conceal his opinions. He said that the people were a "great beast." At the convention he declared: "Take mankind in general, they are vicious." Of course, he did not mean the aristocratic mankind; he meant the poor portion of mankind. Here is a characteristic passage from one of his speeches at the Federal Convention:

> Take mankind as they are, and what are they governed by? Their passions. . . . One great error is that we suppose mankind more honest than they are. Our prevailing passions are ambition and interest; and it will ever be the duty of a wise government

to avail itself of those passions, in order to make them subservient to the public good. . . . All communities divide themselves into the few and the many. The first are the rich and well-born, the other the mass of the people. . . . The people are turbulent and changing; they seldom judge or determine right. Give, therefore, to the first class a distinct, permanent share in the government. They will check the unsteadiness of the second, and, as they cannot receive any advantage by a change, they therefore will ever maintain good government. . . . Nothing but a permanent body can check the imprudence of democracy. Their turbulent and uncontrollable disposition requires checks.

Had Hamilton had his way, the United States might have become an aristocratic republic; but fortunately his views did not prevail. Instead he gave the Constitution and later the new republic the benefit of his penetrating mind and brilliant ability. Whatever his shortcomings, he was one of the great men of the American republic, his cold skepticism serving as a balance, especially after the government was set up, against the warm idealism of a Jefferson.

MADISON

James Madison, delegate from Virginia and future president of the United States, was then thirty-six years old and deeply learned in history and politics, both ancient and contemporary. He knew more about American affairs than probably any man present. Though small and frail, he was a powerful and lucid debater. Despite his youth, his greatness was universally acknowledged. A disciple of Jefferson, whose lifelong friend he was to become, Madison was a middle-of-the-road statesman, conservative in economic matters and liberal in civil liberties. He was humane and yet skeptical. Unlike Jefferson, Madison was not given to illusions about human nature, but, on the contrary, considered man a self-interested creature capable of evil, although not necessarily always evil. Since history taught him that humanity was nearly always its own enemy and that governments in the past had usually ended in tyranny, Madison visualized the creation of a new type of government that would not have the power or temptation to tyrannize over the citizens. This required careful and delicate safeguards that would be built into the governmental structure and become an integral part of it.

In one of the profoundest paragraphs on politics that was ever written, Madison thus summarized his basic skeptical views of government in general:

> It may be a reflection on human nature, that such devices should be necessary to control the abuses of government. But what is government itself, but the greatest of all reflections on human nature? If men were angels, no government would be necessary. If angels were to govern men, neither external or internal controls on government would be necessary. In framing a government which is to be administered by men over men, the great difficulty lies in this: you must first enable the government to control the governed; and in the next place oblige it to control itself. A dependence on the people is, no doubt, the primary control on the government; but experience has taught mankind the necessity of auxiliary precautions.
>
> *(Federalist, No. 51)*

This, in a nutshell, may be said to be the underlying philosophy of the American Constitution, for which Madison, more than any other single individual, was mainly responsible. It was Madison who gave the Constitution its basic shape, its essential conservatism, and yet flexibility sufficient to meet the changing needs of future times.

Beginnings

In the middle of May 1787, the delegates began to arrive in Philadelphia. The first act of the Convention was to elect a president. There were many eminent candidates available—Governor Edmund Randolph of Virginia, Justice Oliver Ellsworth of Connecticut, General Thomas Mifflin of Pennsylvania, to mention but a few. But only two, Washington and Franklin, commanded universal approval. Pennsylvania's Robert Morris nominated General Washington. "The nomination," wrote James Madison, "came with particular grace from Pennsylvania, as Doctor Franklin alone could have been thought of as a competitor. The Doctor was himself to have made the nomination of General Washington, but the state of the weather and his health confined him to his house."

Washington was unanimously elected president of the Convention.

He rose and thanked the gentlemen for their confidence and apologized for his inexperience in such matters, but hoped, he said, that he would not make too many mistakes. A committee was then appointed to draw up the rules for the Convention and the delegates adjourned for the weekend.

The Rules

They reassembled on Monday, May 28, and adopted the rules. These were strict and businesslike. One of the rules shows that the Convention had a high regard for its dignity. The rule required that "Every member, rising to speak, shall address the President; and whilst he shall be speaking, none shall pass between them, or hold discourse with another, or read a book, pamphlet or paper, printed or manuscript." The tight-lipped George Washington, who could freeze the boldest with a look, saw to it that this was severely enforced.

Another rule demanded absolute secrecy of the proceedings: "that nothing spoken in the House be printed, or otherwise published or communicated." This was a wise regulation, for the country was in a pitch of excitement, and the wildest kind of gossip—for instance, that the Duke of York was being invited to become king of the United States—was being repeated. The press, too, was irresponsible and factional, given to vitriolic personal attacks and political character assassination. In order, therefore, to safeguard the debates and to guarantee the fullest freedom of speech on the floor, it was essential not to let anything leak out. An iron curtain thus hung over the Convention, and for thirty-two years the secret of what went on inside was kept from the American public. Not until 1819, in the administration of President Monroe, was the first *Journal* of the convention printed.

The fear of Washington's wrath kept the members careful. When an important project was being debated, copies of it were made and distributed to every member. One morning a delegate accidentally dropped his copy; it was picked up by General Mifflin, who handed it over to the president. Washington put it in his pocket and said not a word. He waited until the debates of the day were over and then he stood up and spoke coldly:

"Gentlemen—I am sorry to find that some member of this Body has been so neglectful of the secrets of the Convention as to drop a copy. . . . I must entreat Gentlemen to be more careful, lest our transactions get into the News Papers, and disturb the public repose by premature speculations. I know not whose Paper it is, but there it is''—he threw it on the table—''let him who owns it take it.''

Then he bowed, picked up his hat and, in the words of one of the delegates, ''quitted the room with a dignity so severe that every Person seemed alarmed.'' No member ever dared claim that copy.

Madison's Notes

Most of what we know of what happened in the Convention is due to James Madison. By common consent young Madison became the more or less official recorder of the Convention. He sat out in front, his back to Washington, facing the delegates. ''In this favorable position for hearing all that passed,'' he tells, ''I noted in terms legible and in abbreviations and marks intelligible to myself what was read from the Chair or spoken by the members; and losing not a moment . . . I was enabled to write out my daily notes during the session or within a few finishing days after its close.'' At the same time he participated vigorously in the debates and contributed greatly to the clarification of many issues. Evenings he would check up with the delegates to make sure that his shorthand record was accurate. It was a grueling task which, Madison said years later, almost killed him. His notes, which were not published until after his death, constitute the most complete and priceless record of the Convention.

The Debates

The debates were opened by Governor Edmund Randolph of Virginia. He started out with a vigorous attack on the Articles of Confederation, that makeshift constitution under which the states then maintained an ineffectual union, and then he moved a series of fifteen carefully prepared (mostly by Madison) resolutions. This so-called Virginia Plan became the basis of the whole subsequent discussion. It called for a strong *national* government, consisting of an executive, a judiciary, and a legislature; the latter was to have two branches, one elected by freemen and the other chosen by the state legislatures.

On this the debate got into high gear and rolled along for two weeks. Reduced to its essentials, the great arguments centered on the two issues of democracy and states' rights. Should the people elect their representatives? Could the people be trusted with self-government? If they were permitted to vote, was there not a danger that the numerous poor would outvote the few rich, and, therefore, property would no longer be safe? Was it not better that gentlemen of social position, wealth, and education do the ruling? These were the most hotly debated questions. Then there was the matter of the states. What should be the relation between the big and the little ones? Was it right that tiny Delaware should have as many representatives as populous Virginia, Pennsylvania, or Massachusetts? And were not the little states in danger of being swallowed up by the Big Three?

DEMOCRACY

On the question of democracy a large number of the delegates were outright skeptical and even hostile. The distinguished-looking Randolph started the debate with an attack on the dangers of democracy and the need to curb the people. Massachusetts's rich Elbridge Gerry (from whom we get the word *gerrymander*) remarked: "The evils we experience flow from the excess of democracy." His colleague Rufus King agreed with him.

Pennsylvania's wealthy and brilliant Gouverneur Morris said: "The people never act from reason alone," but are the "dupes of those who have more knowledge."

New York's Alexander Hamilton spoke contemptuously of the "imprudence of democracy," because "the people seldom judge or determine right."

Democracy had few champions. Old George Mason, aristocratic Virginia liberal (who used to refer to George Washington in the old days as "that damned young surveyor"), observed philosophically that the upper classes had always been selfish and indifferent to human needs, and he warned against going to extremes. "We ought to attend," he said, "to the rights of every class of people."

Scottish-born James Wilson, a signer of the Declaration of Independence and an eminent jurist, argued strenuously for a broadening of the franchise and insisted that at least one branch of the legislature be elected by the people. "No government," he reminded the delegates, "could long subsist without the confidence of the people."

James Madison talked in the same way. "The great fabric to be raised," he said, "would be more stable and durable if it should rest on the solid foundation of the people themselves."

Finally there was Benjamin Franklin, who was not afraid of the people, who believed in full democracy, in giving everybody the right to vote and elect the government. "It is of great consequence," he said, "that we should not depress the virtue and public spirit of our common people; of which they displayed a great deal during the war, and which contributed principally to the favorable issue of it." This was a diplomatic way of reminding the assembled gentlemen that if the common people were good enough to fight in the Revolution, which they won, they were also good enough to govern themselves.

POSITION OF THE STATES

The bitterest arguments, which led to weeks of deadlock, concerned the position of the individual states within any federal framework. Big states like Virginia, Pennsylvania, and Massachusetts naturally favored representation in Congress according to population; the little states were terrified that this would swamp them. William Paterson of New Jersey proposed a plan whereby each state, regardless of size, would have the same representation in the national legislature. This was, of course, unfair and undemocratic, but Paterson, speaking for the small states, ridiculed the whole idea of numbers.

"What, pray," he cried angrily, "is representation founded on numbers? If State sovereignty is to be kept up, shall I submit the welfare of New Jersey with five votes in a council where Virginia has sixteen?" This, he said, would lead to autocracy. "Neither my State nor myself will ever submit to despotism or to tyranny."

THE GREAT COMPROMISE

After weeks of wrangling which, in the Philadelphia summer heat, produced ragged tempers, Connecticut brought in the Great Compromise. According to this, the national legislature would consist of two branches—a Senate in which every state, regardless of size, would have an equal vote, and a House of Representatives, in which representation would be based on the numbers of the free population plus three-fifths of the slaves. This was actually a double compromise, for the House was to be more or less democratically elected, and the Senate, appointed by the state legislatures, was to serve as a check on democratically inspired legislation.

THE SENATE

The Senate idea was a victory for both the small states and the conservative interests. When Jefferson returned from France he had a visit with George Washington and asked him critically why he had favored the Senate in the Convention. "Why," countered General Washington, "did you pour that coffee into your saucer?"

"To cool it," said Jefferson.

"Even so," replied Washington, "we pour legislation in the senatorial saucer to cool it."

The Senate, in other words, was to serve as the balance wheel in the governmental mechanism. Its members enjoying a six-year term of office and not being subject to popular election, it was designed to be the stabilizing force in the new government. The makers of the Constitution, it is clear, took no undue chances. They were cautious about indulging in too much democracy, fearing that the common people, who were then mostly without education, and even illiterate, would not have sufficient wisdom and knowledge to govern themselves intelligently. Nevertheless, in order to maintain a balance between conservatism and liberalism, the House of Representatives was made subject to popular and direct election by the people.

Franklin's Concluding Speech

After the fundamental problems were finally settled, a committee "on stile," headed by Gouverneur Morris, drew up the completed document of the Constitution. On September 17, after sixteen weeks of continuous work, the Convention met for the last time. The Constitution lay on the table for signature. There were several minutes of silence. Then Benjamin Franklin stood up, holding a paper, but his voice was too weak, and he handed it to James Wilson to read for him. Franklin's words best summarized the mood of that historic moment:

Mr. President, I confess that there are several parts of this Constitution which I do not at present approve, but I am not sure I shall never approve them. For, having lived long, I have experienced many instances of being obliged, by better information or fuller consideration, to change opinions, even on important subjects, which I once thought right, but found to be otherwise. It is therefore that, the older I grow, the more apt I am to doubt my own judgment, and to pay more respect to the judgment of others. . . .

I agree to this Constitution, with all its faults, if they are such; because I think a general government necessary for us, and there is no form of government, but what may be a blessing to the people if well administered; and believe further, that this is likely to be well administered for a course of years, and can only end in despotism, as other forms have done before it, when the people shall become so corrupted as to need despotic government, being incapable of any other. I doubt, too, whether any other convention we can obtain may be able to make a better constitution. For, when you assemble a number of men to have the advantage of their joint wisdom, you inevitably assemble with those men all their prejudices, their passions, their errors of opinion, their local interests, and their selfish views. From such an assembly can a perfect production be expected? It therefore astonishes me, sir, to find this system approaching so near to perfection as it does; and I think it will astonish our enemies, who are waiting with confidence to hear that our councils are confounded, like those of the builders of Babel, and that our States are on the point of separation, only to meet hereafter for the purpose of cutting one another's throats. Thus I consent, sir, to this Constitution, because I expect no better, and because I am not sure that it is not the best. The opinions I have had of its errors I sacrifice to the public good. I have never whispered a syllable of them abroad. Within these walls they were born, and here they shall die. If every one of us, in returning to our constituents, were to report the objections he has had to it, and endeavor to gain partisans in support of them, we might prevent its being generally received, and thereby lose all the salutary effects and great advantages resulting naturally in our favor among foreign nations, as well as among ourselves, from our real or apparent unanimity. Much of the strength and efficiency of any government, in procuring and securing happiness to the people, depends on opinion—on the general opinion of the goodness of the government, as well as of the wisdom and integrity of its governors. I hope, therefore, that for our own sakes, as a part of the people, and for the sake of posterity, we shall act heartily and unanimously in recommending this Constitution (if approved by Congress and confirmed by the conventions) wherever our influence may extend, and turn our future thoughts and endeavors to the means of having it well administered. . . .

On the whole, sir, I cannot help expressing a wish that every member of the Convention, who may still have objections to it, would with me, on this occasion, doubt a little of his own infallibility, and, to make manifest our unanimity, put his name to this instrument.

While the members were signing, Franklin, looking at the president's chair, on the back of which a sun was painted, said: "I have, often and often, in the course of this session, and the vicissitudes of my hopes and fears as to its issue, looked at that behind the president, without being able to tell whether it was rising or setting; but now, at length, I have the happiness to know that it is a rising, and not a setting sun."

The Ratification Debates

Class Divisions

As soon as the Constitution was submitted to the states for ratification, there broke out an intense and often bitter conflict over its adoption. Article VII of the Constitution provided that nine out of the thirteen states would be needed to ratify it. For a while it looked as if this could not be achieved. A considerable portion of public opinion—especially in the big and populous states like New York and Virginia—seemed to be against the Constitution. Both the defenders and opponents of the Constitution girded for a tough fight.

The struggle produced at least two first-rate publications in the field of political literature. One, defending the Constitution, was *The Federalist*, a series of eighty-five essays mostly written by Madison and Hamilton. The other, criticizing the Constitution as being undemocratic, was Richard Henry Lee's *Letters from the Federal Farmer to the Republican.*

Influenced by the findings of the historian Charles Beard, scholars until recently believed that the battle was drawn mainly across class lines, with propertied and educated people as a rule favoring the Constitution, and the poor and nonprivileged usually opposing it. Current research, however, indicates that the cleavage cut through class lines. One thing is certain: some of the most formidable opposition came from those who objected that the Constitution contained no bill of rights for the protection of individual liberties.

Arguments of Those Who Favored the Constitution

The most outspoken and searching opinions about the Constitution were expressed by members—often ordinary farmers—of the state ratification conventions. This was especially true of the conventions of Massachusetts, New York, and Virginia. Other opinions were stated in private letters by leading individuals. The Constitution's defenders generally followed the line (1) that it was the best that could be had in an imperfect world, (2) that if it had undesirable features, there were means of amending them, and (3) that, in the last analysis, it did provide for a government by the people.

Some of America's ablest men defended the Constitution.

The following are a few samples of letters and speeches of the Constitution's supporters:

George Washington
Letter to Colonel David Humphreys, October 10, 1787

The Constitution that is submitted [to the states for ratification], is not free from imperfections, but there are as few radical defects in it as could well be expected, considering the heterogeneous mass of which the Convention was composed and the diversity of interests that are to be attended to. As a Constitutional door is opened for future amendments and alterations, I think it would be wise in the People to accept what is offered to them and I wish it may be by as great a majority of them as it was by that of the Convention.

George Washington
Letter to Bushrod Washington, November 10, 1787

The warmest friends and the best supporters the Constitution has, do not contend that it is free from imperfections; but they found them unavoidable, and are sensible, if evil is likely to arise therefrom, the remedy must come hereafter; for in the present moment it is not to be obtained; and, as there is a constitutional door open for it, I think the people (for it is with them to judge), can, as they will have the advantage of experience on their side, decide with as much propriety on the alterations and amendments which are necessary, as ourselves. I do not think we are more inspired, have more wisdom, or possess more virtue, than those who will come after us.

The power under the Constitution will always be in the people. It is intrusted for certain defined purposes, and for a certain limited period, to representatives of their own choosing; and, whenever it is executed contrary to their interest, or not agreeable to their wishes, their servants can and undoubtedly will be recalled.

Dr. Benjamin Rush
Letter to John Coakley Lettsom, September 28, 1787

Our new federal government is very acceptable to a great majority of our citizens and will certainly be adopted immediately by *nine* and in the course of a year or 18 months by *all* the States. When this shall happen, *then* to be a citizen of the United States *with all its consequences* will be to be a citizen of the freest, purest, and happiest government upon the face of the earth. It contains all the theoretical and practical advantages of the British Constitution without any of its defects or corruptions. While the nations of Europe have waded into order through seas of *blood*, you see we have traveled peaceably into order only through seas of *blunders*.

Dr. Benjamin Rush
Letter to David Ramsay, March or April 1788

The objections which have been urged against the federal Constitution, from its wanting a bill of rights, have been reasoned and ridiculed out of credit in every state that has adopted it. There can be only two securities for liberty in any government, viz., representation and checks. By the first the rights of the people, and by the second the rights of representation, are effectually secured. Every part of a free constitution hangs upon these two points; and these form the two capital features of the proposed Constitution of the United States. Without them, a volume of rights would avail nothing; and with them, a declaration of rights is absurd and unnecessary; for the people, where their liberties are committed to an equal representation and to a compound legislature such as we observe in the new government, will always be the sovereigns of their rulers and hold all their rights in their own hands. To hold them at the mercy of their servants is disgraceful to the dignity of freemen. Men who call for a bill of rights have not recovered from the habits they acquired under the monarchical government of Great Britain.

I have the same opinion with the Antifederalists of the danger of trusting arbitrary power to any single body of men, but no such power will be committed to our new rulers. Neither the House of Representatives, the Senate, or the President can perform a single legislative act by themselves. An hundred principles in man will lead them to watch, to check, and to oppose each other should an attempt be made by either of them upon the liberties of the people. If we may judge of their conduct by what we have so often observed in all the state governments, the members of the federal legislature will much oftener injure their constituents by voting agreeably to their inclinations than against them. . . .

Is not history as full of the vices of the people as it is of the crimes of the kings? What is the present moral character of the citizens of the United States? I need not describe it. It proves too plainly that the people are as much disposed to vice as their rulers, and that nothing but a vigorous and efficient government can prevent their degenerating into savages or devouring each other like beasts of prey.

A simple democracy has been very aptly compared by Mr. Ames of Massachusetts to a volcano that contained within its bowels the fiery materials of its own destruction. A citizen of one of the cantons of Switzerland, in the year 1776, refused in my presence to drink ''the commonwealth of America'' as a toast, and gave as a reason for it ''that a simple democracy was the devil's own government.'' The experience of the American states under the present confederation has in too many instances justified these two accounts of a simple popular government. . . .

To look up to a government that establishes justice, insures order, cherishes virtue, secures property, and protects from every species of violence, affords a pleasure that can only be exceeded by looking up, in all circumstances, to an overruling providence. Such a pleasure I hope is before us and our posterity under the influence of the new government. . . .

Think, then, my friend, of the expansion and dignity the American mind will acquire by having its powers transferred from the contracted objects of a state to the more unbounded objects of a national government!—A citizen and a legislator of the free and united states of America will be one of the first characters in the world.

I would not have you suppose, after what I have written, that I believe the new government to be without faults. . . . But who ever saw anything perfect come from the hands of man? It realizes notwithstanding, in a great degree, every wish I ever entertained in every state of the Revolution for the happiness of my country.

Mr. Smith, in Massachusetts Constitutional Convention,
January–February 1788

I am a plain man, and get my living by the plough. I am not used to speak in public, but I beg your leave to say a few words to my brother ploughjoggers in this house. . . .

I formed my own opinion, and was pleased with this Constitution. . . . I never had any post, nor do I want one. But I don't think the worse of the Constitution because lawyers, and men of learning, and moneyed men, are fond of it. I don't suspect they want to get into Congress and abuse their power. I am not of such a jealous make. They that are honest men themselves are not apt to suspect other people.

Zachariah Johnson, in Virginia Constitutional Convention,
June 1788

It is my lot to be among the poor people. The most that I can claim or flatter myself with, is to be of the middle rank. . . . But I shall give my opinion unbiased and uninfluenced, without erudition or eloquence

. . . ; and in so doing I will satisfy my conscience. If this Constitution be bad, it will bear equally as hard on me as on any other member of the society. It will bear hard on my children. . . . Having their felicity and happiness at heart, the vote I shall give in its favor can only be imputed to a conviction of its utility and propriety. When I look for responsibility, I full find it in that paper [Constitution]. When the members of the government depend on ourselves for their appointment, and will bear an equal share of the burdens imposed on the people . . . , I conceive there can be no danger.

Arguments Against the Constitution

Those who opposed the Constitution, known as the Anti-federalists, had some able spokesmen on their side, too. Perhaps the most eloquent opponent was Patrick Henry in Virginia. The opposition argued (1) that the Constitution was undemocratic, (2) that it threatened the people's liberties by providing for a too-strong central government, and (3) that it was an instrument of the rich for the oppression of the poor.

The following extracts, which have a special flavor, are from speeches against the adoption of the Constitution:

Patrick Henry, in Virginia Constitutional Convention, June 1788

I have the highest veneration for those gentlemen [who attended the Philadelphia Constitutional Convention]; but, sir, give me leave to demand, What right they had to say, *We, the people?* . . . Who authorized them to speak the language of, *We, the people*, instead of *We, the States?* . . . The people gave them no power to use their name. . . . I wish to hear the real, actual, existing danger, which should lead us to take those steps, so dangerous in my conception. . . . The federal Convention ought to have amended the old system; for this purpose they were solely delegated. . . .

The principles of this system [the Constitution] are extremely pernicious, impolitic, and dangerous. . . . It is not a democracy, wherein the people retain all their rights securely. . . . The rights of conscience, trial by jury, liberty of the press, all your immunities and franchises, all pretensions to human rights and privileges, are rendered insecure, if not lost, by this change [of government]. . . . Is this tame relinquishment of rights worthy of freemen? Is it worthy of that manly fortitude that ought to characterize republicans?

William Grayson, in Virginia Constitutional Convention, June 1788

Will this Constitution remedy the fatal inconveniences of the clashing state interests? . . . Will the liberty and property of this country be secure under such a government? What, sir, is the present Constitution? A republican government founded on the principles of monarchy, with the three estates. . . . There is an executive fetter in some parts, and as unlimited in others as a Roman dictator. A democratic branch marked with the strong features of aristocracy, and an aristocratic branch with all the impurities and imperfections of the British House of Commons, arising from the inequality of representation and want of responsibility. . . . Are not all defects and corruption founded on the inequality of representation and want of responsibility . . . ? We have asked for bread, and they have given us a stone.

Mr. Randall, in Massachusetts Constitutional Convention, January–February 1788

I hope, sir, these great men of eloquence and learning will not try to *make* arguments to make this Constitution go down, right or wrong. An old saying, sir, is, that a "good thing don't need praising"; but, sir, it takes the best men in the state to gloss this Constitution, which they say is the best that human wisdom can invent. In praise of it we hear the reverend clergy, the judges of the Supreme Court, and the ablest lawyers, exerting their utmost abilities. Now, sir, suppose all this artillery turned the other way, and these great men would speak half as much against it, we might complete our business and go home in forty-eight hours.

*Amos Singletary, in Massachusetts Constitutional
Convention, January–February 1788*

We contended with Great Britain . . . because they claimed a
right to tax and bind us in all cases, whatever. And does not this
Constitution do the same? Does it not take away all we have—
all our property? Does it not lay *all* taxes, duties, imposts, and
excises? . . . They tell us Congress won't lay dry taxes upon us,
but collect all the money they want by impost. I say . . . they
won't be able to raise money enough by impost, and then they
will lay it on the land, and take all we have got. These lawyers
and men of learning and moneyed men, that talk so finely, and
gloss over matters so smoothly, to make us poor illiterate people
swallow down the pill, expect to be the manager of this Constitution, and get all the power and all the money into their own
hands, and then they will swallow up all us little folks, like the
great Leviathan, Mr. President; yes, just as the whale swallowed
up Jonah. This is what I am afraid of.

*Thomas Tredwell, in New York Constitutional Convention,
June–July 1788*

In this Constitution, sir, we have departed widely from the
principles and political faith of '76, when the spirit of liberty ran
high, and danger put a curb on ambition. Here we find no security
for the rights of individuals, no security for the existence of our
state governments; here is no bill of rights, no proper restriction
of power; our lives, our property, and our consciences, are left
wholly at the mercy of the legislature, and the powers of the
judiciary may be extended to any degree short of almighty. . . .
Is this, sir, a government for freedom? Are we thus to be duped
out of our liberties? I hope, sir, our affairs have not yet arrived
to that long-wished-for pitch of confusion, that we are under the
necessity of accepting such a system of government as this.

Jefferson's Criticism of the Constitution

Jefferson was the most cogent spokesman of the middle group, that is, those who thought the Constitution had good features but needed some fundamental amending.

Thomas Jefferson to James Madison, December 20, 1787

I like much the general idea of framing a government, which should go on of itself, peaceably, without needing continual recurrence to the State legislatures. I like the organization of the government into legislative, judiciary and executive. I like the power given the legislature to levy taxes, and for that reason solely, I approve of the greater House being chosen by the people directly. For though I think a House so chosen, will be very far inferior to the present Congress, will be very illy qualified to legislate for the Union, for foreign nations, etc., yet this evil does not weigh against the good, of preserving inviolate the fundamental principle, that the people are not to be taxed but by representatives chosen immediately by themselves. I am captivated by the compromise of the opposite claims of the great and little States, of the latter to equal, and the former to proportional influence. I am much pleased too, with the substitution of the method of voting by person, instead of that of voting by States; and I like the negative given to the Executive, conjointly with a third of either House; though I should have liked it better, had the judiciary been associated for that purpose, or invested separately with a similar power. There are other good things of less moment.

I will now tell you what I do not like. First, the omission of a bill of rights, providing clearly, and without the aid of sophism, for freedom of religion, freedom of the press, protection against standing armies, restriction of monopolies, the eternal and unremitting force for the habeas corpus laws, and trials by jury in all matters of fact triable by the laws of the land, and not by the laws of nations. To say, as Mr. Wilson does, that a bill of rights was not necessary, because all is reserved in the case of the general government which is not given, while in the particular ones, all is given which is not reserved, might do for the audience to which it was addressed; but it is . . . opposed by strong inferences from the body of the instrument. . . . Let me add, that a bill of rights is what the people are entitled to against every government on earth, general or particular; and what no just government should refuse, or rest on inference.

I own I am not a friend to a very energetic government. It is always oppressive. It places the governors indeed more at their ease, at the expense of the people. The late rebellion in Massachusetts [Shay's Rebellion] has given more alarm, than I think it should have done. Calculate that one rebellion in thirteen States in the course of eleven years, is but one for each State in a century and a half. No country should be so long without one.

And say, finally, whether peace is best preserved by giving energy to the government, or information to the people. This last is the most certain, and the most legitimate engine of government. Educate and inform the whole mass of the people. Enable them to see that it is their interest to preserve peace and order, and they will preserve them. And it requires no very high degree of education to convince them of this. They are the only sure reliance for the preservation of our liberty. After all, it is my principle that the will of the majority should prevail. If they approve the proposed constitution in all its parts, I shall concur in it cheerfully, in hope they will amend it, whenever they shall find it works wrong.

Ratification of the Constitution

There was little debate in the smaller states. Four of them—Delaware, New Jersey, Georgia, and Connecticut—promptly ratified the Constitution. Elsewhere, however, the struggle continued to be intense and close.

In the end the supporters of the Constitution did carry the day, but the margin of victory was slim. Massachusetts ratified by 187 against 168. In Virginia 89 delegates voted yes and 79 no. In New York the Constitution squeezed through by a mere three votes—30 to 27. But by June 21, 1788, when New Hampshire ratified (57 to 47), the Constitution already had the required nine states, and so it went into effect. In two states, North Carolina and Rhode Island, the opposition was so great that the Constitution was not ratified until the federal government was already set up. Rhode Island ratified on May 29, 1790, well over a year after the new government had been inaugurated.

Bill of Rights

To allay the widespread public criticism and to obtain ratification, defenders of the Constitution promised a Bill of Rights to protect the citizens against the government. A series of amendments were thus introduced in the first Congress, the first ten of which came to be known as the Bill of Rights, containing strict and permanent guarantees against undue and illegal government encroachments upon the individual. The Bill of Rights went into effect by November 1791. An integral part of the Constitution, the Bill of Rights may be considered as one of the noblest and most massive achievements of the American democracy.

Later Comments on the Constitution

Abraham Lincoln

Lincoln viewed the Constitution as a basic frame of government for freedom and union. He expressed his ideas in the following unusual "Fragment on the Constitution and the Union," written about 1860:

> All this is not the result of accident. It has a philosophical cause. Without the *Constitution* and the *Union*, we could not have attained the result; but even these, are not the primary cause of our great prosperity. There is something back of these, entwining itself more closely about the human heart. That something, is the principle of "Liberty to all"—the principle that clears the *path* for all—gives *hope* to all—and, by consequence, *enterprise*, and *industry* to all.
>
> The *expression* of that principle, in our Declaration of Independence, was most happy, and fortunate. *Without* this, as well as *with* it, we could have declared our independence of Great Britain; but without it, we could not, I think, have secured our free government, and consequent prosperity. No oppressed people will *fight*, and *endure*, as our fathers did, without the promise of something better, than a mere change of masters.

The assertion of that *principle*, at *that time*, was *the* word,
"*fitly spoken*" which has proved an "apple of gold" to us. The
Union, and the *Constitution*, are the *picture* of *silver*, subsequently framed around it. The picture was made, not to *conceal*,
or *destroy* the apple; but to *adorn*, and *preserve* it. The *picture*
was made *for* the apple—*not* the apple for the picture.

Woodrow Wilson

Long before he became president of the United States, Woodrow Wilson, one of the profoundest students of American history and politics,
thus analyzed the importance of the Constitution in his book *Congressional Government* (1885):

The Constitution is now, like Magna Carta and the Bill of
Rights, only the sap-centre of a system of government vastly
larger than the stock from which it has branched—a system some
of whose forms have only very indistinct and rudimental begin-
nings in the simple substance of the Constitution, and which exercises many functions apparently quite foreign to the primitive
properties contained in the fundamental law.

The Constitution itself is not a complete system; it takes none
but the first steps in organization. It does little more than lay a
foundation of principles. It provides with all possible brevity for
the establishment of a government having, in several distinct
branches, executive, legislative, and judicial powers. It vests executive power in a single chief magistrate, for whose election and
inauguration it makes carefully definite provision, and whose
privileges and prerogatives it defines with succinct clearness; it
grants specifically enumerated powers of legislation to a representative Congress, outlining the organization of the two houses
of that body . . . ; and it establishes a Supreme Court with ample
authority. . . . Here the Constitution's work of organization ends,
and the fact that it attempts nothing more is its chief strength.
For it to go beyond elementary provisions would be to lose elasticity and adaptability. The growth of the nation and the consequent development of the governmental system would snap
asunder a constitution which could not adapt itself to the measure
of the new conditions of an advancing society. If it could not

stretch itself to the measure of the times, it must be thrown off and left behind, as a by-gone device; and there can, therefore, be no question that our Constitution has proved lasting because of its simplicity. It is a cornerstone, not a complete building; or, rather, to return to the old figure, it is a root, not a perfect vine.

Lord Bryce

In his book *The American Commonwealth* (1888), Bryce, one of the keenest British observers of American life, wrote of the Constitution:

The Constitution of 1789 deserves the veneration with which the Americans have been accustomed to regard it. It is true that many criticisms have been passed upon its arrangement, upon its omissions, upon the artificial character of some of the institutions it creates. . . . Yet, after all deductions, it ranks above every other written constitution for the intrinsic excellence of its scheme, its adaptation to the circumstances of the people, the simplicity, brevity, and precision of its language, its judicious mixture of definiteness in principle with elasticity in details.

Appendix I.1:
Delegates and Signers

Of the delegates elected to the Constitutional Convention, a few did not attend the sessions at all. Some others were not pleased with the final outcome. The result was that when the Constitution was completed, only thirty-nine delegates signed it.

a. List of Delegates
(by States)

The following were present at some time during the deliberations of the Convention:

1. *Connecticut:*
   Oliver Ellsworth
   William Samuel Johnson*
   Roger Sherman*

2. *Delaware:*
   Richard Bassett*
   Gunning Bedford, Jr.*
   Jacob Broom*
   John Dickinson*
   George Read*

3. *Georgia:*
   Abraham Baldwin*
   William Few*
   William Houston
   William Pierce

4. *Maryland:*
   Daniel Carroll*
   Daniel Jenifer*
   James McHenry*
   Luther Martin
   John Francis Mercer

5. *Massachusetts:*
   Elbridge Gerry
   Nathaniel Gorham*
   Rufus King*
   Caleb Strong

6. *New Hampshire:*
   Nicholas Gilman*
   John Langdon*

7. *New Jersey:*
   David Brearly*
   Jonathan Dayton*
   William Churchill Houston
   William Livingston*
   William Paterson*

8. *New York:*
   Alexander Hamilton*
   John Lansing
   Robert Yates

9. *North Carolina:*
   William Blount*
   William R. Davie
   Alexander Martin
   Richard Dobbs Spaight*
   Hugh Williamson*

10. *Pennsylvania:*
    George Clymer*
    Thomas Fitzsimmons*
    Benjamin Franklin*
    Jared Ingersoll*

* Those who signed the Constitution.

Thomas Mifflin*
Gouverneur Morris*
Robert Morris*
James Wilson*

11. *Rhode Island:*
None

12. *South Carolina:*
Pierce Butler*
Charles Pinckney*
Charles Cotesworth
    Pinckney*
John Rutledge*

13. *Virginia:*
John Blair*
James McClurg
James Madison, Jr.*
George Mason
Edmund Randolph
George Washington*
George Wythe

b. Signers
(Alphabetical)

Last Name	Given Name	State	Occupation	Dates
1. Baldwin	Abraham	Ga.	Lawyer	1754–1807
2. Bassett	Richard	Del.	Lawyer	1745–1815
3. Bedford	Gunning	Del.	Lawyer	1747–1812
4. Blair	John	Va.	Lawyer	1732–1800
5. Blount	William	N.C.	Politician	1744–1800
6. Brearly	David	N.J.	Lawyer	1745–1790
7. Broom	Jacob	Del.	Politician	1752–1810
8. Butler	Pierce	S.C.	Planter	1744–1822
9. Carroll	Daniel	Md.	Politician	1730–1796
10. Clymer	George	Pa.	Merchant	1739–1813
11. Dayton	Jonathan	N.J.	Politician	1760–1824
12. Dickinson	John	Del.	Lawyer	1732–1808
13. Few	William	Ga.	Soldier, banker	1748–1828
14. Fitzsimmons	Thomas	Pa.	Businessman	1741–1811
15. Franklin	Benjamin	Pa.	Philosopher	1706–1790
16. Gilman	Nicholas	N.H.	Lawyer	1755–1814
17. Gorham	Nathaniel	Mass.	Merchant	1738–1796
18. Hamilton	Alexander	N.Y.	Lawyer	1757–1804
19. Ingersoll	Jared	Pa.	Lawyer	1749–1822
20. Jenifer	Daniel, of St. Thomas	Md.	Politician	1723–1790

21. Johnson	William Samuel	Conn.	Lawyer	1727–1819
22. King	Rufus	Mass.	Lawyer	1755–1827
23. Langdon	John	N.H.	Merchant	1741–1819
24. Livingston	William	N.J.	Lawyer	1723–1790
25. McHenry	James	Md.	Physician	1753–1816
26. Madison	James	Va.	Lawyer	1751–1836
27. Mifflin	Thomas	Pa.	General	1744–1800
28. Morris	Gouverneur	Pa.	Lawyer	1752–1816
29. Morris	Robert	Pa.	Merchant	1734–1806
30. Paterson	William	N.J.	Lawyer	1745–1806
31. Pinckney	Charles	S.C.	Lawyer	1757–1824
32. Pinckney	Charles Cotesworth	S.C.	General	1746–1825
33. Read	George	Del.	Lawyer	1733–1798
34. Rutledge	John	S.C.	Lawyer	1739–1800
35. Sherman	Roger	Conn.	Lawyer	1721–1793
36. Spaight	Richard Dobbs	N.C.	Politician	1758–1802
37. Washington	George	Va.	Planter	1732–1799
38. Williamson	Hugh	N.C.	Physician	1735–1819
39. Wilson	James	Pa.	Lawyer	1742–1798

Appendix I.2: Contemporary Pen Portraits of the Delegates

A number of the delegates to the Constitutional Convention were, or subsequently became, famous. At least two—Washington and Franklin—were world figures. Some—particularly Hamilton and Madison—became important American statesmen. Others continued to play great roles in their states or in the Congress. A few are not well known to posterity. The following portrait sketches by contemporaries are, therefore, of special interest. They throw a fresh light on the delegates, both on the historically known and the obscure ones.

A. Major Pierce's Character Sketches

Following are extracts from sketches of the delegates written by Major William Pierce, who represented Georgia at the Convention. Major Pierce thus described himself:

William Pierce (c. 1740–1789)

My own character I shall not attempt to draw, but leave those who may chose to speculate on it, to consider it in any light that their fancy or imagination may depict. I am conscious of having discharged my duty as a Soldier through the course of the late revolution with honor and propriety; . . . I possess ambition, and it was that, and the flattering opinion which some of my Friends had of me, that gave me a seat in the wisest Council in the World, and furnished me with an opportunity of giving these short Sketches of the Characters who composed it.

Abraham Baldwin (1754–1807)

Mr. Baldwin is a Gentleman of superior abilities, and joins in a public debate with great art and eloquence. Having laid the foundation of a compleat classical education at Harvard College, he pursues every other study with ease.

Richard Bassett (1745–1815)

He is a Man of plain sense, and has modesty enough to hold his Tongue.

Gunning Bedford (1747–1812)

Mr. Bedford was educated for the Bar, and in his profession, I am told, has merit. He is a bold and nervous Speaker, and has a very commanding and striking manner;—but he is warm and impetuous in his temper, and precipitate in his judgment.

John Blair (1732–1800)

Mr. Blair is one of the most respectable Men in Virginia, both on account of his Family as well as fortune. He is one of the Judges of the Supreme Court in Virginia, and acknowledged to have a very extensive knowledge of the Laws. Mr. Blair is, however, no Orator, but his good sense, and most excellent principles, compensate for other deficiencies.

William Blount (1744–1800)

Mr. Blount is a character strongly marked for integrity and honor. He has been twice a Member of Congress, and in that office discharged his duty with ability and faithfulness. He is no Speaker, nor does he possess any of those talents that make Men shine;—he is plain, honest, and sincere.

David Brearly (1745–1790)

Mr. Brearly is a man of good, rather than of brilliant parts. He is a Judge of the Supreme Court of New Jersey and is very much in the esteem of the people. As an Orator he has little to boast of, but as a Man he has every virtue to recommend him.

Jacob Broom (1752–1810)

Mr. Broom is a plain good Man, with some abilities, but nothing to render him conspicuous. He is silent in public, but chearful and conversable in private.

Pierce Butler (1744–1822)

Mr. Butler is a character much respected for the many excellent virtues which he possesses. But as a politician or an Orator, he has no pretentions to either. He is a Gentleman of fortune, and takes rank among the first in South Carolina. He has been appointed to Congress, and is now a Member of the Legislature of South Carolina.

Daniel Carroll (1730–1796)

Mr. Carroll is a Man of large fortune, and influence in his State. He possesses plain good sense, and is in the full confidence of his Countrymen.

George Clymer (1739–1813)

Mr. Clymer is a Lawyer of some abilities;—he is a respectable man, and much esteemed.

William Richardson Davie (1756–1820)

Mr. Davey is a Lawyer of some eminence in his State. He is said to have a good classical education, and is a Gentleman of considerable literary talents. He was silent in the Convention, but his opinion was always respected.

Jonathan Dayton (1760–1824)

Capt. Dayton is a young Gentleman of talents, with an ambition to exert them. He possesses a good education and reading; he speaks well, and seems desirous of improving himself in Oratory. There is an impetuosity in his temper that is injurious to him; but there is an honest rectitude about him that makes him a valuable Member of Society, and secures to him the esteem of all good Men [at twenty-seven, he was the youngest member of the convention].

John Dickinson (1732–1808)

Mr. Dickinson has been famed through all America, for his Farmers Letters; he is a Scholar, and said to be a Man of very extensive information. When I saw him in the Convention I was induced to pay the greatest attention to him whenever he spoke. I had often heard that he was a great Orator, but I found him an indifferent Speaker. With an affected air of wisdom he labors to produce a trifle,—his language is irregular and incorrect,—his flourishes (for he sometimes attempts them), are like expiring flames, they just shew themselves and go out;—no traces of them are left on the mind to clear or animate it. He is, however, a good writer and will ever be considered one of the most important characters in the United States.

Oliver Ellsworth (1745–1807)

Mr. Ellsworth is a Judge of the Supreme Court in Connecticut; —he is a Gentleman of a clear, deep, and copious understanding; eloquent, and connected in public debate; and always attentive to his duty. He is very happy in a reply, and choice in selecting such parts of his adversary's arguments as he finds make the strongest impressions,—in order to take off the force of them, so as to admit the power of his own. Mr. Ellsworth is . . . a Man much respected for his integrity, and venerated for his abilities.

William Few (1748–1828)

Mr. Few possesses a strong natural Genius, and from application has acquired some knowledge of legal matters;—he practices at the bar of Georgia, and speaks tolerably well in the Legislature. He has been twice a Member of Congress, and served in that capacity with fidelity to his State, and honor to himself.

Thomas Fitzsimmons (1741–1811)

Mr. Fitzsimmons is a Merchant of considerable talents, and speaks very well I am told, in the Legislature of Pennsylvania.

Benjamin Franklin (1706–1790)

Dr. Franklin is well known to be the greatest philosopher of the present age;—all the operation of nature he seems to understand—the very heavens obey him, and the Clouds yield up their Lightning to be imprisoned in his rod. But what claim he has to the politician, posterity must determine. It is certain that he does not shine much in public Council,—he is no Speaker, nor does he seem to let politics engage his attention. He is, however, a most extraordinary Man, and tells a story in a style more engaging than anything I ever heard. Let his Biographer finish his character. He is 82 years old, and possesses an activity of mind equal to a youth of 25 years of age.

Elbridge Gerry (1744–1814)

Mr. Gerry's character is marked for integrity and perseverance. He is a hesitating and laborious speaker;—possesses a great degree of confidence and goes extensively into all subjects that he speaks on, without respect to elegance or flower of diction. He is connected and sometimes clear in his arguments, conceives well, and cherishes as his first virtue, a love for his Country. Mr. Gerry is very much of a Gentleman in his principles and manners; —he has been engaged in the mercantile line and is a Man of property.

Nicholas Gilman (1755–1814)

Mr. Gilman is modest, genteel, and sensible. There is nothing brilliant or striking in his character, but there is something respectable and worthy in the Man.

Nathaniel Gorham (1738–1796)

Mr. Gorham is a Merchant in Boston, high in reputation, and much in the esteem of his Country-men. He is a Man of very good sense, but not much improved in his education. He is eloquent and easy in public debate, but has nothing fashionable or elegant in his style;—all he aims at is to convince, and where he fails it never is from his auditors not understanding him, for no Man is more perspicuous and full. He has been President of Congress, and three years a Member of that Body. Mr. Gorham is . . . rather lusty, and has an agreeable and pleasing manner.

Alexander Hamilton (1757–1804)

Colo. Hamilton is deservedly celebrated for his talents. He is a practitioner of the Law, and reputed to be a finished Scholar. To a clear and strong judgment he unites the ornaments of fancy, and whilst he is able, convincing, and engaging in his eloquence the Heart and Head sympathize in approving him. Yet there is something too feeble in his voice to be equal to the strains of oratory;—it is my opinion that he is rather a convincing Speaker,

than a blazing Orator. Colo. Hamilton requires time to think,—
he enquires into every part of his subject with the searchings of
philosophy, and when he comes forward he comes highly charged
with interesting matter, there is no skimming over the surface of
a subject with him, he must sink to the bottom to see what foundation it rests on.—His language is not always equal, sometimes
didactic like Bolingbroke's and at others light and tripping like
Stern's. His eloquence is not so defusive as to trifle with the
senses, but he rambles just enough to strike and keep up the
attention. He is . . . of small stature, and lean. His manners are
tinctured with stiffness, and sometimes with a degree of vanity
that is highly disagreeable.

William Churchill Houston (c. 1746–1788)

Mr. Houston is an Attorney at Law, and has been a Member
of Congress for the State of Georgia. He is a Gentleman of Family, and was educated in England. As to his legal or political
knowledge he has very little to boast of. Nature seems to have
done more for his corporeal than mental powers. His Person is
striking, but his mind very little improved with useful or elegant
knowledge. He has none of the talents requisite for the Orator,
but in public debate is confused and irregular. Mr. Houston is
. . . of an amiable and sweet temper, and of good and honorable
principles.

Jared Ingersoll (1749–1822)

Mr. Ingersoll is a very able Attorney, and possesses a clear
legal understanding. He is well educated in the Classic's, and is
a Man of very extensive reading. Mr. Ingersol speaks well, and
comprehends his subject fully. There is a modesty in his character
that keeps him back.

Daniel Jenifer of St. Thomas (1723–1790)

Mr. Jenifer is a Gentleman of fortune in Maryland;—he is
always in good humour, and never fails to make his company

pleased with him. He sits silent in the Senate, and seems to be conscious that he is no politician.

William Samuel Johnson (1727–1819)

Dr. Johnson is a character much celebrated for his legal knowledge; he is said to be one of the first classics in America, and certainly possesses a very strong and enlightened understanding.

As an Orator in my opinion, there is nothing in him that warrants the high reputation which he has for public speaking. There is something in the tone of his voice not pleasing to the Ear,— but he is eloquent and clear,—always abounding with information and instruction. He was once employed as an Agent for the State of Connecticut to state her claims to certain landed territory before the British House of Commons; this Office he discharged with so much dignity, and made such an ingenious display of his powers, that he laid the foundation of a reputation which will probably last much longer than his own life. Dr. Johnson . . . possesses the manners of a Gentleman, and engages the Hearts of Men by the sweetness of his temper, and that affectionate style of address with which he accosts his acquaintance.

Rufus King (1755–1827)

Mr. King is a Man much distinguished for his eloquence and great parliamentary talents. He was educated in Massachusetts, and is said to have good classical as well as legal knowledge. He has served for three years in the Congress of the United States with great and deserved applause, and is at this time high in the confidence and approbation of his Country-men. This Gentleman is about thirty-three years of age, about five feet ten Inches high, well formed, an handsome face, with a strong expressive Eye, and a sweet high toned voice. In his public speaking there is something peculiarly strong and rich in his expression, clear and convincing in his arguments, rapid and irresistible at times in his eloquence but he is not always equal. His action is natural, swimming, and graceful, but there is a rudeness of manner sometimes accompanying it. But take him *tout en semble*, he may with propriety be ranked among the Luminaries of the present Age.

John Langdon (1741–1819)

Mr. Langdon is a Man of considerable fortune, possesses a liberal mind, and a good plain understanding.

John Lansing (1754–1829)

Mr. Lansing is a practising Attorney at Albany, and Mayor of that Corporation. He has a hesitation in his speech, that will prevent his being an Orator of any eminence;—his legal knowledge I am told is not extensive, nor his education a good one. He is however a Man of good sense, plain in his manners, and sincere in his friendships.

William Livingston (1723–1790)

Governor Livingston is confessedly a Man of the first rate talents, but he appears to me rather to indulge a sportiveness of wit, than a strength of thinking. He is however equal to anything, from the extensiveness of his education and genius. His writings teem with satyr and a neatness of style. But he is no Orator, and seems little acquainted with the guiles of policy.

James Madison (1751–1836)

Mr. Madison is a character who has long been in public life; and what is very remarkable every Person seems to acknowledge his greatness. He blends together the profound politician, with the Scholar. In the management of every great question he evidently took the lead in the Convention, and tho' he cannot be called an Orator, he is a most agreeable, eloquent, and convincing Speaker. From a spirit of industry and application which he possesses in a most eminent degree, he always comes forward the best informed Man of any point in debate. The affairs of the United States, he perhaps, has the most correct knowledge of, of any Man in the Union. He has been twice a Member of Congress, and was always thought one of the ablest Members that ever sat in that Council. Mr. Madison is . . . a Gentleman of great modesty,—with a remarkable sweet temper. He is easy and unreserved among acquaintance, and has a most agreeable style of conversation.

Alexander Martin (*1740–1807*)

Mr. Martin was lately Governor of North Carolina, which office he filled with credit. He is a Man of sense, and undoubtedly is a good politician, but he is not formed to shine in public debate, being no Speaker. Mr. Martin was once a Colonel in the American Army, but proved unfit for the field.

Luther Martin (*1748–1826*)

Mr. Martin was educated for the Bar, and is Attorney general for the State of Maryland. This Gentleman possesses a good deal of information, but he has a very bad delivery, and so extremely prolix, that he never speaks without tiring the patience of all who hear him.

George Mason (*1725–1792*)

Mr. Mason is a Gentleman of remarkable strong powers, and possesses a clear and copious understanding. He is able and convincing in debate, steady and firm in his principles, and undoubtedly one of the best politicians in America.

James McClurg (*c. 1746–1823*)

Mr. McClurg is a learned physician, but having never appeared before in public life his character as a politician is not sufficiently known. He attempted once or twice to speak, but with no great success. It is certain that he has a foundation of learning, on which, if he pleases, he may erect a character of high renown. The Doctor is . . . a Gentleman of great respectability, and a fair and unblemished character.

James McHenry (*1753–1816*)

Mr. McHenry was bred a physician, but he afterwards turned Soldier and acted as Aid to Genl. Washington and the Marquis de la Fayette. He is a Man of specious talents, with nothing of genious to improve them. As a politician there is nothing remarkable in him, nor has he any of the graces of the Orator. He is however, a very respectable young Gentleman, and deserves the honor which his Country has bestowed on him.

Thomas Mifflin (1744–1800)

General Mifflin is well known for the activity of his mind, and the brilliancy of his parts. He is well informed and a graceful Speaker.

Gouverneur Morris (1752–1816)

Mr. Gouverneur Morris is one of those Genius's in whom every species of talents combine to render him conspicuous and flourishing in public debate:—He winds through all the mazes of rhetoric, and throws around him such a glare that he charms, captivates, and leads away the senses of all who hear him. With an infinite stretch of fancy he brings to view things when he is engaged in deep argumentation, that render all the labor of reasoning easy and pleasing. But with all these powers he is fickle and inconstant,—never pursuing one train of thinking—nor ever regular. He has gone through a very extensive course of reading, and is acquainted with all the sciences. No Man has more wit,—nor can any one engage the attention more than Mr. Morris. He was bred to the Law, but I am told he disliked the profession, and turned merchant. He is engaged in some great mercantile matters with his namesake Mr. Robt. Morris. This Gentleman . . . has been unfortunate in losing one of his Legs, and getting all the flesh taken off his right arm by a scald, when a youth.

Robert Morris (1734–1806)

Robert Morris is a merchant of great eminence and wealth; an able Financier, and a worthy Patriot. He has an understanding equal to any public object, and possesses an energy of mind that few Men can boast of. Although he is not learned, yet he is as great as those who are. I am told that when he speaks in the

Assembly of Pennsylvania, that he bears down all before him. What could have been his reason for not Speaking in the Convention I know not—but he never once spoke on any point.

William Paterson (1745–1806)

Mr. Paterson is one of those kind of Men whose powers break in upon you, and create wonder and astonishment. He is a Man of great modesty, with looks that bespeak talents of no great extent—but he is a Classic, a Lawyer, and an Orator;—and of a disposition so favorable to his advancement that every one seemed ready to exalt him with their praises. He is very happy in the choice of time and manner of engaging in a debate, and never speaks but when he understands his subject well. This Gentleman is . . . of a very low stature.

Charles Pinckney (1757–1824)

Mr. Charles Pinckney is a young Gentleman of the most promising talents. He is . . . in possession of a very great variety of knowledge. Government, Law, History and Phylosophy are his favorite studies, but he is intimately acquainted with every species of polite learning, and has a spirit of application and industry beyond most Men. He speaks with great neatness and perspicuity, and treats every subject as fully, without running into prolixity, as it requires. He has been a Member of Congress, and served in that Body with ability and eclat.

Charles Cotesworth Pinckney (1746–1825)

Mr. Chs Cotesworth Pinckney is a Gentleman of Family and fortune in his own State. He has received the advantage of a liberal education, and possesses a very extensive degree of legal knowledge. When warm in a debate he sometimes speaks well, —but he is generally considered an indifferent Orator. Mr. Pinckney was an Officer of high rank in the American army, and served with great reputation through the War.

Edmund Randolph (1753–1813)

Mr. Randolph is Governor of Virginia,—a young Gentleman in whom unite all the accomplishments of the Scholar, and the States-man. He came forward with the postulate, or first principles, on which the Convention acted, and he supported them with a force of eloquence and reasoning that did him great honor. He has a most harmonious voice, a fine person and striking manner.

George Read (1733–1798)

Mr. Read is a Lawyer and a Judge:—his legal abilities are said to be very great, but his powers of Oratory are fatiguing and tiresome to the last degree;—his voice is feeble, and his articulation so bad that few can have patience to attend to him. He is a very good Man, and bears an amiable character with those who know him.

John Rutledge (1739–1800)

Mr. Rutledge is one of those characters who was highly mounted at the commencement of the late revolution;—his reputation in the first Congress gave him a distinguished rank among the American Worthies. He was bred to the Law, and now acts as one of the Chancellors of South Carolina. This Gentleman is much famed in his own State as an Orator, but in my opinion he is too rapid in his public speaking to be denominated an agreeable Orator. He is undoubtedly a man of abilities, and a Gentleman of distinction and fortune. Mr. Rutledge was once Governor of South Carolina.

Roger Sherman (1721–1793)

Mr. Sherman exhibits the oddest shaped character I ever remember to have met with. He is awkward, un-meaning, and unaccountably strange in his manner. But in his train of thinking there is something regular, deep and comprehensive; yet the oddity of his address, the vulgarisms that accompany his public speaking, and that strange New England cant which runs through his public as well as his private speaking make everything that is connected with him grotesque and laughable:—and yet he deserves infinite praise—no Man has a better Heart or a clearer Head. If he cannot embellish he can furnish thoughts that are wise and useful. He is an able politician, and extremely artful in accomplishing any particular object;—it is remarked that he seldom fails. I am told he sits on the Bench in Connecticut, and is very correct in the discharge of his Judicial functions. In the early part of his life he was a Shoe-maker;—but despising the lowness of his condition, he turned Almanack maker, and so progressed upwards to a Judge. He has been several years a Member of Congress, and discharged the duties of Office with honor and credit to himself, and advantage to the State he represented.

Richard Dobbs Spaight (1758–1802)

Mr. Spaight is a worthy Man, of some abilities, and fortune: Without possessing a Genius to render him brilliant, he is able to discharge any public trust that his Country may repose in him.

Caleb Strong (1745–1819)

Mr. Strong is a lawyer of some eminence,—he has received a liberal education, and has good connections to recommend him. As a Speaker he is feeble, and without confidence. This Gentn. is . . . greatly in the esteem of his Colleagues.

George Washington (1732–1799)

Genl. Washington is well known as the Commander in chief of the late American Army. Having conducted these states to independence and peace, he now appears to assist in framing a Government to make the People happy. Like Gustavus Vasa, he may be said to be the deliverer of his Country;—like Peter the Great he appears as the politician and the States-man; and like Cincinnatus he returned to his farm perfectly contented with being only a plain Citizen, after enjoying the highest honor of the Confederacy,—and now only seeks for the approbation of his Country-men by being virtuous and useful. The General was conducted to the Chair as President of the Convention by the unanimous voice of its Members.

Hugh Williamson (1735–1819)

Mr. Williamson is a Gentleman of education and talents. He enters freely into public debate from his close attention to most subjects, but he is no Orator. There is a great degree of good humour and pleasantry in his character; and in his manners there is a strong trait of the Gentleman.

James Wilson (1742–1798)

Mr. Wilson ranks among the foremost in legal and political knowledge. He has joined to a fine genius all that can set him off and show him to advantage. He is well acquainted with Man, and understands all the passions that influence him. Government seems to have been his peculiar Study, all the political institutions of the World he knows in detail, and can trace the causes and effects of every revolution from the earliest stages of the Greecian commonwealth down to the present time. No man is more clear, copious, and comprehensive than Mr. Wilson, yet he is no great Orator. He draws the attention not by the charm of his eloquence, but by the force of his reasoning.

George Wythe (1726–1806)

Mr. Wythe is the famous Professor of Law at the University of William and Mary. He is confessedly one of the most learned legal Characters of the present age. From his close attention to the study of general learning he has acquired a compleat knowledge of the dead languages and all the sciences. He is remarked for his exemplary life, and universally esteemed for his good principles. No Man it is said understands the history of Government better than Mr. Wythe,—nor any one who understands the fluctuating conditions to which all societies are liable better than he does, yet from his too favorable opinion of Men, he is no great politician. He is a neat and pleasing Speaker, and a most correct and able Writer.

Robert Yates (1724–1796)

Mr. Yates is said to be an able Judge. He is a Man of great legal abilities, but not distinguished as an Orator. Some of his Enemies say he is an anti-federal Man, but I discovered no such disposition in him.

B. **French Character Sketches***
The following sketches are from the report of the French minister to Foreign Minister Montmorin in Paris. They were written in 1788.

John Dickinson

Author of the Letters of a Pennsylvania Farmer; very rich; had been anti-English at the beginning of the Revolution, without however favoring independence, having actually voted against it publicly. He is old, feeble and without influence.

Oliver Ellsworth

Mr. Ellsworth, former member of Congress, is absolutely of the same outlook and disposition [as Benjamin Huntington, a friend of France]. The same may be said of Mr. [Roger] Sherman. In general, the men of that State [Connecticut] have a national outlook which is rarely found elsewhere on the continent. They show a greater republican simplicity; they are well off without being opulent. The rural economy and domestic industry have developed quite far in Connecticut; the people there are happy.

Benjamin Franklin

Dr. Franklin, the present President of the State [Pennsylvania], is too well known to need deserved praising. He feels, more than any other American, that in order to be a true patriot it is necessary to be a friend of France. Unfortunately, this philosopher, who has known how to brave the lightning of heaven and of the English Parliament, will not long continue to fight against the

---

* Translated from the French by Saul K. Padover.

infirmities of age. We must regret that immortality belongs only to his name and writings.

Elbridge Gerry

Mr. Elb. Gerry is a little man, very intriguing and full of small shrewdnesses, which have hitherto brought him sufficient success. Of all the members of the Congress, he has been active the longest. He has acquired a great knowledge of public affairs, which he uses to arouse esteem among his fellow-citizens. In 1782 he had delivered a pretty effective speech in the legislature at Boston against ratification of the Consular Convention. He pretends a great liking for Chevalier de La Luzerne, but one should be on guard against his fine claims. In general, we have very few friends among the powerful men of Massachusetts; our commerce does not interest them and our fisheries are in their way. . . . The people in general like the French, since they often saw our fleet and recall the services which we have rendered them.

Alexander Hamilton

Great orator; intrepid in public debate. Zealous and even extremist partisan of the new Constitution and a declared enemy of Gov. Clinton. . . . He is one of these rare men who has distinguished himself equally on the field of battle and at the bar. He owes everything to his talents. . . . He has a bit too much affectation and too little prudence. . . . He is too impetuous and owing to a desire to lead everything, he fails of his goal. His eloquence is often out of place in public debates, where precision and clarity are preferred to brilliant imagination. It is believed that Mr. H. is the author of the pamphlet entitled *The Federalist*. Here again he has failed of his goal. That work is of no use to the educated, and it is too learned and too long for the ignorant. Nevertheless, it has given him great fame, and has led to the giving of the name *Hamilton* to a small frigate which was carried through the streets of New York during the great Federal procession. . . . A stranger in this State, where he was educated through charity, Mr. Hamilton has found a means of carrying off the daughter of General Schuyler, a great landowner and very influential.

William Livingston

William Livingston, Esq., Governor [of New Jersey] since the beginning of the Revolution, very well informed, firm, patriotic, preferring the public welfare to popularity and having often endangered his position by opposing bad laws in the legislature. Although he does not cease to criticize the people, he is always re-elected, since even his enemies agree that he is one of the cleverest and most virtuous men on the continent.

James Madison

Well-informed, wise, moderate, docile, studious; perhaps more profound than Mr. Hamilton, but less brilliant; intimate friend of Mr. Jefferson and sincerely attached to France. He was at the Congress very young and he appears to be particularly dedicated to public affairs. He could be some day Governor of his State, if his modesty would permit him to accept that place. Last time he refused to accept the presidency of the Congress. He is a man who should be studied a long time in order to form a just opinion of him.

Luther Martin

A distinguished lawyer who has written much against the resolutions of the Philadelphia Convention, of which he was a member.

Gouverneur Morris

Citizen of the State of New York, but always in contact with Rob. Morris and having represented Pennsylvania several times. Celebrated lawyer; one of the best organized heads on the continent, but without manners, and, if his enemies are to be believed, without principles; infinitely interesting in conversation, having made a special study of finances. He works constantly with Mr. Rob. Morris. He is more feared than admired, but few people esteem him.

Robert Morris

Superintendent of Finances during the war, the most powerful merchant in his State. A good head above all, and experienced, but not studious. He has grown a bit cold towards France. . . . Still it will be easy to win him back through proper handling. This is a man of the greatest weight, to whose friendship we cannot be indifferent.

Edmund Randolph

Present Governor [of Virginia], one of the most distinguished men in America by his talents and influence; nevertheless, he has lost a bit of his standing through his too-violent opposition to the ratification of the new Constitution. . . . We may consider him as being very indifferent to France.

John Rutledge

Governor [of South Carolina] during the war, member of Congress and of the [Philadelphia] Convention, as well as of other great conferences. The most eloquent, but also the proudest and most imperious man in the Unites States. He uses his great influence and his knowledge as a lawyer for not paying his debts, which greatly exceed his fortune. His son is traveling in France for his education.

Hugh Williamson

Physician and former professor of astronomy. Excessively bizarre, loving to hold forth, but speaking with spirit. It is difficult to know his character well; it is even possible that he does not have any; but his activity has given him much influence in Congress for some time.

James Wilson

Distinguished jurist. It was he who was designated by Mr. Gerard to be the lawyer of the French nation, a place which has since been recognized as useless. A haughty man, an intrepid aristocrat, active, eloquent, profound, a dissembler, known by the name of *James the Caledonian* which his enemies have given him. His participation in public affairs has led to a disorganization of his fortune. Indifferently attached to France.

Appendix I.3: Chronological Table

1786 September 11. Conference at Annapolis recommended a Constitutional Convention

1787 February 21. Congress resolved in favor of a Constitutional Convention
May 14. Delegates convened in Philadelphia
May 25. First formal meeting of the Convention
September 17. Constitution completed and signed
September 19. Constitution printed in Philadelphia newspapers
December 7. Delaware ratified Constitution (Unanimous)
December 12. Pennsylvania ratified Constitution (46–23)
December 18. New Jersey ratified Constitution (Unanimous)

1788 January 2. Georgia ratified Constitution (Unanimous)
January 4. Connecticut ratified Constitution (128–40)
February 6. Massachusetts ratified Constitution (187–168)
April 28. Maryland ratified Constitution (63–11)
May 23. South Carolina ratified Constitution (149–73)
June 21. Constitution became effective when New Hampshire ratified (57–47)
June 25. Virginia ratified Constitution (89–79)
July 26. New York ratified Constitution (30–27)

1789 March 4. Federal government inaugurated in New York
April 1. First House of Representatives organized
April 6. George Washington elected president
April 30. Washington inaugurated
September 25. First ten amendments adopted by Congress
November 21. North Carolina ratified Constitution (195–77)

1790 May 29. Rhode Island ratified Constitution (34–32)

1791 December 15. First ten amendments (Bill of Rights) declared to be in force

CHAPTER II

The Judicial Power

"The judicial power of the United States, shall be vested in one Supreme Court . . ."—Art. III, Sec. 1

"The judicial power shall extend to all cases, in law and equity, arising under the Constitution . . ."—Art. III, Sec. 2

"In all cases affecting ambassadors, other public ministers and consuls, and those in which a state shall be party, the supreme court shall have original jurisdiction. In all the other cases beforementioned, the supreme court shall have appellate jurisdiction, both as to law and fact, with such exceptions, and under such regulations as the Congress shall make."—Art. III, Sec. 2

The Supreme Court has the power to void legislation repugnant to the Constitution.

1. *Marbury v. Madison* (1803)

The importance of this case lies in the fact that it was the first one in which the Supreme Court ruled a law of Congress void. This established a precedent that has been followed ever since.

Background: On the eve of his retirement from the presidency, John Adams appointed William Marbury as a justice of the peace but, owing to an oversight, his commission was not delivered to him. The new president, Thomas Jefferson, ordered his secretary of state, James Madison, not to deliver the commission to Marbury. The latter then sued for a writ of mandamus requiring Madison to give him his commission. In the forepart of his opinion, Chief Justice Marshall made two points. One was that the president had no right to deny Marbury his commission; the second was that Section 13 of the Judiciary Act of 1789, which gave the Supreme Court the power to issue writs of mandamus, was contrary to the Constitution because it enlarged the Court's "original jurisdiction." In the main section, reproduced below, Marshall justified the now unquestioned power of the Court to declare acts of Congress unconstitutional and, therefore, void.

MR. CHIEF JUSTICE MARSHALL DELIVERED
THE OPINION OF THE COURT:

The question, whether an act, repugnant to the constitution, can become the law of the land, is a question deeply interesting to the United States; but, happily, not of an intricacy proportioned to its interest. It seems only necessary to recognize certain principles, supposed to have been long and well established, to decide it.

That the people have an original right to establish, for their future government, such principles, as, in their opinion, shall most conduce to their own happiness is the basis on which the whole American fabric has been erected. The exercise of this original right is a very great exertion; nor can it, nor ought it, to be frequently repeated. The principles, therefore, so established, are deemed fundamental. And as the authority from which they proceed is supreme, and can seldom act, they are designed to be permanent.

This original and supreme will organizes the government, and assigns to different departments their respective powers. It may either stop here, or establish certain limits not to be transcended by those departments.

The government of the United States is of the latter description. The powers of the legislature are defined and limited; and that those limits may not be mistaken, or forgotten, the constitution is written. To what purpose are powers limited, and to what purpose is that limitation committed to writing, if these limits may, at any time, be passed by those intended to be restrained? The distinction between a government with limited and unlimited powers is abolished, if those limits do not confine the persons on whom they are imposed, and if acts prohibited and acts allowed, are of equal obligation. It is a proposition too plain to be contested, that the constitution controls any legislative act repugnant to it; or, that the legislature may alter the constitution by an ordinary act.

Between these alternatives there is no middle ground. The constitution is either a superior paramount law, unchangeable by ordinary means, or it is on a level with ordinary legislative acts, and, like other acts, is alterable when the legislature shall please to alter it.

If the former part of the alternative be true, then a legislative act contrary to the constitution is not law: if the latter part be true, then written constitutions are absurd attempts, on the part of the people, to limit a power in its own nature illimitable.

Certainly all those who have framed written constitutions contemplate them as forming the fundamental and paramount law of the nation, and, consequently, the theory of every such government must be, that an act of the legislature, repugnant to the constitution, is void.

This theory is essentially attached to a written constitution, and, is consequently, to be considered, by this court, as one of the fundamental principles of our society. It is not therefore to be lost sight of in the further consideration of this subject.

If an act of the legislature, repugnant to the constitution, is void, does it, notwithstanding its invalidity, bind the courts, and oblige them to give it effect? Or, in other words, though it be not law, does it constitute a rule as operative as if it was a law? This would be to overthrow in fact what was established in theory; and would seem, at first view, an absurdity too gross to be insisted on. It shall, however, receive a more attentive consideration.

It is emphatically the province and duty of the judicial department to say what the law is. Those who apply the rule to particular cases, must of necessity expound and interpret that rule. If two laws conflict with each other, the courts must decide on the operation of each.

So if a law be in opposition to the constitution; if both the law and the constitution apply to a particular case, so that the court must either decide that case conformably to the law, disregarding the constitution; or conformably to the constitution, disregarding the law; the court must determine which of these conflicting rules governs the case. This is of the very essence of judicial duty.

If, then, the courts are to regard the constitution, and the constitution is superior to any ordinary act of the legislature, the constitution, and not such ordinary act, must govern the case to which they both apply.

Those, then, who controvert the principle that the constitution is to be considered, in court, as a paramount law, are reduced to the necessity of maintaining that courts must close their eyes on the constitution, and see only the law.

This doctrine would subvert the very foundation of all written constitutions. It would declare that an act which, according to the principles and theory of our government, is entirely void, is yet, in practice, completely obligatory. It would declare that if the legislature shall do what is expressly forbidden, such act, notwithstanding the express prohibition, is in reality effectual. It would be giving to the legislature a practical and real omnipotence, with the same breath which professes to restrict their powers within narrow limits. It is prescribing limits, and declaring that those limits may be passed at pleasure.

That it thus reduces to nothing what we have deemed the greatest improvement on political institutions, a written constitution, would of itself be sufficient, in America, where written constitutions have been viewed with so much reverence, for rejecting the construction. But the peculiar expressions of the constitution of the United States furnish additional arguments in favour of its rejection.

The judicial power of the United States is extended to all cases arising under the constitution.

Could it be the intention of those who gave this power, to say that in using it the constitution should not be looked into? That a case arising under the constitution should be decided without examining the instrument under which it arises?

This is too extravagant to be maintained.

In some cases, then, the constitution must be looked into by the judges. And if they can open it at all, what part of it are they forbidden to read or to obey?

There are many other parts of the constitution which serve to illustrate this subject.

It is declared that "no tax or duty shall be laid on articles exported from any state." Suppose a duty on the export of cotton, of tobacco, or of flour; and a suit instituted to recover it. Ought judgment to be rendered in such a case? Ought the judges to close their eyes on the constitution, and only see the law?

The constitution declares "that no bill of attainder or ex post facto law shall be passed."

If, however, such a bill should be passed, and a person should be prosecuted under it; must the court condemn to death those victims whom the constitution endeavors to preserve?

"No person," says the constitution, "shall be convicted of treason unless on the testimony of two witnesses to the same overt act, or on confession in open court."

Here the language of the constitution is addressed especially to the courts. It prescribes, directly for them, a rule of evidence not to be departed from. If the legislature should change that rule, and declare one witness, or a confession out of court, sufficient for conviction, must the constitutional principle yield to the legislative act?

From these, and many other selections which might be made, it is apparent, that the framers of the constitution contemplated that instrument as a rule for the government of courts, as well as of the legislature.

Why otherwise does it direct the judges to take an oath to support it? This oath certainly applies in an especial manner, to their conduct in their official character. How immoral to impose it on them, if they were to be used as the instruments, and the knowing instruments, for violating what they swear to support!

The oath of office, too, imposed by the legislature, is completely demonstrative of the legislative opinion on this subject. It is in these words: "I do solemnly swear that I will administer justice without respect to persons, and do equal right to the poor and to the rich; and that I will faithfully and impartially discharge all the duties incumbent on me as —— according to the best of my abilities and understanding agreeably to the constitution and laws of the United States."

Why does a judge swear to discharge his duties agreeably to the constitution of the United States, if that constitution forms no rule for his government? if it is closed upon him, and cannot be inspected by him?

If such be the real state of things, this is worse than solemn mockery. To prescribe, or to take this oath, becomes equally a crime.

It is also not entirely unworthy of observation, that in declaring what shall be the supreme law of the land, the constitution itself is first mentioned; and not the laws of the United States generally, but those only which shall be made in pursuance of the constitution, have that rank.

Thus, the particular phraseology of the constitution of the United States confirms and strengthens the principle, supposed to be essential to all written constitutions, that a law repugnant to the constitution is void; and that courts, as well as other departments, are bound by that instrument.

What is the proper scope of Supreme Court review?
A judicial debate in 1798.

2. *Calder v. Bull* (1798)

Background: Several years before Chief Justice Marshall's great decision in *Marbury v. Madison*, Justices Samuel Chase and James Iredell agreed on the authority of the Court to nullify legislation, but engaged in a vigorous debate on the nature and scope of this power. (The balance of the case, which dealt with the meaning of the *ex post facto* provision in Art. I, Sec. 10, is omitted.)

Justice Chase

I cannot subscribe to the omnipotence of a state legislature, or that it is absolute and without control; although its authority should not be expressly restrained by the Constitution, or fundamental law of the State. The people of the United States erected their constitutions or forms of government, to establish justice, to promote the general welfare, to secure the blessings of liberty; and to protect their persons and property from violence. The purposes for which men enter into society will determine the nature and terms of the social compact; and as they are the foundation of the legislative power, they will decide what are the proper objects of it. . . . There are acts which the federal or state legislature cannot do, without exceeding their authority. There are certain vital principles in our free republican governments which will determine and overrule an apparent and flagrant abuse of legislative power; as to authorize manifest injustice by positive law; or to take away that security for personal liberty, or private property, for the protection whereof the Government was established. An Act of the legislature (for I cannot call it a law), contrary to the great first principles of the social compact, cannot be considered a rightful exercise of legislative authority.

Justice Iredell

If any Act of Congress, or of the legislature of a State, violates those constitutional provisions, it is unquestionably void; though, I admit, that as the authority to declare it void is of a delicate and awful nature, the Court will never resort to that authority, but in a clear and urgent case. If, on the other hand, the legislature of the Union, or the legislature of any member of the Union, shall pass a law, within the general scope of their constitutional power, the Court cannot pronounce it to be void, merely because it is, in their judgment, contrary to the principles of natural justice. The ideas of natural justice are regulated by no fixed standard: the ablest and the purest men have differed upon the subject; and all that the Court could properly say, in such an event, would be, that the legislature (possessed of an equal right of opinion) had passed an Act which, in the opinion of the judges, was inconsistent with the abstract principles of natural justice.

Congress may limit the appellate jurisdiction of the Supreme Court even in constitutional cases.

3. *Ex Parte McCardle* (1869)

The ''original jurisdiction'' of the Supreme Court (under which the Court decides the case in the first instance, rather than on appeal from a state or lower federal court) is defined in Art. III, Sec. 2, of the Constitution as extending to ''all cases affecting ambassadors, and other public ministers and consuls, and those in which a state shall be a party.'' (''Original jurisdiction'' accounts for only the tiniest fraction of the Court's cases.) In contrast, the appellate jurisdiction is left to Congress to define: ''The Supreme Court shall have appellate jurisdiction, both as to law and fact, with such exceptions and under such regulations as the Congress shall make.'' In the *McCardle* case, the Supreme Court held that Congress is empowered to define the appellate jurisdiction so as to withdraw from the Court even cases raising constitutional issues.

This case illustrates the other side of judicial review: for all its power, the Supreme Court remains at the mercy of the congressional authority to define its appellate jurisdiction. That Congress has not seen fit to interfere more frequently with the Court's jurisdiction, even during times of acute constitutional controversy, is testimony to both the Court's prestige and congressional responsibility.

Background: McCardle, a Mississippi newspaper editor, was arrested on charges of publishing incendiary articles, and held for trial by a military commission established under the Reconstruction Acts. His petition for a writ of habeas corpus was denied by the circuit court. After the Supreme Court had heard argument in his case, Congress, fearing that the court might declare the Reconstruction Acts unconstitutional, legislated to withdraw the appellate jurisdiction over habeas corpus cases that it had granted the Court only one year earlier (Habeas Corpus Act of 1867). The Court, in a unanimous opinion by Chief Justice Chase, acquiesced.

MR. CHIEF JUSTICE CHASE DELIVERED
THE OPINION OF THE COURT:

The first question necessarily is that of jurisdiction; for, if the Act of March, 1868, takes away the jurisdiction defined by the Act of February, 1867, it is useless, if not improper, to enter into any discussion of other questions.

It is quite true, as was argued by the counsel for the petitioner, that the appellate jurisdiction of this court is not derived from Acts of Congress. It is, strictly speaking, conferred by the Constitution. But it is conferred "with such exceptions and under such regulations as Congress shall make."

It is unnecessary to consider whether, if Congress had made no exceptions and no regulations, this court might not have exercised general appellate jurisdiction under rules prescribed by itself. From among the earliest Acts of the first Congress, at its first session, was the Act of September 24th, 1789, to establish the judicial courts of the United States. That Act provided for the organization of this court, and prescribed regulations for the exercise of its jurisdiction.

The source of that jurisdiction, and the limitations of it by the Constitution and by statute, have been on several occasions subjects of consideration here. In the case of *Durousseau v. U.S.* [1810] particularly, the whole matter was carefully examined, and the court held, that while "the appellate powers of this court are not given by the Judicial

Act, but are given by the Constitution,'' they are, nevertheless, ''limited and regulated by that Act, and by such other Acts as have been passed on the subject.'' The court said, further, that the Judicial Act was an exercise of the power given by the Constitution to Congress ''of making exceptions to the appellate jurisdiction of the Supreme Court.''

''They have described affirmatively,'' said the court, ''its jurisdiction, and this affirmative description has been understood to imply a negation of the exercise of such appellate power as is not comprehended within it.''

The principle that the affirmation of appellate jurisdiction implies the negation of all such jurisdiction not affirmed having been thus established, it was an almost necessary consequence that Acts of Congress, providing for the exercise of jurisdiction, should come to be spoken of as Acts granting jurisdiction, and not as Acts making exceptions to the constitutional grant of it.

The exception to appellate jurisdiction in the case before us, however, is not an inference from the affirmation of other appellate jurisdiction. It is made in terms. The provision of the Act of 1867, affirming the appellate jurisdiction of this court in cases of habeas corpus, is expressly repealed. It is hardly possible to imagine a plainer instance of positive exception. . . .

What, then, is the effect of the repealing Act upon the case before us? We cannot doubt as to this. Without jurisdiction the court cannot proceed at all in any cause. Jurisdiction is power to declare the law, and when it ceases to exist, the only function remaining to the court is that of announcing the fact and dismissing the cause. And this is not less clear upon authority than upon principle. . . .

It is quite clear, therefore, that this court cannot proceed to pronounce judgment in this case, for it has no longer jurisdiction of the appeal; and judicial duty is not less fitly performed by declining ungranted jurisdiction than in exercising firmly that which the Constitution and the laws confer.

Counsel seem to have supposed, if effect be given to the repealing Act in question, that the whole appellate power of the court, in cases of habeas corpus, is denied. But this is in error. The Act of 1868 does not except from that jurisdiction any cases but appeals from circuit courts under the Act of 1867. It does not affect the jurisdiction which was previously exercised.

The appeal of the petitioner in this case must be dismissed for want of jurisdiction.

Federal courts may not impose taxes directly to finance remedial orders, but may require the state to impose such levies.

4. *Missouri v. Jenkins* (1990)

This case well illustrates the enormous expansion of federal judicial power since *Marbury v. Madison* was decided. At issue was a district court's direct imposition of a property tax increase in a school district (doubling the tax, and overriding a state constitutional taxing limit) to help pay the huge sums mandated by that court to remove "vestiges of discrimination." The Supreme Court ruled that while direct imposition of taxes is indeed beyond judicial authority, it would be permissible for the district court to order the school district to levy the same tax. The dissenters derided the majority's distinction as "mere formalism."

Background: After a trial following a complaint filed in 1977, a district court ordered the Kansas City, Missouri, School District to eliminate segregation in its schools. The court initially estimated the cost of its remedial order at $88 million over three years, to be divided between the state and the district. Within a few years, however, the expense of the court's ever-escalating remedies (which eventually included such things as a "25 acre farm and 25 acre woodland area" for science studies and the construction of new schools rather than the renovation of existing ones, in order to achieve "visual attractiveness") would run to over $450 million. The proceedings in the district court and court of appeals, important for an understanding of the case, are summarized in the Court's opinion.

Justice White delivered the opinion of the Court:

The United States District Court for the Western District of Missouri imposed an increase in the property taxes levied by the Kansas City, Missouri, School District (KCMSD) to ensure funding for the desegregation of KCMSD's public schools. . . . For the reasons given below, we hold that the District Court abused its discretion in imposing the tax increase. We also hold, however, that the modifications of the District Court's order made by the Court of Appeals do satisfy equitable and constitutional principles governing the District Court's power.

In 1977, KCMSD and a group of KCMSD students filed a complaint alleging that the State of Missouri and surrounding school districts had operated a segregated public school system in the Kansas City metropolitan area. . . . After a lengthy trial, the District Court found that KCMSD and the State had operated a segregated school system within the KCMSD.

The District Court thereafter issued an order detailing the remedies necessary to eliminate the vestiges of segregation and the financing necessary to implement those remedies. The District Court originally estimated the total cost of the desegregation remedy to be almost $88 million over three years, of which it expected the State to pay $67,592,072 and KCMSD to pay $20,140,472. . . .

A year later, the District Court approved KCMSD's proposal to operate six magnet schools during the 1986–1987 school year. . . .

In November 1986, the District Court endorsed a marked expansion of the magnet school program. It adopted in substance a KCMSD proposal that every high school, every middle school, and half of the elementary schools in KCMSD become magnet schools by the 1991–1992 school year. It also approved the $142,736,025 budget proposed by KCMSD for implementation of the magnet school plan, as well as the expenditure of $52,858,301 for additional capital improvements. . . .

Three months later, the District Court adopted a plan requiring $187,450,334 in further capital improvements. By then it was clear that KCMSD would lack the resources to pay for its 25% share of the desegregation cost. . . . Finding itself with "no choice but to exercise its broad equitable powers and enter a judgment that will enable the KCMSD to raise its share of the cost of the plan," . . . the court ordered the KCMSD property tax levy raised from $2.05 to $4.00 per $100 of assessed valuation through the 1991–1992 fiscal year. KCMSD was also directed to issue $150 million in capital improvement bonds.

A subsequent order directed that the revenues generated by the property tax increase be used to retire the capital improvement bonds. . . .

Although the Court of Appeals "affirm[ed] the actions that the [District] [C]ourt has taken to this point," it agreed with the states that principles of federal/state comity required the District Court to use "minimally obtrusive methods to remedy constitutional violations." The Court of Appeals thus required that in the future, the District Court should not set the property tax rate itself but should authorize KCMSD to submit a levy to the state tax collection authorities and should enjoin the operation of state laws hindering KCMSD from adequately funding the remedy. The Court of Appeals reasoned that permitting the school board to set the levy itself would minimize disruption of state laws and processes and would ensure maximum consideration of the views of state and local officials. . . .

It is accepted by all the parties, as it was by the courts below, that the imposition of a tax increase by a federal court was an extraordinary event. In assuming for itself the fundamental and delicate power of taxation the District Court not only intruded on local authority but circumvented it altogether. . . .

The District Court believed that it had no alternative to imposing a tax increase. But there was an alternative, the very one outlined by the Court of Appeals: it could have authorized or required KCMSD to levy property taxes at a rate adequate to fund the desegregation remedy and could have enjoined the operation of state laws that would have prevented KCMSD from exercising this power. The difference between the two approaches is far more than a matter of form. Authorizing and directing local government institutions to devise and implement remedies not only protects the function of those institutions but, to the extent possible, also places the responsibility for solutions to the problems of segregation upon those who have themselves created the problems.

The District Court therefore abused its discretion in imposing the tax itself. The Court of Appeals should not have allowed the tax increase to stand and should have reversed the District Court in this respect. . . .

[T]he State argues that an order to increase taxes cannot be sustained under the judicial power of Article III. Whatever the merits of this argument when applied to the District Court's own order increasing taxes, a point we have not reached, a court order directing a local government body to levy its own taxes is plainly a judicial act within the power of a federal court. . . .

The State maintains, however, that even under [our earlier] cases, the federal judicial power can go no further than to require local governments to levy taxes *as authorized under state law*. In other words, the State argues that federal courts cannot set aside state-imposed limitations on local taxing authority because to do so is to do more than to require the local government "to exercise the power *that is theirs.*" We disagree. . . .

It is . . . clear that a local government with taxing authority may be ordered to levy taxes in excess of the limit set by state statute where there is reason based in the Constitution for not observing the statutory limitation. . . . Here, the KCMSD may be ordered to levy taxes despite the statutory limitations on its authority in order to compel the discharge of an obligation imposed on KCMSD by the Fourteenth Amendment. To hold otherwise would fail to take account of the obligations of local governments, under the Supremacy Clause, to fulfill the requirements that the Constitution imposes on them.

Accordingly the judgment of the Court of Appeals is affirmed insofar as it required the District Court to modify its funding order and reversed insofar as it allowed the tax increase imposed by the District Court to stand.

JUSTICE KENNEDY, WITH WHOM THE CHIEF JUSTICE,
JUSTICE O'CONNOR, AND JUSTICE SCALIA JOIN,
CONCURRING IN PART AND CONCURRING IN THE JUDGMENT:

I agree . . . that the District Court exceeded its authority by attempting to impose a tax. . . .

In my view, however, the Court transgresses these same principles when it goes further, much further, to embrace by broad dictum an expansion of power in the Federal Judiciary beyond all precedent. Today's casual embrace of taxation imposed by the unelected, life-tenured Federal Judiciary disregards fundamental precepts for the democratic control of public institutions. . . .

Some essential litigation history is necessary for a full understanding of what is at stake here and what will be wrought if the implications of all the Court's statements are followed to the full extent. The District Court's remedial plan was proposed for the most part by the Kansas City, Missouri, School District (KCMSD) itself, which is in name a defendant in the suit. But in the context of this dispute, it is of vital importance to note the KCMSD demonstrated little concern for the fiscal consequences of the remedy that it helped design.

As the District Court acknowledged, the plaintiffs and the KCMSD pursued a "friendly adversary" relationship. Throughout the remedial phase of the litigation, the KCMSD proposed ever more expensive capital improvements with the agreement of the plaintiffs, and the State objected. Some of these improvements involved basic repairs to deteriorating facilities within the school system. The KCMSD, however, devised a broader concept for districtwide improvement, and the District Court approved it. The plan involved a variation of the magnet school concept. Magnet schools, as the majority opinion notes, offer special programs, often used to encourage voluntary movement of students within the district in a pattern that aids desegregation.

Although we have approved desegregation plans involving magnet schools of this conventional definition, the District Court found this insufficient. Instead, the court and the KCMSD decided to make a magnet of the district as a whole. The hope was to draw new non-minority students from outside the district. The KCMSD plan adopted by the court provided that "every senior high school, every middle school, and approximately one-half of the elementary schools in the KCMSD will become magnet schools by the school year 1991–92." The plan was intended to "improve the quality of education of all KCMSD students." The District Court was candid to acknowledge that the "long term goal of this Court's remedial order is to make available to *all* KCMSD students educational opportunities equal to or greater than those presently available in the average Kansas City, Missouri metropolitan suburban school district" (emphasis in original).

It comes as no surprise that the cost of this approach to the remedy far exceeded KCMSD's budget, or for that matter, its authority to tax. A few examples are illustrative. Programs such as a "performing arts middle school," a "technical magnet high school" that "will offer programs ranging from heating and air conditioning to cosmetology to robotics," were approved. The plan also included a "25 acre farm and 25 acre wildland area" for science study. The Court rejected various proposals by the State to make "capital improvements necessary to eliminate health and safety hazards and to provide a good learning environment," because these proposals failed to "consider the criteria of suburban comparability." The District Court stated: "This 'patch and repair' approach proposed by the State would not achieve suburban comparability or the visual attractiveness sought by the Court as it would result in floor coverings with unsightly sections of mismatched carpeting and tile, and individual walls possessing different shades of paint." Finding that construction of new schools would result in more "attractive" facilities than renovation of existing ones, the District Court approved new construction at a cost ranging from $61.80 per square foot to $95.70 per square foot as distinct from renovation at $45 per square foot.

By the time of the order at issue here, the District Court's remedies included some "$260 million in capital improvements and a magnet-school plan costing over $200 million." And the remedial orders grew more expensive as shortfalls in revenue became more severe. . . .

The premise of the Court's analysis, I submit, is infirm. Any purported distinction between direct imposition of a tax by the federal court and an order commanding the school district to impose the tax is but a convenient formalism where the court's action is predicated on elimination of state-law limitations on the school district's taxing authority. . . . Local government bodies in Missouri, as elsewhere, must derive their power from a sovereign, and that sovereign is the State of Missouri. . . .

The power of taxation is one that the Federal Judiciary does not possess. In our system "the legislative department alone has access to the pockets of the people," *The Federalist* No. 48, for it is the Legislature that is accountable to them and represents their will. The authority that would levy the tax at issue here shares none of these qualities. Our Federal Judiciary, by design, is not representative or responsible to the people in a political sense; it is independent. Federal judges do not depend on the popular will for their office. They may not even share the burden of taxes they attempt to impose, for they may live outside the jurisdiction their orders affect. And federal judges have no fear that the competition for scarce public resources could result in a diminution of their salaries. It is not surprising that imposition of taxes by an authority so insulated from public communication or control can lead to deep feelings of frustration, powerlessness, and anger on the part of taxpaying citizens. . . .

[W]hile this case happens to arise in the compelling context of school desegregation, the principles involved are not limited to that context. There is no obvious limit to today's discussion that would prevent judicial taxation in cases involving prisons, hospitals, or other public institutions. . . . This assertion of judicial power in one of the most sensitive of policy areas, that involving taxation, begins a process that over time could threaten fundamental alteration of the form of government our Constitution embodies.

Appendix II.1:
The Supreme Court
on Precedent

The doctrine of *stare decisis*—meaning adherence to precedent—has long been a cardinal principle of Anglo-American law. The following excerpt from the joint opinion of Justices O'Connor, Kennedy, and Souter in *Planned Parenthood v. Casey* (1992) discusses the role of precedent in *constitutional* cases. (For additional discussion of this subject by these Justices, see pp. 254ff., below.)

The obligation to follow precedent begins with necessity, and a contrary necessity marks its outer limit. With [Justice] Cardozo, we recognize that no judicial system could do society's work if it eyed each issue afresh in every case that raised it. Indeed, the very concept of the rule of law underlying our own Constitution requires such continuity over time that a respect for precedent is, by definition, indispensable. At the other extreme, a different necessity would make itself felt if a prior judicial ruling should come to be seen so clearly as error that its enforcement was for that very reason doomed.

Even when the decision to overrule a prior case is not, as in the rare, latter instance, virtually foreordained, it is common wisdom that the rule of stare decisis is not an "inexorable command," and certainly it is not such in every constitutional case. Rather, when this Court reexamines a prior holding, its judgment is customarily informed by a series of prudential and pragmatic considerations designed to test the consistency of overruling a prior decision with the ideal of the rule of law, and to gauge the respective costs of reaffirming and overruling a prior case. Thus, for example, we may ask whether the rule has proved to be intolerable simply in defying practical workability; whether the rule is subject to a kind of reliance that would lend a special hardship to the consequences of overruling and add inequity to the cost of repudiation, whether related principles of law have so far developed as to have left the old rule no more than a remnant of abandoned doctrine, or whether facts have so changed or come to be seen so differently, as to have robbed the old rule of significant application or justification.

Appendix II.2:
The Supreme Court
on Democracy

How to reconcile judicial review with majority rule has been a basic issue, at times a critical one, in our polity. In 1938 Justice Stone, in his famous footnote 4 to *U.S. v. Carolene Products*, articulated a justification for judicial activism in the field of individual rights when he suggested that, unlike challenges to "ordinary commercial transactions," "there may be narrower scope for operation of the presumption of constitutionality when legislation appears on its face to be within a specific prohibition of the Constitution, such as those of the first ten amendments, which are deemed equally specific when held to be embraced within the Fourteenth." The same was true with regard to "legislation which restricts [the] political processes," or is directed at "discrete and insular" (i.e., vulnerable) minority groups; these situations might call for a "more searching judicial inquiry." In other words, ordinarily the political system is adequate to defend individual liberties. When it is not, the Court's role must be redefined to allow broader judicial review as a substitute for the political review which these groups were unable effectively to obtain. In effect, the Court appoints itself a surrogate legislature, judicially awarding the legislative bargains it believes these groups would themselves have struck were they politically influential. In such circumstances, judicial activism becomes defensible as a safeguard for democratic principles, for the Court can be seen as aiding democracy rather than blocking it, as giving expression to the political process rather than negating it.

Footnote 4 has served as a cornerstone of contemporary constitutional law in the field of individual rights.

Appendix II.3:
American Statesmen
and Supreme Court Justices
on Judicial Review

Thomas Jefferson

Nothing in the Constitution has given them [the judges] a right to decide for the Executive, more than to the Executive to decide for them. Both magistracies are equally independent in the sphere of action assigned to them. The judges, believing the [sedition] law constitutional, had a right to pass a sentence of fine and imprisonment; because that power was placed in their hands by the Constitution. But the Executive, believing the law to be unconstitutional, was bound to remit the execution of it; because that power has been confided to him by the Constitution. That instrument meant that its co-ordinate branches should be checks on each other. But the opinion which gives to the judges the right to decide what laws are constitutional, and what not, not only for themselves in their own sphere of action, but for the Legislature & Executive also, in their spheres, would make the judiciary a despotic branch. (Letter to Mrs. John Adams, September 11, 1804)

James Madison

But it is objected, that the judicial authority is to be regarded as the sole expositor of the Constitution in the last resort; and it may be asked for what reason the declaration by the General Assembly [of Virginia, in opposition to the Alien and Sedition laws], supposing it to be theoretically true, could be required at the present day, and in so solemn a manner. . . .

The resolution supposes that dangerous powers, not delegated, may not only be usurped and executed by the other departments, but that the judicial department, also, may exercise or sanction dangerous powers beyond the grant of the Constitution; and, consequently, that the ultimate right of the parties to the Constitution, to judge whether the compact has been dangerously violated, must extend to violations by one delegated authority as well as by another—by the judiciary as well as by the executive, or the legislature.

However true, therefore, it may be, that the judicial department is, in all questions submitted to it by the forms of the Constitution, to decide in the last resort, this resort must necessarily be deemed the last in relation to the authorities of the other departments of the government; not in relation to the rights of the parties to the constitutional compact, from which the judicial, as well as the other departments, hold their delegated trusts. (Report on the Virginia Resolutions, 1800)

Andrew Jackson

[The decision of the Supreme Court] ought not to control the coordinate authorities of this Government. The Congress, the Executive, and the Court must each for itself be guided by its own opinion of the Constitution. Each public officer who takes an oath to support the Constitution swears that he will support it as he understands it, and not as it is understood by others. It is as much the duty of the House of Representatives, of the Senate, and of the President to decide upon the constitutionality of any bill or resolution which may be presented to them for passage or approval as it is of the supreme judges when it may be brought before them for judicial decision. The opinion of the judges has no more authority over Congress than the opinion of Congress has over the judges, and on that point the President is independent of both. The authority of the Supreme Court must not, therefore, be permitted to control the Congress or the Executive when acting in their legislative capacities, but to have only such influence as the force of their reasoning may deserve. (Veto of the Bank Bill, July 10, 1832)

Abraham Lincoln

I do not forget the position assumed by some that constitutional questions are to be decided by the Supreme Court, nor do I deny that such decisions must be binding in any case upon the parties to a suit as to the object of that suit, while they are also entitled to very high respect and consideration in all parallel cases by all other departments of the Government. And while it is obviously possible that such decision may be erroneous in any given case, still the evil effect following it, being limited to that particular case, with the chance that it may be overruled and never become a precedent for other cases, can better be borne than could the evils of a different practice. At the same time, the candid citizen must confess that if the policy of the Government upon vital questions affecting the whole people is to be irrevocably fixed by decisions of the Supreme Court, the instant they are made in ordinary litigation between parties in personal actions the people will have ceased to be their own rulers, having to that extent practically resigned their Government into the hands of that eminent tribunal. Nor is there in this view any assault upon the court or the judges. It is a duty from which they may not shrink to decide cases properly brought before them, and it is no fault of theirs if others seek to turn their decisions to political purposes. (First Inaugural Address, March 4, 1861)

Franklin D. Roosevelt

The Court in addition to the proper use of its judicial functions has improperly set itself up as a third House of the Congress— a super-legislature, as one of the justices has called it—reading into the Constitution words and implications which are not there, and which were never intended to be there.

We have, therefore, reached the point as a Nation where we must take action to save the Constitution from the Court and the Court from itself. We must find a way to take an appeal from the Supreme Court to the Constitution itself. We want a Supreme Court which will do justice under the Constitution—not over it. In our Courts we want a government of laws and not of men.

I want—as all Americans want—an independent judiciary as proposed by the framers of the Constitution. That means a Supreme Court that will enforce the Constitution as written—that will refuse to amend the Constitution by the arbitrary exercise of judicial power—amendment by judicial say-so. It does not mean a judiciary so independent that it can deny the existence of facts universally recognized. (Fireside Chat, March 9, 1937)

Justice Harlan

The courts have rarely, if ever, felt themselves so restrained by technical rules that they could not find some remedy consistent with the law, for acts, whether done by government or by individual persons, that violated natural justice or were hostile to the fundamental principles devised for the protection of the essential rights of property. (Opinion for the Court in *Monongahela Bridge Co., v. U.S.* [1909])

Justice Holmes

I do not think the United States would come to an end if we lost our power to declare an Act of Congress void. I do think the Union would be imperiled if we could not make that declaration as to the laws of the several States. ("Law and the Court" (1913), in Oliver Wendell Holmes, *Collected Legal Papers* [1920])

Justice Roberts

When an act of Congress is appropriately challenged in the courts as not conforming to the constitutional mandate the judicial branch of the Government has only one duty,—to lay the article of the Constitution which is invoked beside the statute which is challenged and to decide whether the latter squares with the former. All the court does, or can do, is to announce its considered judgment upon the question. The only power it has, if such it may be called, is the power of judgment. This court neither approves nor condemns any legislative policy. (Opinion for the Court in *U.S. v. Butler* [1937])

Justice Stone

The power of courts to declare a statute unconstitutional is subject to two guiding principles of decision which ought never to be absent from judicial consciousness. One is that courts are concerned only with the power to enact statutes, not with their wisdom. The other is that while unconstitutional exercise of power by the executive and legislative branches of the government is subject to judicial restraint, the only check upon our own exercise of power is our own sense of self-restraint. For the removal of unwise laws from the statute books appeal lies not to the courts but to the ballot and to the processes of democratic government. (Dissenting opinion in *U.S. v. Butler* [1937])

Justice Sutherland

The suggestion that the only check upon the exercise of the judicial power, when properly invoked, to declare a constitutional right superior to an unconstitutional statute is the judge's own faculty of self-restraint, is both ill considered and mischievous. Self-restraint belongs in the domain of will and not of judgment. The check upon the judge is that imposed by his oath of office, by the Constitution and by his own conscientious and informed convictions; and since he has the duty to make up his own mind and adjudge accordingly, it is hard to see how there could be any other restraint. . . .

[T]he meaning of the Constitution does not change with the ebb and flow of economic events. We frequently are told in more general words that the Constitution must be construed in the light of the present. If by that it is meant that the Constitution is made up of living words that apply to every new condition which they include, the statement is quite true. But to say, if that be intended, that the words of the Constitution mean today what they did not mean when written—that is, that they do not apply to a situation now to which they would have applied then—is to rob that instrument of the essential element which continues it in force as the people have made it until they, and not their official agents, have made it otherwise. . . .

The judicial function is that of interpretation; it does not include the power of amendment under the guise of interpretation. To miss the point of difference between the two is to miss all that the phrase "supreme law of the land" stands for and to convert what was intended as inescapable and enduring mandates into mere moral reflections. (Dissenting opinion in *West Coast Hotel v. Parrish* [1937])

Justice Black

In interpreting the Bill of Rights, I willingly go as far as a liberal construction of the language takes me, but I simply cannot in good conscience give a meaning to words which they have never before been thought to have and which they certainly do not have in common ordinary usage. I will not distort the words of the Amendment in order to "keep the Constitution up to date" or "to bring it into harmony with the times." It was never meant that this Court have such power, which in effect would make us a continuously functioning constitutional convention. (Dissenting opinion in *Katz v. United States* [1967])

Justice Frankfurter

Judicial review, itself a limitation on popular government, is a fundamental part of our constitutional scheme. But to the legislature no less than to courts is committed the guardianship of deeply-cherished liberties. Where all the effective means of inducing political changes are left free from interference, education in the abandonment of foolish legislation is itself a training in liberty. To fight out the wise use of legislative authority in the forum of public opinion and before legislative assemblies rather than to transfer such a contest to the judicial arena, serves to vindicate the self-confidence of a free people. (Opinion for the Court in *Minersville School District v. Gobitis* [1940])

Justice Brennan

We current Justices read the Constitution in the only way that we can: as Twentieth Century Americans. We look to the history of the time of framing and to the intervening history of interpretation. But the ultimate question must be, what do the words of the text mean in our time. For the genius of the Constitution rests not in any static meaning it might have had in a world that is dead and gone, but in the adaptability of its great principles to cope with current problems and current needs. What the constitutional fundamentals meant to the wisdom of other times cannot be their measure to the vision of our time. (Symposium, Georgetown University, October 12, 1985, Washington, D.C.)

CHAPTER III

The Federal System

"The Congress shall have power to . . . make all laws which shall
be necessary and proper for carrying into execution the foregoing
powers . . ."—Art. I, Sec. 8

"The judicial power shall extend . . . to controversies between two
or more states, between a state and citizens of another state, between
citizens of different states . . ."—Art. III, Sec. 2

"The citizens of each state shall be entitled to all privileges and
immunities of citizens in the several states."—Art. IV, Sec. 2

"This constitution, and the laws of the United States . . . shall be
the supreme law of the land . . ."—Art. VI

"The transportation or importation into any state, territory, or possession of the United States, for delivery or use therein of intoxicating liquors, in violation of the laws thereof, is hereby prohibited."
—Twenty-first Amendment, Sec. 2

**The national government is supreme within its
sphere of authority and has a wide choice of means to
implement its constitutional powers.**

5. *McCulloch v. Maryland* (1819)

This decision, one of the most notable in the Supreme Court's history,
affirmed that the national government must be accorded ample means,

under the Constitution, for the execution of its delegated powers. Chief Justice Marshall's great opinion is an important step in the growth of federal power vis-à-vis the states.

Background: In 1818 Maryland passed a law taxing the notes issued by banks not chartered by the state. The law was aimed at the Bank of the United States; McCulloch, the cashier of its Baltimore branch, refused to pay the $15,000 annual tax. Sued by the state, he lost the case in the Maryland Court of Appeals and brought a writ of error against it to the United States Supreme Court. In this unanimous decision, the Supreme Court held that Maryland had no right to tax the Bank of the United States, and, consequently, the act of the state legislature was "unconstitutional and void."

MR. CHIEF JUSTICE MARSHALL DELIVERED
THE OPINION OF THE COURT:

The first question made in the cause is, has Congress power to incorporate a bank?

It has been truly said that this can scarcely be considered as an open question, entirely unprejudiced by the former proceedings of the nation respecting it. The principle now contested was introduced at a very early period of our history, has been recognized by many successive legislatures, and has been acted upon by the judicial department, in cases of peculiar delicacy, as a law of undoubted obligation. . . .

The power now contested was exercised by the first Congress elected under the present constitution. The bill for incorporating the bank of the United States did not steal upon an unsuspecting legislature, and pass unobserved. Its principle was completely understood, and was opposed with equal zeal and ability. After being resisted, first in the fair and open field of debate, and afterwards in the executive cabinet, with as much persevering talent as any measure has ever experienced, and being supported by arguments which convinced minds as pure and as intelligent as this country can boast, it became a law. The original act was permitted to expire; but a short experience of the embarrassments to which the refusal to revive it exposed the government, convinced those who were most prejudiced against the measure of its necessity and induced the passage of the present law. . . .

In discussing this question, the counsel for the state of Maryland have deemed it of some importance, in the construction of the constitution, to consider that instrument not as emanating from the people, but as the act of sovereign and independent states. The powers of the general government, it has been said, are delegated by the states, who alone are truly sovereign; and must be exercised in subordination to the states, who alone possess supreme dominion.

It would be difficult to sustain this proposition. The convention which framed the constitution was indeed elected by the state legislatures. But the instrument, when it came from their hands, was a mere proposal, without obligation, or pretensions to it. It was reported to the then existing Congress of the United States, with a request that it might "be submitted to a convention of delegates, chosen in each state by the people thereof, under the recommendation of its legislature, for their assent and ratification." This mode of proceeding was adopted; and by the convention, by Congress, and by the state legislatures, the instrument was submitted to the people. They acted upon it in the only manner in which they can act safely, effectively, and wisely, on such a subject, by assembling in convention. It is true, they assembled in their several states—and where else should they have assembled? No political dreamer was ever wild enough to think of breaking down the lines which separate the states, and of compounding the American people into one common mass. Of consequence, when they act, they act, in their states. But the measures they adopt do not, on that account, cease to be the measures of the people themselves, or become the measures of the state governments.

From these conventions the constitution derives its whole authority. The government proceeds directly from the people; is "ordained and established" in the name of the people; and is declared to be ordained, "in order to form a more perfect union, establish justice, insure domestic tranquillity, and secure the blessings of liberty to themselves and to their posterity." The assent of the states, in their sovereign capacity, is implied in calling a convention, and thus submitting that instrument to the people. But the people were at perfect liberty to accept or reject it; and their act was final. It required not the affirmance, and could not be negatived, by the state governments. The constitution, when thus adopted, was of complete obligation, and bound the state sovereignties.

It has been said that the people had already surrendered all their powers to the state sovereignties, and had nothing more to give. But, surely, the question whether they may resume and modify the powers granted to government does not remain to be settled in this country. Much more might the legitimacy of the general government be doubted, had it been created by the states. The powers delegated to the state sovereignties were to be exercised by themselves, not by a distinct and independent sovereignty, created by themselves. To the formation of a league, such as was the confederation, the state sovereignties were certainly competent. But when, "in order to form a more perfect union," it was deemed necessary to change this alliance into an effective government, possessing great and sovereign powers, and acting directly on the people, the necessity of referring it to the people, and of deriving its powers directly from them, was felt and acknowledged by all.

The government of the Union, then (whatever may be the influence of this fact on the case), is emphatically, and truly, a government of the people. In form and in substance it emanates from them. Its powers are granted by them, and are to be exercised directly on them, and for their benefit.

This government is acknowledged by all to be one of enumerated powers. The principle, that it can exercise only the powers granted to it, would seem too apparent to have required to be enforced by all those arguments which its enlightened friends, while it was depending before the people, found it necessary to urge. That principle is now universally admitted. But the question respecting the extent of the powers actually granted, is perpetually arising, and will probably continue to arise, as long as our system shall exist.

In discussing these questions, the conflicting powers of the general and state governments must be brought into view, and the supremacy of their respective laws, when they are in opposition, must be settled.

If any one proposition could command the universal assent of mankind, we might expect it would be this—that the government of the Union, though limited in its powers, is supreme within its sphere of action. This would seem to result necessarily from its nature. It is the government of all; its powers are delegated by all; it represents all, and acts for all. Though any one state may be willing to control its operations, no state is willing to allow others to control them. The nation, on those subjects on which it can act, must necessarily bind its component parts. But this question is not left to mere reason; the people have, in express terms, decided it by saying, "this constitution, and the laws of the United States, which shall be made in pursuance thereof," "shall be the supreme law of the land," and by requiring that the members of the state legislatures, and the officers of the executive and judicial departments of the states shall take the oath of fidelity to it.

The government of the United States, then, though limited in its powers, is supreme; and its laws, when made in pursuance of the constitution, form the supreme law of the land, "anything in the constitution or laws of any state to the contrary notwithstanding."

Among the enumerated powers, we do not find that of establishing a bank or creating a corporation. But there is no phrase in the instrument which, like the articles of confederation, excludes incidental or implied powers: and which requires that everything granted shall be expressly and minutely described. Even the 10th amendment, which was framed for the purpose of quieting the excessive jealousies which had been excited, omits the word "expressly," and declares only that the powers "not delegated to the United States, nor prohibited to the states, are reserved to the states or to the people;" thus leaving the question, whether the particular power which may become the subject of contest has been delegated to the one government, or prohibited to the other, to depend on a fair construction of the whole instrument. The men who drew and adopted this amendment had experienced the embarrassments resulting from the insertion of this word in the articles of confederation, and probably omitted it to avoid those embarrassments. A constitution, to contain an accurate detail of all the subdivisions of which its great powers will admit, and of all the means by which they may be carried into execution, would partake of a prolixity of a legal code, and could scarcely be embraced by the human mind. It would probably never be understood by the public. Its nature, therefore, requires, that only its great outlines should be marked, its important objects designated, and the minor ingredients which compose those objects be deduced from the nature of the objects themselves. That this idea was entertained by the framers of the American constitution, is not only to be inferred from the nature of the instrument, but from the language. Why else were some of the limitations, found in the ninth section of the 1st article, introduced? It is also, in some degree, warranted by their having omitted to use any restrictive term which might prevent its receiving a fair and just interpretation. In considering this question, then, we must never forget that it is *a constitution* we are expounding.

Although, among the enumerated powers of government, we do not find the word "bank" or "incorporation," we find the great powers to lay and collect taxes; to borrow money; to regulate commerce; to declare and conduct a war; and to raise and support armies and navies. The sword and the purse, all the external relations, and no inconsiderable portion of the industry of the nation, are entrusted to its government. It can never be pretended that these vast powers draw after them others of inferior importance, merely because they are inferior. Such an idea can never be advanced. But it may with great reason be contended, that a government, entrusted with such ample powers, on the due execution of which the happiness and prosperity of the nation so vitally depends, must also be entrusted with ample means for their execution. The power being given, it is the interest of the nation to facilitate its execution. It can never be their interest, and cannot be presumed to have been their intention, to clog and embarrass its execution by withholding the most appropriate means. . . . It is not denied that the powers given to the government imply the ordinary means of execution. That, for example, of raising revenue, and applying it to national purposes, is admitted to imply the power of conveying money from place to place, as the exigencies of the nation may require, and of employing the usual means of conveyance. But it is denied that the government has its choice of means; or, that it may employ the most convenient means, if, to employ them, it be necessary to erect a corporation. . . .

The power of creating a corporation, though appertaining to sovereignty, is not, like the power of making war, or levying taxes, or of regulating commerce, a great substantive and independent power, which cannot be implied as incidental to other powers, or used as a means of executing them. It is never the end for which other powers are exercised, but a means by which other objects are accomplished. No contributions are made to charity for the sake of an incorporation, but a corporation is created to administer the charity; no seminary of learning is instituted in order to be incorporated, but the corporate character is conferred to subserve the purposes of education. No city was ever built with the sole object of being incorporated, but is incorporated as affording the best means of being well governed. The power of creating a corporation is never used for its own sake, but for the purpose of effecting something else. No sufficient reason is, therefore, perceived, why it may not pass as incidental to those powers which are expressly given, if it be a direct mode of executing them.

But the constitution of the United States has not left the right of

Congress to employ the necessary means for the execution of the powers conferred on the government to general reasoning. To its enumeration of powers is added that of making "all laws which shall be necessary and proper, for carrying into execution the foregoing powers, and all other powers vested by this constitution, in the government of the United States, or in any department thereof."

The counsel for the State of Maryland have urged various arguments, to prove that this clause, though in terms a grant of power, is not so in effect; but is really restrictive of the general right, which might otherwise be implied, of selecting means for executing the enumerated powers. . . .

But the argument on which most reliance is placed, is drawn from the peculiar language of this clause. Congress is not empowered by it to make all laws, which may have relation to the powers conferred on the government, but such only as may be "necessary and proper" for carrying them into execution. The word "necessary" is considered as controlling the whole sentence, and as limiting the right to pass laws for the execution of the granted powers, to such as are indispensable, and without which the power would be nugatory. That it excludes the choice of means, and leaves to Congress, in each case, that only which is most direct and simple.

Is it true that this is the sense in which the word "necessary" is always used? Does it always import an absolute physical necessity, so strong that one thing, to which another may be termed necessary, cannot exist without that other? We think it does not. If reference be had to its use, in the common affairs of the world, or in approved authors, we find that it frequently imports no more than that one thing is convenient, or useful, or essential to another. To employ the means necessary to an end, is generally understood as employing any means calculated to produce the end, and not as being confined to those single means, without which the end would be entirely unattainable. Such is the character of human language, that no word conveys to the mind, in all situations, one single definite idea; and nothing is more common than to use words in a figurative sense. Almost all compositions contain words, which, taken in their rigorous sense, would convey a meaning different from that which is obviously intended. It is essential to just construction, that many words which import something excessive should be understood in a more mitigated sense—in that sense which common usage justifies. The word "necessary" is of this description.

It has not a fixed character peculiar to itself. It admits to all degrees of comparison; and is often connected with other words, which increase or diminish the impression the mind receives of the urgency it imports. A thing may be necessary, very necessary, absolutely or indispensably necessary. To no mind would the same idea be conveyed by these several phrases. This comment on the word is well illustrated by the passage cited at the bar, from the 10th section of the 1st article of the constitution. It is, we think, impossible to compare the sentence which prohibits a state from laying "imposts or duties on imports or exports, except what may be absolutely necessary for executing its inspection laws," with that which authorizes Congress "to make all laws which shall be necessary and proper for carrying into execution" the powers of the general government, without feeling a conviction that the convention understood itself to change materially the meaning of the word "necessary," by prefixing the word *"absolutely."* This word, then, like others, is used in various senses; and, in its construction, the subject, the context, the intention of the person using them, are all to be taken into view.

Let this be done in the case under consideration. The subject is the execution of those great powers on which the welfare of a nation essentially depends. It must have been the intention of those who gave these powers, to insure, as far as human prudence could insure, their beneficial execution. This could not be done by confiding the choice of means to such narrow limits as not to leave it in the power of Congress to adopt any which might be appropriate, and which were conducive to the end. This provision is made in a constitution intended to endure for ages to come, and, consequently, to be adapted to the various *crises* of human affairs. To have prescribed the means by which government should, in all future time, execute its powers, would have been to change, entirely, the character of the instrument, and give it the properties of a legal code. It would have been an unwise attempt to provide, by immutable rules, for exigencies which, if foreseen at all, must have been seen dimly, and which can be best provided for as they occur. To have declared that the best means shall not be used, but those alone without which the power given would be nugatory, would have been to deprive the legislature of the capacity to avail itself of experience, to exercise its reason, and to accommodate its legislation to circumstances. If we apply this principle of construction to any of the powers of the government, we shall find it so pernicious in its operation that we shall be compelled to discard it. . . .

But the argument which most conclusively demonstrates the error of the construction contended for by the counsel for the state of Maryland, is founded on the intention of the convention, as manifested in the whole clause. To waste time and argument in proving that without it Congress might carry its powers into execution, would be not much less idle than to hold a lighted taper to the sun. As little can it be required to prove, that in the absence of this clause, Congress would have some choice of means. That it might employ those which, in its judgment, would most advantageously effect the object to be accomplished. That any means adapted to the end, any means which tended directly to the execution of the constitutional powers of the government, were in themselves constitutional. This clause, as construed by the state of Maryland, would abridge, and almost annihilate this useful and necessary right of the legislature to select its means. That this could not be intended, is, we should think, had it not been already controverted, too apparent for controversy. We think so for the following reasons:

1st. The clause is placed among the powers of Congress, not among the limitations on those powers.

2d. Its terms purport to enlarge, not to diminish the powers vested in the government. It purports to be an additional power, not a restriction on those already granted. No reason has been, or can be assigned for thus concealing an intention to narrow the discretion of the national legislature under words which purport to enlarge it. The framers of the constitution wished its adoption, and well knew that it would be endangered by its strength, not by its weakness. Had they been capable of using language which would convey to the eye one idea, and, after deep reflection, impress on the mind another, they would rather have disguised the grant of power than its limitation. If, then, their intention had been, by this clause, to restrain the free use of means which might otherwise have been implied, that intention would have been inserted in another place, and would have been expressed in terms resembling these. "In carrying into execution the foregoing powers, and all others," etc., "no laws shall be passed but such as are necessary and proper." Had the intention been to make this clause restrictive, it would unquestionably have been so in form as well as in effect.

The result of the most careful and attentive consideration bestowed upon this clause is, that if it does not enlarge, it cannot be construed to restrain the powers of Congress, or to impair the right of the legislature to exercise its best judgment in the selection of measures to carry into execution the constitutional powers of the government. If no other motive for its insertion can be suggested, a sufficient one is found in the desire to remove all doubts respecting the right to legislate on that vast mass of incidental powers which must be involved in the constitution, if that instrument be not a splendid bauble.

We admit, as all must admit, that the powers of the government are limited, and that its limits are not to be transcended. But we think the sound construction of the constitution must allow to the national legislature that discretion, with respect to the means by which the powers it confers are to be carried into execution, which will enable that body to perform the high duties assigned to it, in the manner most beneficial to the people. Let the end be legitimate, let it be within the scope of the constitution, and all means which are appropriate, which are plainly adapted to that end, which are not prohibited, but consist with the letter and spirit of the constitution, are constitutional. . . .

It being the opinion of the court that the act incorporating the bank is constitutional, and that the power of establishing a branch in the state of Maryland might be properly exercised by the bank itself, we proceed to inquire:

2. Whether the state of Maryland may, without violating the constitution, tax that branch?

That the power of taxation is one of vital importance; that it is retained by the states; that it is not abridged by the grant of a similar power to the government of the Union; that it is to be concurrently exercised by the two governments; are truths which have never been denied. But, such is the paramount character of the constitution that its capacity to withdraw any subject from the action of even this power, is admitted. The states are expressly forbidden to lay any duties on imports or exports, except what may be absolutely necessary for executing their inspection laws. If the obligation of this prohibition must be conceded—if it may restrain a state from the exercise of its taxing power on imports and exports—the same paramount character would seem to restrain, as it certainly may restrain, a state from such other exercise of this power, as is in its nature incompatible with, and repugnant to, the constitutional laws of the Union. A law, absolutely repugnant to another, as entirely repeals that other as if express terms of repeal were used.

On this ground the counsel for the bank place its claim to be exempted from the power of a state to tax its operations. There is no express provision for the case, but the claim has been sustained on a principle which so entirely pervades the constitution, is so intermixed with the materials which compose it, so interwoven with its web, so blended with its texture, as to be incapable of being separated from it without rendering it into shreds.

This great principle is, that the constitution and the laws made in pursuance thereof are supreme; that they control the constitution and laws of the respective states, and cannot be controlled by them. From this, which may be almost termed an axiom, other propositions are deduced as corollaries, on the truth or error of which, and on their application to this case, the cause has been supposed to depend. These are, 1st. that a power to create implies a power to preserve. 2d. That a power to destroy, if wielded by a different hand, is hostile to, and incompatible with these powers to create and to preserve. 3d. That where this repugnancy exists, that authority which is supreme must control, not yield to that over which it is supreme. . . .

That the power of taxing it by the states may be exercised so as to destroy it, is too obvious to be denied. But taxation is said to be an absolute power, which acknowledges no other limits than those expressly prescribed in the constitution, and like sovereign power of every other description, is trusted to the discretion of those who use it. But the very terms of this argument admit that the sovereignty of the state, in the article of taxation itself, is subordinate to, and may be controlled by the constitution of the United States. How far it has been controlled by that instrument must be a question of construction. In making this construction, no principle not declared can be admissible, which would defeat the legitimate operations of a supreme government. It is of the very essence of supremacy to remove all obstacles to its action within its own sphere, and so to modify every power vested in subordinate governments as to exempt its own operations from their own influence. This effect need not be stated in terms. It is so involved in the declaration of supremacy, so necessarily implied in it, that the expression of it could not make it more certain. We must, therefore, keep it in view while construing the constitution. . . .

The sovereignty of a state extends to everything which exists by its own authority, or is introduced by its permission; but does it extend to those means which are employed by Congress to carry into execution —powers conferred on that body by the people of the United States? We think it demonstrable that it does not. Those powers are not given by the people of a single state. They are given by the people of the United States, to a government whose laws, made in pursuance of the constitution, are declared to be supreme. Consequently, the people of a single state cannot confer a sovereignty which will extend over them.

If we measure the power of taxation residing in a state, by the extent of sovereignty which the people of a single state possess, and can confer on its government, we have an intelligible standard, applicable to every case to which the power may be applied. We have a principle which leaves the power of taxing the people and property of a state unimpaired; which leaves to a state the command of all its resources, and which places beyond its reach, all those powers which are conferred by the people of the United States on the government of the Union, and all those means which are given for the purpose of carrying those powers into execution. We have a principle which is safe for the states, and safe for the Union. We are relieved, as we ought to be, from clashing sovereignty; from interfering powers; from a repugnancy between a right in one government to pull down what there is an acknowledged right in another to build up; from the incompatibility of a right in one government to destroy what there is a right in another to preserve. We are not driven to the perplexing inquiry, so unfit for the judicial department, what degree of taxation is the legitimate use, and what degree may amount to the abuse of the power. The attempt to use it on the means employed by the government of the Union, in pursuance of the constitution, is itself an abuse, because it is the usurpation of a power which the people of a single state cannot give.

We find, then, on just theory, a total failure of this original right to tax the means employed by the government of the Union, for the execution of its powers. The right never existed, and the question whether it has been surrendered, cannot arise.

But, waiving this theory for the present, let us resume the inquiry, whether this power can be exercised by the respective states, consistently with a fair construction of the constitution.

That the power to tax involves the power to destroy; that the power to destroy may defeat and render useless the power to create; that there is a plain repugnance, in conferring on one government a power to control the constitutional measures of another, which other, with respect to those very measures, is declared to be supreme over that which exerts the control, are propositions not to be denied. But all inconsistencies are to be reconciled by the magic of the word confidence. Taxation, it is said, does not necessarily and unavoidably destroy. To carry it to the excess of destruction would be an abuse, to presume which, would banish that confidence which is essential to all government.

But is this a case of confidence? Would the people of any one state trust those of another with a power to control the most insignificant operations of their state government? We know they would not. Why, then, should we suppose that the people of any one state should be willing to trust those of another with a power to control the operations of a government to which they have confided the most important and most valuable interests? In the legislature of the Union alone, are all represented. The legislature of the Union alone, therefore, can be trusted by the people with the power of controlling measures which concern all, in the confidence that it will not be abused. This, then, is not a case of confidence, and we must consider it as it really is.

If we apply the principle for which the state of Maryland contends, to the constitution generally, we shall find it capable of changing totally the character of that instrument. We shall find it capable of arresting all the measures of the government, and of prostrating it at the foot of the states. The American people have declared their constitution, and the laws made in pursuance thereof, to be supreme; but this principle would transfer the supremacy, in fact, to the states.

If the states may tax one instrument, employed by the government in the execution of its powers, they may tax any and every other instrument. They may tax the mail; they may tax the mint; they may tax patent-rights; they may tax the papers of the custom-house; they may tax judicial process; they may tax all the means employed by the government, to an excess which would defeat all the ends of government. This was not intended by the American people. They did not design to make their government dependent on the states. . . .

If the controlling power of the states be established; if their supremacy as to taxation be acknowledged; what is to restrain their exercising this control in any shape they may please to give it? Their sovereignty is not confined to taxation. That is not the only mode in which it might be displayed. The question is, in truth, a question of supremacy; and if the right of the states to tax the means employed by the general government be conceded, the declaration that the constitution, and the laws made in pursuance thereof, shall be the supreme law of the land, is empty and unmeaning declamation. . . .

We are unanimously of opinion that the law passed by the legislature of Maryland, imposing a tax on the Bank of the United States, is unconstitutional and void.

This opinion does not deprive the states of any resources which they originally possessed. It does not extend to a tax paid by the real property of the bank, in common with the other real property within the state, nor to a tax imposed on the interest which the citizens of Maryland may hold in this institution, in common with other property of the same description throughout the state. But this is a tax on the operations of the bank, and is, consequently, a tax on the operation of an instrument employed by the government of the Union to carry its powers into execution. Such a tax must be unconstitutional.

The Supreme Court has jurisdiction over the state courts in constitutional matters.

6. *Cohens v. Virginia* (1821)

This case is, in essence, an elaboration of Chief Justice Marshall's basic position that the Supreme Court is the final interpreter of the Constitution.

Background: P. J. and M. J. Cohen were convicted in Virginia for selling lottery tickets in violation of a state statute. They brought a writ of error to the Supreme Court under Sec. 25 of the Judiciary Act of 1789. Virginia's defense was, among other things, that the appellate power of the Supreme Court "cannot . . . be exercised against the judgment of a state court." In this decision, Chief Justice Marshall upheld Virginia on the merits of the case, but reaffirmed at great length the theory that under the Constitution the Supreme Court has jurisdiction over the states in "all cases described" under Art. III, Sec. 2.

MR. CHIEF JUSTICE MARSHALL DELIVERED
THE OPINION OF THE COURT:

The defendant in error moves to dismiss this writ, for want of jurisdiction.

In support of this motion, three points have been made, and argued with the ability which the importance of the question merits. These points are:

1st. That a state is a defendant.

2d. That no writ of error lies from this court to a state court. . . . [The third point has been omitted.]

The questions presented to the court by the two first points made at the bar are of great magnitude, and may be truly said vitally to affect the Union. They exclude the inquiry whether the constitution and laws of the United States have been violated by the judgment which the plaintiffs in error seek to review; and maintain that, admitting such violation, it is not in the power of the government to apply a corrective. They maintain that the nation does not possess a department capable of restraining peaceably, and by authority of law, any attempts which may be made, by a part, against the legitimate powers of the whole; and that the government is reduced to the alternative of submitting to such attempts, or of resisting them by force. They maintain that the constitution of the United States has provided no tribunal for the final construction of itself, or of the laws or treaties of the nation; but that this power may be exercised in the last resort by the courts of every state of the Union. That the constitution, laws, and treaties, may receive as many constructions as there are states; and that this is not a mischief, or, if a mischief, is irremediable. . . .

1st. The first question to be considered is, whether the jurisdiction of this court is excluded by the character of the parties, one of them being a state, and the other a citizen of that state?

The second section of the third article of the constitution defines the extent of the judicial power of the United States. Jurisdiction is given to the courts of the Union in two classes of cases. In the first, their jurisdiction depends on the character of the cause, whoever may be the parties. This class comprehends "all cases in law and equity arising under this constitution, the laws of the United States, and treaties made, or which shall be made, under their authority." This clause extends the jurisdiction of the court to all the cases described, without making in its terms any exception whatever, and without any regard to the condition of the party. If there be any exception, it is to be implied against the express words of the article.

In the second class, the jurisdiction depends entirely on the character of the parties. In this are comprehended "controversies between two or more states, between a state and citizens of another state," "and between a state and foreign states, citizens or subjects." If these be the parties, it is entirely unimportant what may be the subject of controversy. Be it what it may, these parties have a constitutional right to come into the courts of the Union. . . .

The American States, as well as the American people, have believed a close and firm Union to be essential to their liberty and to their happiness. They have been taught by experience, that this Union cannot exist without a government for the whole; and they have been taught by the same experience that this government would be a mere shadow, that must disappoint all their hopes, unless invested with large portions of that sovereignty which belongs to independent states. Under the influence of this opinion, and thus instructed by experience, the American people, in the conventions of their respective states, adopted the present constitution.

If it could be doubted, whether from its nature, it were not supreme in all cases where it is empowered to act, that doubt would be removed by the declaration, that "this constitution, and the laws of the United States, which shall be made in pursuance thereof, and all treaties made, or which shall be made, under the authority of the United States, shall be the supreme law of the land; and the judges in every state shall be bound thereby; anything in the constitution or laws of any state to the contrary notwithstanding."

This is the authoritative language of the American people; and, if gentlemen please, of the American States. It marks, with lines too strong to be mistaken, the characteristic distinction between the government of the Union and those of the states. The general government, though limited as to its objects, is supreme with respect to those objects. This principle is a part of the constitution; and if there be any who deny its necessity, none can deny its authority.

To this supreme government ample powers are confided; and if it were possible to doubt the great purposes for which they were so confided, the people of the United States have declared, that they are given "in order to form a more perfect union, establish justice, ensure domestic tranquillity, provide for the common defense, promote the general welfare, and secure the blessings of liberty to themselves and their posterity."

With the ample powers confided to this supreme government, for these interesting purposes, are connected many express and important limitations on the sovereignty of the states, which are made for the same purposes. The powers of the Union, on the great subjects of war, peace, and commerce, and on many others, are in themselves limitations of the sovereignty of the states; but in addition to these, the sovereignty of the states is surrendered in many instances where the surrender can only operate to the benefit of the people, and where, perhaps, no other power is conferred on Congress than a conservative power to maintain the principles established in the constitution. The maintenance of these principles in their purity, is certainly among the great duties of the government. One of the instruments by which this duty may be peaceably performed, is the judicial department. It is authorized to decide all cases of every description, arising under the constitution or laws of the United States. From this general grant of jurisdiction, no exception is made of those cases in which a state may be a party. When we consider the situation of the government of the Union and of a state, in relation to each other; the nature of our Constitution; the subordination of the state governments to that constitution; the great purpose for which jurisdiction over all cases arising under the constitution and laws of the United States is confided to the judicial department, are we at liberty to insert in this general grant, an exception of those cases in which a state may be a party? Will the spirit of the constitution justify this attempt to control its words? We think it will not. We think a case arising under the constitution or laws of the United States, is cognizable in the courts of the Union, whoever may be the parties to that case. . . .

One of the express objects, then, for which the judicial department was established, is the decision of controversies between states, and between a state and individuals. The mere circumstance, that a state is a party, gives jurisdiction to the court. How, then, can it be contended, that the very same instrument, in the very same section, should be so construed as that this same circumstance should withdraw a case from the jurisdiction of the court, where the constitution or laws of the United States are supposed to have been violated? The constitution gave to every person having a claim upon a state, a right to submit his case to the court of the nation. . . .

The mischievous consequences of the construction contended for on the part of Virginia, are also entitled to great consideration. It would prostrate, it has been said, the government and its laws at the feet of every state in the Union. And would not this be its effect? What power of the government could be executed by its own means, in any state disposed to resist its execution by a course of legislation? The laws must be executed by individuals acting within the several states. If these individuals may be exposed to penalties, and if the courts of the Union cannot correct the judgments by which these penalties may be enforced, the course of the government may be, at any time, arrested by the will of one of its members. Each member will possess a veto on the will of the whole. . . .

These collisions may take place in times of no extraordinary commotion. But a constitution is framed for ages to come, and is designed to approach immortality as nearly as human institutions can approach it. Its course cannot always be tranquil. It is exposed to storms and tempests, and its framers must be unwise statesmen indeed, if they have not provided it, as far as its nature will permit, with the means of self-preservation from the perils it may be destined to encounter. No government ought to be so defective in its organization as not to contain within itself the means of securing the execution of its own laws against other dangers than those which occur every day. Courts of justice are the means most usually employed; and it is reasonable to expect that a government should repose on its own courts, rather than on others. There is certainly nothing in the circumstances under which our constitution was formed; nothing in the history of the times, which would justify the opinion that the confidence reposed in the states was so implicit as to leave in them and their tribunals the power of resisting or defeating, in the form of law, the legitimate measures of the Union. . . .

If jurisdiction depended entirely on the character of the parties, and was not given where the parties have not an original right to come into court, that part of the 2d section of the 3d article which extends the judicial power to all cases arising under the constitution and laws of the United States, would be more surplusage. It is to give jurisdiction where the character of the parties would not give it, that this very important part of the clause was inserted. It may be true, that the partiality of the state tribunals, in ordinary controversies between a state and its citizens, was not apprehended, and therefore the judicial power of the union was not extended to such cases; but this was not the sole nor the greatest object for which this department was created. A more important, a much more interesting object, was the preservation of the constitution and laws of the United States, so far as they can be preserved by judicial authority; and therefore the jurisdiction of the courts of the Union was expressly extended to all cases arising under that constitution and those laws. If the constitution or laws may be violated by proceedings instituted by a state against its own citizens, and if that violation may be such as essentially to affect the constitution and the laws such as to arrest the progress of government in its constitutional course, why should these cases be excepted from that provision which expressly extends the judicial power of the Union to all cases arising under the constitution and laws? . . .

2d. The second objection to the jurisdiction of the court is, that its appellate power cannot be exercised, in any case, over the judgment of a state court.

This objection is sustained chiefly by arguments drawn from the supposed total separation of the judiciary of a state from that of the Union, and their entire independence of each other. The argument considers the federal judiciary as completely foreign to that of a state; and as being no more connected with it, in any respect whatever, than the court of a foreign state. If this hypothesis be just, the argument founded on it is equally so; but if the hypothesis be not supported by the constitution, the argument fails with it.

This hypothesis is not founded on any words in the constitution, which might seem to countenance it, but on the unreasonableness of giving a contrary construction to words which seem to require it; and on the incompatibility of the application of the appellate jurisdiction of the judgments of state courts, with that constitutional relation which subsists between the government of the Union and the governments of those states which compose it.

Let this unreasonableness, this total incompatibility, be examined.

That the United States form, for many, and for most important purposes, a single nation, has not yet been denied. In war, we are one people. In making peace, we are one people. In all commercial regulations, we are one and the same people. In many other respects, the American people are one; and the government which is alone capable of controlling and managing their interests in all these respects, is the government of the Union. It is their government, and in that character they have no other. America has chosen to be, in many respects, and to many purposes, a nation; and for all these purposes, her government is complete; to all these objects, it is competent. The people have declared, that in the exercise of all powers given for these objects it is supreme. It can, then, in effecting these objects, legitimately control all individuals or governments within the American territory. The constitution and laws of a state, so far as they are repugnant to the constitution and laws of the United States, are absolutely void. These states are constituent parts of the United States. They are members of one great empire—for some purposes sovereign, for some purposes subordinate.

In a government so constituted, is it unreasonable that the judicial power should be competent to give efficacy to the constitutional laws of the legislature? That department can decide on the validity of the constitution or law of a state, if it be repugnant to the constitution or to a law of the United States. Is it unreasonable that it should also be empowered to decide on the judgment of a state tribunal enforcing such unconstitutional law? Is it so very unreasonable as to furnish a justification for controlling the words of the constitution?

We think it is not. We think that in a government acknowledgedly supreme, with respect to objects of vital interest to the nation, there is nothing inconsistent with sound reason, nothing incompatible with the nature of government, in making all its departments supreme, so far as respects those objects, and so far as is necessary to their attainment. The exercise of the appellate power over those judgments of the state tribunals which may contravene the constitution or laws of the United States, is, we believe, essential to the attainment of those objects.

Art. IV, Sec. 2, protects only those privileges and immunities "bearing upon the vitality of the nation as a single entity."

7. *Baldwin v. Fish and Game Commission of Montana* (1978)

The clause in Art. IV, Sec. 2 of the Constitution requiring that "The citizens of each state shall be entitled to all the privileges and immunities of citizens in the several states" is rarely litigated in the Supreme Court. Generally speaking, the clause affirms a basic principle of federalism: that each state must accord equality of right to citizens of other states who happen to be within the state. From the first, however, it has been assumed that some legal distinctions between native citizens and the citizens of other states—the right to vote is one such example—may be drawn without violating the provision. The Court in this case attempts to define the rights secured by the Privileges and Immunities Clause.

Background: Montana, our fourth largest state but with a sparse population, is home to large herds of elk. The state attracts hordes of big-game hunters eager for the elk's trophy value. The state charged nonresidents considerably more than residents had to pay for a hunting license. A three-judge district court upheld the state against a claim that the Montana scheme violated Art. IV, Sec. 2, and on direct appeal was sustained by the Supreme Court.

MR. JUSTICE BLACKMUN DELIVERED
THE OPINION OF THE COURT:

This case presents issues, under the Privileges and Immunities Clause of the Constitution's Art IV, § 2, as to the constitutional validity of disparities, as between residents and non-residents, in a State's hunting license system. . . .

The relevant facts are [as follows]: . . .

For the 1976 [hunting] season, the Montana resident could purchase a license solely for elk for $9. The nonresident, in order to hunt elk, was required to purchase a combination license at a cost of $225; this entitled him to take one elk, one deer, one black bear, and game birds, and to fish with hook and line. A resident was not required to buy any combination of licenses, but if he did, the cost to him of all the privileges granted by the nonresident combination license was $30. The nonresident thus paid 7½ times as much as the resident, and if the nonresident wished to hunt only elk, he paid 25 times as much as the resident. . . .

Elk are prized by big-game hunters who come from near and far to pursue the animal for sport. The quest for big game has grown in popularity. During the 10-year period from 1960 to 1970 licenses issued by Montana increased by approximately 67% for residents and by approximately 530% for nonresidents. . . .

Elk are not hunted commercially in Montana. Nonresident hunters seek the animal for its trophy value; the trophy is the distinctive set of antlers. The interest of resident hunters more often may be in the meat. . . .

Elk management is expensive. In regions of the State with significant elk population, more personnel time of the Fish and Game Commission is spent on elk than on any other species of big game. . . .

Perhaps because of the imposition of the Fourteenth Amendment upon our constitutional consciousness and the extraordinary emphasis that the Amendment received, it is not surprising that the contours of Art IV, § 2, cl 1, are not well developed, and that the relationship, if any, between the Privileges and Immunities Clause and the "privileges or immunities" language of the Fourteenth Amendment is less than clear. We are, nevertheless, not without some pronouncements by this Court as to the Clause's significance and reach. . . .

When the Privileges and Immunities Clause has been applied to specific cases, it has been interpreted to prevent a State from imposing unreasonable burdens on citizens of other States in their pursuit of common callings within the State. . . .

It has not been suggested, however, that state citizenship or residency may never be used by a State to distinguish among persons. Suffrage, for example, always has been understood to be tied to an individual's identification with a particular State. No one would suggest that the Privileges and Immunities Clause requires a State to open its polls to a person who declines to assert that the State is the only one where he claims a right to vote. . . . Some distinctions between residents and nonresidents merely reflect the fact that this is a Nation composed of individual States, and are permitted; other distinctions are prohibited because they hinder the formation, the purpose, or the development of a single Union of those States. Only with respect to those "privileges" and "immunities" bearing upon the vitality of the Nation as a single entity must the State treat all citizens, resident and nonresident, equally. Here we must decide into which category falls a distinction with respect to access to recreational big-game hunting. . . .

Does the distinction made by Montana between residents and nonresidents in establishing access to elk hunting threaten a basic right in a way that offends the Privileges and Immunities Clause? Merely to ask the question seems to provide the answer. . . . Elk hunting by nonresidents in Montana is a recreation and a sport. In itself—wholly apart from license fees—it is costly and obviously available only to the wealthy nonresident or to the one so taken with the sport that he sacrifices other values in order to indulge in it and to enjoy what it offers. It is not a means to the nonresident's livelihood. The mastery of the animal and the trophy are the ends that are sought; appellants are not totally excluded from these. The elk supply, which has been entrusted to the care of the State by the people of Montana, is finite and must be carefully tended in order to be preserved.

Appellants' interest in sharing this limited resource on more equal terms with Montana residents simply does not fall within the purview of the Privileges and Immunities Clause. Equality in access to Montana elk is not basic to the maintenance or well-being of the Union. Appellants do not—and cannot—contend that they are deprived of a means of a livelihood by the system or of access to any part of the State to which they may seek to travel. . . . Whatever rights or activities may be "fundamental" under the Privileges and Immunities Clause, we are persuaded, and hold, that elk hunting by nonresidents in Montana is not one of them.

[Mr. Chief Justice Burger wrote a concurring opinion.]

MR. JUSTICE BRENNAN, WITH WHOM MR. JUSTICE WHITE AND MR. JUSTICE MARSHALL JOIN, DISSENTING:

[A]n inquiry into whether a given right is "fundamental" has no place in our analysis of whether a State's discrimination against nonresidents . . . violates the Clause. Rather, our primary concern is the State's justification for its discrimination. . . . [A] State's discrimination against nonresidents is permissible where (1) the presence or activity of nonresidents is the source or cause of the problem or effect with which the State seeks to deal, and (2) the discrimination practiced against nonresidents bears a substantial relation to the problem they present. . . .

It is clear that under a proper privileges and immunities analysis Montana's discriminatory treatment of nonresident big-game hunters in this case must fall. . . . [T]here are three possible justifications for charging nonresident elk hunters an amount at least 7.5 times the fee imposed on resident big-game hunters. The first is conservation. . . . [T]here is nothing in the record to indicate that the influx of nonresident hunters created a special danger to Montana's elk or to any of its other wildlife species. In the most recent year for which statistics are available, 1974–1975, there were 198,411 resident hunters in Montana and only 31,406 nonresident hunters. Nonresidents thus constituted only 13% of all hunters pursuing their sport in the State. . . .

The second possible justification for the fee differential Montana imposes on nonresident elk hunters—the one presented in the District

Court and principally relied upon here—is a cost justification. Appel-lants have never contended that the Privileges and Immunities Clause requires that identical fees be assessed residents and nonresidents. . . . Their position throughout this litigation has been that the higher fee extracted from nonresident elk hunters is not a valid effort by Montana to recoup state expenditures on their behalf, but a price gouged from those who can satisfactorily pursue their avocation in no other State in the Union. . . .

The third possible justification for Montana's licensing scheme, the doctrine of *McCready v. Virginia* (1877), is actually no justification at all, but simply an assertion that a State "owns" the wildlife within its borders in trust for its citizens and may therefore do with it what it pleases. . . .

In unjustifiably discriminating against nonresident elk hunters, Mon-tana has not "exercised its police power in conformity with the . . . Constitution." The State's police power interest in its wildlife cannot override the appellants' constitutionally protected privileges and im-munities right. I respectfully dissent and would reverse.

Congress may regulate wages and hours of state employees.

8. *Garcia v. San Antonio Metropolitan Transit Authority* (1985)

National League of Cities v. Usery (1976) was the first decision in forty years to nullify an act of Congress grounded in the Commerce Clause. The Court held that in regulating wages and hours for state employees, Congress impermissibly interfered with the powers of the states to function effectively in a federal system. Only eight years later, in *Garcia*, the Court overruled *National League*. Each case was decided by a bare five-to-four majority. The only member of the Court to be in the majority both times was Justice Blackmun, who switched sides and wrote the Court's opinion in *Garcia*.

More disturbing to the *Garcia* dissenters than the quick reversal of precedent was the Court's announced reliance on Congress to draw the proper lines of demarcation between national and state authority (where the Constitution is vague or silent). This has always been considered one of the principal functions of the Court. If the Court holds fast to its abnegation of this traditional role, it could mark a sea change in federal-state relations.

Background: Legislation passed by Congress in 1974 extended the maximum-hours and minimum-wage provisions of the Fair Labor Standards Act to employees of state and local governments. The district court had held, in reliance on *National League*, that the Transit Authority was exempt from the requirements of the act.

JUSTICE BLACKMUN DELIVERED
THE OPINION OF THE COURT:

We revisit in these cases an issue raised in *National League of Cities v. Usery* (1976). In that litigation, this Court, by a sharply divided vote, ruled that the Commerce Clause does not empower Congress to enforce the minimum-wage and overtime provisions of the Fair Labor Standards Act (FLSA) against the States "in areas of traditional governmental functions." Although *National League of Cities* supplied some examples of "traditional governmental functions," it did not offer a general explanation of how a "traditional" function is to be distinguished from a "nontraditional" one. Since then, federal and state courts have struggled with the task, thus imposed, of identifying a traditional function for purposes of state immunity under the Commerce Clause. . . .

Our examination of this "function" standard applied in . . . cases over the last eight years now persuades us that the attempt to draw the boundaries of state regulatory immunity in terms of "traditional governmental function" is not only unworkable but is also inconsistent with established principles of federalism and, indeed, with those very federalism principles on which *National League of Cities* purported to rest. That case, accordingly, is overruled. . . .

The most obvious defect of a historical approach to state immunity is that it prevents a court from accommodating changes in the historical functions of States, changes that have resulted in a number of once-private functions like education being assumed by the States and their subdivisions. At the same time, the only apparent virtue of a rigorous historical standard, namely, its promise of a reasonably objective measure for state immunity, is illusory. Reliance on history as an organizing principle results in linedrawing of the most arbitrary sort; the genesis of state governmental functions stretches over a historical continuum from before the Revolution to the present, and courts would have to decide by fiat precisely how longstanding a pattern of state involvement had to be for federal regulatory authority to be defeated.

A nonhistorical standard for selecting immune governmental functions is likely to be just as unworkable as is a historical standard. The goal of identifying "uniquely" governmental functions, for example, has been rejected by the Court in the field of government tort liability in part because the notion of a "uniquely" governmental function is unmanageable.

Another possibility would be to confine immunity to "necessary" governmental services, that is, services that would be provided inadequately or not at all unless the government provided them. The set of services that fits into this category, however, may well be negligible. The fact that an unregulated market produces less of some service than a State deems desirable does not mean that the State itself must provide the service; in most if not all cases, the State can "contract out" by hiring private firms to provide the service or simply by providing subsidies to existing suppliers. It also is open to question how well equipped courts are to make this kind of determination about the workings of economic markets.

We believe, however, that there is a more fundamental problem at work here. . . . The problem is that neither the governmental/proprietary distinction nor any other that purports to separate out important governmental functions can be faithful to the role of federalism in a democratic society. The essence of our federal system is that within the realm of authority left open to them under the Constitution, the States must be equally free to engage in any activity that their citizens choose for the common weal, no matter how unorthodox or unnecessary anyone else—including the judiciary—deems state involvement to be. Any rule of state immunity that looks to the "traditional," "integral," or "necessary" nature of governmental functions inevitably invites an unelected federal judiciary to make decisions about which state policies it favors and which ones it dislikes. . . .

The central theme of *National League of Cities* was that the States occupy a special position in our constitutional system and that the scope of Congress' authority under the Commerce Clause must reflect that position.

We doubt that courts ultimately can identify principled constitutional limitations on the scope of Congress' Commerce Clause powers over the States merely by relying on a priori definitions of state sovereignty. In part, this is because of the elusiveness of objective criteria for "fundamental" elements of state sovereignty, a problem we have witnessed in the search for "traditional governmental functions." There is, however, a more fundamental reason: the sovereignty of the States is limited by the Constitution itself. A variety of sovereign powers, for example, are withdrawn from the States by [various provisions of the Constitution]. . . .

Apart from the limitation on federal authority inherent in the delegated nature of Congress' Article I powers, the principal means chosen by the Framers to ensure the role of the States in the federal system lies in the structure of the Federal Government itself. It is no novelty to observe that the composition of the Federal Government was designed in large part to protect the States from overreaching by Congress. The Framers thus gave the States a role in the selection both of the Executive and the Legislative Branches of the Federal Government. The States were vested with indirect influence over the House of Representatives and the Presidency by their control of electoral qualifications and their role in Presidential elections. US Const, Art I, § 2, and Art II, § 1. They were given more direct influence in the Senate, where each State received equal representation and each Senator was to be selected by the legislature of his State. Art I, § 3. The significance attached to the States' equal representation in the Senate is underscored by the prohibition of any constitutional amendment divesting a State of equal representation without the State's consent. Art V.

The extent to which the structure of the Federal Government itself was relied on to insulate the interests of the States is evident in the views of the Framers. James Madison explained that the Federal Government "will partake sufficiently of the spirit [of the States], to be disinclined to invade the rights of the individual States, or the prerogatives of their governments." *The Federalist* No. 46. . . . Madison placed particular reliance on the equal representation of the States in the Senate, which he saw as "at once a constitutional recognition of the portion of sovereignty remaining in the individual States, and an instrument for preserving that residuary sovereignty." *The Federalist* No. 62. He further noted that "the residuary sovereignty of the States [is] implied *and secured* by that principle of representation in one branch of the [federal] legislature" (emphasis added). *The Federalist* No. 43. In short, the Framers chose to rely on a federal system in which special restraints on federal power over the States inhered principally in the workings of the National Government itself, rather than in discrete limitations on the objects of federal authority. State sovereign interests, then, are more properly protected by procedural safeguards inherent in the structure of the federal system than by judicially created limitations on federal power. . . .

We realize that changes in the structure of the Federal Government have taken place since 1789, not the least of which has been the substitution of popular election of Senators by the adoption of the Seventeenth Amendment in 1913, and that these changes may work to alter the influence of the States in the federal political process. Nonetheless, against this background, we are convinced that the fundamental limitation that the constitutional scheme imposes on the Commerce Clause to protect the ''States as States'' is one of process rather than one of result.

This analysis makes clear that Congress' action in affording SAMTA employees the protections of the wage and hour provisions of the FLSA contravened no affirmative limit on Congress' power under the Commerce Clause. . . .

[T]he principal and basic limit on the federal commerce power is that inherent in all congressional action—the built-in restraints that our system provides through state participation in federal governmental action. The political process ensures that laws that unduly burden the States will not be promulgated. In the factual setting of these cases the internal safeguards of the political process have performed as intended.

We do not lightly overrule recent precedent. We have not hesitated, however, when it has become apparent that a prior decision has departed from a proper understanding of congressional power under the Commerce Clause. Due respect for the reach of congressional power within the federal system mandates that we do so now.

National League of Cities v. Usery, (1976), is overruled.

JUSTICE POWELL, WITH WHOM THE CHIEF JUSTICE,
JUSTICE REHNQUIST, AND JUSTICE O'CONNOR
JOIN, DISSENTING:

Because I believe this decision substantially alters the federal system embodied in the Constitution, I dissent.

There are, of course, numerous examples over the history of this

Court in which prior decisions have been reconsidered and overruled. There have been few cases, however, in which the principle of stare decisis and the rationale of recent decisions were ignored as abruptly as we now witness. . . .

Whatever effect the Court's decision may have in weakening the application of stare decisis, it is likely to be less important than what the Court has done to the Constitution itself. A unique feature of the United States is the *federal* system of government guaranteed by the Constitution and implicit in the very name of our country. Despite some genuflecting in the Court's opinion to the concept of federalism, today's decision effectively reduces the Tenth Amendment to meaningless rhetoric when Congress acts pursuant to the Commerce Clause. . . .

[T]he extent to which the States may exercise their authority, when Congress purports to act under the Commerce Clause, henceforth is to be determined from time to time by political decisions made by members of the Federal Government, decisions the Court says will not be subject to judicial review. I note that it does not seem to have occurred to the Court that *it*—an unelected majority of five Justices—today rejects almost 200 years of the understanding of the constitutional status of federalism. . . .

Today's opinion does not explain how the States' role in the electoral process guarantees that particular exercises of the Commerce Clause power will not infringe on residual state sovereignty. Members of Congress are elected from the various States, but once in office they are Members of the Federal Government. Although the States participate in the Electoral College, this is hardly a reason to view the President as a representative of the States' interest against federal encroachment. The Court offers no reason to think that this pressure will not operate when Congress seeks to invoke its powers under the Commerce Clause, notwithstanding the electoral role of the States. . . .

More troubling than the logical infirmities in the Court's reasoning is the result of its holding, i.e., that federal political officials, invoking the Commerce Clause, are the sole judges of the limits of their own power. This result is inconsistent with the fundamental principles of our constitutional system. At least since *Marbury v. Madison* (1803), it has been the settled province of the federal judiciary "to say what the law is" with respect to the constitutionality of acts of Congress. In rejecting the role of the judiciary in protecting the States from federal overreaching, the Court's opinion offers no explanation for ignoring the teaching of the most famous case in our history.

In our federal system, the States have a major role that cannot be pre-empted by the National Government. As contemporaneous writings and the debates at the ratifying conventions make clear, the States' ratification of the Constitution was predicated on this understanding of federalism. Indeed, the Tenth Amendment was adopted specifically to ensure that the important role promised the States by the proponents of the Constitution was realized.

Much of the initial opposition to the Constitution was rooted in the fear that the National Government would be too powerful and eventually would eliminate the States as viable political entities. This concern was voiced repeatedly until proponents of the Constitution made assurances that a Bill of Rights, including a provision explicitly reserving powers in the States, would be among the first business of the new Congress. . . .

[E]ight States voted for the Constitution only after proposing amendments to be adopted after ratification. All eight of these included among their recommendations some version of what later became the Tenth Amendment. So strong was the concern that the proposed Constitution was seriously defective without a specific bill of rights, including a provision reserving powers to the States, that in order to secure the votes for ratification, the Federalists eventually conceded that such provisions were necessary. . . .

The Framers believed that the separate sphere of sovereignty reserved to the States would ensure that the States would serve as an effective "counterpoise" to the power of the Federal Government. The States would serve this essential role because they would attract and retain the loyalty of their citizens. . . .

[T]he harm to the States that results from federal overreaching under the Commerce Clause is not simply a matter of dollars and cents. Nor is it a matter of the wisdom or folly of certain policy choices. Rather, by usurping functions traditionally performed by the States, federal overreaching under the Commerce Clause undermines the constitutionally mandated balance of power between the States and the Federal Government, a balance designed to protect our fundamental liberties. . . .

To be sure, this Court has construed the Commerce Clause to accommodate unanticipated changes over the past two centuries. As these changes have occurred, the Court has had to decide whether the Federal Government has exceeded its authority by regulating activities beyond the capability of a single State to regulate or beyond legitimate federal interests that outweighed the authority and interests of the States. In so doing, however, the Court properly has been mindful of the essential role of the States in our federal system. . . .

The Court maintains that the standard approved in *National League of Cities* "disserves principles of democratic self-governance." In reaching this conclusion, the Court looks myopically only to persons elected to positions in the Federal Government. It disregards entirely the far more effective role of democratic self-government at the state and local levels. One must compare realistically the operation of the state and local governments with that of the Federal Government. Federal legislation is drafted primarily by the staffs of the congressional committees. In view of the hundreds of bills introduced at each session of Congress and the complexity of many of them, it is virtually impossible for even the most conscientious legislators to be truly familiar with many of the statutes enacted. Federal departments and agencies customarily are authorized to write regulations. Often these are more important than the text of the statutes. As is true of the original legislation, these are drafted largely by staff personnel. The administration and enforcement of federal laws and regulations necessarily are largely in the hands of staff and civil service employees. These employees may have little or no knowledge of the States and localities that will be affected by the statutes and regulations for which they are responsible. In any case, they hardly are as accessible and responsive as those who occupy analogous positions in state and local governments. . . .

[M]embers of the immense federal bureaucracy are not elected, know less about the services traditionally rendered by States and localities, and are inevitably less responsive to recipients of such services, than are state legislatures, city councils, boards of supervisors, and state and local commissions, boards, and agencies. It is at these state and local levels—not in Washington as the Court so mistakenly thinks—that "democratic self-government" is best exemplified.

The question presented in these cases is whether the extension of the FLSA to the wages and hours of employees of a city-owned transit system unconstitutionally impinges on fundamental state sovereignty. The Court's sweeping holding does far more than simply answer this question in the negative. In overruling *National League of Cities*, today's opinion apparently authorizes federal control, under the auspices of the Commerce Clause, over the terms and conditions of employment of all state and local employees. Thus, for purposes of federal regulation, the Court rejects the distinction between public and private employers that had been drawn carefully in *National League of Cities*. The Court's action reflects a serious misunderstanding, if not an outright rejection, of the history of our country and the intention of the Framers of the Constitution.

JUSTICE O'CONNOR, WITH WHOM JUSTICE POWELL
AND JUSTICE REHNQUIST JOIN, DISSENTING:

In my view, federalism cannot be reduced to the weak "essence" distilled by the majority today. . . . The central issue of federalism, of course, is whether any realm is left open to the States by the Constitution—whether any area remains in which a State may act free of federal interference. . . .

The true "essence" of federalism is that the States *as* States have legitimate interests which the National Government is bound to respect even though its laws are supreme. If federalism so conceived and so carefully cultivated by the Framers of our Constitution is to remain meaningful, this Court cannot abdicate its constitutional responsibility to oversee the Federal Government's compliance with its duty to respect the legitimate interests of the States.

[Mr. Justice Rehnquist also wrote a dissenting opinion.]

Congress may encourage a national minimum drinking age despite the states' authority over liquor consumption.

9. *South Dakota v. Dole* (1987)

This case demonstrates the far-reaching scope of federal spending power when Congress attaches conditions to its grants. May Congress require states receiving federal highway construction funds to establish a minimum drinking age of twenty-one (as it did in the National Minimum Drinking Age Amendment of 1984), or else lose 5 percent of the obtainable funds? The Court answered in the affirmative, distinguishing between impermissible federal coercion and permissible "encouragement."

Background: South Dakota permitted the purchase of beer by persons age nineteen and older. It claimed that the federal law was in conflict with the state's constitutional authority over liquor sales. The Supreme Court agreed with the rejection of South Dakota's claim by the district court and court of appeals.

CHIEF JUSTICE REHNQUIST DELIVERED
THE OPINION OF THE COURT:

Petitioner South Dakota permits persons 19 years of age or older to purchase beer containing up to 3.2% alcohol. In 1984 Congress enacted [a law] which directs the Secretary of Transportation to withhold a percentage of federal highway funds otherwise allocable from States "in which the purchase or public possession . . . of any alcoholic beverage by a person who is less than twenty-one years of age is lawful." . . .

[T]he parties direct most of their efforts to defining the proper scope of the Twenty-first Amendment. Relying on our statement in [a 1980 decision] that the "Twenty-first Amendment grants the States virtually complete control over whether to permit importation or sale of liquor and how to structure the liquor distribution system," South Dakota asserts that the setting of minimum drinking ages is clearly within the "core powers" reserved to the States under § 2 of the Amendment. . . . The Secretary in response asserts that the Twenty-first Amendment is simply not implicated by [the Act]; the plain language of § 2 confirms the States' broad power to impose restrictions on the sale and distribution of alcoholic beverages but does not confer on them any power to *permit* sales that Congress seeks to *prohibit*. That Amendment, under this reasoning, would not prevent Congress from affirmatively enacting a national minimum drinking age more restrictive than that provided by the various state laws; and it would follow a fortiori that the indirect inducement involved here is compatible with the Twenty-first Amendment.

These arguments present questions of the meaning of the Twenty-first Amendment, the bounds of which have escaped precise definition. Despite the extended treatment of the question by the parties, however, we need not decide in this case whether that Amendment would prohibit an attempt by Congress to legislate directly a national minimum drinking age. Here, Congress has acted indirectly under its spending power to encourage uniformity in the States' drinking ages. As we explain below, we find this legislative effort within constitutional bounds even if Congress may not regulate drinking ages directly.

The Constitution empowers Congress to "lay and collect Taxes, Duties, Imposts, and Excises, to pay the Debts and provide for the common Defense and general Welfare of the United States." Art I, § 8, cl 1. Incident to this power, Congress may attach conditions on the receipt of federal funds, and has repeatedly employed the power "to further broad policy objectives by conditioning receipt of federal moneys upon compliance by the recipient with federal statutory and administrative directives." . . .

The spending power is of course not unlimited, but is instead subject to several general restrictions articulated in our cases. The first of these limitations is derived from the language of the Constitution itself: the exercise of the spending power must be in pursuit of "the general welfare." In considering whether a particular expenditure is intended to serve general public purposes, courts should defer substantially to the judgment of Congress. Second, we have required that if Congress desires to condition the States' receipt of federal funds, it "must do so unambiguously . . . , enabl[ing] the States to exercise their choice knowingly, cognizant of the consequences of their participation." Third, our cases have suggested (without significant elaboration) that conditions on federal grants might be illegitimate if they are unrelated "to the federal interest in particular national projects or programs." Finally, we have noted that other constitutional provisions may provide an independent bar to the conditional grant of federal funds.

South Dakota does not seriously claim that [this Act] is inconsistent with any of the first three restrictions mentioned above. We can readily conclude that the provision is designed to serve the general welfare. Congress found that the differing drinking ages in the States created particular incentives for young persons to combine their desire to drink with their ability to drive, and that this interstate problem required a national solution. The means it chose to address this dangerous situation were reasonably calculated to advance the general welfare. The conditions upon which States receive the funds, moreover, could not be more clearly stated by Congress. And the State itself, rather than challenging the germaneness of the condition to federal purposes, admits that it "has never contended that the congressional action was . . . unrelated to a national concern in the absence of the Twenty-first Amendment." Indeed, the condition imposed by Congress is directly related to one of the main purposes for which highway funds are expended—safe interstate travel. This goal of the interstate highway system had been frustrated by varying drinking ages among the States. A Presidential commission appointed to study alcohol-related accidents and fatalities on the Nation's highways concluded that the lack of uniformity in the States' drinking ages created "an incentive to drink and drive" because "young persons commut[e] to border States where the drinking age is lower." By enacting [this law], Congress conditioned the receipt of federal funds in a way reasonably calculated to address this particular impediment to a purpose for which the funds are expended.

The remaining question about the validity of [the Act]—and the basic point of disagreement between the parties—is whether the Twenty-first Amendment constitutes an "independent constitutional bar" to the conditional grant of federal funds. Petitioner, relying on its view that the Twenty-first Amendment prohibits *direct* regulation of drinking ages by Congress, asserts that "Congress may not use the spending power to regulate that which it is prohibited from regulating directly under the Twenty-first Amendment." But our cases show that this "independent constitutional bar" limitation on the spending power is not of the kind petitioner suggests . . . the constitutional limitations on Congress when exercising its spending power are less exacting than those on its authority to regulate directly.

Our decisions have recognized that in some circumstances the financial inducement offered by Congress might be so coercive as to pass the point at which "pressure turns into compulsion." Here, however, Congress has directed only that a State desiring to establish a minimum drinking age lower than 21 lose a relatively small percentage of certain federal highway funds. Petitioner contends that the coercive nature of this program is evident from the degree of success it has achieved. We cannot conclude, however, that a conditional grant of federal money of this sort is unconstitutional simply by reason of its success in achieving the congressional objective.

When we consider, for a moment, that all South Dakota would lose if she adheres to her chosen course as to a suitable minimum drinking age is 5% of the funds otherwise obtainable under specified highway grant programs, the argument as to coercion is shown to be more rhetoric than fact. . . .

Here Congress has offered relatively mild encouragement to the States to enact higher minimum drinking ages than they would otherwise choose. But the enactment of such laws remains the prerogative of the States not merely in theory but in fact. Even if Congress might lack the power to impose a national minimum drinking age directly, we conclude that encouragement to state action found in [the Act] is a valid use of the spending power.

JUSTICE BRENNAN, DISSENTING:

I agree with Justice O'Connor that regulation of the minimum age of purchasers of liquor falls squarely within the ambit of those powers reserved to the States by the Twenty-first Amendment. Since States possess this constitutional power, Congress cannot condition a federal grant in a manner that abridges this right. The Amendment, itself, strikes the proper balance between federal and state authority. I therefore dissent.

JUSTICE O'CONNOR, DISSENTING:

My disagreement with the Court is relatively narrow on the spending power issue: it is a disagreement about the application of a principle rather than a disagreement on the principle itself. I agree with the Court that Congress may attach conditions on the receipt of federal funds to further "the federal interest in particular national projects or programs." I also subscribe to the established proposition that the reach of the spending power "is not limited by the direct grants of legislative power found in the Constitution." . . .

But the Court's application of the requirement that the condition imposed be reasonably related to the purpose for which the funds are expended is cursory and unconvincing. We have repeatedly said that Congress may condition grants under the spending power only in ways reasonably related to the purpose of the federal program. In my view, establishment of a minimum drinking age of 21 is not sufficiently related to interstate highway construction to justify so conditioning funds appropriated for that purpose. . . .

[T]he Court asserts the reasonableness of the relationship between the supposed purpose of the expenditure—"safe interstate travel"—and the drinking age condition. The Court reasons that Congress wishes that the roads it builds may be used safely, that drunken drivers threaten highway safety, and that young people are more likely to drive while under the influence of alcohol under existing law than would be the case if there were a uniform national drinking age of 21. It hardly needs saying, however, that if the purpose of [this law] is to deter drunken driving, it is far too over- and under-inclusive. It is over-inclusive because it stops teenagers from drinking even when they are not about to drive on interstate highways. It is under-inclusive because teenagers pose only a small part of the drunken driving problem in this Nation.

When Congress appropriates money to build a highway, it is entitled to insist that the highway be a safe one. But it is not entitled to insist as a condition of the use of highway funds that the State impose or change regulations in other areas of the State's social and economic life because of an attenuated or tangential relationship to highway use or safety. Indeed, if the rule were otherwise, the Congress could effectively regulate almost any area of a State's social, political, or economic life on the theory that use of the interstate transportation system is somehow enhanced. If, for example, the United States were to condition highway moneys upon moving the state capital, I suppose it might argue that interstate transportation is facilitated by locating local governments in places easily accessible to interstate highways—or, conversely, that highways might become overburdened if they had to carry traffic to and from the state capital. In my mind, such a relationship is hardly more attenuated than the one which the Court finds supports [the Act]. . . .

Accordingly, Congress simply lacks power under the Commerce Clause to displace state regulation of this kind.

The immense size and power of the Government of the United States ought not obscure its fundamental character. It remains a Government of enumerated powers.

Separation of Powers

"All legislative powers herein granted shall be vested in a Congress of the United States, which shall consist of a Senate and a House of Representatives."—Art. I, Sec. 1

"Every Bill which shall have passed the House of Representatives and the Senate, shall, before it becomes a Law, be presented to the President of the United States."—Art. I, Sec. 7, cl. 2.

"Every Order, Resolution, or Vote to which the Concurrence of the Senate and House of Representatives may be necessary (except on a question of Adjournment) shall be presented to the President of the United States; and before the same shall take Effect, shall be approved by him, shall be repassed by two thirds of the Senate and House of Representatives, according to the Rules and Limitations prescribed in the Case of a Bill."—Art. I, Sec. 7, cl. 3.

"The executive power shall be vested in a president of the United States of America."—Art. II, Sec. 1

"The president shall be commander in chief of the army and navy of the United States . . ."—Art. II, Sec. 2

"[The president] shall nominate, and by and with the advice and consent of the Senate, shall appoint ambassadors, other public ministers and consuls, judges of the supreme court, and all other officers of the United States . . ."—Art. II, Sec. 2

"[The president] shall take care that the laws be faithfully executed . . ."—Art. II, Sec. 3

"The judicial power of the United States shall be vested in one supreme court . . ."—Art. III, Sec. 1

The president's power to remove executive officials does not extend to independent agencies.

10. *Humphrey's Executor v. United States* (1935)

In *Myers v. United States* (1926) the Supreme Court took up the question of whether the president had the power to remove executive officials of the federal government. The problem had come up after the Civil War, in connection with President Andrew Johnson, who was impeached largely for defying the Tenure of Office Act of 1867 (which required the Senate to approve the president's dismissal of executive officials whose appointments had received Senate confirmation), but it did not reach the Supreme Court. Not until 1926 did the Court rule that the Congress could not limit the president's power of removal.

However, in *Humphrey's Executor v. United States*, the Court retracted some of the broader implications of the *Myers* decision. While that decision was left intact as far as officials within the executive branch are concerned, the Court ruled in the *Humphrey* case that the president may not, at his own discretion, remove officials of "independent agencies" exercising "quasi-legislative" or "quasi-judicial" powers.

Background: Humphrey was appointed to the Federal Trade Commission (FTC) by President Hoover for a term due to expire in 1938. When the newly elected president, Franklin D. Roosevelt, sought his resignation in 1933, Humphrey refused. The president then removed him from office. Humphrey died shortly after his removal. The suit was brought to the court of claims by the executor of his estate for payment of Humphrey's salary from the time of his removal to the time of his death. The Supreme Court ruled in Humphrey's favor.

MR. JUSTICE SUTHERLAND DELIVERED
THE OPINION OF THE COURT:

The commission is to be nonpartisan; and it must, from the very nature of its duties, act with entire impartiality. It is charged with the enforcement of no policy except the policy of the law. Its duties are neither political nor executive, but predominantly quasi-judicial and quasi-legislative. Like the Interstate Commerce Commission, its members are called upon to exercise the trained judgment of a body of experts "appointed by law and informed by experience."

The legislative reports in both houses of Congress clearly reflect the view that a fixed term was necessary to the effective and fair administration of the law. . . .

The debates in both houses demonstrate that the prevailing view was that the commission was not to be "subject to anybody in the government but . . . only to the people of the United States," free from "political domination or control," or the "probability or possibility of such a thing;" to be "separate and apart from any existing department of the government—not subject to the orders of the President."

More to the same effect appears in the debates, which were long and thorough and contain nothing to the contrary. . . .

Thus, the language of the act, the legislative reports and the general purposes of the legislation as reflected by the debates, all combine to demonstrate the Congressional intent to create a body of experts who shall gain experience by length of service—a body which shall be independent of Executive authority, *except in its selection*, and free to exercise its judgment without the leave or hindrance of any other official or any department of the government. To the accomplishment of these purposes it is clear that Congress was of opinion that length and certainty of tenure would vitally contribute. And to hold that, nevertheless, the members of the commission continue in office at the mere will of the President, might be to thwart, in large measure, the very ends which Congress sought to realize by definitely fixing the term of office.

We conclude that the intent of the act is to limit the executive power of removal to the causes enumerated, the existence of none of which is claimed here; and we pass to the second question.

To support its contention that the removal provision . . . as we have just construed it, is an unconstitutional interference with the executive power of the President, the government's chief reliance is *Myers v. United States* [1926]. . . . Nevertheless, the narrow point actually decided was only that the President had power to remove a postmaster of the first class, without the advice and consent of the Senate, as required by act of Congress. In the course of the opinion of the court, expressions occur which tend to sustain the government's contention, but these are beyond the point involved, and therefore, do not come within the rule of *stare decisis*. In so far as they are out of harmony with the views here set forth, these expressions are disapproved. . . .

The office of a postmaster is so essentially unlike the office now involved that the decision in the *Myers case* cannot be accepted as controlling our decision here. A postmaster is an executive officer restricted to the performance of executive functions. He is charged with no duty at all related to either the legislative or judicial power. The actual decision in the *Myers case* finds support in the theory that such an officer is merely one of the units in the executive department and hence inherently subject to the exclusive and illimitable power of removal by the chief executive, whose subordinate and aide he is. Putting aside dicta, which may be followed if sufficiently persuasive but which are not controlling, the necessary reach of the decision goes far enough to include all purely executive officers. It goes no farther;—much less does it include an officer who occupies no place in the executive department and who exercises no part of the executive power vested by the Constitution in the President.

The Federal Trade Commission is an administrative body created by Congress to carry into effect legislative policies embodied in the statute, in accordance with the legislative standard therein prescribed, and to perform other specified duties as a legislative or as a judicial aid. Such a body cannot in any proper sense be characterized as an arm or an eye of the executive. Its duties are performed without executive leave and, in the contemplation of the statute, must be free from executive control. In administering the provisions of the statute in respect of "unfair methods of competition"—that is to say in filling in and administering the details embodied by the general standard—the commission acts in part quasi-legislatively and in part quasi-judicially. . . .

If Congress is without authority of prescribe causes for removal of members of the Trade Commission and limit executive power of removal accordingly, that power at once becomes practically all inclusive in respect of civil officers, with the exception of the judiciary provided for by the Constitution. . . . We are thus confronted with the serious question whether not only the members of these quasi-legislative and quasi-judicial bodies, but the judges of the legislative court of claims, exercising judicial power, continue in office only at the pleasure of the President.

We think it plain under the Constitution that illimitable power of removal is not possessed by the President in respect to officers of the character of those just named. The authority of Congress, in creating quasi-legislative or quasi-judicial agencies, to require them to act in discharge of their duties independently of executive control, cannot well be doubted; and that authority includes, as an appropriate incident, power to fix the period during which they shall continue, and to forbid their removal except for cause in the meantime. For it is quite evident that one who holds his office only during the pleasure of another cannot be depended upon to maintain an attitude of independence against the latter's will. . . .

The result of what we now have said is this: Whether the power of the President to remove an officer shall prevail over the authority of Congress to condition the power by fixing a definite term and precluding a removal except for cause will depend upon the character of the office. The *Myers* decision, affirming the power of the President alone to make the removal, is confined to purely executive officers. And as to officers of the kind here under consideration, we hold that no removal can be made during the prescribed term for which the officer is appointed, except for one or more of the causes named in the applicable statute.

The president may not seize private property without congressional authorization.

11. *Youngstown Sheet and Tube Co. v. Sawyer* (1952)

The significance of this decision is that it attempts to put some restraints on presidential power, which had been expanding steadily for decades. Specifically, the case dealt with the crucial problem of whether the president had a constitutional right to seize private property even during a war emergency.

Background: After President Truman ordered his secretary of commerce, Charles Sawyer, to seize the steel companies in order to avert a threatened strike and continue production for the Korean War, Youngstown Sheet and Tube Company, joined by other steel companies, appealed to the Supreme Court. Acting with rare swiftness (the arguments were heard on May 12, 1952, and the decision was handed down on June 2), the Court, by a vote of six to three, ruled that since the president had no statutory authority for his action, it must be considered void.

In his dissent, Chief Justice Vinson defended the president's seizure order as being within his power and duty as commander-in-chief. National emergencies call for prompt executive action, he asserted, ''with or without explicit statutory authorization.''

MR. JUSTICE BLACK DELIVERED
THE OPINION OF THE COURT:

We are asked to decide whether the President was acting within his constitutional power when he issued an order directing the Secretary of Commerce to take possession of and operate most of the Nation's steel mills. The mill owners argue that the President's order amounts to lawmaking, a legislative function which the Constitution has expressly confided to the Congress and not to the President. The Government's position is that the order was made on findings of the President that his action was necessary to avert a national catastrophe which would inevitably result from a stoppage of steel production and that in meeting this grave emergency the President was acting within the aggregate of his constitutional powers as the Nation's Chief Executive and the Commander in Chief of the Armed Forces of the United States. The issue emerges here from the following series of events:

In the latter part of 1951, a dispute arose between the steel companies and their employees over terms and conditions that should be included in new collective bargaining agreements. Long-continued conferences failed to resolve the dispute. . . . On April 4, 1952, the Union gave notice of a nation-wide strike called to begin at 12:01 a.m. April 9. The indispensability of steel as a component of substantially all weapons and other war materials led the President to believe that the proposed work stoppage would immediately jeopardize our national defense and that governmental seizure of the steel mills was necessary in order to assure the continued availability of steel. Reciting these considerations for his action, the President, a few hours before the strike was to begin, issued Executive Order 10340. . . . The order directed the Secretary of Commerce to take possession of most of the steel mills and keep them running. . . .

The President's power, if any, to issue the order must stem either from an act of Congress or from the Constitution itself. There is no statute that expressly authorizes the President to take possession of property as he did here. Nor is there any act of Congress to which our attention has been directed from which such a power can fairly be implied. Indeed, we do not understand the Government to rely on statutory authorization for this seizure. . . .

Moreover, the use of the seizure technique to solve labor disputes in order to prevent work stoppages was not only unauthorized by any congressional enactment; prior to this controversy Congress had refused to adopt that method of settling labor disputes. When the Taft-Hartley Act was under consideration in 1947, Congress rejected an amendment which would have authorized such governmental seizures in cases of emergency. . . .

It is clear that if the President had authority to issue the order he did, it must be found in some provision of the Constitution. And it is not claimed that express constitutional language grants this power to the President. The contention is that presidential power should be implied from the aggregate of his powers under the Constitution. Particular reliance is placed on provisions in Article II which say that ''The executive Power shall be vested in a President . . .''; that ''he shall take Care that the Laws be faithfully executed''; and that he ''shall be Commander in Chief of the Army and Navy of the United States.''

The order cannot properly be sustained as an exercise of the President's military power as Commander in Chief of the Armed Forces. The Government attempts to do so by citing a number of cases upholding broad powers in military commanders engaged in day-to-day fighting in a theater of war. Such cases need not concern us here. Even though ''theater of war'' be an expanding concept, we cannot with faithfulness to our constitutional system hold that the Commander in Chief of the Armed Forces has the ultimate power as such to take possession of private property in order to keep labor disputes from stopping production. This is a job for the Nation's lawmakers, not for its military authorities.

Nor can the seizure order be sustained because of the several constitutional provisions that grant executive power to the President. In the framework of our Constitution, the President's power to see that the laws are faithfully executed refutes the idea that he is to be a lawmaker. The Constitution limits his functions in the lawmaking process to the recommending of laws he thinks wise and the vetoing of laws he thinks bad. And the Constitution is neither silent nor equivocal about who shall make laws which the President is to execute. The first section of the first article says that "All legislative Powers herein granted shall be vested in a Congress of the United States. . . ." After granting many powers to the Congress, Article I goes on to provide that Congress may "make all Laws which shall be necessary and proper for carrying into Execution the foregoing Powers, and all other Powers vested by this Constitution in the Government of the United States, or in any Department or Officer thereof. . . ."

It is said that other Presidents without congressional authority have taken possession of private business enterprises in order to settle labor disputes. But even if this be true, Congress has not thereby lost its exclusive constitutional authority to make laws necessary and proper to carry out the powers vested by the Constitution "in the Government of the United States, or any Department or Officer thereof."

The Founders of this Nation entrusted the lawmaking power to the Congress alone in both good and bad times. It would do no good to recall the historical events, the fears of power and the hopes for freedom that lay behind their choice. Such a review would but confirm our holding that this seizure order cannot stand.

MR. JUSTICE FRANKFURTER, CONCURRING:

In adopting the provisions which it did, by the Labor Management Relations Act of 1947, for dealing with a "national emergency" arising out of a breakdown in peaceful industrial relations, Congress was very familiar with Governmental seizure as a protective measure. On a balance of considerations Congress chose not to lodge this power in the President. It chose not to make available in advance a remedy to which both industry and labor were fiercely hostile. . . .

[N]othing can be plainer than that Congress made a conscious choice of policy in a field full of perplexity and peculiarly within legislative responsibility for choice. In formulating legislation for dealing with industrial conflicts, Congress could not more clearly and emphatically have withheld authority than it did in 1947. . . .

By the Labor Management Relations Act of 1947, Congress said to the President, "You may not seize. Please report to us and ask for seizure power if you think it is needed in a specific situation. . . ."

A scheme of government like ours no doubt at times feels the lack of power to act with complete, all-embracing, swiftly moving authority. No doubt a government with distributed authority, subject to be challenged in the courts of law, at least long enough to consider and adjudicate the challenge, labors under restrictions from which other governments are free. It has not been our tradition to envy such governments.

MR. JUSTICE DOUGLAS, CONCURRING:

We pay a price for our system of checks and balances, for the distribution of power among the three branches of the government. It is a price that today may seem exorbitant to many. Today a kindly President uses the seizure power to effect a wage increase and to keep the steel furnaces in production. Yet tomorrow another President might use the same power to prevent a wage increase, to curb trade-unionists, to regiment labor as oppressively as industry thinks it has been regimented by this seizure.

MR. JUSTICE JACKSON, CONCURRING:

Assuming that we are in a war *de facto*, whether it is or is not a war *de jure*, does that empower the Commander-in-Chief to seize industries he thinks necessary to supply our army? The Constitution expressly places in Congress power "to raise and *support* Armies" and "to *provide* and *maintain* a Navy." (Emphasis supplied.) This certainly lays upon Congress primary responsibility for supplying the armed forces. Congress alone controls the raising of revenues and their appropriation and may determine in what manner and by what means they shall be spent for military and naval procurement. I suppose no one would doubt that Congress can take over war supply as a Government enterprise. . . .

We should not use this occasion to circumscribe, much less to contract, the lawful role of the President as Commander-in-Chief. I should indulge the widest latitude of interpretation to sustain his exclusive function to command the instruments of national force, at least when turned against the outside world for security of our society. But, when it is turned inward, not because of rebellion but because of a lawful economic struggle between industry and labor it should have no such indulgence. . . .

The essence of our free Government is "leave to live by no man's leave, underneath the law"—to be governed by those impersonal forces which we call law. Our Government is fashioned to fulfill this concept so far as humanly possible. The Executive, except for recommendation and veto, has no legislative power. The executive action we have here originates in the individual will of the President and represents an exercise of authority without law. . . . With all its defects, delays and inconveniences, men have discovered no technique for long preserving free government except that the Executive be under the law, and that the law be made by parliamentary deliberations.

Such institutions may be destined to pass away. But it is the duty of the Court to be last, not first, to give them up.

MR. JUSTICE BURTON, CONCURRING:

The controlling fact here is that Congress, within its constitutional delegated power, has prescribed for the President specific procedures, exclusive of seizure, for his use in meeting the present type of emergency. Congress has reserved to itself the right to determine where and when to authorize the seizure of property in meeting such an emergency. Under these circumstances, the President's order of April 8 invaded the jurisdiction of Congress. It violated the essence of the principle of the separation of governmental powers. Accordingly, the injunction against its effectiveness should be sustained.

MR. JUSTICE CLARK, CONCURRING:

In my view—taught me not only by the decision of Mr. Chief Justice Marshall in *Little v. Barreme* [1804], but also by a score of other pronouncements of distinguished members of this bench—the Constitution does grant to the President extensive authority in times of grave and imperative national emergency. In fact, to my thinking, such a grant may well be necessary to the very existence of the Constitution itself.

As Lincoln aptly said, "[is] it possible to lose the nation and yet preserve the Constitution?" In describing this authority I care not whether one calls it "residual," "inherent," "moral," "implied," "aggregate," "emergency," or otherwise. I am of the conviction that those who have had the gratifying experience of being the President's lawyer have used one or more of these adjectives only with the utmost of sincerity and the highest of purpose.

I conclude that where Congress has laid down specific procedures to deal with the type of crisis confronting the President, he must follow those procedures in meeting the crisis; but that in the absence of such action by Congress, the President's independent power to act depends upon the gravity of the situation confronting the nation. I cannot sustain the seizure in question because here, as in *Little v. Barreme*, Congress had prescribed methods to be followed by the President in meeting the emergency at hand.

MR. CHIEF JUSTICE VINSON, WITH WHOM MR. JUSTICE REED AND MR. JUSTICE MINTON JOIN, DISSENTING:

The President of the United States directed the Secretary of Commerce to take temporary possession of the Nation's steel mills during the existing emergency because "a work stoppage would immediately jeopardize and imperil our national defense and the defense of those joined with us in resisting aggression, and would add to the continuing danger of our soldiers, sailors, and airmen engaged in combat in the field." . . .

Some members of the Court are of the view that the President is without power to act in time of crisis in the absence of express statutory authorization. Other members of the Court affirm on the basis of their reading of certain statutes. Because we cannot agree that affirmance is proper on any ground, and because of the transcending importance of the questions presented not only in this critical litigation but also to the powers of the President and of future Presidents to act in time of crisis, we are compelled to register this dissent.

In passing upon the question of Presidential powers in this case, we must first consider the context in which those powers were exercised.

Those who suggest that this is a case involving extraordinary powers should be mindful that these are extraordinary times. A world not yet recovered from the devastation of World War II has been forced to face the threat of another and more terrifying global conflict. . . .

Under this view, the President is left powerless at the very moment when the need for action may be most pressing and when no one, other than he, is immediately capable of action. Under this view, he [the President] is left powerless because a power not expressly given to Congress is nevertheless found to rest exclusively with Congress. . . .

A review of executive action demonstrates that our Presidents have on many occasions exhibited the leadership contemplated by the Framers when they made the President Commander in Chief, and imposed upon him the trust to "take Care that the Laws be faithfully executed." With or without explicit statutory authorization, Presidents have at such times dealt with national emergencies by acting promptly and resolutely to enforce legislative programs, at least to save those programs until Congress could act. Congress and the courts have responded to such executive initiative with consistent approval.

The executive's privilege to withhold information is not absolute.

12. *United States v. Nixon* (1974)

Beginning with George Washington, nearly all presidents of the United States have claimed an executive privilege to withhold information from other agencies of government (usually the Congress) in order to protect the integrity of sources and confidentiality of discussion in the executive branch. Surprisingly enough, *United States v. Nixon* was the first occasion on which the Supreme Court passed upon the executive privilege. The Court recognized the validity of the privilege in general but ruled that it was not an absolute, and withheld it from President Nixon for reasons explained in the opinion.

Background: A federal grand jury in the District of Columbia indicted several high officials, including two presidential assistants and a former attorney general, charging them with a number of offenses, including conspiracy to defraud the United States and to obstruct justice. The grand jury also named President Nixon as a co-conspirator, though he was not indicted. At the request of the special prosecutor, the district court issued a third-party subpoena, directing the president to produce, for use at the pending criminal trial, certain tape recordings and documents relating to his conversations with aides and advisers. President Nixon's counsel moved to quash this subpoena on the ground that the materials were within his executive privilege against disclosure of confidential communications. The district court denied the motion. The case went to the United States Supreme Court, which bypassed the court of appeals at the request of the special prosecutor, and was argued on July 8, 1974. On July 24 the Supreme Court upheld the district court, rejecting President Nixon's claim to executive privilege in the circumstances of this case.

Chief Justice Burger delivered the opinion of the Court, in which all members (except Justice Rehnquist, who did not participate) joined.

Shortly after the decision, articles of impeachment were voted against President Nixon by the House Judiciary Committee. In the face of these dual setbacks, Nixon became the first United States president to resign his office, on August 9, 1974.

MR. JUSTICE BURGER DELIVERED
THE OPINION OF THE COURT:

[W]e turn to the claim that the subpoena should be quashed because it demands "confidential conversations between a President and his close advisers that it would be inconsistent with the public interest to produce." The first contention is a broad claim that the separation of powers doctrine precludes judicial review of a President's claim of privilege. The second contention is that if he does not prevail on the claim of absolute privilege, the court should hold as a matter of constitutional law that the privilege prevails over the subpoena *duces tecum.* . . .

In support of his claim of absolute privilege, the President's counsel urges two grounds, one of which is common to all governments and one of which is peculiar to our system of separation of powers. The first ground is the valid need for protection of communications between high Government officials and those who advise and assist them in the performance of their manifold duties; the importance of this confidentiality is too plain to require further discussion. Human experience teaches that those who expect public dissemination of their remarks may well temper candor with a concern for appearances and for their own interests to the detriment of the decisionmaking process. Whatever the nature of the privilege of confidentiality of Presidential communications in the exercise of Art II powers, the privilege can be said to derive from the supremacy of each branch within its own assigned area of constitutional duties. Certain powers and privileges flow from the nature of enumerated powers; the protection of the confidentiality of Presidential communications has similar constitutional underpinnings.

The second ground asserted by the President's counsel in support of the claim of absolute privilege rests on the doctrine of separation of powers. Here it is argued that the independence of the Executive Branch within its own sphere insulates a President from a judicial subpoena in an ongoing criminal prosecution, and thereby protects confidential Presidential communications.

However, neither the doctrine of separation of powers, nor the need for confidentiality of high-level communications, without more, can sustain an absolute, unqualified Presidential privilege of immunity from judicial process under all circumstances. The President's need for complete candor and objectivity from advisers calls for great deference from the courts. However, when the privilege depends solely on the broad, undifferentiated claim of public interest in the confidentiality of such conversations, a confrontation with other values arises. Absent a claim of need to protect military, diplomatic, or sensitive national security secrets, we find it difficult to accept the argument that even the very important interest in confidentiality of Presidential communications is significantly diminished by production of such material for *in camera* inspection with all the protection that a district court will be obliged to provide.

The impediment that an absolute, unqualified privilege would place in the way of the primary constitutional duty of the Judicial Branch to do justice in criminal prosecutions would plainly conflict with the function of the courts under Art III. In designing the structure of our Government and dividing and allocating the sovereign power among three co-equal branches, the Framers of the Constitution sought to provide a comprehensive system, but the separate powers were not intended to operate with absolute independence.

"While the Constitution diffuses power the better to secure liberty, it also contemplates that practice will integrate the dispersed powers into a workable government. It enjoins upon its branches separateness but interdependence, autonomy but reciprocity." *Youngstown Sheet & Tube Co. v. Sawyer* [1952] (Jackson, J., concurring). To read the Art ll powers of the President as providing an absolute privilege as against a subpoena essential to enforcement of criminal statutes on no more than a generalized claim of the public interest in confidentiality of non-military and nondiplomatic discussions would upset the constitutional balance of "a workable government" and gravely impair the role of the courts under Art III.

Since we conclude that the legitimate needs of the judicial process may outweigh Presidential privilege, it is necessary to resolve those competing interests in a manner that preserves the essential functions of each branch. . . .

The expectation of a President to the confidentiality of his conversations and correspondence, like the claim of confidentiality of judicial deliberations, for example, has all the values to which we accord deference for the privacy of all citizens and added to those values the necessity for protection of the public interest in candid, objective, and even blunt or harsh opinions in Presidential decision making. . . . These are the considerations justifying a presumptive privilege for Presidential communications. The privilege is fundamental to the operation of government and inextricably rooted in the separation of powers under the Constitution. . . .

But this presumptive privilege must be considered in light of our historic commitment to the rule of law. This is nowhere more profoundly manifest than in our view that "the twofold aim [of criminal justice] is that guilt shall not escape or innocence suffer." We have elected to employ an adversary system of criminal justice in which the parties contest all issues before a court of law. The need to develop all relevant facts in the adversary system is both fundamental and comprehensive. The ends of criminal justice would be defeated if judgments were to be founded on a partial or speculative presentation of the facts. The very integrity of the judicial system and public confidence in the system depend on full disclosure of all the facts, within the framework of the rules of evidence. To ensure that justice is done, it is imperative to the function of courts that compulsory process be available for the production of evidence needed either by the prosecution or by the defense. . . .

In this case the President challenges a subpoena served on him as a third party requiring the production of materials for use in a criminal prosecution; he does so on the claim that he has a privilege against disclosure of confidential communications. He does not place his claim of privilege on the ground they are military or diplomatic secrets. As to these areas of Art II duties the courts have traditionally shown the utmost deference to Presidential responsibilities. . . . No case of the Court, however, has extended this high degree of deference to a President's generalized interest in confidentiality. Nowhere in the Constitution, as we have noted earlier, is there any explicit reference to a privilege of confidentiality, yet to the extent this interest relates to the effective discharge of a President's powers, it is constitutionally based.

The right to the production of all evidence at a criminal trial similarly has constitutional dimensions. The Sixth Amendment explicitly confers upon every defendant in a criminal trial the right "to be confronted with the witnesses against him" and "to have compulsory process for obtaining witnesses in his favor." Moreover, the Fifth Amendment also guarantees that no person shall be deprived of liberty without due process of law. It is the manifest duty of the courts to vindicate those guarantees, and to accomplish that it is essential that all relevant and admissible evidence be produced.

In this case we must weigh the importance of the general privilege of confidentiality of Presidential communications in performance of his responsibilities against the inroads of such a privilege on the fair administration of criminal justice. The interest in preserving confidentiality is weighty indeed and entitled to great respect. However, we cannot conclude that advisers will be moved to temper the candor of their remarks by the infrequent occasions of disclosure because of the possibility that such conversations will be called for in the context of a criminal prosecution.

On the other hand, the allowance of the privilege to withhold evidence that is demonstrably relevant in a criminal trial would cut deeply into the guarantee of due process of law and gravely impair the basic function of the courts. A President's acknowledged need for confidentiality in the communications of his office is general in nature, whereas the constitutional need for production of relevant evidence in a criminal proceeding is specific and central to the fair adjudication of a particular criminal case in the administration of justice. Without access to specific facts a criminal prosecution may be totally frustrated. The President's broad interest in confidentiality of communications will not be vitiated by disclosure of a limited number of conversations preliminarily shown to have some bearing on the pending criminal cases.

We conclude that when the ground for asserting privilege as to subpoenaed materials sought for use in a criminal trial is based only on the generalized interest in confidentiality, it cannot prevail over the fundamental demands of due process of law in the fair administration of criminal justice. The generalized assertion of privilege must yield to the demonstrated, specific need for evidence in a pending criminal trial.

There are limitations on the power of Congress to investigate.

13. *Watkins v. United States* (1957)

The congressional power to conduct investigations is not expressly granted by the Constitution but is derived from the power to legislate. Thus only investigations conducted with an eye toward legislation can pass constitutional muster; investigations that seek to hold up to public opprobrium the witness's actions or views ("exposure for the sake of exposure," as the Supreme Court has called it) are beyond the pale. Reversals in the Supreme Court of convictions for refusing to testify are quite rare, but one such reversal took place in *Watkins v. United States*.

Background: Watkins was a labor union official who freely testified concerning his own Communist background before the House Un-American Activities Committee, but he refused to testify concerning others whom he had known as party members. The Court reversed his conviction for contempt on the ground that the pertinence of the Committee's questions, and hence his obligation to testify, had not been properly clarified for him by the Committee.

MR. CHIEF JUSTICE WARREN DELIVERED
THE OPINION OF THE COURT:

The character of petitioner's testimony on these matters can perhaps best be summarized by the Government's own appraisal in its brief:
"A more complete and candid statement of his past political associations and activities (treating the Communist Party for present purposes as a mere political party) can hardly be imagined. Petitioner certainly was not attempting to conceal or withhold from the Committee his own past political associations, predilections, and preferences.

Furthermore, petitioner told the Committee that he was entirely willing to identify for the Committee, and answer any questions it might have concerning, 'those persons whom I knew to be members of the Communist Party,' provided that, 'to [his] best knowledge and belief,' they still were members of the Party. . . .''

[When he was asked by the Committee's counsel about the Communist affiliations of a number of persons, Watkins] stated that he did not know several of the persons. Of those whom he did know, he refused to tell whether he knew them to have been members of the Communist Party. He explained to the Subcommittee why he took such a position: . . .

''I do not believe that such questions are relevant to the work of this committee nor do I believe that this committee has the right to undertake the public exposure of persons because of their past activities. I may be wrong, and the committee may have this power, but until and unless a court of law so holds and directs me to answer, I most firmly refuse to discuss the political activities of my past associates.'' . . .

We start with several basic premises on which there is general agreement. The power of the Congress to conduct investigations is inherent in the legislative process. That power is broad. It encompasses inquiries concerning the administration of existing laws as well as proposed or possibly needed statutes. It includes surveys of defects in our social, economic or political system for the purpose of enabling the Congress to remedy them. It comprehends probes into departments of the Federal Government to expose corruption, inefficiency or waste. But broad as is this power of inquiry, it is not unlimited. There is no general authority to expose the private affairs of individuals without justification in terms of the functions of the Congress. . . .

It is unquestionably the duty of all citizens to cooperate with the Congress in its efforts to obtain the facts needed for intelligent legislative action. It is their unremitting obligation to respond to subpoenas, to respect the dignity of the Congress and its committees and to testify fully with respect to matters within the province of proper investigation. This, of course, assumes that the constitutional rights of witnesses will be respected by the Congress as they are in a court of justice. . . .

In the decade following World War II, there appeared a new kind of congressional inquiry unknown in prior periods of American history. Principally this was the result of the various investigations into the threat of subversion of the United States Government, but other subjects of congressional interest also contributed to the changed scene. This new phase of legislative inquiry involved a broad-scale intrusion into the lives and affairs of private citizens. It brought before the courts novel questions of the appropriate limits of congressional inquiry. Prior cases . . . had defined the scope of investigative power in terms of the inherent limitations of the sources of that power. In the more recent cases, the emphasis shifted to problems of accommodating the interest of the Government with the rights and privileges of individuals. The central theme was the application of the Bill of Rights as a restraint upon the assertion of governmental power in this form.

It was during this period that the Fifth Amendment privilege against self-incrimination was frequently invoked and recognized as a legal limit upon the authority of a committee to require that a witness answer its questions. Some early doubts as to the applicability of that privilege before a legislative committee never matured. When the matter reached this Court, the Government did not challenge in any way that the Fifth Amendment protection was available to the witness, and such a challenge could not have prevailed. It confined its argument to the character of the answers sought and to the adequacy of the claim of privilege.

A far more difficult task evolved from the claim by witnesses that the committees' interrogations were infringements upon the freedoms of the First Amendment. Clearly, an investigation is subject to the command that the Congress shall make no law abridging freedom of speech or press or assembly. While it is true that there is no statute to be reviewed, and that an investigation is not a law, nevertheless an investigation is part of lawmaking. It is justified solely as an adjunct to the legislative process. The First Amendment may be invoked against infringement of the protected freedoms by law or by law-making.

Abuses of the investigative process may imperceptibly lead to abridgment of protected freedoms. The mere summoning of a witness and compelling him to testify, against his will, about his beliefs, expressions or associations is a measure of governmental interference. And when those forced revelations concern matters that are unorthodox, unpopular, or even hateful to the general public, the reaction in the life of the witness may be disastrous. This effect is even more harsh when it is past beliefs, expressions or associations that are disclosed and judged by current standards rather than those contemporary with the matters exposed. Nor does the witness alone suffer the consequences. Those who are identified by witnesses and thereby placed in the same glare of publicity are equally subject to public stigma, scorn and obloquy. . . .

We have no doubt that there is no congressional power to expose for the sake of exposure. The public is, of course, entitled to be informed concerning the workings of its government. That cannot be inflated into a general power to expose where the predominant result can only be an invasion of the private rights of individuals. But a solution to our problem is not to be found in testing the motives of committee members for this purpose. Such is not our function. Their motives alone would not vitiate an investigation which had been instituted by a House of Congress if that assembly's legislative purpose is being served. . . .

It is the responsibility of the Congress, in the first instance, to insure that compulsory process is used only in furtherance of a legislative purpose. That requires that the instructions to an investigating committee spell out that group's jurisdiction and purpose with sufficient particularity. Those instructions are embodied in the authorizing resolution. That document is the committee's charter. Broadly drafted and loosely worded, however, such resolutions can leave tremendous latitude to the discretion of the investigators. The more vague the committee's charter is, the greater becomes the possibility that the committee's specific actions are not in conformity with the will of the parent House of Congress.

The authorizing resolution of the Un-American Activities Committee was adopted in 1938 when a select committee, under the chairmanship of Representative Dies, was created. Several years later, the Committee was made a standing organ of the House with the same mandate. It defines the Committee's authority as follows:

"The Committee on Un-American Activities, as a whole or by subcommittee, is authorized to make from time to time investigations of (i) the extent, character, and objects of un-American propaganda activities in the United States, (ii) the diffusion within the United States of subversive and un-American propaganda that is instigated from foreign countries or of a domestic origin and attacks the principle of the form of government as guaranteed by our Constitution, and (iii) all other questions in relation thereto that would aid Congress in any necessary remedial legislation."

It would be difficult to imagine a less explicit authorizing resolution. Who can define the meaning of "un-American"? What is that single, solitary "principle of the form of government as guaranteed by our Constitution"? . . .

When the definition of jurisdictional pertinency is as uncertain and wavering as in the case of the Un-American Activities Committee, it becomes extremely difficult for the Committee to limit its inquiries to statutory pertinency.

In fulfillment of their obligation under this statute, the courts must accord to the defendants every right which is guaranteed to defendants in all other criminal cases. Among these is the right to have available, through a sufficiently precise statute, information revealing the standard of criminality before the commission of the alleged offense. . . . [T]his raises a special problem in that the statute defines the crime as refusal to answer "any question pertinent to the question under inquiry." Part of the standard of criminality, therefore, is the pertinency of the questions propounded to the witness.

The problem attains proportion when viewed from the standpoint of the witness who appears before a congressional committee. He must decide at the time the questions are propounded whether or not to answer. . . .

It is obvious that a person compelled to make this choice is entitled to have knowledge of the subject to which the interrogation is deemed pertinent. That knowledge must be available with the same degree of explicitness and clarity that the Due Process Clause requires in the expression of any element of a criminal offense. The "vice of vagueness" must be avoided here as in all other crimes. . . .

The statement of the Committee Chairman in this case, in response to petitioner's protest, was woefully inadequate to convey sufficient information as to the pertinency of the questions to the subject under inquiry. Petitioner was thus not accorded a fair opportunity to determine whether he was within his rights in refusing to answer, and his conviction is necessarily invalid under the Due Process Clause of the Fifth Amendment.

We are mindful of the complexities of modern government and the ample scope that must be left to the Congress as the sole constitutional depository of legislative power. Equally mindful are we of the indispensable function, in the exercise of that power, of congressional investigations. The conclusions we have reached in this case will not prevent the Congress, through its committees, from obtaining any information it needs for the proper fulfillment of its role in our scheme of government. The legislature is free to determine the kinds of data that should be collected. It is only those investigations that are conducted by use of compulsory process that give rise to a need to protect the rights of individuals against illegal encroachment. That protection can be readily achieved through procedures which prevent the separation of power from responsibility and which provide the constitutional requisites of fairness for witnesses. A measure of added care on the part of the House and the Senate in authorizing the use of compulsory process and by their committees in exercising that power would suffice. That is a small price to pay if it serves to uphold the principles of limited, constitutional government without constricting the power of the Congress to inform itself.

[Mr. Justice Burton and Mr. Justice Whittaker took no part in the consideration or decision of this case. Mr. Justice Frankfurter wrote a concurring opinion. Mr. Justice Clark wrote a dissenting opinion.]

The "legislative veto" is unconstitutional.

14. *Immigration and Naturalization Service v. Chadha* (1983)

As the volume of national legislation continues to grow, Congress has increasingly sought the aid of executive agencies to make rules (having the force of law) and so "fill up the gaps" in the often vague legislation it passes. Though wholesale delegation is forbidden as a violation of the principle of separation of powers, the Court has allowed delegation where Congress prescribes standards to guide the rule makers. What if the legislators are dissatisfied with a rule drafted by an agency? Both houses of Congress can, of course, act to override the agency and cancel the rule by writing a new law. But this is a time-consuming and cumbersome procedure. During the Hoover administration, Congress hit upon the idea of a one-house veto of agency rules. This procedure came to be known as the legislative veto. In *Chadha*, one of the most important separation-of-powers cases in decades, the Court declared the legislative veto unconstitutional, thereby invalidating veto provisions in nearly 200 laws.

Background: Chadha, an immigrant, was ordered deported following a one-house veto of an INS action which would have allowed him to remain in the United States. The court of appeals ruled the congressional veto unconstitutional and the Supreme Court agreed.

CHIEF JUSTICE BURGER DELIVERED
THE OPINION OF THE COURT:

[This case] presents a challenge to the constitutionality of the provision in the Immigration and Nationality Act, authorizing one House of Congress, by resolution, to invalidate the decision of the Executive Branch, pursuant to authority delegated by Congress to the Attorney General of the United States, to allow a particular deportable alien to remain in the United States. . . .

Chadha is an East Indian who was born in Kenya and holds a British passport. He was lawfully admitted to the United States in 1966 on a nonimmigrant student visa. His visa expired on June 30, 1972. On October 11, 1973, the District Director of the Immigration and Naturalization Service ordered Chadha to show cause why he should not be deported for having "remained in the United States for a longer time than permitted." [A] deportation hearing was held before an Immigration Judge on January 11, 1974. Chadha conceded that he was deportable for overstaying his visa and the hearing was adjourned to enable him to file an application for suspension of deportation. . . .

After Chadha submitted his application for suspension of deportation, the deportation hearing was resumed on February 7, 1974. On the basis of evidence adduced at the hearing . . . the Immigration Judge, on June 25, 1974, ordered that Chadha's deportation be suspended. The Immigration Judge found that Chadha . . . had resided continuously in the United States for over seven years, was of good moral character, and would suffer "extreme hardship" if deported. . . .

Once the Attorney General's recommendation for suspension of Chadha's deportation was conveyed to Congress, Congress had the power under [this] Act, to veto the Attorney General's determination that Chadha should not be deported. . . .

The resolution [to deport Chadha] was passed without debate or recorded vote. . . .

We turn now to the question whether action of one House of Congress under [the Act] violates strictures of the Constitution. . . .

Explicit and unambiguous provisions of the Constitution prescribe and define the respective functions of the Congress and of the Executive in the legislative process. Since the precise terms of those familiar provisions are critical to the resolution of these cases, we set them out verbatim. Article I provides:

"All legislative Powers herein granted shall be vested in a Congress of the United States, which shall consist of a Senate *and* House of Representatives." Art I, § 1. (Emphasis added.)

"Every Bill which shall have passed the House of Representatives *and* the Senate, *shall*, before it becomes a Law, be presented to the President of the United States. . . ." Art I, § 7, cl 2. (Emphasis added.)

"*Every* Order, Resolution, or Vote to which the Concurrence of the Senate and House of Representatives may be necessary (except on a question of Adjournment) *shall be* presented to the President of the United States; and before the Same shall take Effect, *shall be* approved by him, or being disapproved by him, *shall be* repassed by two thirds of the Senate and House of Representatives, according to the Rules and Limitations prescribed in the Case of a Bill." Art I, § 7, cl 3. (Emphasis added.)

These provisions of Art I are integral parts of the constitutional design for the separation of powers. . . .

The records of the Constitutional Convention reveal that the requirement that all legislation be presented to the President before becoming law was uniformly accepted by the Framers. . . .

The decision to provide the President with a limited and qualified power to nullify proposed legislation by veto was based on the profound conviction of the Framers that the powers conferred on Congress were the powers to be most carefully circumscribed. It is beyond doubt that lawmaking was a power to be shared by both Houses and the President. . . .

The President's role in the lawmaking process also reflects the Framers' careful efforts to check whatever propensity a particular Congress might have to enact oppressive, improvident, or ill-considered measures. . . .

The bicameral requirement of Art I, §§ 1, 7, was of scarcely less concern to the Framers than was the Presidential veto and indeed the two concepts are interdependent. By providing that no law could take effect without the concurrence of the prescribed majority of the Members of both Houses, the Framers reemphasized their belief . . . that legislation should not be enacted unless it has been carefully and fully considered by the Nation's elected officials.

We see therefore that the Framers were acutely conscious that the bicameral requirement and the Presentment Clauses would serve essential constitutional functions. The President's participation in the legislative process was to protect the Executive Branch from Congress and to protect the whole people from improvident laws. The division of the Congress into two distinctive bodies assures that the legislative power would be exercised only after opportunity for full study and debate in separate settings. The President's unilateral veto power, in turn, was limited by the power of two-thirds of both Houses of Congress to overrule a veto thereby precluding final arbitrary action of one person. . . .

Examination of the action taken here by one House reveals that it was essentially legislative in purpose and effect. In purporting to exercise power defined in Art I, § 8, cl 4, to "establish an uniform Rule of Naturalization," the House took action that had the purpose and effect of altering the legal rights, duties, and relations of persons, including the Attorney General, Executive Branch officials and Chadha, all outside the Legislative Branch . . . The one-House veto operated in these cases to overrule the Attorney General and mandate Chadha's deportation; absent the House action, Chadha would remain in the United States. Congress has *acted* and its action has altered Chadha's status.

The legislative character of the one-House veto in these cases is confirmed by the character of the congressional action it supplants. Neither the House of Representatives nor the Senate contends that, absent the veto provision [the Act], either of them, or both of them acting together, could effectively require the Attorney General to deport an alien once the Attorney General, in the exercise of legislatively delegated authority, had determined the alien should remain in the United States. Without the challenged provision in [the Act], this could have been achieved, if at all, only by legislation requiring deportation.

The nature of the decision implemented by the one-House veto in these cases further manifests its legislative character. After long experience with the clumsy, time-consuming private bill procedure, Congress made a deliberate choice to delegate to the Executive Branch, and specifically to the Attorney General, the authority to allow deportable aliens to remain in this country in certain specified circumstances.

It is not disputed that this choice to delegate authority is precisely the kind of decision that can be implemented only in accordance with the procedures set out in Art I. Disagreement with the Attorney General's decision on Chadha's deportation—that is, Congress' decision to deport Chadha—no less than Congress' original choice to delegate to the Attorney General the authority to make that decision, involves determinations of policy that Congress can implement in only one way; bicameral passage followed by presentment to the President. Congress must abide by its delegation of authority until that delegation is legislatively altered or revoked. . . .

The choices we discern as having been made in the Constitutional Convention impose burdens on governmental processes that often seem clumsy, inefficient, even unworkable, but those hard choices were consciously made by men who had lived under a form of government that permitted arbitrary governmental acts to go unchecked. There is no support in the Constitution or decisions of this Court for the proposition that the cumbersomeness and delays often encountered in complying with explicit constitutional standards may be avoided, either by the Congress or by the President. With all the obvious flaws of delay, untidiness, and potential for abuse, we have not yet found a better way to preserve freedom than by making the exercise of power subject to the carefully crafted restraints spelled out in the Constitution.

JUSTICE POWELL, CONCURRING IN THE JUDGMENT:

The Court's decision, based on the Presentment Clauses, Art I, § 7, cls 2 and 3, apparently will invalidate every use of the legislative veto. The breadth of this holding gives one pause. Congress has included the veto in literally hundreds of statutes, dating back to the 1930's. Congress clearly views this procedure as essential to controlling the delegation of power to administrative agencies. . . . [T]he respect due its judgment as a coordinate branch of Government cautions that our holding should be no more extensive than necessary to decide these cases. In my view, the cases may be decided on a narrower ground. When Congress finds that a particular person does not satisfy the statutory criteria for permanent residence in this country it has assumed a judicial function in violation of the principle of separation of powers. Accordingly, I concur only in the judgment. . . .

One abuse that was prevalent during the Confederation was the exercise of judicial power by the state legislatures. The Framers were well acquainted with the danger of subjecting the determination of the rights of one person to the "tyranny of shifting majorities." . . .

It was to prevent the recurrence of such abuses that the Framers vested the executive, legislative, and judicial powers in separate branches. Their concern that a legislature should not be able unilaterally to impose a substantial deprivation on one person was expressed not only in this general allocation of power, but also in more specific provisions, such as the Bill of Attainder Clause, Art I, § 9, cl 3. . . . This Clause, and the separation of powers doctrine generally, reflect the Framers' concern that trial by a legislature lacks the safeguards necessary to prevent the abuse of power.

JUSTICE WHITE, DISSENTING:

Today the Court not only invalidates [a section] of the Immigration and Nationality Act, but also sounds the death knell for nearly 200 other statutory provisions in which Congress has reserved a "legislative veto." . . .

The prominence of the legislative veto mechanism in our contemporary political system and its importance to Congress can hardly be overstated. It has become a central means by which Congress secures the accountability of executive and independent agencies. Without the legislative veto, Congress is faced with a Hobson's choice: either to refrain from delegating the necessary authority, leaving itself with a hopeless task of writing laws with the requisite specificity to cover endless special circumstances across the entire policy landscape, or in the alternative, to abdicate its lawmaking function to the Executive Branch and independent agencies. To choose the former leaves major national problems unresolved; to opt for the latter risks unaccountable policy-making by those not elected to fill that role. Accordingly, over the past five decades, the legislative veto has been placed in nearly 200 statutes. The device is known in every field of governmental concern: reorganization, budgets, foreign affairs, war powers, and regulation of trade, safety, energy, the environment, and the economy.

I

The legislative veto developed initially in response to the problems of reorganizing the sprawling Government structure created in response to the Depression. . . .

Over the quarter century following World War II, Presidents continued to accept legislative vetoes by one or both Houses as constitutional, while regularly denouncing provisions by which congressional Committees reviewed Executive activity. . . .

II

The Constitution does not directly authorize or prohibit the legislative veto. Thus, our task should be to determine whether the legislative veto is consistent with the purposes of Art I and the principles of separation of powers which are reflected in that Article and throughout the Constitution.

We should not find the lack of a specific constitutional authorization for the legislative veto surprising, and I would not infer disapproval of the mechanism from its absence. From the summer of 1787 to the present the Government of the United States has become an endeavor far beyond the contemplation of the Framers. Only within the last half century has the complexity and size of the Federal Government's responsibilities grown so greatly that the Congress must rely on the legislative veto as the most effective if not the only means to insure its role as the Nation's lawmaker. But the wisdom of the Framers was to anticipate that the Nation would grow and new problems of governance would require different solutions. Accordingly, our Federal Government was intentionally chartered with the flexibility to respond to contemporary needs without losing sight of fundamental democratic principles. . . .

This is the perspective from which we should approach the novel constitutional questions presented by the legislative veto. In my view, neither Art I of the Constitution nor the doctrine of separation of powers is violated by this mechanism by which our elected Representatives preserve their voice in the governance of the Nation. . . .

III

The power to exercise a legislative veto is not the power to write new law without bicameral approval or Presidential consideration. The veto must be authorized by statute and may only negate what an Executive department or independent agency has proposed. On its face, the legislative veto no more allows one House of Congress to make law than does the Presidential veto confer such power upon the President. . . .

The Court's holding today that all legislative-type action must be enacted through the lawmaking process ignores that legislative authority is routinely delegated to the Executive Branch, to the independent regulatory agencies, and to private individuals and groups. . . .

For some time, the sheer amount of law—the substantive rules that regulate private conduct and direct the operation of government—made by the agencies has far outnumbered the lawmaking engaged in by Congress through the traditional process. There is no question but that agency rulemaking is lawmaking in any functional or realistic sense of the term. . . .

If Congress may delegate lawmaking power to independent and Executive agencies, it is most difficult to understand Art I as prohibiting Congress from also reserving a check on legislative power for itself. Absent the veto, the agencies receiving delegations of legislative or quasi-legislative power may issue regulations having the force of law without bicameral approval and without the President's signature. It is thus not apparent why the reservation of a veto over the exercise of that legislative power must be subject to a more exacting test. In both cases, it is enough that the initial statutory authorizations comply with the Art I requirements. . . .

Under the Court's analysis, the Executive Branch and the independent agencies may make rules with the effect of law while Congress, in whom the Framers confided the legislative power, Art I, § 1, may not exercise a veto which precludes such rules from having operative force. If the effective functioning of a complex modern government requires the delegation of vast authority which, by virtue of its breadth, is legislative or "quasi-legislative" in character, I cannot accept that Art I—which is, after all, the source of the nondelegation doctrine—should forbid Congress to qualify that grant with a legislative veto.

[Justice Rehnquist also wrote a dissenting opinion.]

Congress may delegate power to a commission to establish sentencing guidelines.

15. *Mistretta v. United States* (1989)

Serious disparities in sentencing by judges have long been a source of dissatisfaction with the federal court system. After wrestling with the problem for years, Congress passed the Sentencing Reform Act of 1984 which established a Sentencing Commission with power to formulate sentencing guidelines that are binding on federal judges. Details of the act and of the guidelines that have emerged are spelled out in the Court's opinion.

Background: Mistretta, convicted of selling drugs, challenged the power of Congress to establish the Commission, arguing that the delegation of power was so broad as to violate the separation-of-powers principle. Despite the far-reaching nature of the delegation, it was upheld by the Supreme Court, leading dissenting Justice Scalia to remark that the act had really created "a junior-varsity Congress."

JUSTICE BLACKMUN DELIVERED
THE OPINION OF THE COURT:

In this litigation, we consider the constitutionality of the Sentencing Guidelines promulgated by the United States Sentencing Commission. The Commission is a body created under the Sentencing Reform Act of 1984. . . .

I

A
Background

For almost a century, the Federal Government employed in criminal cases a system of indeterminate sentencing. Statutes specified the penalties for crimes but nearly always gave the sentencing judge wide discretion to decide whether the offender should be incarcerated and for how long, whether he should be fined and how much, and whether some lesser restraint, such as probation, should be imposed instead of imprisonment or fine. This indeterminate-sentencing system was supplemented by the utilization of parole, by which an offender was returned to society under the "guidance and control" of a parole officer.

Both indeterminate sentencing and parole were based on concepts of the offender's possible, indeed probable, rehabilitation, a view that it was realistic to attempt to rehabilitate the inmate and thereby to minimize the risk that he would resume criminal activity upon his return to society. It obviously required the judge and the parole officer to make their respective sentencing and release decisions upon their own assessments of the offender's amenability to rehabilitation. As a result, the court and the officer were in positions to exercise, and usually did exercise, very broad discretion. This led almost inevitably to the conclusion on the part of a reviewing court that the sentencing judge "sees more and senses more" than the appellate court; thus, the judge enjoyed the "superiority of his nether position," for that court's determination as to what sentence was appropriate met with virtually unconditional deference on appeal. The decision whether to parole was also "predictive and discretionary." The correction official possessed almost absolute discretion over the parole decision.

Historically, federal sentencing—the function of determining the scope and extent of punishment—never has been thought to be assigned by the Constitution to the exclusive jurisdiction of any one of the three Branches of Government. Congress, of course, has the power to fix the sentence for a federal crime, and the scope of judicial discretion with respect to a sentence is subject to congressional control. Congress early abandoned fixed-sentence rigidity, however, and put in place a system of ranges within which the sentencer could choose the precise punishment. . . . Congress delegated almost unfettered discretion to the sentencing judge to determine what the sentence should be within the customarily wide range so selected. This broad discretion was further enhanced by the power later granted the judge to suspend the sentence and by the resulting growth of an elaborate probation system. Also, with the advent of parole, Congress moved toward a "three-way sharing" of sentencing responsibility by granting corrections personnel in the Executive Branch the discretion to release a prisoner before the expiration of the sentence imposed by the judge.

Thus, under the indeterminate-sentence system, Congress defined the maximum, the judge imposed a sentence within the statutory range (which he usually could replace with probation), and the Executive Branch's parole official eventually determined the actual duration of imprisonment. . . .

[The Senate report on this legislation] observed that the indeterminate-sentencing system had two "unjustifi[ed]" and "shameful" consequences. The first was the great variation among sentences imposed by different judges upon similarly situated offenders. The second was the uncertainty as to the time the offender would spend in prison. Each was a serious impediment to an evenhanded and effective operation of the criminal justice system. . . .

Before settling on a mandatory-guideline system, Congress considered other competing proposals for sentencing reform. It rejected strict determinate sentencing because it concluded that a guideline system would be successful in reducing sentence disparities while retaining the flexibility needed to adjust for unanticipated factors arising in a particular case. The Judiciary Committee rejected a proposal that would have made the sentencing guidelines only advisory.

B
The Act

The Act, as adopted, revises the old sentencing process in several ways:

1. It rejects imprisonment as a means of promoting rehabilitation, and it states that punishment should serve retributive, educational, deterrent, and incapacitative goals.

2. It consolidates the power that had been exercised by the sentencing judge and the Parole Commission to decide what punishment an offender should suffer. This is done by creating the United States Sentencing Commission, directing that Commission to devise guidelines to be used for sentencing, and prospectively abolishing the Parole Commission.

3. It makes all sentences basically determinate. A prisoner is to be released at the completion of his sentence reduced only by any credit earned by good behavior while in custody.

4. It makes the Sentencing Commission's guidelines binding on the courts, although it preserves for the judge the discretion to depart from

the guideline applicable to a particular case if the judge finds an aggravating or mitigating factor present that the Commission did not adequately consider when formulating guidelines. The Act also requires the court to state its reasons for the sentence imposed and to give "the specific reason" for imposing a sentence different from that described in the guideline.

5. It authorizes limited appellate review of the sentence. It permits a defendant to appeal a sentence that is above the defined range, and it permits the Government to appeal a sentence that is below that range. It also permits either side to appeal an incorrect application of the guideline.

Thus, guidelines were meant to establish a range of determinate sentences for categories of offenses and defendants according to various specified factors, "among others." The maximum of the range ordinarily may not exceed the minimum by more than the greater of 25% of six months, and each sentence is to be within the limit provided by existing law.

C

The Sentencing Commission

The Commission is established "as an independent commission in the judicial branch of the United States." It has seven voting members (one of whom is the Chairman) appointed by the President "by and with the advice and consent of the Senate." "At least three of the members shall be Federal judges selected after considering a list of six judges recommended to the President by the Judicial Conference of the United States." No more than four members of the Commission shall be members of the same political party. The Attorney General, or his designee, is an ex officio nonvoting member. The Chairman and other members of the Commission are subject to removal by the President "only for neglect of duty or malfeasance in office or for other good cause shown." Except for initial staggering of terms, a voting member serves for six years and may not serve more than two full terms. . . .

III
Delegation of Power

Petitioner argues that in delegating the power to promulgate sentencing guidelines for every federal criminal offense to an independent Sentencing Commission, Congress has granted the Commission excessive legislative discretion in violation of the constitutionally based nondelegation doctrine. We do not agree.

The nondelegation doctrine is rooted in the principle of separation of powers that underlies our tripartite system of Government. The Constitution provides that "[a]ll legislative Powers herein granted shall be vested in a Congress of the United States," US Const, Art I, § 1, and we long have insisted that "the integrity and maintenance of the system of government ordained by the Constitution" mandate that Congress generally cannot delegate its legislative power to another Branch. We also have recognized, however, that the separation-of-powers principle, and the nondelegation doctrine in particular, do not prevent Congress from obtaining the assistance of its coordinate Branches. So long as Congress "shall lay down by legislative act an intelligible principle to which the person or body authorized to [exercise the delegated authority] is directed to conform, such legislative action is not a forbidden delegation of legislative power."

Applying this "intelligible principle" test to congressional delegations, our jurisprudence has been driven by a practical understanding that in our increasingly complex society, replete with ever changing and more technical problems, Congress simply cannot do its job absent an ability to delegate power under broad general directives. . . . Accordingly, this Court has deemed it "constitutionally sufficient if Congress clearly delineates the general policy, the public agency which is to apply it, and the boundaries of this delegated authority." . . .

[W]e harbor no doubt that Congress' delegation of authority to the Sentencing Commission is sufficiently specific and detailed to meet constitutional requirements. Congress charged the Commission with three goals: to "assure the meeting of the purposes of sentencing as set forth" in the Act; to "provide certainty and fairness in meeting the purposes of sentencing, avoiding unwarranted sentencing disparities among defendants with similar records . . . while maintaining sufficient flexibility to permit individualized sentences," where appropriate; and to "reflect, to the extent practicable, advancement in knowledge of human behavior as it relates to the criminal justice process." Congress further specified four "purposes" of sentencing that the Commission must pursue in carrying out its mandate: "to reflect the seriousness of the offense, to promote respect for the law, and to provide just punishment for the offense"; "to afford adequate deterrence to criminal conduct"; "to protect the public from further crimes of the defendant"; and "to provide the defendant with needed . . . correctional treatment."

In addition, Congress prescribed the specific tool—the guidelines system—for the Commission to use in regulating sentencing. More particularly, Congress directed the Commission to develop a system of "sentencing ranges" applicable "for each category of offense involving each category of defendant." Congress instructed the Commission that these sentencing ranges must be consistent with pertinent provisions of Title 18 of the United States Code and could not include sentences in excess of the statutory maxima. Congress also required that for sentences of imprisonment, "the maximum of the range established for such a term shall not exceed the minimum of that range by more than the greater of 25 percent or 6 months, except that, if the minimum term of the range is 30 years or more, the maximum may be life imprisonment." Moreover, Congress directed the Commission to use current average sentences "as a starting point" for its structuring of the sentencing ranges.

To guide the Commission in its formulation of offense categories, Congress directed it to consider seven factors: the grade of the offense; the aggravating and mitigating circumstances of the crime; the nature and degree of the harm caused by the crime; the community view of the gravity of the offense; the public concern generated by the crime; the deterrent effect that a particular sentence may have on others; and the current incidence of the offense. Congress set forth 11 factors for the Commission to consider in establishing categories of defendants. These include the offender's age, education, vocational skills, mental and emotional condition, physical condition (including drug dependence), previous employment record, family ties and responsibilities, community ties, role in the offense, criminal history, and degree of dependence upon crime for a livelihood. Congress also prohibited the Commission from considering the "race, sex, national origin, creed, and socioeconomic status of offenders," and instructed that the guidelines should reflect the "general inappropriateness" of considering certain other factors, such as current unemployment, that might serve as proxies for forbidden factors.

In addition to these overarching constraints, Congress provided even more detailed guidance to the Commission about categories of offenses and offender characteristics. Congress directed that guidelines require a term of confinement at or near the statutory maximum for certain crimes of violence and for drug offenses, particularly when committed by recidivists. Congress further directed that the Commission assure a substantial term of imprisonment for an offense constituting a third felony conviction, for a career felon, for one convicted of a managerial role in a racketeering enterprise, for a crime of violence by an offender on release from a prior felony conviction, and for an offense involving a substantial quantity of narcotics. Congress also instructed "that the guidelines reflect . . . the general appropriateness of imposing a term of imprisonment" for a crime of violence that resulted in serious bodily injury. On the other hand, Congress directed that guidelines reflect the general inappropriateness of imposing a sentence of imprisonment "in cases in which the defendant is a first offender who has not been convicted of a crime of violence or an otherwise serious offense." Congress also enumerated various aggravating and mitigating circumstances, such as, respectively, multiple offenses or substantial assistance to the Government, to be reflected in the guidelines. In other words, although Congress granted the Commission substantial discretion in formulating guidelines, in actuality it legislated a full hierarchy of punishment—from near maximum imprisonment, to substantial imprisonment, to some imprisonment, to alternatives—and stipulated the most important offense and offender characteristics to place defendants within these categories.

We cannot dispute petitioner's contention that the Commission enjoys significant discretion in formulating guidelines. The Commission does have discretionary authority to determine the relative severity of federal crimes and to assess the relative weight of the offender characteristics that Congress listed for the Commission to consider. The Commission also has significant discretion to determine which crimes have been punished too leniently, and which too severely. Congress has called upon the Commission to exercise its judgment about which types of crimes and which types of criminals are to be considered similar for the purposes of sentencing. . . .

Developing proportionate penalties for hundreds of different crimes by a virtually limitless array of offenders is precisely the sort of intricate, labor-intensive task for which delegation to an expert body is especially appropriate. Although Congress has delegated significant discretion to the Commission to draw judgments from its analysis of existing sentencing practice and alternative sentencing models, "Congress is not confined to that method of executing its policy which involves the least possible delegation of discretion to administrative officers." . . .

IV
Separation of Powers

Having determined that Congress has set forth sufficient standards for the exercise of the Commission's delegated authority, we turn to Mistretta's claim that the Act violates the constitutional principle of separation of powers.

This Court consistently has given voice to, and has reaffirmed, the central judgment of the Framers of the Constitution that, within our political scheme, the separation of governmental powers into three coordinate Branches is essential to the preservation of liberty.

Although the unique composition and responsibilities of the Sentencing Commission give rise to serious concerns about a disruption of the appropriate balance of governmental power among the coordinate Branches, we conclude, upon close inspection, that petitioner's fears for the fundamental structural protections of the Constitution prove, at least in this case, to be "more smoke than fire," and do not compel us to invalidate Congress' considered scheme for resolving the seemingly intractable dilemma of excessive disparity in criminal sentencing.

Location of the Commission

[T]he sentencing function long has been a peculiarly shared responsibility among the Branches of Government and has never been thought of as the exclusive constitutional province of any one Branch. For more than a century, federal judges have enjoyed wide discretion to determine the appropriate sentence in individual cases and have exercised special authority to determine the sentencing factors to be applied in any given case. Indeed, the legislative history of the Act makes clear that Congress' decision to place the Commission within the Judicial Branch reflected Congress' "strong feeling" that sentencing has been and should remain "primarily a judicial function." That Congress should vest such rulemaking in the Judicial Branch, far from being "incongruous" or vesting within the Judiciary responsibilities that more appropriately belong to another Branch, simply acknowledges the role that the Judiciary always has played, and continues to play, in sentencing. . . .

V

We conclude that in creating the Sentencing Commission—an unusual hybrid in structure and authority—Congress neither delegated excessive legislative power nor upset the constitutionally mandated balance of powers among the coordinate Branches. The Constitution's structural protections do not prohibit Congress from delegating to an expert body located within the Judicial Branch the intricate task of formulating sentencing guidelines consistent with such significant statutory direction as is present here. Nor does our system of checked and balanced authority prohibit Congress from calling upon the accumulated wisdom and experience of the Judicial Branch in creating policy on a matter uniquely within the ken of judges. Accordingly, we hold that the Act is constitutional.

JUSTICE SCALIA, DISSENTING:

While the products of the Sentencing Commission's labors have been given the modest name "Guidelines," they have the force and effect of laws, prescribing the sentences criminal defendants are to receive. A judge who disregards them will be reversed. I dissent from today's decision because I can find no place within our constitutional system for an agency created by Congress to exercise no governmental power other than the making of laws.

I

There is no doubt that the Sentencing Commission has established significant, legally binding prescriptions governing application of governmental power against private individuals—indeed, application of the ultimate governmental power, short of capital punishment. Statutorily permissible sentences for particular crimes cover as broad a range as zero years to life, and within those ranges the Commission was given broad discretion to prescribe the "correct" sentence. Average prior sentences were to be a starting point for the Commission's inquiry, but it could and regularly did deviate from those averages as it thought appropriate. It chose, for example, to prescribe substantial increases over average prior sentences for white-collar crimes such as public corruption, antitrust violations, and tax evasion. For antitrust violations, before the Guidelines only 39% of those convicted served any imprisonment, and the average imprisonment was only 45 days, whereas the Guidelines prescribe base sentences (for defendants with no prior criminal conviction) ranging from 2-to-8 months to 10-to-16 months, depending upon the volume of commerce involved.

The Commission also determined when probation was permissible, imposing a strict system of controls because of its judgment that probation had been used for an "inappropriately high percentage of offenders guilty of certain economic crimes." Moreover, the Commission had free rein in determining whether statutorily authorized fines should be imposed in addition to imprisonment, and if so, in what amounts. It ultimately decided that every nonindigent offender should pay a fine according to a schedule devised by the Commission.

Congress also gave the Commission discretion to determine whether 7 specified characteristics of offenses, and 11 specified characteristics of offenders, "have any relevance," and should be included among the factors varying the sentence. Of the latter, it included only three among the factors required to be considered, and declared the remainder not ordinarily relevant.

It should be apparent from the above that the decisions made by the Commission are far from technical, but are heavily laden (or ought to be) with value judgments and policy assessments. . . .

It is difficult to imagine a principle more essential to democratic government than that upon which the doctrine of unconstitutional delegation is founded: Except in a few areas constitutionally committed to the Executive Branch, the basic policy decisions governing society are to be made by the Legislature. Our Members of Congress could not, even if they wished, vote all power to the President and adjourn sine die. . . .

II

The focus of controversy, in the long line of our so-called excessive delegation cases, has been whether the *degree* of generality contained in the authorization for exercise of executive or judicial powers in a particular field is so unacceptably high as to *amount* to a delegation of legislative powers. I say "so-called excessive delegation" because although that convenient terminology is often used, what is really at issue is whether there has been *any* delegation of legislative power, which occurs (rarely) when Congress authorizes the exercise of executive or judicial power without adequate standards. Strictly speaking, there is *no* acceptable delegation of legislative power. . . . In the present case, however, a pure delegation of legislative power is precisely what we have before us. It is irrelevant whether the standards are adequate, because they are not standards related to the exercise of executive or judicial powers; they are, plainly and simply, standards for further legislation.

The lawmaking function of the Sentencing Commission is completely divorced from any responsibility for execution of the law or adjudication of private rights under the law. . . .

And the Commission's lawmaking is completely divorced from the exercise of judicial powers since, not being a court, it has no judicial powers itself, nor is it subject to the control of any other body with judicial powers. The power to make law at issue here, in other words, is not ancillary but quite naked. The situation is no different in principle from what would exist if Congress gave the same power of writing sentencing laws to a congressional agency such as the General Accounting Office, or to members of its staff.

The delegation of lawmaking authority to the Commission is, in short, unsupported by any legitimating theory to explain why it is not a delegation of legislative power. . . .

By reason of today's decision, I anticipate that Congress will find delegation of its lawmaking powers much more attractive in the future. If rulemaking can be entirely unrelated to the exercise of judicial or executive powers, I foresee all manner of "expert" bodies, insulated from the political process, to which Congress will delegate various portions of its lawmaking responsibility. How tempting to create an expert Medical Commission (mostly M.D.'s, with perhaps a few

Ph.D.'s in moral philosophy) to dispose of such thorny, "no-win" political issues as the withholding of life-support systems in federally funded hospitals, or the use of fetal tissue for research. This is an undemocratic precedent that we set—not because of the scope of the delegated power, but because its recipient is not one of the three Branches of Government. The only governmental power the Commission possesses is the power to make law; and it is not the Congress.

* * *

Today's decision follows the regrettable tendency of our recent separation-of-powers jurisprudence, to treat the Constitution as though it were no more than a generalized prescription that the functions of the Branches should not be commingled too much—how much is too much to be determined, case-by-case, by this Court. The Constitution is not that. Rather, as its name suggests, it is a prescribed structure, a framework, for the conduct of government. In designing that structure, the Framers *themselves* considered how much commingling was, in the generality of things, acceptable, and set forth their conclusions in the document. . . .

I think the Court errs, in other words, not so much because it mistakes the degree of commingling, but because it fails to recognize that this case is not about commingling, but about the creation of a new Branch altogether, a sort of junior-varsity Congress. It may well be that in some circumstances such a Branch would be desirable; perhaps the agency before us here will prove to be so. But there are many desirable dispositions that do not accord with the constitutional structure we live under. And in the long run the improvisation of a constitutional structure on the basis of currently perceived utility will be disastrous.

CHAPTER V

Foreign Affairs and National Security

"The Congress shall have power . . . To declare war, grant letters of marque and reprisal, and make rules concerning captures on land and water."—Art. I, Sec. 8

"The privilege of the writ of *habeas corpus* shall not be suspended unless when in cases of rebellion or invasion the public safety may require it."—Art. I, Sec. 9

"The executive power shall be vested in a president of the United States of America."—Art. II, Sec. 1

"The president shall be commander in chief of the army and navy of the United States . . ."—Art. II, Sec. 2

"He [the President] shall have power, by and with the advice and consent of the Senate, to make treaties provided two-thirds of the senators present concur; and he shall nominate, and by and with the consent of the Senate, shall appoint ambassadors, other public ministers and consuls . . ."—Art. II, Sec. 2

". . . he shall take care that the laws be faithfully executed . . ." —Art. II, Sec. 3

"This constitution, and the laws of the United States which shall be made in pursuance thereof; and all treaties made, or which shall be made, under the authority of the United States, shall be the supreme law of the land . . ."—Art. VI

**The president is authorized to respond to
an armed attack on the nation.**

16. *The Prize Cases* (1863)

Though decided during the Civil War, this case remains a landmark on
the scope of presidential power to deal with military emergency. The
closeness of the vote (5–4) sustaining the president led to an increase
in the size of the Court to ten justices, the largest it has ever been. The
tenth appointee was Stephen J. Field, a reliable Union Democrat from
California.

Background: The Civil War broke out while Congress was not in
session. President Lincoln, on his own initiative, took a number of
strong military measures to preserve the Union, including a proclamation of a blockade on Confederate ports. Several vessels attempting
to run the blockade were captured and confiscated as prizes of war.
The owners sued for return of the vessels, claiming that Lincoln had
acted unconstitutionally. The Supreme Court upheld Lincoln in a far-
reaching statement.

MR. JUSTICE GRIER DELIVERED
THE OPINION OF THE COURT:

Had the President a right to institute a blockade of ports in possession of persons in armed rebellion against the government, on the
principles of international law, as known and acknowledged among
civilized States? . . .

That a blockade *de facto* actually existed, and was formally declared
and notified by the President on the 27th and 30th of April, 1861, is
an admitted fact in these cases. . . .

The right of prize and capture has its origin in the *"jus belli,"* and
is governed and adjudged under the laws of nations. To legitimate the
capture of a neutral vessel or property on the high seas, a war must
exist *de facto*, and the neutral must have a knowledge or notice of the
intention of one of the parties belligerent to use this mode of coercion
against a port, city or territory, in possession of the other.

Let us inquire whether, at the time this blockade was instituted, a
state of war existed which would justify a resort to these means of
subduing the hostile force.

War has been well defined to be, "That state in which a nation prosecutes its right by force."

The parties belligerent in a public war are independent nations. But it is not necessary, to constitute war, that both parties should be acknowledged as independent nations or sovereign States. A war may exist where one of the belligerents claims sovereign rights as against the other. . . .

A civil war is never solemnly declared; it becomes such by its accidents—the number, power, and organization of the persons who originate and carry it on. When the party in rebellion occupy and hold in a hostile manner a certain portion of territory; have declared their independence; have cast off their allegiance; have organized armies; have commenced hostilities against their former Sovereign, the world acknowledges them as belligerents, and the contest a war. . . .

By the Constitution, Congress alone has the power to declare a national or foreign war. . . .

The Constitution confers on the President the whole executive power. He is bound to take care that the laws be faithfully executed. He is Commander-in-Chief of the Army and Navy of the United States, and of the militia of the several States when called into the actual service of the United States. He has no power to initiate or declare a war either against a foreign nation or a domestic State. But by the Acts of Congress of Feb. 28th, 1795, and 3d of March, 1807, he is authorized to call out the militia and use the military and naval forces of the United States in case of invasion by foreign nations, and to suppress insurrection against the government of a State or of the United States.

If a war be made by invasion of a foreign nation, the President is not only authorized but bound to resist force, by force. He does not initiate the war, but is bound to accept the challenge without waiting for any special legislative authority. And whether the hostile party be a foreign invader, or States organized in rebellion, it is none the less a war, although the declaration of it be *"unilateral."* . . .

As soon as the news of the attack on Fort Sumter, and the organization of a government by the seceding States, assuming to act as belligerents, could become known in Europe, to wit: on the 13th of May, 1861, the Queen of England issued her proclamation of neutrality, "recognizing hostilities as existing between the Government of the United States of America and certain States styling themselves the Confederate States of America." This was immediately followed by similar declarations or silent acquiescence by other nations.

After such an official recognition by the sovereign, a citizen of a foreign State is estopped to deny the existence of a war, with all its consequences, as regards neutrals. They cannot ask a court to affect a technical ignorance of the existence of a war, which all the world acknowledges to be the greatest civil war known in the history of the human race, and thus cripple the arm of the government and paralyze its power by subtle definitions and ingenious sophisms. . . .

Whether the President in fulfilling his duties, as Commander-in-Chief, in suppressing an insurrection, has met with such armed hostile resistence, and a civil war of such alarming proportions as will compel him to accord to them the character of belligerents, is a question to be decided by him, and this court must be governed by the decisions and acts of the Political Department of the government to which this power was intrusted. "He must determine what degree of force the crisis demands." The proclamation of blockade is, itself, official and conclusive evidence to the court that a state of war existed which demanded and authorized a recourse to such a measure, under the circumstances peculiar to the case. . . .

If it were necessary to the technical existence of a war, that it should have a legislative sanction, we find it in almost every Act passed at the extraordinary session of the Legislature of 1861, which was wholly employed in enacting laws to enable the government to prosecute the war with vigor and efficiency. And finally, in 1861 we find Congress *"ex majore cautela"* and in anticipation of such astute objections, passing an Act "approving, legalizing and making valid all the acts, proclamations, and orders of the President, &c., as if they had been issued and done under the previous express authority and direction of the Congress of the United States."

Without admitting that such an Act was necessary under the circumstances, it is plain that if the President had in any manner assumed powers which it was necessary should have the authority or sanction of Congress, . . . this ratification has operated to perfectly cure the defect. . . .

The objection made to this act of ratification, that it is *ex post facto* and, therefore, unconstitutional and void, might possibly have some weight on the trial of an indictment in a criminal court. But precedents from that source cannot be received as authoritative in a tribunal administering public and international law.

[W]e are of the opinion that the President had a right, *jure belli*, to institute a blockade of ports in possession of the States in rebellion which neutrals are bound to regard.

MR. JUSTICE NELSON, DISSENTING:

By our Constitution this power [of making war] is lodged in Congress. Congress shall have power "to declare war, grant letters of marque and reprisal, and make rules concerning captures on land and water." . . .

An idea seemed to be entertained that all that was necessary to constitute a war was organized hostility in the district or country in a state of rebellion—that conflicts on land and on sea—and taking of towns and capture of fleets—in fine, the magnitude and dimensions of the resistance against the government—constituted war with all the belligerent rights belonging to civil war. . . .

Now, in one sense, no doubt this is war, and may be a war of the most extensive and threatening dimensions and effects, but it is a statement simply of its existence in a material sense, and has no relevancy or weight when the question is what constitutes war in a legal sense, in the sense of the law of nations, and of the Constitution of the United States? For it must be a war in this sense to attach to it all the consequences that belong to belligerent rights. Instead, therefore, of inquiring after armies and navies, and victories lost and won, or organized rebellion against the General Government, the inquiry should be into the law of nations and into the municipal fundamental laws of the government. For we find there that to constitute a civil war in the sense in which we are speaking, before it can exist, in contemplation of law, it must be recognized or declared by the sovereign power of the State, and which sovereign power by our Constitution is lodged in the Congress of the United States—civil war, therefore, under our system of government, can exist only by an Act of Congress, which requires the assent of two of the great departments of the government, the Executive and Legislative. . . .

Congress assembled on the call for an extra session the 4th July, 1861, and among the first Acts passed was one in which the President was authorized by proclamation to interdict all trade and intercourse between all the inhabitants of States in insurrection and rest of the United States, subjecting vessel and cargo to capture and condemnation as prize, and also to direct the capture of any ship or vessel belonging in whole or in part to any inhabitant of a State whose inhabitants are declared by the proclamation to be in a state of insurrection, found at sea or in any part of the rest of the United States. . . .

This Act of Congress, we think, recognized a state of civil war between the government and the Confederate States, and made it territorial. . . .

Congress, on the 6th of August, 1862, passed an Act confirming all acts, proclamations, and orders of the President, after the 4th of March, 1861, respecting the Army and Navy, and legalizing them, so far as was competent for that body and it has been suggested, but scarcely argued, that this legislation on the subject had the effect to bring into existence an *ex post facto* civil war with all the rights of capture and confiscation, *jure belli*, from the date referred to. . . .

Here the captures were without any constitutional authority, and void; and, on principle, no subsequent ratification could make them valid. . . . I am compelled to the conclusion that no civil war existed between this Government and the States in insurrection till recognized by the Act of Congress 13th July, 1861; that the President does not possess the power under the Constitution to declare war or recognize its existence within the meaning of the law of nations, which carries with it belligerent rights, and thus change the country and all its citizens from a state of peace to a state of war; that this power belongs exclusively to the Congress of the United States and, consequently, that the President had no power to set on foot a blockade under the law of nations.

[Chief Justice Taney and Justices Catron and Clifford joined in this dissent.]

**The treaty-making power of Congress
has supremacy over the States.**

17. *Missouri v. Holland* (1920)

In this decision the Supreme Court held the treaty-making power of the
national government to be extremely broad and superior to state law.

Background: The case involved the constitutionality of the Migratory
Bird Treaty Act of 1918, which, pursuant to a treaty between the United
States and Great Britain, undertook to regulate and protect bird migration between Canada and the United States. (A similar act of Congress,
passed independently of the treaty power, had previously been held
unconstitutional in the district court.) The state of Missouri sought to
prevent a federal game warden from enforcing the act and, upon losing
the case in the district court, appealed to the Supreme Court. Speaking
for the Court, Justice Holmes declared the act constitutional under the
treaty-making provision of the Constitution.

MR. JUSTICE HOLMES DELIVERED
THE OPINION OF THE COURT:

[T]he question raised is the general one whether the treaty and
statute are void as an interference with the rights reserved to
the states.

To answer this question it is not enough to refer to the 10th Amendment, reserving the powers not delegated to the United States, because
by article 2, § 2, the power to make treaties is delegated expressly, and
by article 6, treaties made under the authority of the United States,
along with the Constitution and laws of the United States, made in
pursuance thereof, are declared the supreme law of the land. If the
treaty is valid, there can be no dispute about the validity of the statute
under article 1, § 8, as a necessary and proper means to execute the
powers of the government. The language of the Constitution as to the
supremacy of treaties being general, the question before us is narrowed
to an inquiry into the ground upon which the present supposed exception is placed.

It is said that a treaty cannot be valid if it infringes the Constitution;
that there are limits, therefore, to the treaty-making power; and that one
such limit is that what an act of Congress could not do unaided, in

derogation of the powers reserved to the states, a treaty cannot do. An earlier act of Congress that attempted by itself, and not in pursuance of a treaty, to regulate the killing of migratory birds within the states, had been held bad in the district court. *United States v. Shauver*, 214 Fed. 154; *United States v. McCullagh*, 221 Fed. 288.

Those decisions were supported by arguments that migratory birds were owned by the states in their sovereign capacity, for the benefit of their people, and that . . . this control was one that Congress had no power to displace. The same argument is supposed to apply now with equal force.

Whether the two cases cited were decided rightly or not, they cannot be accepted as a test of the treaty power. Acts of Congress are the supreme law of the land only when made in pursuance of the Constitution, while treaties are declared to be so when made under the authority of the United States. It is open to question whether the authority of the United States means more than the formal acts prescribed to make the convention. We do not mean to imply that there are no qualifications to the treaty-making power; but they must be ascertained in a different way. It is obvious that there may be matters of the sharpest exigency for the national well-being that an act of Congress could not deal with, but that a treaty followed by such an act could, and it is not lightly to be assumed that, in matters requiring national action, "a power which must belong to and somewhere reside in every civilized government" is not to be found. What [has just been said] with regard to the powers of the states applies with equal force to the powers of the nation in cases where the states individually are incompetent to act. We are not yet discussing the particular case before us, but only are considering the validity of the test proposed. With regard to that, we may add that when we are dealing with words that also are a constituent act, like the Constitution of the United States, we must realize that they have called into life a being the development of which could not have been foreseen completely by the most gifted of its begetters. It was enough for them to realize or to hope that they had created an organism; it has taken a century and has cost their successors much sweat and blood to prove that they created a nation. The case before us must be considered in the light of our whole experience, and not merely in that of what was said a hundred years ago. The treaty in question does not contravene any prohibitory words to be found in the Constitution. The only question is whether it is forbidden by some invisible radiation from the general terms of the 10th Amendment. We must consider what this country has become in deciding what that amendment has reserved.

The state, as we have intimated, founds its claim of exclusive authority upon an assertion of title to migratory birds,—an assertion that is embodied in statute. No doubt it is true that, as between a state and its inhabitants, the state may regulate the killing and sale of such birds, but it does not follow that its authority is exclusive of paramount powers. To put the claim of the state upon title is to lean upon a slender reed. Wild birds are not in the possession of anyone; and possession is the beginning of ownership. The whole foundation of the state's rights is the presence within their jurisdiction of birds that yesterday had not arrived, to-morrow may be in another state, and in a week a thousand miles away. If we are to be accurate, we cannot put the case of the state upon higher ground than that the treaty deals with creatures that for the moment are within the state borders, that it must be carried out by officers of the United States within the same territory, and that, but for the treaty, the state would be free to regulate this subject itself. . . .

Here a national interest of very nearly the first magnitude is involved. It can be protected only by national action in concert with that of another power. The subject-matter is only transitorily within the state, and has no permanent habitat therein. But for the treaty and the statute, there soon might be no birds for any powers to deal with. We see nothing in the Constitution that compels the government to sit by while a food supply is cut off and the protectors of our forests and of our crops are destroyed. It is not sufficient to rely upon the states. The reliance is vain, and were it otherwise, the question is whether the United States is forbidden to act. We are of opinion that the treaty and statute must be upheld.

In the field of foreign policy, Congress has the power to delegate broad authority to the president.

18. *United States v. Curtiss-Wright Export Corp.* (1936)

This is an extremely important decision regarding presidential power in foreign affairs. After analyzing the president's functions in international relations, the Court concludes by interpreting the Constitution in such a way as to grant him "broad discretion" in conducting foreign policy.

Background: In 1934 the Curtiss-Wright Export Corporation sold fifteen machine guns to Bolivia, which was then at war with Paraguay. The president's proclamation of May 28, 1934, issued pursuant to a joint resolution of Congress, prohibited the sale of arms and munitions to these nations. Indicted, the Curtiss-Wright Corporation objected on the ground that such a delegation of power to the president was not valid. The district court upheld Curtiss-Wright. The Supreme Court reversed the lower court and sustained the president.

MR. JUSTICE SUTHERLAND DELIVERED
THE OPINION OF THE COURT:

It is contended that by the Joint Resolution, the going into effect and continued operation of the resolution was conditioned (a) upon the President's judgment as to its beneficial effect upon the reestablishment of peace between the countries engaged in armed conflict in the Chaco; (b) upon the making of a proclamation, which was left to his unfettered discretion, thus constituting an attempted substitution of the President's will for that of Congress; (c) upon the making of a proclamation putting an end to the operation of the resolution, which again was left to the President's unfettered discretion; and (d) further, that the extent of its operation in particular cases was subject to limitation and exception by the President, controlled by no standard. In each of these particulars, appellees urge that Congress abdicated its essential functions and delegated them to the Executive.

Whether, if the Joint Resolution had related solely to internal affairs it would be open to the challenge that it constituted an unlawful delegation of legislative power to the Executive, we find it unnecessary to determine. The whole aim of the resolution is to affect a situation entirely external to the United States, and falling within the category of foreign affairs. The determination which we are called to make, therefore, is whether the Joint Resolution, as applied to that situation, is vulnerable to attack under the rule that forbids a delegation of the lawmaking power. In other words, assuming (but not deciding) that the challenged delegation, if it were confined to internal affairs, would be invalid, may it nevertheless be sustained on the ground that its exclusive aim is to afford a remedy for a hurtful condition within foreign territory?

It will contribute to the elucidation of the question if we first consider the differences between the powers of the Federal government in respect of foreign or external affairs and those in respect of domestic or internal affairs. That there are differences between them, and that these differences are fundamental, may not be doubted.

The two classes of powers are different, both in respect of their origin and their nature. The broad statement that the Federal government can exercise no powers except those specifically enumerated in the Constitution, and such implied powers as are necessary and proper to carry into effect the enumerated powers, is categorically true only in respect of our internal affairs. In that field, the primary purpose of the Constitution was to carve from the general mass of legislative powers *then possessed by the states* such portions as it was thought desirable to vest in the Federal government, leaving those not included in the enumeration still in the states. That this doctrine applies only to powers which the states had, is self-evident. And since the states severally never possessed international powers, such powers could not have been carved from the mass of state powers but obviously were transmitted to the United States from some other source. During the colonial period, those powers were possessed exclusively by and were entirely under the control of the Crown. By the Declaration of Independence, "the Representatives of the United States of America" declared the United [not the several] Colonies to be free and independent states, and as such to have "full Power to levy War, conclude Peace, contract Alliances, establish Commerce and to do all other Acts and Things which Independent States may of right do."

As a result of the separation from Great Britain by the colonies, acting as a unit, the powers of external sovereignty passed from the Crown not to the colonies severally, but to the colonies in their collective and corporate capacity as the United States of America. Even before the Declaration, the colonies were a unit in foreign affairs, acting through a common agency—namely the Continental Congress, composed of delegates from the thirteen colonies. That agency exercised the powers of war and peace, raised an army, created a navy, and finally adopted the Declaration of Independence. Rulers come and go; governments end and forms of government change; but sovereignty survives. A political society cannot endure without a supreme will somewhere. Sovereignty is never held in suspense. When, therefore, the external sovereignty of Great Britain in respect of the colonies ceased, it immediately passed to the Union. That fact was given practical application almost at once. The treaty of peace, made on September 3, 1783, was concluded between his Britannic Majesty and the "United States of America."

The Union existed before the Constitution, which was ordained and established among other things to form "a more perfect Union." Prior to that event, it is clear that the Union, declared by the Articles of Confederation to be "perpetual," was the sole possessor of external sovereignty, and in the Union it remained without change save in so far as the Constitution in express terms qualified its exercise. . . .

It results that the investment of the Federal government with the powers of external sovereignty did not depend upon the affirmative grants of the Constitution. The powers to declare and wage war, to conclude peace, to make treaties, to maintain diplomatic relations with other sovereignties, if they had never been mentioned in the Constitution, would have vested in the Federal government as necessary concomitants of nationality. Neither the Constitution nor the laws passed in pursuance of it have any force in foreign territory unless in respect of our own citizens; and operations of the nation in such territory must be governed by treaties, international understandings and compacts, and the principles of international law. As a member of the family of nations, the right and power of the United States in that field are equal to the right and power of the other members of the international family. Otherwise, the United States is not completely sovereign. . . .

Not only, as we have shown, is the Federal power over external affairs in origin and essential character different from that over internal affairs, but participation in the exercise of the power is significantly limited. In this vast external realm, with its important, complicated, delicate and manifold problems, the President alone has the power to speak or listen as a representative of the nation. He *makes* treaties with the advice and consent of the Senate; but he alone negotiates. Into the field of negotiation the Senate cannot intrude; and Congress itself is powerless to invade it. . . .

It is important to bear in mind that we are here dealing not alone with an authority vested in the President by an exertion of legislative power, but with such an authority plus the very delicate, plenary and exclusive power of the President as the sole organ of the Federal government in the field of international relations—a power which does not require as a basis for its exercise an act of Congress, but which, of course, like every other governmental power, must be exercised in subordination to the applicable provisions of the Constitution. It is quite apparent that if, in the maintenance of our international relations, embarrassment—perhaps serious embarrassment—is to be avoided and success for our aims achieved, congressional legislation which is to be made effective through negotiation and inquiry within the international field must often accord to the President a degree of discretion and freedom from statutory restriction which would not be admissible were domestic affairs alone involved. Moreover, he, not Congress, has the better opportunity of knowing the conditions which prevail in foreign countries, and especially is this true in time of war. He has his confidential sources of information. He has his agents in the form of diplomatic, consular and other officials. Secrecy in respect of information gathered by them may be highly necessary, and the premature disclosure of it productive of harmful results. Indeed, so clearly is this true that the first President refused to accede to a request to lay before the House of Representatives the instructions, correspondence and documents relating to the negotiation of the Jay Treaty—a refusal the wisdom of which was recognized by the House itself and has never since been doubted. . . .

In the light of the foregoing observations, it is evident that this court should not be in haste to apply a general rule which will have the effect of condemning legislation like that under review as constituting an unlawful delegation of legislative power. The principles which justify such legislation find overwhelming support in the unbroken legislative practice which has prevailed almost from the inception of the national government to the present day. . . .

Practically every volume of the United States Statutes contains one or more acts or joint resolutions of Congress authorizing action by the President in respect of subjects affecting foreign relations, which either leave the exercise of the power to his unrestricted judgment, or provide a standard far more general than that which has always been considered requisite with regard to domestic affairs. . . .

A legislative practice such as we have here, evidenced not by only occasional instances, but marked by the movement of a steady stream for a century and a half of time, goes a long way in the direction of proving the presence of unassailable ground for the constitutionality of the practice, to be found in the origin and history of the power involved, or in its nature, or in both combined.

**Prior restraint on publication bears
"a heavy presumption" of unconstitutionality.**

19. *New York Times Co. v. United States* (1971)

This case concerns the purloined "History of U.S. Decision-Making on Viet Nam Policy," popularly known as the "Pentagon Papers," which *The New York Times* and the *Washington Post* proposed to publish, even though the material was classified. The government's effort to enjoin the publication of the papers on grounds of national security was rebuffed in two district courts. The United States Courts of Appeals for the Second Circuit and the District of Columbia Circuit divided on the matter. The Supreme Court affirmed, by a vote of six to three, the decisions of the district courts, holding that the government had not met the burden of proof necessary to impose prior restraints on expression.

The decision was announced in the form of a brief *per curiam* (unsigned) opinion, with each member of the Court also filing an individual opinion. Concurring opinions were written by Justices Black, Douglas, Brennan, Stewart, White, and Marshall; dissenting opinions by Chief Justice Burger and Justices Harlan and Blackmun. Observe that Justices Black and Douglas took an "absolutist" position, holding that direct restraints on freedom of expression can *never* be justified.

PER CURIAM:

We granted certiorari in these cases in which the United States seeks to enjoin the New York Times and the Washington Post from publishing the contents of a classified study entitled "History of U.S. Decision-Making Process on Viet Nam Policy."

"Any system of prior restraints of expression comes to this Court bearing a heavy presumption against its constitutional validity." *Bantam Books, Inc. v. Sullivan* (1963); see also *Near v. Minnesota* (1931). The government "thus carries a heavy burden of showing justification for the imposition of such a restraint." *Organization for a Better Austin v. Keefe* (1971). The District Court for the Southern District of New York in the New York Times case and the District Court for the District of Columbia and the Court of Appeals for the District of Columbia Circuit in the Washington Post case held that the Government had not met that burden. We agree.

The judgment of the Court of Appeals for the District of Columbia Circuit is therefore affirmed. The order of the Court of Appeals for the Second Circuit is reversed and the case is remanded with directions to enter a judgment affirming the judgment of the District Court for the Southern District of New York. The stays entered June 25, 1971, by the Court are vacated. The judgments shall issue forthwith.

Mr. Justice Black, with whom Mr. Justice Douglas joins, concurring:

I believe that every moment's continuance of the injunctions against these newspapers amounts to a flagrant, indefensible, and continuing violation of the First Amendment. . . .

In seeking injunctions against these newspapers and in its presentation to the Court, the Executive Branch seems to have forgotten the essential purpose and history of the First Amendment. When the Constitution was adopted, many people strongly opposed it because the document contained no Bill of Rights to safeguard certain basic freedoms. They especially feared that the new powers granted to a central government might be interpreted to permit the government to curtail freedom of religion, press, assembly, and speech. In response to an overwhelming public clamor, James Madison offered a series of amendments to satisfy citizens that these great liberties would remain safe and beyond the power of government to abridge. . . .

In the First Amendment the Founding Fathers gave the free press the protection it must have to fulfill its essential role in our democracy. The press was to serve the governed, not the governors. The Government's power to censor the press was abolished so that the press would remain forever free to censure the Government. The press was protected so that it could bare the secrets of government and inform the people. Only a free and unrestrained press can effectively expose deception in government. And paramount among the responsibilities of a free press is the duty to prevent any part of the government from deceiving the people and sending them off to distant lands to die of foreign fevers

and foreign shot and shell. . . . In revealing the workings of government
that led to the Vietnam war, the newspapers nobly did precisely that
which the Founders hoped and trusted they would do. . . .

The word "security" is a broad, vague generality whose contours
should not be invoked to abrogate the fundamental law embodied in
the First Amendment. The guarding of military and diplomatic secrets
at the expense of informed representative government provides no real
security for our Republic.

MR. JUSTICE DOUGLAS, WITH WHOM MR. JUSTICE BLACK
JOINS, CONCURRING:

It should be noted at the outset that the First Amendment provides
that "Congress shall make no law . . . abridging the freedom of
speech, or of the press." That leaves, in my view, no room for governmental restraint on the press.

There is, moreover, no statute barring the publication by the press
of the material which the Times and the Post seek to use. . . .

It is common knowledge that the First Amendment was adopted
against the widespread use of the common law of seditious libel to
punish the dissemination of material that is embarrassing to the powers-
that-be. . . . The present cases will, I think, go down in history as the
most dramatic illustration of that principle. A debate of large proportions goes on in the Nation over our posture in Vietnam. That debate
antedated the disclosure of the contents of the present documents. The
latter are highly relevant to the debate in progress.

MR. JUSTICE BRENNAN, CONCURRING:

So far as I can determine, never before has the United States sought
to enjoin a newspaper from publishing information in its possession. . . .

[O]nly governmental allegation and proof that publication must inevitably, directly, and immediately cause the occurrence of an event
kindred to imperiling the safety of a transport already at sea can support
even the issuance of an interim restraining order. In no event may mere
conclusions be sufficient: for if the Executive Branch seeks judicial aid
in preventing publication, it must inevitably submit the basis upon
which that aid is sought to scrutiny by the judiciary.

MR. JUSTICE STEWART, WITH WHOM MR. JUSTICE WHITE
JOINS, CONCURRING:

In the absence of the governmental checks and balances present in other areas of our national life, the only effective restraint upon executive policy and power in the areas of national defense and international affairs may lie in an enlightened citizenry—in an informed and critical public opinion which alone can here protect the values of democratic government. For this reason, it is perhaps here that a press that is alert, aware, and free most vitally serves the basic purpose of the First Amendment. For without an informed and free press there cannot be an enlightened people.

Yet it is elementary that the successful conduct of international diplomacy and the maintenance of an effective national defense require both confidentiality and secrecy. Other nations can hardly deal with this Nation in an atmosphere of mutual trust unless they can be assured that their confidences will be kept. And within our own executive departments, the development of considered and intelligent international policies would be impossible if those charged with their formulation could not communicate with each other freely, frankly, and in confidence. In the area of basic national defense the frequent need for absolute secrecy is, of course, self-evident.

I think there can be but one answer to this dilemma, if dilemma it be. The responsibility must be where the power is. If the Constitution gives the Executive a large degree of unshared power in the conduct of foreign affairs and the maintenance of our national defense, then under the Constitution the Executive must have the largely unshared duty to determine and preserve the degree of internal security necessary to exercise that power successfully. It is an awesome responsibility, requiring judgment and wisdom of a high order. I should suppose that moral, political, and practical considerations would dictate that a very first principle of that wisdom would be an insistence upon avoiding secrecy for its own sake. For when everything is classified, then nothing is classified, and the system becomes one to be disregarded by the cynical or the careless, and to be manipulated by those intent on self-protection or self-promotion. I should suppose, in short, that the hallmark of a truly effective internal security system would be the maximum possible disclosure, recognizing that secrecy can best be preserved only when credibility is truly maintained. But be that as it may, it is clear to me that it is the constitutional duty of the Executive—as a matter of sovereign prerogative and not as a matter of law as the courts know law—through the promulgation and enforcement of executive regulations, to protect the confidentiality necessary to carry out its responsibilities in the fields of international relations and national defense. . . .

[I]n the cases before us we are asked neither to construe specific regulations nor to apply specific laws. We are asked, instead, to perform a function that the Constitution gave to the Executive, not the Judiciary. We are asked, quite simply, to prevent the publication by two newspapers of material that the Executive Branch insists should not, in the national interest, be published. I am convinced that the Executive is correct with respect to some of the documents involved. But I cannot say that disclosure of any of them will surely result in direct, immediate, and irreparable damage to our Nation or its people. That being so, there can under the First Amendment be but one judicial resolution of the issues before us. I join the judgments of the Court.

MR. JUSTICE WHITE, WITH WHOM MR. JUSTICE STEWART JOINS, CONCURRING:

I concur in today's judgments, but only because of the concededly extraordinary protection against prior restraints enjoyed by the press under our constitutional system. I do not say that in no circumstances would the First Amendment permit an injunction against publishing information about government plans or operations. Nor, after examining the materials the Government characterizes as the most sensitive and destructive, can I deny that revelation of these documents will do substantial damage to public interests. Indeed, I am confident that their disclosure will have that result. But I nevertheless agree that the United States has not satisfied the very heavy burden that it must meet to warrant an injunction against publication in these cases, at least in the absence of express and appropriately limited congressional authorization for prior restraints in circumstances such as these. . . .

At least in the absence of legislation by Congress, based on its own investigations and findings, I am quite unable to agree that the inherent powers of the Executive and the courts reach so far as to authorize remedies having such sweeping potential for inhibiting publications by the press. . . . To sustain the Government in these cases would start the courts down a long and hazardous road that I am not willing to travel, at least without congressional guidance and direction.

It is not easy to reject the proposition urged by the United States and to deny relief on its good-faith claims in these cases that publication will work serious damage to the country. But that discomfiture is considerably dispelled by the infrequency of prior-restraint cases. Normally, publication will occur and the damage be done before the Government has either opportunity or grounds for suppression. So here, publication has already begun and a substantial part of the threatened damage has already occurred. The fact of a massive breakdown in security is known, access to the documents by many unauthorized people is undeniable, and the efficacy of equitable relief against these or other newspapers to avert anticipated damage is doubtful at best.

MR. JUSTICE MARSHALL, CONCURRING:

The problem here is whether in these particular cases the Executive Branch has authority to invoke the equity jurisdiction of the courts to protect what it believes to be the national interest. . . .

It would . . . be utterly inconsistent with the concept of separation of powers for this Court to use its power of contempt to prevent behavior that Congress has specifically declined to prohibit. . . . The Constitution . . . did not provide for government by injunction in which the courts and the Executive Branch can "make law" without regard to the action of Congress. It may be more convenient for the Executive Branch if it need only convince a judge to prohibit conduct rather than ask the Congress to pass a law, and it may be more convenient to enforce a contempt order than to seek a criminal conviction in a jury trial. Moreover, it may be considered politically wise to get a court to share the responsibility for arresting those who the Executive Branch has probable cause to believe are violating the law. But convenience and political considerations of the moment do not justify a basic departure from the principles of our system of government.

In these cases we are not faced with a situation where Congress has failed to provide the Executive with broad power to protect the Nation from disclosure of damaging state secrets. Congress has on several occasions given extensive consideration to the problem of protecting the military and strategic secrets of the United States. This consideration has resulted in the enactment of statutes making it a crime to receive, disclose, communicate, withhold, and publish certain documents, photographs, instruments, appliances, and information. . . .

Either the Government has the power under statutory grant to use traditional criminal law to protect the country or, if there is no basis for arguing that Congress has made the activity a crime, it is plain that Congress has specifically refused to grant the authority the Government seeks from this Court. In either case this Court does not have authority to grant the requested relief. It is not for this Court to fling itself into every breach perceived by some Government official nor is it for this Court to take on itself the burden of enacting law, especially a law that Congress has refused to pass.

MR. CHIEF JUSTICE BURGER, DISSENTING:

We do not know the facts of the cases. No District Judge knew all the facts. No Court of Appeals judge knew all the facts. No member of this Court knows all the facts.

Why are we in this posture, in which only those judges to whom the First Amendment is absolute and permits of no restraint in any circumstances or for any reason, are really in a position to act?

I suggest we are in this posture because these cases have been conducted in unseemly haste. . . . [P]rompt judicial action does not mean unjudicial haste.

Here, moreover, the frenetic haste is due in large part to the manner in which the Times proceeded from the date it obtained the purloined documents. It seems reasonably clear now that the haste precluded reasonable and deliberate judicial treatment of these cases and was not warranted. The precipitate action of this Court aborting trials not yet completed is not the kind of judicial conduct that ought to attend the disposition of a great issue.

The newspapers make a derivative claim under the First Amendment; they denominate this right as the public "right to know"; by implication, the Times asserts a sole trusteeship of that right by virtue of its journalistic "scoop." . . . An issue of this importance should be tried and heard in a judicial atmosphere conducive to thoughtful, reflective deliberation, especially when haste, in terms of hours, is unwarranted in light of the long period the Times, by its own choice, deferred publication.

It is not disputed that the Times has had unauthorized possession of the documents for three to four months, during which it has had its expert analysts studying them, presumably digesting them and preparing the material for publication. During all of this time, the Times, presumably in its capacity as trustee of the public's "right to know," has held up publication for purposes it considered proper and thus public knowledge was delayed. No doubt this was for a good reason; the analysis of 7,000 pages of complex material drawn from a vastly greater volume of material would inevitably take time and the writing of good news stories takes time. But why should the United States Government, from whom this information was illegally acquired by someone, along with all the counsel, trial judges, and appellate judges be placed under needless pressure? After these months of deferral, the alleged "right to know" has somehow and suddenly become a right that must be vindicated instanter. . . .

The consequence of all this melancholy series of events is that we literally do not know what we are acting on. . . .

We all crave speedier judicial processes but when judges are pressured as in these cases the result is a parody of the judicial function.

MR. JUSTICE HARLAN, WITH WHOM THE CHIEF JUSTICE AND MR. JUSTICE BLACKMUN JOIN, DISSENTING:

With all respect, I consider that the Court has been almost irresponsibly feverish in dealing with these cases. . . . Forced as I am to reach the merits of these cases, I dissent from the opinion and judgments of the Court. . . .

It is plain to me that the scope of the judicial function in passing upon the activities of the Executive Branch of the Government in the field of foreign affairs is very narrowly restricted. This view is, I think, dictated by the concept of separation of powers upon which our constitutional system rests. . . .

I agree that, in performance of its duty to protect the values of the First Amendment against political pressures, the judiciary must review the initial Executive determination to the point of satisfying itself that the subject matter of the dispute does lie within the proper compass of the President's foreign relations power. . . . Moreover, the judiciary may properly insist that the determination that disclosure of the subject matter would irreparably impair the national security be made by the head of the Executive Department concerned—here the Secretary of

State or the Secretary of Defense—after actual personal consideration by that officer. This safeguard is required in the analogous area of executive claims of privilege for secrets of state.

But in my judgment the judiciary may not properly go beyond these two inquiries and redetermine for itself the probable impact of disclosure on the national security.

MR. JUSTICE BLACKMUN, DISSENTING:

Two federal district courts, two United States courts of appeals, and this Court—within a period of less than three weeks from inception until today—have been pressed into hurried decision of profound constitutional issues on inadequately developed and largely assumed facts without the careful deliberation that, one would hope, should characterize the American judicial process. . . .

The First Amendment, after all, is only one part of an entire Constitution. Article II of the great document vests in the Executive Branch primary power over the conduct of foreign affairs and places in that branch the responsibility for the Nation's safety. Each provision of the Constitution is important, and I cannot subscribe to a doctrine of unlimited absolutism for the First Amendment at the cost of downgrading other provisions.

Martial law cannot operate where civil courts are open.

20. *Ex Parte Milligan* (1866)

The significance of this case lies in its rejection of military tribunals of justice in areas where civilian courts are in operation. The case is, therefore, basic to civil liberties. It is an eloquent reaffirmation of the rights of Americans under the Constitution.

Background: On October 15, 1863, President Lincoln, after authorization by Congress, suspended the writ of habeas corpus in cases of persons arrested for military offenses. The following year the army jailed Lambdin P. Milligan, a pro-Southern Indiana lawyer and teacher, tried him by a military commission for disloyalty, and condemned him to be hanged. The Supreme Court, in the following opinion by Justice Davis (a friend of Lincoln's), reversed the military sentence and ruled that Milligan should have been given a civilian trial with all the constitutional safeguards.

MR. JUSTICE DAVIS DELIVERED THE OPINION OF THE COURT:

During the late wicked Rebellion the temper of the times did not allow that calmness in deliberation and discussion so necessary to a correct conclusion of a purely judicial question. Then, considerations of safety were mingled with the exercise of power, and feelings and interests prevailed which are happily terminated. Now that the public safety is assured, this question, as well as all others, can be discussed and decided without passion or the admixture of any element not required to form a legal judgment. We approach the investigation of this case fully sensible of the magnitude of the inquiry and the necessity of full and cautious deliberation. . . .

The controlling question in the case is this: . . . had the Military Commission mentioned in it jurisdiction, legally, to try and sentence him? Milligan, not a resident of one of the rebellious states, or a prisoner of war, but a citizen of Indiana for twenty years past, and never in the military or naval service, is, while at his home, arrested by the military power of the United States, imprisoned and, on certain criminal charges preferred against him, tried, convicted, and sentenced to be hanged by a military commission, organized under the direction of the military commander of the military district of Indiana. Had this tribunal the legal power and authority to try and punish this man?

No graver question was ever considered by this court, nor one which more nearly concerns the rights of the whole people; for it is the birthright of every American citizen when charged with crime, to be tried and punished according to law. The power of punishment is alone through the means which the laws have provided for that purpose, and if they are ineffectual, there is an immunity from punishment, no matter how great an offender the individual may be, or how much his crimes may have shocked the sense of justice of the country, or endangered its safety. By the protection of the law human rights are secured; withdraw that protection, and they are at the mercy of wicked rulers, or the clamor of an excited people. If there was law to justify this military trial, it is not our province to interfere; if there was not, it is our duty to declare the nullity of the whole proceedings.

The Constitution of the United States is a law for rulers and people, equally in war and in peace, and covers with the shield of its protection all classes of men, at all times, and under all circumstances. No doctrine, involving more pernicious consequences, was ever invented by the wit of man than that any of its provisions can be suspended during any of the great exigencies of government. Such a doctrine leads directly to anarchy or despotism, but the theory of necessity on which it is based is false; for the government, within the Constitution, has all the powers granted to it which are necessary to preserve its existence, as has been happily proved by the result of the great effort to throw off its just authority.

Have any of the rights guaranteed by the Constitution been violated in the case of Milligan? and if so, what are they?

Every trial involves the exercise of judicial power; and from what source did the Military Commission that tried him derive their authority? Certainly no part of the judicial power of the country was conferred on them; because the Constitution expressly vests it "in one Supreme Court and such inferior courts as the Congress may from time to time ordain and establish," and it is not pretended that the commission was a court ordained and established by Congress. They cannot justify on the mandate of the President; because he is controlled by law, and has his appropriate sphere of duty, which is to execute, not to make, the laws: and there is "no unwritten criminal code to which resort can be had as a source of jurisdiction."

But it is said that the jurisdiction is complete under the "laws and usages of war."

It can serve no useful purpose to inquire what those laws and usages are, whence they originated, where found, and on whom they operate; they can never be applied to citizens in states which have upheld the authority of the government, and where the courts are open and their process unobstructed. This court has judicial knowledge that in Indiana the Federal authority was always unopposed, and its courts always open to hear criminal accusations and redress grievances; and no usage of war could sanction a military trial there for any offense whatever of a citizen in civil life, in nowise connected with the military service. Congress could grant no such power; and to the honor of our national legislature be it said, it has never been provoked by the state of the country even to attempt its exercise. One of the plainest constitutional provisions was, therefore, infringed when Milligan was tried by a court not ordained and established by Congress, and not composed of judges appointed during good behavior.

Why was he not delivered to the circuit court of Indiana to be proceeded against according to law? No reason of necessity could be urged against it; because Congress had declared penalties against the offenses charged, provided for their punishment, and directed that court to hear and determine them. And soon after this military tribunal was ended, the circuit court met, peacefully transacted its business, and adjourned. It needed no bayonets to protect it, and required no military aid to execute its judgments. It was held in a state, eminently distinguished for patriotism, by judges commissioned during the Rebellion, who were provided with juries, upright, intelligent, and selected by a marshal appointed by the President. The government had no right to conclude that Milligan, if guilty, would not receive in that court merited punishment; for its records disclose that it was constantly engaged in the trial of similar offenses, and was never interrupted in its administration of criminal justice. . . .

Another guarantee of freedom was broken when Milligan was denied a trial by jury. . . . [U]ntil recently no one ever doubted that the right of trial by jury was fortified in the organic law against the power of attack. It is now assailed; but if ideas can be expressed in words, and language has any meaning, this right—one of the most valuable in a free country—is preserved to every one accused of crime who is not attached to the Army or Navy or Militia in actual service.

It is claimed that martial law covers with its broad mantle the proceedings of this Military Commission. The proposition is this: That in a time of war the commander of an armed force (if in his opinion the exigencies of the country demand it, and of which he is to judge), has the power, within the lines of his military district, to suspend all civil rights and their remedies, and subject citizens as well as soldiers to the rule of his will; and in the exercise of his lawful authority cannot be restrained, except by his superior officer or the President of the United States.

If this position is sound to the extent claimed, then when war exists, foreign or domestic, and the country is subdivided into military departments for mere convenience, the commander of one of them can, if he chooses, within the limits, on the plea of necessity, with the approval of the Executive, substitute military force for and the exclusion of the laws, and punish all persons, as he thinks right and proper, without fixed or certain rules.

The statement of this proposition shows its importance; for, if true, republican government is a failure, and there is an end of liberty regulated by law. Martial law, established on such a basis, destroys every guaranty of the Constitution, and effectually renders the "military independent of and superior to the civil power"—the attempt to do which by the King of Great Britain was deemed by our fathers such an offense, that they assigned it to the world as one of the causes which impelled them to declare their independence. Civil liberty and this kind of martial law cannot endure together; the antagonism is irreconcilable and, in the conflict, one or the other must perish. . . .

If, in foreign invasion or civil war, the courts are actually closed, and it is impossible to administer criminal justice according to law, then, on the theater of actual military operations, where war really prevails, there is a necessity to furnish a substitute for the civil authority, thus overthrown, to preserve the safety of the army and society; and as no power is left but the military, it is allowed to govern by martial rule until the laws can have their free course. As necessity creates the rule, so it limits its duration; for, if this government is continued after the courts are reinstated, it is a gross usurpation of power. Martial rule can never exist where the courts are open, and in the proper and unobstructed exercise of their jurisdiction. It is also confined to the locality of actual war. Because, during the late Rebellion it could have been enforced in Virginia, where the national authority was overturned and the courts driven out, it does not follow that it should obtain in Indiana, where that authority was never disputed, and justice was always administered. And so in the case of a foreign invasion, martial rule may become a necessity, in one state, when, in another, it would be "mere lawless violence."

CHIEF JUSTICE CHASE CONCURRING IN THE JUDGMENT
JOINED BY JUSTICES WAYNE, SWAYNE, AND MILLER:

[T]he opinion . . . asserts not only that the Military Commission held in Indiana was not authorized by Congress, but that it was not in the power of Congress to authorize it. . . .

We cannot agree to this. . . .

We cannot doubt that, in such a time of public danger, Congress had power, under the Constitution, to provide for the organization of a military commission, and for trial by that commission of persons engaged in this conspiracy. The fact that the Federal courts were open was regarded by Congress as a sufficient reason for not exercising the power; but that fact could not deprive Congress of the right to exercise it. Those courts might be open and undisturbed in the execution of their functions, and yet wholly incompetent to avert threatened danger, or to punish, with adequate promptitude and certainty, the guilty conspirators.

In Indiana, the judges and officers of the courts were loyal to the government. But it might have been otherwise. In times of rebellion and civil war it may often happen, indeed, that judges and marshals will be in active sympathy with the rebels, and courts their most efficient allies.

We have confined ourselves to the question of power. It was for Congress to determine the question of expediency. And Congress did determine it. That body did not see fit to authorize trials by military commission in Indiana, but by the strongest implication prohibited them.

The exigencies of war may justify the detention of American citizens.

21. *Korematsu v. United States* (1944)

This case, better than any other, illustrates the pressures militating against judicial enforcement of constitutional guarantees in time of war.

Background: On the authorization of an executive order issued by President Roosevelt shortly after the Japanese attack on Pearl Harbor (Congress quickly gave substantial assent to the president's directive through legislation), General DeWitt, the commander of the Western Defense Command, ordered the removal of "all persons of Japanese ancestry, both alien and non-alien," from the San Francisco area. The evacuees remained in relocation centers until their loyalty was established. Korematsu, an American citizen, was convicted for refusing to leave his home. After the court of appeals affirmed the conviction, Korematsu carried his appeal to the Supreme Court, which likewise turned him down, Justice Black cautioning that "hardships are part of war, and war is an aggregation of hardships.'' A curfew order aimed at persons of Japanese descent was earlier upheld by the Court, in *Hirabayashi v. United States* (1943).

MR. JUSTICE BLACK DELIVERED
THE OPINION OF THE COURT:

It should be noted, to begin with, that all legal restrictions which curtail the civil rights of a single racial group are immediately suspect. That is not to say that all such restrictions are unconstitutional. It is to say that courts must subject them to the most rigid scrutiny. Pressing public necessity may sometimes justify the existence of such restrictions; racial antagonism never can. . . .

In the light of the principles we announced in the *Hirabayashi Case* [1943], we are unable to conclude that it was beyond the war power of Congress and the Executive to exclude those of Japanese ancestry from the West Coast war area at the time they did. True, exclusion from the area in which one's home is located is a far greater deprivation than constant confinement to the home from 8 p.m. to 6 a.m. Nothing short of apprehension by the proper military authorities of the gravest imminent danger to the public safety can constitutionally justify either. But exclusion from a threatened area, no less than curfew, has a definite and close relationship to the prevention of espionage and sabotage. The military authorities, charged with the primary responsibility of defending our shores, concluded that curfew provided inadequate protection and ordered exclusion. They did so, as pointed out in our *Hirabayashi* opinion, in accordance with congressional authority to the military to say who should, and who should not, remain in the threatened areas. . . .

Like curfew, exclusion of those of Japanese origin was deemed necessary because of the presence of an unascertained number of disloyal members of the group, most of whom we have no doubt were loyal to this country. It was because we could not reject the finding of the military authorities that it was impossible to bring about an immediate segregation of the disloyal from the loyal that we sustained the validity of the curfew order as applying to the whole group. In the instant case, temporary exclusion of the entire group was rested by the military on the same ground. The judgment that exclusion of the whole group was for the same reason a military imperative answers the contention that the exclusion was in the nature of group punishment based on antagonism to those of Japanese origin. That there were members of the group who retained loyalties to Japan has been confirmed by investigations made subsequent to the exclusion. Approximately five thousand American citizens of Japanese ancestry refused to swear unqualified allegiance to the United States and to renounce allegiance to the Japanese Emperor, and several thousand evacuees requested repatriation to Japan.

We uphold the exclusion order as of the time it was made and when the petitioner violated it. In doing so, we are not unmindful of the hardships imposed by it upon a large group of American citizens. But hardships are part of war, and war is an aggregation of hardships. All citizens alike, both in and out of uniform, feel the impact of war in greater or lesser measure. Citizenship has its responsibilities as well as its privileges, and in time of war the burden is always heavier. Compulsory exclusion of large groups of citizens from their homes, except under circumstances of direst emergency and peril, is inconsistent with our basic governmental institutions. But when under conditions of modern warfare our shores are threatened by hostile forces, the power to protect must be commensurate with the threatened danger. . . .

It is said that we are dealing here with the case of imprisonment of a citizen in a concentration camp solely because of his ancestry, without evidence or inquiry concerning his loyalty and good disposition towards the United States. Our task would be simple, our duty clear, were this a case involving the imprisonment of a loyal citizen in a concentration camp because of racial prejudice. Regardless of the true nature of the assembly and relocation centers—and we deem it unjustifiable to call them concentration camps with all the ugly connotations that term implies—we are dealing specifically with nothing but an exclusion order. To cast this case into outlines of racial prejudice, without reference to the real military dangers which were presented, merely confuses the issue. Korematsu was not excluded from the Military Area because of hostility to him or his race. He *was* excluded because we are at war with the Japanese Empire, because the properly constituted military authorities feared an invasion of our West Coast and felt constrained to take proper security measures, because they decided that the military urgency of the situation demanded that all citizens of Japanese ancestry be segregated from the West Coast temporarily, and finally, because Congress, reposing its confidence in this time of war in our military leaders—as inevitably it must—determined that they should have the power to do just this. There was evidence of disloyalty on the part of some, the military authorities considered that the need for action was great, and time was short. We cannot—by availing ourselves of the calm perspective of hindsight—now say that at that time these actions were unjustified.

[Mr. Justice Frankfurter wrote a concurring opinion.]

MR. JUSTICE JACKSON, DISSENTING:

In the very nature of things military decisions are not susceptible of intelligent judicial appraisal. They do not pretend to rest on evidence, but are made on information that often would not be admissible and on assumptions that could not be proved. Information in support of an order could not be disclosed to courts without danger that it would reach the enemy. Neither can courts act on communications made in confidence. Hence courts can never have any real alternative to accepting the mere declaration of the authority that issued the order that it was reasonably necessary from a military viewpoint.

Much is said of the danger to liberty from the Army program for deporting and detaining these citizens of Japanese extraction. But a judicial construction of the due process clause that will sustain this order is a far more subtle blow to liberty than the promulgation of the order itself. A military order, however unconstitutional, is not apt to last longer than the military emergency. Even during that period a succeeding commander may revoke it all. But once a judicial opinion rationalizes such an order to show that it conforms to the Constitution, or rather rationalizes the Constitution to show that the Constitution sanctions such an order, the Court for all time has validated the principle of racial discrimination in criminal procedure and of transplanting American citizens. The principle then lies about like a loaded weapon ready for the hand of any authority that can bring forward a plausible claim of an urgent need. Every repetition imbeds that principle more deeply in our law and thinking and expands it to new purposes. All who observe the work of courts are familiar with what Judge Cardozo described as "the tendency of a principle to expand itself to the limit of its logic." A military commander may overstep the bounds of constitutionality, and it is an incident. But if we review and approve, that passing incident becomes the doctrine of the Constitution.

I should hold that a civil court cannot be made to enforce an order which violates constitutional limitations even if it is a reasonable exercise of military authority. The courts can exercise only the judicial power, can apply only law, and must abide by the Constitution, or they cease to be civil courts and become instruments of military policy.

My duties as a justice as I see them do not require me to make a military judgment as to whether General DeWitt's evacuation and detention program was a reasonable military necessity. I do not suggest that the courts should have attempted to interfere with the Army in carrying out its task. But I do not think they may be asked to execute a military expedient that has no place in law under the Constitution. I would reverse the judgment and discharge the prisoner.

[Mr. Justice Roberts and Mr. Justice Murphy also wrote dissenting opinions.]

CHAPTER VI

The Commerce Power

"The Congress shall have power to . . . regulate commerce with foreign nations, and among the several states . . ."—Art. I, Sec. 8

Commerce is more than mere "traffic." It involves a whole range of interconnected activities protected by the Constitution.

22. *Gibbons v. Ogden* (1824)

In this decision, Chief Justice Marshall, following his general philosophy of strengthening the central authority, interpreted the Constitution's Commerce Clause as a broad and ample grant of power to Congress to regulate and encourage commerce in all its forms.

Background: Robert Livingston and Robert Fulton had been given the exclusive right by the state of New York to navigate steamboats on the waters of the state. Aaron Ogden, who acquired this right, sued a competitor named Gibbons in order to prevent him from operating his boats (which were licensed under a federal act) on the Hudson River. Ogden won an injunction in the New York courts but lost the case in the Supreme Court.

MR. CHIEF JUSTICE MARSHALL DELIVERED
THE OPINION OF THE COURT:

The words are: "Congress shall have power to regulate commerce with foreign nations, and among the several states, and with the Indian tribes."

The subject to be regulated is commerce; and our constitution being, as was aptly said at the bar, one of enumeration, and not of definition, to ascertain the extent of the power it becomes necessary to settle the meaning of the word. The counsel for the appellee would limit it to traffic, to buying and selling, or the interchange of commodities, and do not admit that it comprehends navigation. This would restrict a general term, applicable to many objects, to one of its significations. Commerce, undoubtedly, is traffic, but it is something more; it is intercourse. It describes the commercial intercourse between nations, and parts of nations, in all its branches, and is regulated by prescribing rules for carrying on that intercourse. The mind can scarcely conceive a system for regulating commerce between nations, which shall exclude all laws concerning navigation, which shall be silent on the admission of the vessels of the one nation into the ports of the other, and be confined to prescribing rules for the conduct of individuals, in the actual employment of buying and selling or of barter.

If commerce does not include navigation, the government of the Union has no direct power over the subject, and can make no law prescribing what shall constitute American vessels, or requiring that they shall be navigated by American seamen. Yet this power has been exercised from the commencement of the government, has been exercised with the consent of all, and has been understood by all to be a commercial regulation. All America understands, and has uniformly understood, the word "commerce" to comprehend navigation. It was so understood, and must have been so understood, when the constitution was framed. The power over commerce, including navigation, was one of the primary objects for which the people of America adopted their government, and must have been contemplated in forming it. The convention must have used the words in that sense; because all have understood it in that sense, and the attempt to restrict it comes too late. . . .

The word used in the constitution, then, comprehends, and has been always understood to comprehend, navigation within its meaning; and a power to regulate navigation is as expressly granted as if that term had been added to the word "commerce."

To what commerce does this power extend? The constitution informs us, to commerce "with foreign nations, and among the several states, and with the Indian tribes."

It has, we believe, been universally admitted that these words comprehend every species of commercial intercourse between the United States and foreign nations. No sort of trade can be carried on between this country and any other, to which this power does not extend. It has been truly said, that commerce, as the word is used in the constitution, is a unit, every part of which is indicated by the term.

If this be the admitted meaning of the word, in its application to foreign nations, it must carry the same meaning throughout the sentence, and remain a unit, unless there be some plain intelligible cause which alters it.

The subject to which the power is next applied, is to commerce "among the several states." The word "among" means intermingled with. A thing which is among others, is intermingled with them. Commerce among the states cannot stop at the external boundary line of each state, but may be introduced into the interior.

It is not intended to say that these words comprehend that commerce which is completely internal, which is carried on between man and man in a state, or between different parts of the same state, and which does not extend to or affect other states. Such a power would be inconvenient, and is certainly unnecessary.

Comprehensive as the word "among" is, it may very properly be restricted to that commerce which concerns more states than one. The phrase is not one which would probably have been selected to indicate the completely interior traffic of a state, because it is not an apt phrase for that purpose; and the enumeration of the particular classes of commerce to which the power was to be extended, would not have been made had the intention been to extend the power to every description. The enumeration presupposes something not enumerated; and that something, if we regard the language or the subject of the sentence, must be the exclusively internal commerce of a state. The genius and character of the whole government seem to be, that its action is to be applied to all the external concerns of the nation, and to those internal concerns which affect the states generally; but not to those which are completely within a particular state, which do not affect other states, and with which it is not necessary to interfere, for the purpose of executing some of the general powers of the government. The completely internal commerce of a state, then, may be considered as reserved for the state itself.

But, in regulating commerce with foreign nations, the power of Congress does not stop at the jurisdictional lines of the several states. It would be a very useless power if it could not pass those lines. The commerce of the United States with foreign nations, is that of the whole United States. Every district has a right to participate in it. The deep streams which penetrate our country in every direction, pass through the interior of almost every state in the Union, and furnish the means of exercising this right. If Congress has the power to regulate it, that power must be exercised whenever the subject exists. If it exists within the states, if a foreign voyage may commence or terminate at a port within a state, then the power of Congress may be exercised within a state.

This principle is, if possible, still more clear, when applied to commerce ''among the several states.'' They either join each other, in which case they are separated by a mathematical line, or they are remote from each other, in which case other states lie between them. What is commerce ''among'' them; and how is it to be conducted? Can a trading expedition between two adjoining states commence and terminate outside of each? And if the trading intercourse be between two states remote from each other, must it not commence in one, terminate in the other, and probably pass through a third? Commerce among the states must, of necessity, be commerce with the states. In the regulation of trade with the Indian tribes, the action of the law, especially when the constitution was made, was chiefly within a state. The power of Congress, then, whatever it may be, must be exercised within the territorial jurisdiction of the several states. The sense of the nation, on this subject, is unequivocally manifested by the provisions made in the laws for transporting goods, by land, between Baltimore and Providence, between New York and Philadelphia, and between Philadelphia and Baltimore.

We are now arrived at the inquiry. What is this power?

It is the power to regulate; that is, to prescribe the rule by which commerce is to be governed. This power, like all others vested in Congress, is complete in itself, may be exercised to its utmost extent, and acknowledges no limitations, other than are prescribed in the constitution. These are expressed in plain terms, and do not affect the questions which arise in this case, or which have been discussed at the bar. If, as has always been understood, the sovereignty of Congress, though limited to specified objects, is plenary as to those objects, the power over commerce with foreign nations, and among the several States is vested in Congress as absolutely as it would be in a single government, having in its constitution the same restrictions on the exercise of the power as are found in the constitution of the United States. The wisdom and the discretion of Congress, their identity with the people, and the influence which their constituents possess at election, are, in this, as in many other instances, as that, for example, of declaring war, the sole restraints on which they have relied, to secure them from its abuse. They are the restraints on which the people must often rely solely, in all representative governments. . . .

The power of Congress, then, comprehends navigation within the limits of every state in the Union; so far as that navigation may be, in any manner, connected with ''commerce with foreign nations, or among the several states, or with the Indian tribes.'' It may, of consequence, pass the jurisdictional line of New York, and act upon the very waters to which the prohibition now under consideration applies.

But it has been urged with great earnestness, that although the power of Congress to regulate commerce with foreign nations, and among the several states, be co-extensive with the subject itself, and have no other limits than are prescribed in the constitution, yet the states may severally exercise the same power within their respective jurisdictions. In support of this argument, it is said that they possessed it as an inseparable attribute of sovereignty, before the formation of the constitution, and still retain it, except so far as they have surrendered it by that instrument; that this principle results from the nature of the government, and is secured by the tenth amendment; that an affirmative grant of power is not exclusive, unless in its own nature it be such that the continued exercise of it by the former possessor is inconsistent with the grant, and that this is not of that description.

The appellant, conceding these postulates, except the last, contends that full power to regulate a particular subject, implies the whole power, and leaves no residuum; that a grant of the whole is incompatible with the existence of a right in another to any part of it. . . .

The grant of the power to lay and collect taxes is, like the power to regulate commerce, made in general terms, and has never been understood to interfere with the exercise of the same power by the States; and hence has been drawn an argument which has been applied to the question under consideration. But the two grants are not, it is conceived, similar in their terms or their nature. Although many of the powers formerly exercised by the States are transferred to the Government of the Union, yet the State Governments remain, and constitute a most important part of our system. The power of taxation is indispensable to their existence, and is a power which, in its own nature, is capable of residing in, and being exercised by, different authorities at the same time. We are accustomed to see it placed, for different purposes, in different hands. Taxation is the simple operation of taking small portions from a perpetually accumulating mass, susceptible of almost infinite division; and a power in one to take what is necessary for certain purposes, is not in its nature incompatible with a power in another to take what is necessary for other purposes. Congress is authorized to lay and collect taxes, etc., to pay the debts, and provide for the common defense and general welfare of the United States. This does not interfere with the power of the States to tax for the support of their own governments; nor is the exercise of that power by the States an exercise of any portion of the power that is granted to the United States. In imposing taxes for state purposes, they are not doing what Congress is empowered to do. Congress is not empowered to tax for those purposes which are within the exclusive province of the States. When, then, each government exercises the power of taxation, neither is exercising the power of the other. But when a State proceeds to regulate commerce with foreign nations, or among the several States, it is exercising the very power that is granted to Congress, and is doing the very thing which Congress is authorized to do. There is no analogy, then, between the power of taxation and the power of regulating commerce. . . .

But the inspection laws are said to be regulations of commerce, and are certainly recognized in the constitution, as being passed in the exercise of a power remaining with the states.

That inspection laws may have a remote and considerable influence on commerce, will not be denied; but that a power to regulate commerce is the source from which the right to pass them is derived, cannot be admitted. The objects of inspection laws is to improve the quality of articles produced by the labor of the country; to fit them for exportation; or, it may be, for domestic use. They act upon the subject before it becomes an article of foreign commerce, or of commerce among the states, and prepared it for that purpose. They form a portion of that immense mass of legislation which embraces everything within the territory of a state not surrendered to the general government; all which can be most advantageously exercised by the states themselves. Inspection laws, quarantine laws, health laws of every description, as well as laws for regulating the internal commerce of a state, and those which respect turnpike-roads, ferries, etc., are component parts of this mass.

No direct general power over these objects is granted to Congress; and, consequently, they remain subject to state legislation. If the legislative power of the Union can reach them, it must be for national purposes; it must be where the power is expressly given for a special purpose, or is clearly incidental to some power which is expressly given. It is obvious, that the government of the Union, in the exercise of its express powers, that, for example, of regulating commerce with foreign nations and among the states, may use means that may also be employed by a state, in the exercise of its acknowledged power; that, for example, of regulating commerce within the state. If Congress license vessels to sail from one port to another, in the same state, the act is supposed to be, necessarily, incidental to the power expressly granted to Congress, and implies no claim of a direct power to regulate the purely internal commerce of a state, or to act directly on its system of police. So, if a state, in passing laws on subjects acknowledged to be within its control, and with a view to those subjects, shall adopt a measure of the same character with one which Congress may adopt, it does not derive its authority from the particular power which has been granted, but from some other, which remains with the state, and may be executed by the same means. . . .

Since, however, in exercising the power of regulating their own purely internal affairs, whether of trading or police, the states may sometimes enact laws, the validity of which depends on their interfering with, and being contrary to, an act of Congress passed in pursuance of the constitution, the court will enter upon the inquiry, whether the laws of New York, as expounded by the highest tribunal of that state, have, in their application to this case, come into collision with an act of Congress, and deprived a citizen of a right to which that act entitles him. Should this collision exist, it will be immaterial whether those laws were passed in virtue of a concurrent power ''to regulate commerce with foreign nations and among the several states,'' or in virtue of a power to regulate their domestic trade and police. In one case and the other, the acts of New York must yield to the law of Congress; and the decision sustaining the privilege they confer, against a right given by a law of the Union, must be erroneous. . . .

The nullity of any act, inconsistent with the constitution, is produced by the declaration that the constitution is the supreme law. The appropriate application of that part of the clause which confers the same supremacy on laws and treaties, is to such acts of the state legislatures as do not transcend their powers, but, though enacted in the execution of acknowledged state powers, interfere with, or are contrary to the laws of Congress, made in pursuance of the constitution, or some treaty made under the authority of the United States. In every such case, the act of Congress, or the treaty, is supreme; and the law of the state, though enacted in the exercise of powers not controverted, must yield to it.

Mr. Justice Johnson:

The "power to regulate commerce," here meant to be granted, was that power to regulate commerce which previously existed in the states. But what was that power? The states were, unquestionably, supreme, and each possessed that power over commerce which is acknowledged to reside in every sovereign state. . . . The power of a sovereign state over commerce, therefore, amounts to nothing more than a power to limit and restrain it at pleasure. And since the power to prescribe the limits to its freedom necessarily implies the power to determine what shall remain unrestrained, it follows that the power must be exclusive; it can reside but in one potentate; and hence, the grant of this power carries with it the whole subject, leaving nothing for the state to act upon. . . .

Power to regulate foreign commerce is given in the same words, and in the same breath, as it were, with that over the commerce of the states and with the Indian tribes. But the power to regulate foreign commerce is necessarily exclusive. The states are unknown to foreign nations; their sovereignty exists only with relation to each other and the general government. . . .

It is impossible, with the views which I entertain of the principle on which the commercial privileges of the people of the United States, among themselves, rests, to concur in the view which this court takes of the effect of the coasting license in this cause. I do not regard it as the foundation of the right set up in behalf of the appellant. If there was any one object riding over every other in the adoption of the Constitution, it was to keep the commercial intercourse among the States free from all invidious and partial restraints. And I cannot overcome the conviction, that if the licensing act was repealed tomorrow, the rights of the appellant to a reversal of the decision complained of, would be as strong as it is under this license.

States may regulate local incidents of interstate commerce when Congress has not occupied the field.

23. *Cooley v. Board of Wardens* (1851)

Gibbons v. Ogden had granted ample power over commerce to the national government, but this power went largely unused until the latter part of the nineteenth century. (The first major piece of federal economic legislation was the Interstate Commerce Commission Act of 1886.) In consequence, the burden of regulation fell on the states. Yet a knotty problem remained: Is the federal power plenary, excluding state regulation on interstate matters even in the absence of federal regulation, or are the states authorized to legislate until such time as Congress chooses to occupy the field? In the post-Marshall period, the Court divided sharply in several cases on this issue, until the matter was finally laid to rest in *Cooley v. Board of Wardens*. Justice Curtis's opinion took a middle position, distinguishing between subjects national in scope, which require uniform national regulation, and those of a more local character, over which the states might exercise jurisdiction so long as Congress did not.

Background: Ships sailing from Philadelphia were required under state law to pay a one-half pilotage fee in the event a pilot was not hired. Cooley, the consignee of two vessels leaving that port, refused to pay the fee. The Supreme Court affirmed the judgment of the Supreme Court of Pennsylvania upholding the state law.

Mr. Justice Curtis delivered
the opinion of the Court:

It remains to consider the objection, that [the Pennsylvania law] is repugnant to the third clause of the eighth section of the first article. "The Congress shall have power to regulate commerce with foreign nations and among the several States, and with the Indian tribes."

That the power to regulate commerce includes the regulation of navigation, we consider settled. And when we look to the nature of the service performed by pilots, to the relations which that service and its compensations bear to navigation between the several States, and between the ports of the United States, and foreign countries, we are brought to the conclusion, that the regulation of the qualifications of pilots, of the modes and times of offering and rendering their services, of the responsibilities which shall rest upon them, of the powers they shall possess, of the compensation they may demand, and of the penalties by which their rights and duties may be enforced, do constitute regulations of navigation, and consequently of commerce, within the just meaning of this clause of the Constitution. . . .

[W]e are brought directly and unavoidably to the consideration of the question, whether the grant of the commercial power to Congress, did per se deprive the States of all power to regulate pilots. This question has never been decided by this court, nor, in our judgment, has any case depending upon all the considerations which must govern this one, come before this court. The grant of commercial power to Congress does not contain any terms which expressly exclude the States from exercising an authority over its subject matter. If they are excluded it must be because the nature of the power, thus granted to Congress, requires that a similar authority should not exist in the States. If it were conceded on the one side, that the nature of this power, like that to legislate for the District of Columbia, is absolutely and totally repugnant to the existence or similar power in the States, probably no one would deny that the grant of the power to Congress, as effectually and perfectly excludes the States from all future legislation on the subject, as if express words had been used to exclude them. And on the other hand, if it were admitted that the existence of this power in Congress, like the power of taxation, is compatible with the existence of a similar power in the States, then it would be in conformity with the contemporary exposition of the Constitution (*Federalist*, No. 32), and with the judicial construction, given from time to time by this court, after the most deliberate consideration, to hold that the mere grant of such a power to Congress, did not imply a prohibition on the States to exercise the same power; that it is not the mere existence of such a power, but its exercise by Congress, which may be incompatible with the exercise of the same power by the States, and that the States may legislate in the absence of congressional regulations.

The diversities of opinion, therefore, which have existed on this subject, have arisen from the different views taken of the nature of this power. But when the nature of a power like this is spoken of, when it is said that the nature of the power requires that it should be exercised exclusively by Congress, it must be intended to refer to the subjects of that power, and to say they are of such a nature as to require exclusive legislation by Congress. Now, the power to regulate commerce, embraces a vast field, containing not only many, but exceedingly various subjects, quite unlike in their nature; some imperatively demanding a single uniform rule, operating equally on the commerce of the United States in every port; and some, like the subject now in question, as imperatively demanding that diversity, which alone can meet the local necessities of navigation.

Either absolutely to affirm, or deny, that the nature of this power requires exclusive legislation by Congress, is to lose sight of the nature of the subjects of this power, and to assert concerning all of them, what is really applicable but to a part. Whatever subjects of this power are in their nature national, or admit only of one uniform system, or plan of regulation, may justly be said to be of such a nature as to require exclusive legislation by Congress. . . .

We are of opinion that this state law was enacted by virtue of a power, residing in the State to legislate; that it is not in conflict with any law of Congress; that it does not interfere with any system which Congress has established by making regulations, or by intentionally leaving individuals to their own unrestricted action; that this law is therefore valid, and the judgment of the Supreme Court of Pennsylvania in each case must be affirmed.

[Mr. Justice Daniel wrote an opinion concurring in the judgment. Mr. Justice McLean wrote a dissenting opinion.]

Congress has broad authority to regulate social conditions that affect interstate commerce.

24a. *Hammer v. Dagenhart* (1918)
24b. *United States v. Darby* (1941)

Hammer v. Dagenhart presents an extremely narrow interpretation of the Commerce Clause. The decision followed a series of cases in which the Supreme Court had construed the clause as granting a federal "police power," that is, as authorizing legislation directed not so much to the regulation of commerce per se as to the regulation of social problems that adversely affect interstate commerce. Thus, Congress's prohibition of lottery tickets from interstate channels was sustained in *Champion v. Ames* (1903); the power to regulate was considered to embrace clearly the power to prohibit. Vehemently protested by Justice Holmes, the decision in *Hammer v. Dagenhart* was badly eroded by *N.L.R.B. v. Jones and Laughlin Steel Corp.* (1937), and was finally overruled in *United States v. Darby*.

Background: *Hammer v. Dagenhart* concerned an act of Congress that banned the products of child labor from interstate commerce. The Court declared the act unconstitutional, affirming a district court's decision to the same effect.

United States v. Darby upheld the Fair Labor Standards Act of 1938, which established maximum hours and minimum wages for industries engaged in interstate commerce. The Supreme Court reversed a district court's finding of unconstitutionality.

Hammer v. Dagenhart

MR. JUSTICE DAY DELIVERED
THE OPINION OF THE COURT:

The controlling question for decision is: Is it within the authority of Congress in regulating commerce among the states to prohibit the transportation in interstate commerce of manufactured goods, the product of a factory in which, within thirty days prior to their removal therefrom, children under the age of fourteen have been employed or permitted to work, or children between the ages of fourteen and sixteen years have been employed or permitted to work, more than eight hours in any day, or more than six days in any week, or after the hour of 7 o'clock P.M. or before the hour of 6 o'clock A.M.?

The power essential to the passage of this act, the government contends, is found in the commerce clause of the Constitution, which authorizes Congress to regulate commerce with foreign nations and among the states. . . .

But it is insisted that adjudged cases in this court establish the doctrine that the power to regulate given to Congress incidentally includes the authority to prohibit the movement of ordinary commodities, and therefore that the subject is not open for discussion. The cases demonstrate the contrary. They rest upon the character of the particular subjects dealt with and the fact that the scope of governmental authority, state or national, possessed over them, is such that the authority to prohibit is, as to them, but the exertion of the power to regulate.

The first of these cases is *Champion v. Ames* [1903], the so-called Lottery Case, in which it was held that Congress might pass a law having the effect to keep the channels of commerce free from use in the transportation of tickets used in the promotion of lottery schemes. In *Hipolite Egg Co. v. United States* [1911], this court sustained the power of Congress to pass the Pure Food and Drug Act, which prohibited the introduction into the states by means of interstate commerce of impure foods and drugs. In *Hoke v. United States* [1913], this court sustained the constitutionality of the so-called "White Slave Traffic Act," whereby transportation of a woman in interstate commerce for the purpose of prostitution was forbidden. . . .

In *Caminetti v. United States* [1917], we held that Congress might prohibit the transportation of women in interstate commerce for the purposes of debauchery and kindred purposes. In *Clark Distilling Co. v. Western Maryland R. Co.* [1917], the power of Congress over the transportation of intoxicating liquors was sustained. . . .

In each of these instances the use of interstate transportation was necessary to the accomplishment of harmful results. In other words, although the power over interstate transportation was to regulate, that could only be accomplished by prohibiting the use of the facilities of interstate commerce to effect the evil intended.

This element is wanting in the present case. The thing intended to be accomplished by this statute is the denial of the facilities of interstate commerce to those manufacturers in the states who employ children within the prohibited ages. The act in its effect does not regulate transportation among the states, but aims to standardize the ages at which children may be employed in mining and manufacturing within the states. The goods shipped are of themselves harmless. The act permits them to be freely shipped after thirty days from the time of their removal from the factory. When offered for shipment, and before transportation begins, the labor of their production is over, and the mere fact that they were intended for interstate commerce transportation does not make their production subject to Federal control under the commerce power.

Commerce "consists of intercourse and traffic . . . and includes the transportation of persons and property, as well as the purchase, sale and exchange of commodities." The making of goods and the mining of coal are not commerce, nor does the fact that these things are to be afterwards shipped, or used in interstate commerce, make their production a part thereof. . . .

The grant of authority over a purely Federal matter was not intended to destroy the local power always existing and carefully reserved to the states in the 10th Amendment to the Constitution. . . .

That there should be limitations upon the right to employ children in mines and factories in the interest of their own and the public welfare, all will admit. That such employment is generally deemed to require regulation is shown by the fact that the brief of counsel states that every state in the Union has a law upon the subject, limiting the right to thus employ children. In North Carolina, the state wherein is located the factory in which the employment was had in the present case, no child under twelve years of age is permitted to work.

In may be desirable that such laws be uniform, but our Federal government is one of enumerated powers; "this principle," declared Chief Justice Marshall in *M'Culloch v. Maryland* [1819] "is universally admitted." . . .

In our view the necessary effect of this act is, by means of a prohibition against the movement in interstate commerce of ordinary commercial commodities, to regulate the hours of labor of children in factories and mines within the states,—a purely state authority. Thus the act in a twofold sense is repugnant to the Constitution. It not only transcends the authority delegated to Congress over commerce, but also exerts a power as to a purely local matter to which the Federal authority does not extend. The far-reaching result of upholding the act cannot be more plainly indicated than by pointing out that if Congress can thus regulate matters intrusted to local authority by prohibition of the movement of commodities in interstate commerce, all freedom of commerce will be at an end, and the power of the states over local matters may be eliminated, and thus our system of government be practically destroyed.

For these reasons we hold that this law exceeds the constitutional authority of Congress.

MR. JUSTICE HOLMES, DISSENTING:

The first step in my argument is to make plain what no one is likely to dispute,—that the statute in question is within the power expressly given to Congress if considered only as to its immediate effects, and that if invalid it is so only upon some collateral ground. The statute confines itself to prohibiting the carriage of certain goods in interstate or foreign commerce. Congress is given power to regulate such commerce in unqualified terms. It would not be argued to-day that the power to regulate does not include the power to prohibit. Regulation means the prohibition of something, and when interstate commerce is the matter to be regulated I cannot doubt that the regulations may prohibit any part of such commerce that Congress sees fit to forbid. At all events it is established by the *Lottery Case* and others that have followed it that a law is not beyond the regulative power of Congress merely because it prohibits certain transportation out and out. So I repeat that this statute in its immediate operation is clearly within the Congress's constitutional power.

The question, then, is narrowed to whether the exercise of its otherwise constitutional power by Congress can be pronounced unconstitutional because of its possible reaction upon the conduct of the sales in a matter upon which I have admitted that they are free from direct control. I should have thought that that matter had been disposed of so fully as to leave no room for doubt. I should have thought that the most conspicuous decisions of this court had made it clear that the power to regulate commerce and other constitutional powers could not be cut down or qualified by the fact that it might interfere with the carrying out of the domestic policy of any state. . . .

The notion that prohibition is any less prohibition when applied to things now thought evil I do not understand. But if there is any matter upon which civilized countries have agreed,—far more unanimously than they have with regard to intoxicants and some other matters over which this country is now emotionally aroused,—it is the evil of premature and excessive child labor. I should have thought that if we were to introduce our own moral conceptions where, in my opinion, they do not belong, this was pre-eminently a case for upholding the exercise of all its powers by the United States.

But I had thought that the propriety of the exercise of a power admitted to exist in some cases was for the consideration of Congress alone, and that this court always had disavowed the right to intrude its judgment upon questions of policy or morals. It is not for this court to pronounce when prohibition is necessary to regulation if it ever may be necessary,—to say that it is permissible as against strong drink, but not as against the product of ruined lives.

The act does not meddle with anything belonging to the states. They may regulate their internal affairs and their domestic commerce as they like. But when they seek to send their products across the state line they are no longer within their rights. If there were no Constitution and no Congress their power to cross the line would depend upon their neighbors. Under the Constitution such commerce belongs not to the states, but to Congress to regulate. It may carry out its views of public policy whatever indirect effect they may have upon the activities of the states. Instead of being encountered by a prohibitive tariff at her boundaries, the state encounters the public policy of the United States which it is for Congress to express. The public policy of the United States is shaped with a view to the benefit of the nation as a whole. If, as has been the case within the memory of men still living, a state should take a different view of the propriety of sustaining a lottery from that which generally prevails, I cannot believe that the fact would require a different decision from that reached in *Champion v. Ames*. Yet in that case it would be said with quite as much force as in this that Congress was attempting to intermeddle with the state's domestic affairs. The national welfare as understood by Congress may require a different attitude within its sphere from that of some self-seeking state. It seems to me entirely constitutional for Congress to enforce its understanding by all the means at its command.

[Mr. Justice McKenna, Mr. Justice Brandeis, and Mr. Justice Clarke concurred in this opinion.]

United States v. Darby

MR. JUSTICE STONE DELIVERED
THE OPINION OF THE COURT:

The two principal questions raised by the record in this case are, *first*, whether Congress has constitutional power to prohibit the shipment in interstate commerce of lumber manufactured by employees whose wages are less than a prescribed minimum or whose weekly hours of labor at that wage are greater than a prescribed maximum, and, *second*, whether it has power to prohibit the employment of workmen in the production of goods "for interstate commerce" at other than prescribed wages and hours. . . .

While manufacture is not of itself interstate commerce the shipment of manufactured goods interstate is such commerce and the prohibition of such shipment by Congress is indubitably a regulation of the commerce. The power to regulate commerce is the power "to prescribe the rule by which commerce is governed." *Gibbons v. Ogden* [1824]. It extends not only to those regulations which aid, foster and protect the commerce, but embraces those which prohibit it. It is conceded that the power of Congress to prohibit transportation in interstate commerce includes noxious articles, stolen articles, kidnapped persons, and articles such as intoxicating liquor or convict made goods, traffic in which is forbidden or restricted by the laws of the state of destination.

But it is said that . . . while the prohibition is nominally a regulation of the commerce its motive or purpose is regulation of wages and hours of persons engaged in manufacture, the control of which has been reserved to the states. . . .

The motive and purpose of the present regulation are plainly to make effective the Congressional conception of public policy that interstate commerce should not be made the instrument of competition in the distribution of goods produced under substandard labor conditions, which competition is injurious to the commerce and to the states from and to which the commerce flows. . . . Whatever their motive and purpose, regulations of commerce which do not infringe some constitutional prohibition are within the plenary power conferred on Congress by the Commerce Clause. . . .

In the more than a century which has elapsed since the decision of *Gibbons v. Ogden*, these principles of constitutional interpretation have been so long and repeatedly recognized by this Court as applicable to the Commerce Clause, that there would be little occasion for repeating them now were it not for the decision of this Court twenty-two years ago in *Hammer v. Dagenhart* [1918]. In that case it was held by a bare majority of the Court over the powerful and now classic dissent of Mr. Justice Holmes setting forth the fundamental issues involved, that Congress was without power to exclude the products of child labor from interstate commerce. . . .

Hammer v. Dagenhart has not been followed. The distinction on which the decision was rested that Congressional power to prohibit interstate commerce is limited to articles which in themselves have some harmful or deleterious property—a distinction which was novel when made and unsupported by any provision of the Constitution—has long since been abandoned. . . .

The conclusion is inescapable that *Hammer v. Dagenhart* was a departure from the principles which have prevailed in the interpretation of the commerce clause both before and since the decision and that such vitality, as a precedent, as it then had has long since been exhausted. It should be and now is overruled.

Validity of the wage and hour requirements. [The act requires] employers to conform to the wage and hour provisions with respect to all employees engaged in the production of goods for interstate commerce. . . .

The power of Congress over interstate commerce . . . extends to those activities intrastate which so affect interstate commerce or the exercise of the power of Congress over it as to make regulation of them appropriate means to the attainment of a legitimate end, the exercise of the granted power of Congress to regulate interstate commerce. . . .

Congress, having by the present Act adopted the policy of excluding from interstate commerce all goods produced for the commerce which do not conform to the specified labor standards, it may choose the means reasonably adapted to the attainment of the permitted end, even though they involve control of intrastate activities. . . .

The Sherman Act and the National Labor Relations Act are familiar examples of the exertion of the commerce power to prohibit or control activities wholly intrastate because of their effect on interstate commerce. . . .

Our conclusion is unaffected by the Tenth Amendment which provides: "The powers not delegated to the United States by the Constitution nor prohibited by it to the states are reserved to the states respectively or to the people." The amendment states but a truism that all is retained which has not been surrendered. There is nothing in the history of its adoption to suggest that it was more than declaratory of the relationship between the national and state governments as it had been established by the Constitution before the amendment or that its purpose was other than to allay fears that the new national government might seek to exercise powers not granted, and that the states might not be able to exercise fully their reserved powers.

The congressional power of economic regulation extends to production for personal consumption.

25. *Wickard v. Filburn* (1942)

Does the Commerce Clause authorize Congress to regulate agricultural production for home use on the farm? The answer, in this decision, is yes.

Background: Under the Agricultural Adjustment Act (AAA) of 1938, the secretary of agriculture was empowered to proclaim an annual allocation of wheat acreage per farmer. Filburn, a wheat farmer, produced wheat in excess of his quota, and his refusal to pay the resulting penalty (on the ground, among others, that he used the excess for home consumption) was upheld by the district court. Secretary of Agriculture Claude R. Wickard appealed to the Supreme Court, which ruled in the government's favor.

MR. JUSTICE JACKSON DELIVERED
THE OPINION OF THE COURT:

It is urged that under the Commerce Clause of the Constitution, Article 1, § 8, clause 3, Congress does not possess the power it has in this instance sought to exercise. The question would merit little consideration since our decision in *United States v. Darby* [1941], sustaining the federal power to regulate production of goods for commerce except for the fact that this Act extends federal regulation to production not intended in any part for commerce but wholly for consumption on the farm. . . . The sum of this is that the Federal Government fixes a quota including all that the farmer may harvest for sale or for his own farm needs, and declares that wheat produced on excess acreage may neither be disposed of nor used except upon payment of the penalty or except it is stored as required by the Act or delivered to the Secretary of Agriculture.

Appellee says that this is a regulation of production and consumption of wheat. Such activities are, he urges, beyond the reach of congressional power under the Commerce Clause, since they are local in character, and their effects upon interstate commerce are at most "indirect." In answer the Government argues that the statute regulates neither production nor consumption, but only marketing; and, in the alternative, that if the Act does go beyond the regulation of marketing it is sustainable as a "necessary and proper" implementation of the power of Congress over interstate commerce.

The Government's concern lest the Act be held to be a regulation of production or consumption rather than of marketing is attributable to a few dicta and decisions of this Court which might be understood to lay it down that activities such as "production," "manufacturing," and "mining" are strictly "local" and, except in special circumstances which are not present here, cannot be regulated under the commerce power because their effects upon interstate commerce are, as matter of law, only "indirect." Even today, when this power has been held to have great latitude, there is no decision of this Court that such activities may be regulated where no part of the product is intended for interstate commerce or intermingle with the subjects thereof. . . . [However,] questions of the power of Congress are not to be decided by reference to any formula which would give controlling force to nomenclature such as "production" and "indirect" and foreclose consideration of the actual effects of the activity in question upon interstate commerce. . . .

The Court's recognition of the relevance of the economic effects in the application of the Commerce Clause . . . has made the mechanical application of legal formulas no longer feasible. . . . The present Chief Justice has said in summary of the present state of the law: "The commerce power . . . extends to those activities intrastate which so affect interstate commerce, or the exertion of the power of Congress over it, as to make regulation of them appropriate means to the attainment of a legitimate end, the effective execution of the granted power to regulate interstate commerce. . . ."

Whether the subject of the regulation in question was "production," "consumption," or "marketing" is, therefore, not material for purposes of deciding the question of federal power before us. That an activity is of local character may help in a doubtful case to determine whether Congress intended to reach it. The same consideration might help in determining whether in the absence of congressional action it would be permissible for the state to exert its power on the subject matter, even though in so doing it to some degree affected interstate commerce. But even if appellee's activity be local and though it may not be regarded as commerce, it may still, whatever its nature, be reached by Congress if it exerts a substantial economic effect on interstate commerce, and this irrespective of whether such effect is what might at some earlier time have been defined as "direct" or "indirect." . . .

The effect of consumption of home-grown wheat on interstate commerce is due to the fact that it constitutes the most variable factor in the disappearance of the wheat crop. Consumption on the farm where grown appears to vary in an amount greater than 20 per cent of average production. The total amount of wheat consumed as food varies but relatively little, and use as seed is relatively constant. . . .

It is well established by decisions of this Court that the power to regulate commerce includes the power to regulate the prices at which commodities in that commerce are dealt in and practices affecting such prices. One of the primary purposes of the Act in question was to increase the market price of wheat and to that end to limit the volume thereof that could affect the market. It can hardly be denied that a factor of such volume and variability as home-consumed wheat would have a substantial influence on price and market conditions. This may arise because being in marketable condition such wheat overhangs the market and if induced by rising prices tends to flow into the market and check price increases. But if we assume that it is never marketed, it supplies a need of the man who grew it which would otherwise be reflected by purchases in the open market. Home-grown wheat in this sense competes with wheat in commerce. The stimulation of commerce is a use of the regulatory function quite as definitely as prohibitions or restrictions thereon. This record leaves us in no doubt that Congress may properly have considered that wheat consumed on the farm where grown if wholly outside the scheme of regulation would have a substantial effect in defeating and obstructing its purpose to stimulate trade therein at increased prices.

Interstate train lengths are not subject to state regulation.

26. *Southern Pacific Co. v. Arizona* (1944)

The rule in *Cooley v. Board of Wardens* allows state regulation of local aspects of interstate commerce where Congress has not exercised its power and the subject does not require a uniform national rule. The Arizona train-limit case illustrates the restrictive side of the *Cooley* rule: here the Court struck down a state regulation on the ground that the subject in question—the permissible length of interstate trains—does indeed require national uniformity.

Background: Arizona law limited train lengths to fourteen passenger cars or seventy freight cars in the asserted interests of safety. The railroad brought suit in state court on interstate-commerce grounds and won. The Arizona Supreme Court reversed, and was in turn reversed by the Supreme Court.

MR. CHIEF JUSTICE STONE DELIVERED
THE OPINION OF THE COURT:

The Arizona Train Limit Law of May 16, 1912 makes it unlawful for any person or corporation to operate within the state a railroad train of more than fourteen passenger or seventy freight cars, and authorizes the state to recover a money penalty for each violation of the Act. The question for decision [is] whether the statute contravenes the commerce clause of the federal Constitution.

Although the commerce clause conferred on the national government power to regulate commerce, its possession of the power does not exclude all state power of regulation. [I]t has been recognized that, in the absence of conflicting legislation by Congress, there is a residuum of power in the state to make laws governing matters of local concern which nevertheless in some measure affect interstate commerce or even to some extent, regulate it. . . .

When the regulation of matters of local concern is local in character and effect, and its impact on the national commerce does not seriously interfere with its operation, and the consequent incentive to deal with them nationally is slight, such regulation has been generally held to be within state authority.

But ever since *Gibbons v. Ogden* [1824] the states have not been deemed to have authority to impede substantially the free flow of commerce from state to state, or to regulate those phases of the national commerce which, because of the need of national uniformity, demand that their regulation, if any, be prescribed by a single authority. *Cooley v. Port Wardens* [1851]. . . .

For a hundred years it has been accepted constitutional doctrine that the commerce clause, without the aid of Congressional legislation, thus affords some protection from state legislation inimical to the national commerce, and that in such cases, where Congress has not acted, this Court, and not the state legislature, is under the commerce clause the final arbiter of the competing demands of state and national interests.

Congress has undoubted power to redefine the distribution of power over interstate commerce. It may either permit the states to regulate the commerce in a manner which would otherwise not be permissible, or exclude state regulation even of matters of peculiarly local concern which nevertheless affect interstate commerce.

But in general Congress has left it to the courts to formulate the rules thus interpreting the commerce clause in its application, doubtless because it has appreciated the destructive consequences to the commerce of the nation if their protection were withdrawn. . . . Meanwhile, Congress has accommodated its legislation, as have the states, to these rules as an established feature of our constitutional system. There has thus been left to the states wide scope for the regulation of matters of local state concern, even though it in some measure affects the commerce, provided it does not materially restrict the free flow of commerce across state lines, or interfere with it in matters with respect to which uniformity of regulation is of predominant national concern.

Hence the matters for ultimate determination here are the nature and extent of the burden which the state regulation of interstate trains, adopted as a safety measure, imposes on interstate commerce, and whether the relative weights of the state and national interests involved are such as to make inapplicable the rule, generally observed, that the free flow of interstate commerce and its freedom from local restraints in matters requiring uniformity of regulation are interests safeguarded by the commerce clause from state interference. . . .

The findings [by the State court] show that the operation of long trains, that is trains of more than fourteen passenger and more than seventy freight cars, is standard practice over the main lines of the railroads of the United States, and that, if the length of trains is to be regulated at all, national uniformity in the regulation adopted, such as only Congress can prescribe, is practically indispensable to the operation of an efficient and economical national railway system. On many railroads passenger trains of more than fourteen cars and freight trains of more than seventy cars are operated, and on some systems freight trains are run ranging from one hundred and twenty-five to one hundred and sixty cars in length. . . .

In Arizona, approximately 93% of the freight traffic and 95% of the passenger traffic is interstate. Because of the Train Limit Law appellant is required to haul over 30% more trains in Arizona than would otherwise have been necessary. The record shows a definite relationship between operating costs and the length of trains, the increase in length resulting in a reduction of operating costs per car. The additional cost of operation of trains complying with the Train Limit Law in Arizona amounts for the two railroads traversing that state to about $1,000,000 a year. The reduction in train lengths also impedes efficient operation. More locomotives and more manpower are required; the necessary conversion and reconversion of train lengths at terminals and the delay caused by breaking up and remaking long trains upon entering and leaving the state in order to comply with the law, delays the traffic and diminishes its volume moved in a given time, especially when traffic is heavy. . . .

The unchallenged findings leave no doubt that the Arizona Train Limit Law imposes a serious burden on the interstate commerce conducted by appellant. It materially impedes the movement of appellant's interstate trains through that state and interposes a substantial obstruction to the national policy proclaimed by Congress, to promote adequate, economical and efficient railway transportation service. Enforcement of the law in Arizona, while train lengths remain unregulated or are regulated by varying standards in other states, must inevitably result in an impairment of uniformity of efficient railroad operation because the railroads are subjected to regulation which is not uniform in its application. Compliance with a state statute limiting train lengths requires interstate trains of a length lawful in other states to be broken up and reconstituted as they enter each state according as it may impose varying limitations upon train lengths. The alternative is for the carrier to conform to the lowest train limit restriction of any of the states through which its trains pass, whose laws thus control the carriers' operations both within and without the regulating state. . . .

If one state may regulate train lengths, so may all the others, and they need not prescribe the same maximum limitation. The practical effect of such regulation is to control train operations beyond the boundaries of the state exacting it because of the necessity of breaking up and reassembling long trains at the nearest terminal points before entering and after leaving the regulating state. The serious impediment to the free flow of commerce by the local regulation of train lengths and the practical necessity that such regulation, if any, must be prescribed by a single body having a nation-wide authority are apparent.

The trial court found that the Arizona law had no reasonable relation to safety, and made train operation more dangerous. Examination of the evidence and the detailed findings makes it clear that this conclusion was rested on facts found which indicate that such increased danger of accident and personal injury as may result from the greater length of trains is more than offset by the increase in the number of accidents resulting from the larger number of trains when train lengths are reduced. . . .

Here examination of all the relevant factors makes it plain that the state interest is outweighed by the interest of the nation in an adequate, economical and efficient railway transportation service, which must prevail.

[Mr. Justice Rutledge concurred in the result.]

MR. JUSTICE BLACK, DISSENTING:

[T]he determination of whether it is in the interest of society for the length of trains to be governmentally regulated is a matter of public policy. Someone must fix that policy—either the Congress, or the state, or the courts. A century and a half of constitutional history and government admonishes this Court to leave that choice to the elected legislative representatives of the people themselves, where it properly belongs both on democratic principles and the requirements of efficient government. . . .

This record in its entirety leaves me with no doubt whatever that many employees have been seriously injured and killed in the past, and that many more are likely to be so in the future, because of "slack movement" in trains. . . .

It may be that offsetting dangers are possible in the operation of short trains. The balancing of these probabilities, however, is not in my judgment a matter for judicial determination, but one which calls for legislative consideration. Representatives elected by the people to make their laws, rather than judges appointed to interpret those laws, can best determine the policies which govern the people. That at least is the basic principle on which our democratic society rests.

[Mr. Justice Douglas also wrote a dissenting opinion.]

A state may not prevent the importation of waste from other states.

27. *Philadelphia v. New Jersey* (1978)

One of the principal objects of the Commerce Clause of the Constitution was to create a "common market" for goods throughout the nation and break down the trade barriers that had sprung up between the states in the post-Revolutionary period. When Congress regulates a subject of interstate commerce and evinces an intention to "preempt" the field, the states are automatically excluded from acting. In the absence of congressional preemption, however, may the states, under certain conditions, legislate to protect their interests, when this has the effect of discriminating against the economies of other states? In this case, the Court answered no, though the legislation was prompted by strong environmental concerns.

Background: A New Jersey law banned the importation of waste materials from outside the state. Operators of private landfills in the state, who wished to import waste for disposal, challenged the law and won in the New Jersey trial court. The state's supreme court reversed, only to be reversed itself by the Supreme Court.

MR. JUSTICE STEWART DELIVERED
THE OPINION OF THE COURT:

A New Jersey law prohibits the importation of most "solid or liquid waste which originated or was collected outside the territorial limits of the State. . . ." In this case we are required to decide whether this statutory prohibition violates the Commerce Clause of the United States Constitution. . . .

Although the Constitution gives Congress the power to regulate commerce among the States, many subjects of potential federal regulation under that power inevitably escape congressional attention "because of their local character and their number and diversity." In the absence of federal legislation, these subjects are open to control by the States so long as they act within the restraints imposed by the Commerce Clause itself. The bounds of these restraints appear nowhere in the words of the Commerce Clause, but have emerged gradually in the decisions of this Court giving effect to its basic purpose. . . .

The opinions of the Court through the years have reflected an alertness to the evils of "economic isolation" and protectionism, while at the same time recognizing that incidental burdens on interstate commerce may be unavoidable when a State legislates to safeguard the health and safety of its people. . . .

The crucial inquiry, therefore, must be directed to determining whether [the New Jersey statute] is basically a protectionist measure, or whether it can fairly be viewed as a law directed to legitimate local concerns, with effects upon interstate commerce that are only incidental.

But whatever New Jersey's ultimate purpose, it may not be accomplished by discriminating against articles of commerce coming from outside the State unless there is some reason, apart from their origin, to treat them differently. Both on its face and in its plain effect, [the statute] violates this principle of nondiscrimination. . . .

The New Jersey law at issue in this case falls squarely within the area that the Commerce Clause puts off limits to state regulation. On its face, it imposes on out-of-state commercial interests the full burden of conserving the State's remaining landfill space. . . . [T]he State has overtly moved to slow or freeze the flow of commerce for protectionist reasons. What is crucial is the attempt by one State to isolate itself from a problem common to many by erecting a barrier against the movement of interstate trade.

The appellees argue that not all laws which facially discriminate against out-of-state commerce are forbidden protectionist regulations. In particular, they point to quarantine laws, which this Court has repeatedly upheld even though they appear to single out interstate commerce for special treatment. In the appellees' view, [the statute] is analogous to such health-protective measures, since it reduces the exposure of New Jersey residents to the allegedly harmful effects of landfill sites.

It is true that certain quarantine laws have not been considered forbidden protectionist measures, even though they were directed against out-of-state commerce. But those quarantine laws banned the importation of articles such as diseased livestock that required destruction as soon as possible because their very movement risked contagion and other evils. Those laws thus did not discriminate against interstate commerce as such, but simply prevented traffic in noxious articles, whatever their origin.

The New Jersey statute is not such a quarantine law. There has been no claim here that the very movement of waste into or through New Jersey endangers health, or that waste must be disposed of as soon and as close to its point of generation as possible. The harms caused by waste are said to arise after its disposal in landfill sites, and at that point, as New Jersey concedes, there is no basis to distinguish out-of-state waste from domestic waste. If one is inherently harmful, so is the other. Yet New Jersey has banned the former while leaving its landfill sites open to the latter. The New Jersey law blocks the importation of waste in an obvious effort to saddle those outside the State with the entire burden of slowing the flow of refuse into New Jersey's remaining landfill sites. That legislative effort is clearly impermissible under the Commerce Clause of the Constitution.

Today, cities in Pennsylvania and New York find it expedient or necessary to send their waste into New Jersey for disposal, and New Jersey claims the right to close its borders to such traffic. Tomorrow, cities in New Jersey may find it expedient or necessary to send their waste into Pennsylvania or New York for disposal, and those States might then claim the right to close their borders. The Commerce Clause will protect New Jersey in the future, just as it protects her neighbors now, from efforts by one State to isolate itself in the stream of interstate commerce from a problem shared by all.

MR. JUSTICE REHNQUIST, WITH WHOM THE
CHIEF JUSTICE JOINS, DISSENTING:

A growing problem in our Nation is the sanitary treatment and disposal of solid waste. For many years, solid waste was incinerated. Because of the significant environmental problems attendant on incineration, however, this method of solid waste disposal has declined in use in many localities, including New Jersey. "Sanitary" landfills have replaced incineration as the principal method of disposing of solid waste. . . . [T]he State of New Jersey legislatively recognized the unfortunate fact that landfills also present extremely serious health and safety problems. First, in New Jersey, "virtually all sanitary landfills can be expected to produce leachate, a noxious and highly polluted liquid which is seldom visible and frequently pollutes . . . ground and surface waters." The natural decomposition process which occurs in landfills also produces large quantities of methane and thereby presents a significant explosion hazard. Landfills can also generate "health hazards caused by rodents, fires and scavenger birds" and, "needless to say, do not help New Jersey's aesthetic appearance nor New Jersey's noise or water or air pollution problems." . . .

The question presented in this case is whether New Jersey must also continue to receive and dispose of solid waste from neighboring States, even though these will inexorably increase the health problems discussed above. The Court answers this question in the affirmative. New Jersey must either prohibit *all* landfill operations, leaving itself to cast about for a presently nonexistent solution to the serious problem of disposing of the waste generated within its own borders, or it must accept waste from every portion of the United States, thereby multiplying the health and safety problems which would result if it dealt only with such wastes generated within the State. . . .

According to the Court, the New Jersey law is distinguishable from these other laws, and invalid, because the concern of New Jersey is not with the *movement* of solid waste but with the present inability to safely *dispose* of it once it reaches its destination. But I think it far from clear that the State's law has as limited a focus as the Court imputes to it: Solid waste which is a health hazard when it reaches its destination may in all likelihood be an equally great health hazard in transit. . . .

I do not see why a State may ban the importation of items whose movement risks contagion, but cannot ban the importation of items which, although they may be transported into the State without undue hazard, will then simply pile up in an ever increasing danger to the public's health and safety. The Commerce Clause was not drawn with a view to having the validity of state laws turn on such pointless distinctions.

Congress may forbid discrimination in public accommodations that are related to interstate commerce.

28. *Heart of Atlanta Motel v. United States* (1964)

The Civil Rights Act of 1964—a piece of legislation similar in many ways to the Civil Rights Act of 1875, which the Court had struck down under the Fourteenth Amendment in 1883 (see *Civil Rights Cases*, p. 276)—forbade discrimination obstructing interstate commerce in privately owned places of public accommodations—inns, theaters, restaurants, and the like. Though the manifest object of the legislation was to strike at racial discrimination, Congress specifically premised the act on the Commerce Clause. In upholding the act, the Court gave the Commerce Clause one of the most sweeping applications in its history.

Congress also invoked the Equal Protection Clause in support of the act, but this was not considered by the Court. Justices Douglas and Goldberg, however, would have preferred to sustain the legislation on this ground.

Background: The Heart of Atlanta Motel in Atlanta, Georgia, drew 75 percent of its registered guests from out of state. The motel refused to rent rooms to blacks. It challenged the act on the ground, among others, that Congress had exceeded its powers under the Commerce Clause.

MR. JUSTICE CLARK DELIVERED
THE OPINION OF THE COURT:

Congress first evidenced its interest in civil rights legislation in the Civil Rights or Enforcement Act of April 9, 1866. There followed four Acts, with a fifth, the Civil Rights Act of March 1, 1875, culminating the series. In 1883 this Court struck down the public accommodations sections of the 1875 Act in the *Civil Rights Cases* [1883]. No major legislation in this field had been enacted by Congress for 82 years when the Civil Rights Act of 1957 became law. It was followed by the Civil Rights Act of 1960. Three years later, on June 19, 1963, the late President Kennedy called for civil rights legislation in a message to Congress to which he attached a proposed bill. Its stated purpose was "to promote the general welfare by eliminating discrimination based on race, color, religion, or national origin in . . . public accommodations through the exercise by Congress of the powers conferred upon it . . . to enforce the provisions of the fourteenth and fifteenth amendments, to regulate commerce among the several states, and to make laws necessary and proper to execute the powers conferred upon it by the Constitution." . . .

However, it was not until July 2, 1964, upon the recommendation of President Johnson, that the Civil Rights Act of 1964, here under attack, was finally passed. . . .

The Act as finally adopted was most comprehensive, undertaking to prevent through peaceful and voluntary settlement discrimination in voting, as well as in places of accommodation and public facilities, federally secured programs and in employment. . . .

It is admitted that the operation of the motel brings it within the provisions . . . of the Act and that appellant refused to provide lodging for transient Negroes because of their race or color and that it intends to continue that policy unless restrained. . . .

It is said that the operation of the motel here is of a purely local character. But, assuming this to be true, "[i]f it is interstate commerce that feels the pinch, it does not matter how local the operation which applies the squeeze." . . .

Thus the power of Congress to promote interstate commerce also includes the power to regulate the local incidents thereof, including local activities in both the States of origin and destination, which might have a substantial and harmful effect upon that commerce. One need only examine the evidence which we have discussed above to see that Congress may—as it has—prohibit racial discrimination by motels serving travelers, however "local" their operations may appear.

Nor does the Act deprive appellant of liberty or property under the Fifth Amendment. The commerce power invoked here by the Congress is a specific and plenary one authorized by the Constitution itself. The only questions are: (1) whether Congress had a rational basis for finding that racial discrimination by motels affected commerce, and (2) if it had such a basis, whether the means it selected to eliminate that evil are reasonable and appropriate. If they are, appellant has no "right" to select its guests as it sees fit, free from governmental regulation. . . .

We, therefore, conclude that the action of the Congress in the adoption of the Act as applied here to a motel which concededly serves interstate travelers is within the power granted it by the Commerce Clause of the Constitution, as interpreted by this Court for 140 years. It may be argued that Congress could have pursued other methods to eliminate the obstructions it found in interstate commerce caused by racial discrimination. But this is a matter of policy that rests entirely with the Congress not with the courts. How obstructions in commerce may be removed—what means are to be employed—is within the sound and exclusive discretion of the Congress. It is subject only to one caveat—that the means chosen by it must be reasonably adapted to the end permitted by the Constitution. We cannot say that its choice here was not so adapted. The Constitution requires no more.

MR. JUSTICE BLACK, CONCURRING:

I recognize that every remote, possible, speculative effect on commerce should not be accepted as an adequate constitutional ground to uproot and throw into the discard all our traditional distinctions between what is purely local, and therefore controlled by state laws, and what affects the national interest and is therefore subject to control by federal laws. I recognize too that some isolated and remote lunchroom which sells only to local people and buys almost all its supplies in the locality may possibly be beyond the reach of the power of Congress to regulate commerce, just as such an establishment is not covered by the present Act. But in deciding the constitutional power of Congress in cases like the two before us we do not consider the effect on interstate commerce of only one isolated, individual, local event, without regard to the fact that this single local event when added to many others of a similar nature may impose a burden on interstate commerce by reducing its volume or distorting its flow. . . .

In view of the Commerce Clause it is not possible to deny that the aim of protecting interstate commerce from undue burdens is a legitimate end. In view of the Thirteenth, Fourteenth and Fifteenth Amendments, it is not possible to deny that the aim of protecting Negroes from discrimination is also a legitimate end. The means adopted to achieve these ends are also appropriate, plainly adopted to achieve them and not prohibited by the Constitution but consistent with both its letter and spirit.

MR. JUSTICE DOUGLAS, CONCURRING:

I would prefer to rest on the assertion of legislative power contained in § 5 of the Fourteenth Amendment which states: "The Congress shall have power to enforce, by appropriate legislation, the provisions of this article"—a power which the Court concedes was exercised at least in part in this Act.

A decision based on the Fourteenth Amendment would have a more settling effect, making unnecessary litigation over whether a particular restaurant or inn is within the commerce definitions of the Act or whether a particular customer is an interstate traveler. Under my construction, the Act would apply to all customers in all the enumerated places of public accommodation. And that construction would put an end to all obstructionist strategies and finally close one door on a bitter chapter in American history.

[Mr. Justice Goldberg also wrote a concurring opinion.]

CHAPTER VII

Substantive Due Process

"No person shall . . . be deprived of life, liberty, or property, without due process of law . . ."—Fifth Amendment

"All persons born or naturalized in the United States, and subject to the jurisdiction thereof, are citizens of the United States and of the state wherein they reside. No state shall make or enforce any law which shall abridge the privileges or immunities of citizens of the United States; nor shall any state deprive any person of life, liberty, or property without due process of law; nor deny to any person within its jurisdiction the equal protection of the laws."—Fourteenth Amendment, Sec. 1

A. Economic Rights

The "Privileges or Immunities" and "Due Process" Clauses of the Fourteenth Amendment do not limit state power to legislate on economic matters.

29. *Slaughter-House Cases* (1873)

In this decision, the first under the Fourteenth Amendment, the Court so thoroughly eviscerated the amendment's Privileges or Immunities Clause by narrow interpretation that on only one occasion since has that clause been invoked by the Court to invalidate state legislation (*Colgate v. Harvey* [1935], a decision that was quickly overruled in *Madden v. Kentucky* [1940]). With more justification, Justice Miller's majority opinion confined due process to its traditional meaning of protecting procedural rights, and held it to have no application with regard to the substance of legislation. Justice Field, dissenting, urged a broader view of the amendment's first section, protesting that the Court had turned it into "a vain and idle enactment." The judicial tide soon turned in his favor (see *Lochner v. New York*, p. 222).

Background: In 1869 the legislature of Louisiana granted a twenty-five-year monopoly to a slaughterhouse company to conduct its business in the city of New Orleans. Various butchers brought suit against the monopoly on the ground that it deprived them of the privileges and immunities that the Fourteenth Amendment guaranteed to all citizens.

A fuller description of the facts is contained in the opening paragraphs of the Court's opinion.

Mʀ. Jᴜsᴛɪᴄᴇ Mɪʟʟᴇʀ ᴅᴇʟɪᴠᴇʀᴇᴅ
ᴛʜᴇ ᴏᴘɪɴɪᴏɴ ᴏғ ᴛʜᴇ Cᴏᴜʀᴛ:

This statute is denounced not only as creating a monopoly and conferring odious and exclusive privileges upon a small number of persons at the expense of the great body of the community of New Orleans, but it is asserted that it deprives a large and meritorious class of citizens, the whole of the butchers of the city, of the right to exercise their trade, the business to which they have been trained and on which they depend for the support of themselves and their families; and that the unrestricted exercise of the business of butchering is necessary to the daily subsistence of the population of the city. . . .

It is not, and cannot be successfully controverted, that it is both the right and the duty of the legislative body, the supreme power of the state or municipality, to prescribe and determine the localities where the business of slaughtering for a great city may be conducted. To do this effectively it is indispensable that all persons who slaughter animals for food shall do it in those places and nowhere else.

The statute under consideration defines these localities and forbids slaughtering in any other. It does not, as has been asserted, prevent the butcher from doing his own slaughtering. On the contrary, the Slaughter-House Company is required, under a heavy penalty, to permit any person who wishes to do so, to slaughter in their houses; and they are bound to make ample provision for the convenience of all the slaughtering for the entire city. The butcher, then, is still permitted to slaughter, to prepare, and to sell his own meats; but he is required to slaughter at a specified place and to pay a reasonable compensation for the use of the accommodations furnished him at that place.

The wisdom of the monopoly granted by the legislature may be open to question, but it is difficult to see a justification for the assertion that the butchers are deprived of the right to labor in their occupation, or the people of their daily service in preparing food, or how this statute, with the duties and guards imposed upon the company, can be said to destroy the business of the butcher, or seriously interfere with its pursuit.

The power here exercised by the legislature of Louisiana is, in its essential nature, one which has been, up to the present period in the constitutional history of this country, always conceded to belong to the states, however it may now be questioned in some of its details. . . .

Unless, therefore, it can be maintained that the exclusive privilege granted by this charter to the corporation is beyond the power of the legislature of Louisiana, there can be no just exception to the validity of the statute. And in this respect we are not able to see that these privileges are especially odious or objectionable. The duty imposed as a consideration for the privilege is well defined, and its enforcement well guarded. The prices or charges to be made by the company are limited by the statute, and we are not advised that they are on the whole exorbitant or unjust.

The proposition is, therefore, reduced to these terms: can any exclusive privileges be granted to any of its citizens, or to a corporation, by the legislature of a state? . . .

The plaintiffs in error accepting this issue, allege that the statute is a violation of the Constitution of the United States in these several particulars:

That it creates an involuntary servitude forbidden by the 13th article of amendment;

That it abridges the privileges and immunities of citizens of the United States;

That it denies to the plaintiffs the equal protection of the laws; and,

That it deprives them of their property without due process of law; contrary to the provisions of the 1st section of the 14th article of amendment.

This court is thus called upon for the first time to give construction to these articles. . . .

The most cursory glance at these articles discloses a unity of purpose, when taken in connection with the history of the times, which cannot fail to have an important bearing on any question of doubt concerning their true meaning. Nor can such doubts, when any reasonably exist, be safely and rationally solved without a reference to that history; for in it is found the occasion and the necessity for recurring again to the great source of power in this country, the people of the states, for additional guaranties of human rights; additional powers to the Federal government; additional restraints upon those of the states. Fortunately that history is fresh within the memory of us all, and its leading features, as they bear upon the matter before us, free from doubt. . . .

[I]n the light of this recapitulation of events, almost too recent to be called history, but which are familiar to us all; and on the most casual examination of the language of these amendments, no one can fail to be impressed with the one pervading purpose found in them all, lying at the foundation of each, and without which none of them would have been even suggested; we mean the freedom of the slave race, the security and firm establishment of that freedom, and the protection of the newly made freemen and citizen from the oppressions of those who had formerly exercised unlimited dominion over him. It is true that only the 15th Amendment, in terms, mentions the negro by speaking of his color and his slavery. But it is just as true that each of the other articles was addressed to the grievances of that race, and designed to remedy them as the fifteenth.

We do not say that no one else but the negro can share in this protection. Both the language and spirit of these articles are to have their fair and just weight in any question of construction. Undoubtedly, while negro slavery alone was in the mind of the Congress which proposed the 13th article, it forbids any other kind of slavery, now or hereafter. If Mexican peonage or the Chinese coolie labor system shall develop slavery of the Mexican or Chinese race within our territory, this Amendment may safely be trusted to make it void. And so, if other rights are assailed by the states which properly and necessarily fall within the protection of these articles, that protection will apply though the party interested may not be of African descent. But what we do say, and what we wish to be understood, is, that in any fair and just construction of any section or phrase of these amendments, it is necessary to look to the purpose which we have said was the pervading spirit of them all, the evil which they were designed to remedy, and the process of continued addition to the Constitution until that purpose was supposed to be accomplished, as far as constitutional law can accomplish it. . . .

The next observation is more important in view of the arguments of counsel in the present case. It is that the distinction between citizenship of the United States and citizenship of a state is clearly recognized and established. Not only may a man be a citizen of the United States without being a citizen of a state, but an important element is necessary to convert the former into the latter. He must reside within the state to make him a citizen of it, but it is only necessary that he should be born or naturalized in the United States to be a citizen of the Union.

It is quite clear, then, that there is a citizenship of the United States and a citizenship of a state, which are distinct from each other and which depend upon different characteristics or circumstances in the individual.

We think this distinction and its explicit recognition in this Amendment of great weight in this argument, because the next paragraph of this same section, which is the one mainly relied on by the plaintiffs in error, speaks only of privileges and immunities of citizens of the United States, and does not speak of those of citizens of the several states. The argument, however, in favor of the plaintiffs, rests wholly on the assumption that the citizenship is the same and the privileges and immunities guaranteed by the clause are the same.

The language is: "No state shall make or enforce any law which shall abridge the privileges or immunities of citizens of the United States." It is a little remarkable, if this clause was intended as a protection to the citizen of a state against the legislative power of his own state, that the words "citizen of the state" should be left out when it is so carefully used, and used in contradistinction to "citizens of the United States" in the very sentence which precedes it. It is too clear for argument that the change in phraseology was adopted understandingly and with a purpose.

Of the privileges and immunities of the citizens of the United States, and of the privileges and immunities of the citizen of the state, and what they respectively are, we will presently consider; but we wish to state here that it is only the former which are placed by this clause under the protection of the Federal Constitution, and that the latter, whatever they may be, are not intended to have any additional protection by this paragraph of the Amendment.

If, then, there is a difference between the privileges and immunities belonging to a citizen of the United States as such, and those belonging to the citizen of the state as such, the latter must rest for their security and protection where they have heretofore rested; for they are not embraced by this paragraph of the Amendment. . . .

[U]p to the adoption of the recent Amendments, no claim or pretense was set up that those rights depended on the Federal government for their existence or protection, beyond the very few express limitations which the Federal Constitution imposed upon the states—such, for instance, as the prohibition against *ex post facto* laws, bills of attainder, and laws impairing the obligation of contracts. But with the exception of these and a few other restrictions, the entire domain of the privileges and immunities of citizens of the states, as above defined, lay within the constitutional and legislative power of the states, and without that of the Federal government. Was it the purpose of the 14th Amendment, by the simple declaration that no state should make or enforce any law which shall abridge the privileges and immunities of citizens of the United States, to transfer the security and protection of all the civil rights which we have mentioned, from the states of the Federal government? And where it is declared that Congress shall have the power to enforce that article, was it intended to bring within the power of Congress the entire domain of civil rights, heretofore belonging exclusively to the states?

All this and more must follow, if the proposition of the plaintiffs in error be sound. For not only are these rights subject to the control of Congress whenever in its discretion any of them are supposed to be abridged by state legislation, but that body may also pass laws in advance, limiting and restricting the exercise of legislative power by the states, in their most ordinary and usual functions, as in its judgment it may think proper on all such subjects. And still further, such a construction would constitute this court a perpetual censor upon all legislation of the states, on the civil rights of their own citizens, with authority to nullify such as it did not approve as consistent with those rights, as they existed at the time of the adoption of this Amendment. . . . [W]hen, as in the case before us, these consequences are so serious, so far reaching and pervading, so great a departure from the structure and spirit of our institutions; when the effect is to fetter and degrade the state governments by subjecting them to the control of Congress, in the exercise of powers heretofore universally conceded to them of the most ordinary and fundamental character, when in fact it radically changes the whole theory of the relations of the state and Federal governments to each other and of both these governments to the people; the argument has a force that is irresistible, in the absence of language which expresses such a purpose too clearly to admit of doubt.

We are convinced that no such results were intended by the Congress which proposed these amendments, nor by the legislatures of the states, which ratified them. . . .

But lest it should be said that no . . . privileges and immunities are to be found if those we have been considering are excluded, we venture to suggest some which owe their existence to the Federal government, its national character, its Constitution, or its laws.

One of these is well described in the case of *Crandall v. Nevada* [1868]. It is said to be the right of the citizen of this great country, protected by implied guaranties of its Constitution, "to come to the seat of government to assert any claim he may have upon that government, to transact any business he may have with it, to seek its protection, to share its offices, to engage in administering its functions. He has the right of free access to its seaports, through which all operations of foreign commerce are conducted, to the subtreasuries, land offices, and courts of justice in the several states." . . .

Another privilege of a citizen of the United States is to demand the care and protection of the Federal government over his life, liberty, and property when on the high seas or within the jurisdiction of a foreign government. Of this there can be no doubt, nor that the right depends upon his character as a citizen of the United States. The right to peaceably assemble and petition for redress of grievances, the privilege of the writ of habeas corpus, are rights of the citizen guarantied by the Federal Constitution. The right to use the navigable waters of the United States, however they may penetrate the territory of the several states, and all rights secured to our citizens by treaties with foreign nations, are dependent upon citizenship of the United States, and not citizenship of a state. . . .

The argument has not been much pressed in these cases that the defendant's charter deprives the plaintiffs of their property without due process of law, or that it denies to them the equal protection of the law. The first of these paragraphs has been in the Constitution since the adoption of the 5th Amendment, as a restraint upon the Federal power. It is also to be found in some form of expression in the constitutions of nearly all the states, as a restraint upon the power of the states. . . .

We are not without judicial interpretation, therefore, both state and national, of the meaning of this clause. And it is sufficient to say that under no construction of that provision that we have ever seen, or any that we deem admissible, can the restraint imposed by the State of Louisiana upon the exercise of their trade by the butchers of New Orleans be held to be a deprivation of property within the meaning of that provision.

"Nor shall any state deny to any person within its jurisdiction the equal protection of the laws."

In the light of the history of these amendments, and the pervading purpose of them, which we have already discussed, it is not difficult to give a meaning to this clause. The existence of laws in the states where the newly emancipated negroes resided, which discriminated with gross injustice and hardship against them as a class, was the evil to be remedied by this clause, and by it such laws are forbidden. . . .

We doubt very much whether any action of a state not directed by way of discrimination against the negroes as a class, or on account of their race, will ever be held to come within the purview of this provision. It is so clearly a provision for that race and that emergency, that a strong case would be necessary for its application to any other.

MR. JUSTICE FIELD, DISSENTING:

The question presented is . . . one of the gravest importance, not merely to the parties here, but to the whole country. It is nothing less than the question whether the recent Amendments to the Federal Constitution protect the citizens of the United States against the deprivation of their common rights by state legislation. In my judgment the 14th Amendment does afford such protection, and was so intended by the Congress which framed and the states which adopted it. . . .

The Amendment does not attempt to confer any new privileges or immunities upon citizens or to enumerate or define those already existing. It assumes that there are such privileges and immunities which belong of right to citizens as such, and ordains that they shall not be abridged by state legislation. If this inhibition has no reference to privileges and immunities of this character, but only refers, as held by the majority of the court in their opinion, to such privileges and immunities as were before its adoption specially designated in the Constitution or necessarily implied as belonging to citizens of the United States, it was a vain and idle enactment, which accomplished nothing, and most unnecessarily excited Congress and the people on its passage. With privileges and immunities thus designated no state could ever have interfered by its laws, and no new constitutional provision was required to inhibit such interference. The supremacy of the Constitution and the laws of the United States always controlled any state legislation of that character. But if the Amendment refers to the natural and inalienable rights which belong to all citizens, the inhibition has a profound significance and consequence. . . .

[E]quality of right, with exemption from all disparaging and partial enactments, in the lawful pursuits of life, throughout the whole country, is the distinguishing privilege of citizens of the United States. To them, everywhere, all pursuits, all professions, all avocations are open without other restrictions than such as are imposed equally upon all others of the same age, sex and condition. The state may prescribe such regulations for every pursuit and calling of life as will promote the public health, secure the good order and advance the general prosperity of society, but when once prescribed, the pursuit or calling must be free to be followed by every citizen who is within the conditions designated, and will conform to the regulations. This is the fundamental idea upon which our institutions rest, and unless adhered to in the legislation of the country our government will be a Republic only in name. The 14th Amendment, in my judgment, makes it essential to the validity of the legislation of every state that this equality of right should be respected. How widely this equality has been departed from, how entirely rejected and trampled upon by the act of Louisiana, I have already shown. And it is to me a matter of profound regret that its validity is recognized by a majority of this court, for by it the right of free labor, one of the most sacred and imprescriptible rights of man, is violated. . . .

I am authorized by Mr. Chief Justice Chase, Mr. Justice Swayne and Mr. Justice Bradley, to state that they concur with me in this dissenting opinion.

MR. JUSTICE BRADLEY, DISSENTING:

The right of a state to regulate the conduct of its citizens is undoubtedly a very broad and extensive one, and not to be lightly restricted. But there are certain fundamental rights which this right of regulation cannot infringe. It may prescribe the manner of their exercise, but it cannot subvert the rights themselves. . . .

For the preservation, exercise and enjoyment of these rights the individual citizen, as a necessity, must be left free to adopt such calling, profession or trade as may seem to him most conducive to that end. Without this right he can not be a freeman. This right to choose one's calling is an essential part of that liberty which it is the object of government to protect; and a calling, when chosen, is a man's property and right. Liberty and property are not protected where these rights are arbitrarily assailed. . . .

[C]itizenship is not an empty name, but that, in this country at least, it has connected with it certain incidental rights, privileges, and immunities of the greatest importance. And to say that these rights and immunities attach only to state citizenship, and not to citizenship of the United States, appears to me to evince a very narrow and insufficient estimate of constitutional history and the rights of men, not to say the rights of the American people. . . .

In my judgment, it was the intention of the people of this country in adopting that Amendment to provide national security against violation by the states of the fundamental rights of the citizen.

[Mr. Justice Swayne also wrote a dissenting opinion.]

Maximum-hours legislation is struck down by the Court as interfering with "liberty of contract."

30. *Lochner v. New York* (1905)

Justice Field, in the *Slaughter-House Cases* (see p. 213), had urged the Court to apply the Fourteenth Amendment to prevent the states from infringing unenumerated liberties that the justices considered "fundamental" or basic. This position was adopted by the Court before the close of the nineteenth century, though under the aegis of the Due Process, rather than the Privileges or Immunities, Clause. *Lochner v. New York* is a striking example of the Court's application of "liberty to contract," a judicially discovered "fundamental" right, to void a maximum-hours law. It was also the occasion for one of Justice

Holmes's most celebrated dissents. (The decision was, in effect, over-ruled by *West Coast Hotel Co. v. Parrish*; see p. 228.)

Background: A New York State law limited bakery employees to a ten-hour workday and a sixty-hour workweek. Lochner, a bakery owner, appealed his conviction under this law to the United States Supreme Court, which reversed the judgment of the New York courts.

MR. JUSTICE PECKHAM DELIVERED
THE OPINION OF THE COURT:

The statute necessarily interferes with the right of contract between the employer and employees, concerning the number of hours in which the latter may labor in the bakery of the employer. The general right to make a contract in relation to his business is part of the liberty of the individual protected by the 14th Amendment of the Federal Constitution. Under that provision no state can deprive any person of life, liberty, or property without due process of law. The right to purchase or to sell labor is part of the liberty protected by this amendment, unless there are circumstances which exclude the right. There are, however, certain powers, existing in the sovereignty of each state in the Union, somewhat vaguely termed police powers, the exact description and limitation of which have not been attempted by the courts. Those powers, broadly stated, and without, at present, any attempt at a more specific limitation, relate to the safety, health, morals, and general welfare of the public. Both property and liberty are held on such reasonable conditions as may be imposed by the governing power of the state in the exercise of those powers, and with such conditions the 14th Amendment was not designed to interfere.

The state, therefore, has power to prevent the individual from making certain kinds of contracts, and in regard to them the Federal Constitution offers no protection. If the contract be one which the state, in the legitimate exercise of its police power, has the right to prohibit, it is not prevented from prohibiting it by the 14th Amendment. Contracts in violation of a statute, either of the Federal or state government, or a contract to let one's property for immoral purposes, or to do any other unlawful act, could obtain no protection from the Federal Constitution, as coming under the liberty of person or of free contract. Therefore, when the state, by its legislature, in the assumed exercise of its police powers, has passed an act which seriously limits the rights to labor or the right of contract in regard to their means of livelihood between persons who are *sui juris* (both employer and employee), it becomes of great importance to determine which shall prevail,—the right of the individual to labor for such time as he may choose, or the right of the state to prevent the individual from laboring, or from entering into any contract to labor, beyond a certain time prescribed by the state.

This court has recognized the existence and upheld the exercise of the police powers of the states in many cases. . . . Among the later cases where the state law has been upheld by this court is that of *Holden v. Hardy* [1898]. A provision in the act of the legislature of Utah was there under consideration, the act limiting the employment of workmen in all underground mines or workings, to eight hours per day, "except in cases of emergency, where life or property is in imminent danger." It also limited the hours of labor in smelting and other institutions for the reduction or refining of ores or metals to eight hours per day, except in like cases of emergency. The act was held to be a valid exercise of the police powers of the state. . . .

In every case that comes before this court, therefore, where legislation of this character is concerned, and where the protection of the Federal Constitution is sought, the question necessarily arises: Is this a fair, reasonable, and appropriate exercise of the police power of the state, or is it an unreasonable, unnecessary, and arbitrary interference with the right of the individual to his personal liberty, or to enter into those contracts in relation to labor which may seem to him appropriate or necessary for the support of himself and his family? Of course the liberty of contract relating to labor includes both parties to it. The one has as much right to purchase as the other to sell labor.

This is not a question of substituting the judgment of the court for that of the legislature. If the act be within the power of the state it is valid, although the judgment of the court might be totally opposed to the enactment of such a law. But the question would still remain: Is it within the police power of the state? and that question must be answered by the court.

The question whether this act is valid as a labor law, pure and simple, may be dismissed in a few words. There is no reasonable ground for interfering with the liberty of person or the right of free contract, by determining the hours of labor, in the occupation of a baker. There is no contention that bakers as a class are not equal in intelligence and capacity to men in other trades or manual occupations, or that they are not able to assert their rights and care for themselves without the protecting arm of the state, interfering with their independence of judgment and of action. They are in no sense wards of the state. Viewed in the light of a purely labor law, with no reference whatever to the question of health, we think that a law like the one before us involves neither the safety, the morals, nor the welfare, of the public, and that the interest of the public is not in the slightest degree affected by such an act. The law must be upheld, if at all, as a law pertaining to the health of the individual engaged in the occupation of a baker. It does not affect any other portion of the public than those who are engaged in that occupation. Clean and wholesome bread does not depend upon whether the baker works but ten hours per day or only sixty hours a week. The limitation of the hours of labor does not come within the police power on that ground. . . .

We think the limit of the police power has been reached and passed in this case. There is, in our judgment, no reasonable foundation for holding this to be necessary or appropriate as a health law to safeguard the public health, or the health of the individuals who are following the trade of a baker. If this statute be valid, and if, therefore, a proper case is made out in which to deny the right of an individual, *sui juris*, as employer or employee, to make contracts for the labor of the latter under the protection of the provisions of the Federal Constitution, there would seem to be no length to which legislation of this nature might not go.

We think that there can be no fair doubt that the trade of a baker, in and of itself, is not an unhealthy one to that degree which would authorize the legislature to interfere with the right to labor, and with the right of free contract on the part of the individual, either as employer or employee. In looking through statistics regarding all trades and occupations, it may be true that the trade of a baker does not appear to be as healthy as some other trades, and is also vastly more healthy than still others. To the common understanding the trade of a baker has never been regarded as an unhealthy one. Very likely physicians would not recommend the exercise of that or of any other trade as a remedy for ill health. Some occupations are more healthy than others, but we think there are none which might not come under the power of the legislature to supervise and control the hours of working therein, if the mere fact that the occupation is not absolutely and perfectly healthy is to confer that right upon the legislative department of the government. It might be safely affirmed that almost all occupations more or less affect the health. There must be more than the mere fact of the possible existence of some small amount of unhealthiness to warrant legislative interference with liberty. It is unfortunately true that labor, even in any department, may possibly carry with it the seeds of unhealthiness. But are we all, on that account, at the mercy of legislative majorities? . . .

We do not believe in the soundness of the views which uphold this law. On the contrary, we think that such a law as this, although passed in the assumed exercise of the police power, and as relating to the public health, or the health of the employees named, is not within that power, and is invalid. The act is not, within any fair meaning of the term, a health law, but is an illegal interference with the rights of individuals, both employers and employees, to make contracts regarding labor upon such terms as they may think best, or which they may agree upon with the other parties to such contracts. Statutes of the nature of that under review, limiting the hours in which grown and intelligent men may labor to earn their living, are mere meddlesome interferences with the rights of the individual, and they are not saved from condemnation by the claim that they are passed in the exercise of the police power. . . .

This interference on the part of the legislatures of the several states with the ordinary trades and occupations of the people seems to be on the increase. . . .

It is impossible for us to shut our eyes to the fact that many of the laws of this character, while passed under what is claimed to be the police power for the purpose of protecting the public health or welfare, are, in reality, passed from other motives. We are justified in saying so when, from the character of the law and the subject upon which it legislates, it is apparent that the public health or welfare bears but the most remote relation to the law. . . .

It seems to us that the real object and purpose were simply to regulate the hours of labor between the master and his employees (all being men, *sui juris*), in a private business, not dangerous in any degree to morals, or in any real and substantial degree to the health of the employees.

MR. JUSTICE HARLAN, WITH WHOM MR. JUSTICE WHITE
AND MR. JUSTICE DAY CONCURRED, DISSENTING:

It is plain that this statute was enacted in order to protect the physical
well-being of those who work in bakery and confectionery establishments. It may be that the statute had its origin, in part, in the belief
that employers and employees in such establishments were not upon
an equal footing, and that the necessities of the latter often compelled
them to submit to such exactions as unduly taxed their strength. Be this
as it may, the statute must be taken as expressing the belief of the
people of New York that, as a general rule, and in the case of the
average man, labor in excess of sixty hours during a week in such
establishments may endanger the health of those who thus labor.
Whether or not this be wise legislation it is not the province of the
court to inquire. Under our systems of government the courts are not
concerned with the wisdom or policy of legislation. . . . I find it impossible, in view of common experience, to say that there is here no
real or substantial relation between the means employed by the state
and the end sought to be accomplished by its legislation. . . .

Professor Hirt in his treatise on the "Diseases of the Workers" has
said: "The labor of the bakers is among the hardest and most laborious
imaginable, because it has to be performed under conditions injurious
to the health of those engaged in it. It is hard, very hard, work, not
only because it requires a great deal of physical exertion in an over-
heated workshop and during unreasonably long hours, but more so
because of the erratic demands on the public, compelling the baker to
perform the greater part of his work at night, thus depriving him of an
opportunity to enjoy the necessary rest and sleep,—a fact which is
highly injurious to his health."

MR. JUSTICE HOLMES, DISSENTING:

This case is decided upon an economic theory which a large part of
the country does not entertain. If it were a question whether I
agreed with that theory, I should desire to study it further and long
before making up my mind. But I do not conceive that to be my duty,
because I strongly believe that my agreement or disagreement has nothing to do with the right of a majority to embody their opinions in law.
It is settled by various decisions of this court that state constitutions

and state laws may regulate life in many ways which we as legislators might think as injudicious, or if you like as tyrannical, as this, and which, equally with this, interfere with the liberty to contract. Sunday laws and usury laws are ancient examples. A more modern one is the prohibition of lotteries. The liberty of the citizen to do as he likes so long as he does not interfere with the liberty of others to do the same, which has been a shibboleth for some well-known writers, is interfered with by school laws, by the Postoffice, by every state or municipal institution which takes his money for purposes thought desirable, whether he likes it or not. The 14th Amendment does not enact Mr. Herbert Spencer's *Social Statics*. . . .

[A] Constitution is not intended to embody a particular economic theory, whether of paternalism and the organic relation of the citizen to the state or of *laissez faire*. It is made for people of fundamentally differing views, and the accident of our finding certain opinions natural and familiar, or novel, and even shocking, ought not to conclude our judgment upon the question whether statutes embodying them conflict with the Constitution of the United States.

General propositions do not decide concrete cases. The decision will depend on a judgment or intuition more subtle than any articulate major premise. But I think that the proposition just stated, if it is accepted, will carry us far toward the end. Every opinion tends to become a law. I think that the word "liberty," in the 14th Amendment, is perverted when it is held to prevent the natural outcome of a dominant opinion, unless it can be said that a rational and fair man necessarily would admit that the statute proposed would infringe fundamental principles as they have been understood by the traditions of our people and our law. It does not need research to show that no such sweeping condemnation can be passed upon the statute before us. A reasonable man might think it a proper measure on the score of health.

Minimum-wage regulations by state legislatures or Congress are constitutional.

31. *West Coast Hotel Co. v. Parrish* (1937)

This is the first case in which the Supreme Court upheld minimum-wage regulations. Specifically, the Court overturned a former decision,

Adkins v. Children's Hospital (1923), which, in reasoning similar to that of *Lochner*, had ruled that the setting of minimum wages for women and minors (as provided by an act of Congress of 1918) violated the Due Process Clause of the Fifth Amendment. The *Adkins* decision served as an effective block against wage legislation until 1937.

Background: A Washington State law fixing minimum wages for women and minors was challenged as unconstitutional by the West Coast Hotel Company. Losing in the Supreme Court of the state of Washington, the company carried its appeal to the United States Supreme Court. The latter, by a vote of five to four, validated the Washington State law and, in effect, made possible the enactment of further labor and other social legislation.

MR. CHIEF JUSTICE HUGHES DELIVERED
THE OPINION OF THE COURT:

This case presents the question of the constitutional validity of the minimum wage law of the State of Washington. . . .

The appellant relies upon the decision of this court in *Adkins v. Children's Hospital* . . . which held invalid the District of Columbia Minimum Wage Act which was attacked under the Due Process clause of the Fifth Amendment. . . .

The principle which must control our decision is not in doubt. The constitutional provision invoked is the Due Process clause of the Fourteenth Amendment governing the States, as the Due Process clause invoked in the *Adkins* case governed Congress. In each case the violation alleged by those attacking minimum wage regulation for women is deprivation of freedom of contract. What is this freedom? The Constitution does not speak of freedom of contract. It speaks of liberty and prohibits the deprivation of liberty without the due process of law. In prohibiting that deprivation the Constitution does not recognize an absolute and uncontrollable liberty. Liberty in each of its phases has its history and connotation. But the liberty safeguarded is liberty in a social organization which requires the protection of law against the evils which menace the health, safety, morals and welfare of the people. Liberty under the Constitution is thus necessarily subject to the restraints of due process, and regulation which is reasonable in relation to its subject and is adopted in the interests of the community is due process. . . .

The minimum wage to be paid under the Washington statute is fixed after full consideration by representatives of employers, employees and the public. It may be assumed that the minimum wage is fixed in consideration of the services that are performed in the particular occupations under normal conditions. Provision is made for special licenses at less wages in the case of women who are incapable of full service. The statement of Mr. Justice Holmes in the *Adkins* case is pertinent: "This statute does not compel anybody to pay anything. It simply forbids employment at rates below those fixed as the minimum requirement of health and right living. It is safe to assume that women will not be employed at even the lowest wages allowed unless they earn them, or unless the employer's business can sustain the burden. In short the law in its character and operation is like hundreds of so-called police laws that have been upheld." And Chief Justice Taft forcibly pointed out the consideration which is basic in a statute of this character: "Legislatures which adopt a requirement of maximum hours or minimum wages may be presumed to believe that when sweating employers are prevented from paying unduly low wages by positive law they will continue their business, abating that part of their profits, which were wrung from the necessities of their employees, and will concede the better terms required by the law, and that while in individual cases, hardship may result, the restriction will enure to the benefit of the general class of employees in whose interest the law is passed and so to that of the community at large." . . .

We think that the views thus expressed are sound and that the decision in the *Adkins* case was a departure from the true application of the principles governing the regulation by the State of the relation of employer and employed. . . .

The legislature of the State was clearly entitled to consider the situation of women in employment, the fact that they are in the class receiving the least pay, that their bargaining power is relatively weak, and that they are the ready victims of those who would take advantage of their necessitous circumstances. The legislature was entitled to adopt measures to reduce the evils of the "sweating system," the exploiting of workers at wages so low as to be insufficient to meet the bare cost of living thus making their very helplessness the occasion of a most injurious competition. The legislature had the right to consider that its minimum wage requirements would be an important aid in carrying out its policy of protection. The adoption of similar requirements by many States evidences a deep-seated conviction both as to the presence of the evil and as to the means adapted to check it. Legislative response to that conviction cannot be regarded as arbitrary or capricious and that is all we have to decide. Even if the wisdom of the policy be regarded as debatable and its effects uncertain, still the legislature is entitled to its judgment. . . .

We may take judicial notice of the unparalleled demands for relief which arose during the recent period of depression and still continue to an alarming extent despite the degree of economic recovery which has been achieved. It is unnecessary to cite official statistics to establish what is of common knowledge through the length and breadth of the land. While in the instant case no factual brief has been presented, there is no reason to doubt that the State of Washington has encountered the same social problem that is present elsewhere. The community is not bound to provide what is in effect a subsidy for unconscionable employers. The community may direct its law-making power to correct the abuse which springs from their selfish disregard of the public interest. . . .

Our conclusion is that the case of *Adkins v. Children's Hospital* should be, and it is, overruled.

B. Right to Privacy

The Constitution grants a right of marital privacy.

32. *Griswold v. Connecticut* (1965)

The demise of substantive due process, seemingly sealed in *West Coast Hotel v. Parrish*, was confidently asserted by Justice Black in his opinion for the Court in *Ferguson v. Skrupa* (1963). There Black emphatically denounced half a century of Supreme Court intervention to nullify legislation that the justices thought to be unwise or excessive. Yet such are the vagaries of constitutional interpretation that the ink had hardly dried on Black's opinion before substantive due process was resurrected, albeit in a noneconomic context, in *Griswold*. Here, the Court ruled that a state may not prohibit married couples from using contraceptives because the prohibition violated the right of marital privacy. Although the right of privacy is not directly mentioned in the Constitution, the Court held that "zones of privacy" were created by various guarantees in the Bill of Rights.

Background: The use of contraceptives was made a criminal offense under Connecticut law. Officials of the state's Planned Parenthood League were convicted of violating the law by giving advice on contraceptive use to married couples. Connecticut's Supreme Court of Errors affirmed the conviction, but was reversed by the Supreme Court.

MR. JUSTICE DOUGLAS DELIVERED
THE OPINION OF THE COURT:

Appellant Griswold is Executive Director of the Planned Parenthood League of Connecticut. Appellant Buxton is a licensed physician and a professor at the Yale Medical School who served as Medical Director for the League at its Center in New Haven—a center open and operating from November 1 to November 10, 1961, when appellants were arrested.

They gave information, instruction, and medical advice to *married persons* as to the means of preventing conception. . . .

The appellants were found guilty [of violating Connecticut's anti-contraception statutes] and fined $100 each. . . .

[W]e are met with a wide range of questions that implicate the Due Process Clause of the Fourteenth Amendment. Overtones of some arguments suggest that *Lochner v. New York* [1905] should be our guide. But we decline that invitation. We do not sit as a super-legislature to determine the wisdom, need, and propriety of laws that touch economic problems, business affairs, or social conditions. This law, however, operates directly on an intimate relation of husband and wife and their physician's role in one aspect of that relation.

The association of people is not mentioned in the Constitution nor in the Bill of Rights. The right to educate a child in a school of the parents' choice—whether public or private or parochial—is also not mentioned. Nor is the right to study any particular subject or any foreign language. Yet the First Amendment has been construed to include certain of those rights.

By *Pierce v. Society of Sisters* [1925] the right to educate one's children as one chooses is made applicable to the States by the force of the First and Fourteenth Amendments. By *Meyer v. Nebraska* [1923] the same dignity is given the right to study the German language in a private school. In other words, the State may not, consistently with the spirit of the First Amendment, contract the spectrum of available knowledge. The right of freedom of speech and press includes not only the right to utter or to print, but the right to distribute, the right to receive, the right to read and freedom of inquiry, freedom of thought, and freedom to teach—indeed the freedom of the entire university community. Without those peripheral rights the specific rights would be less secure. And so we reaffirm the principle of the *Pierce* and the *Meyer* cases.

In *NAACP v. Alabama* [1958] we protected the "freedom to associate and privacy in one's associations," noting that freedom of association was a peripheral First Amendment right. Disclosure of membership lists of a constitutionally valid association, we held, was invalid "as entailing the likelihood of a substantial restraint upon the exercise by petitioner's members of their right to freedom of association." In other words, the First Amendment has a penumbra where privacy is protected from governmental intrusion.

The foregoing cases suggest that specific guarantees in the Bill of Rights have penumbras, formed by emanations from those guarantees that help give them life and substance. Various guarantees create zones of privacy. The right of association contained in the penumbra of the First Amendment is one, as we have seen. The Third Amendment in its prohibition against the quartering of soldiers "in any house" in time of peace without the consent of the owner is another facet of that privacy. The Fourth Amendment explicitly affirms the "right of the people to be secure in their persons, houses, papers, and effects, against unreasonable searches and seizures." The Fifth Amendment in its Self-Incrimination Clause enables the citizen to create a zone of privacy which government may not force him to surrender to his detriment. The Ninth Amendment provides: "The enumeration in the Constitution, of certain rights, shall not be construed to deny or disparage others retained by the people."

The Fourth and Fifth Amendments were described in *Boyd v. United States* [1886] as protection against all governmental invasions "of the sanctity of a man's home and the privacies of life." . . .

The present case, then, concerns a relationship lying within the zone of privacy created by several fundamental constitutional guarantees.

And it concerns a law which, in forbidding the *use* of contraceptives rather than regulating their manufacture or sale, seeks to achieve its goals by means having a maximum destructive impact upon that relationship. Such a law cannot stand in light of the familiar principle, so often applied by this Court, that a "governmental purpose to control or prevent activities constitutionally subject to state regulation may not be achieved by means which sweep unnecessarily broadly and thereby invade the area of protected freedoms." Would we allow the police to search the sacred precincts of marital bedrooms for telltale signs of the use of contraceptives? The very idea is repulsive to the notions of privacy surrounding the marriage relationship.

We deal with a right of privacy older than the Bill of Rights—older than our political parties, older than our school system. Marriage is a coming together for better or for worse, hopefully enduring, and intimate to the degree of being sacred. It is an association that promotes a way of life, not causes; a harmony in living, not political faiths; a bilateral loyalty, not commercial or social projects. Yet it is an association for as noble a purpose as any involved in our prior decisions.

MR. JUSTICE GOLDBERG, WITH WHOM THE CHIEF JUSTICE AND MR. JUSTICE BRENNAN JOIN, CONCURRING:

I do agree that the concept of liberty protects those personal rights that are fundamental, and is not confined to the specific terms of the Bill of Rights. My conclusion that the concept of liberty is not so restricted and that it embraces the right of marital privacy though that right is not mentioned explicitly in the Constitution is supported both by numerous decisions of this Court, referred to in the Court's opinion, and by the language and history of the Ninth Amendment. . . .

The [Ninth] Amendment is almost entirely the work of James Madison. It was introduced in Congress by him and passed the House and Senate with little or no debate and virtually no change in language. It was proffered to quiet expressed fears that a bill of specifically enumerated rights could not be sufficiently broad to cover all essential rights and that the specific mention of certain rights would be interpreted as a denial that others were protected. . . .

To hold that a right so basic and fundamental and so deep-rooted in our society as the right of privacy in marriage may be infringed because

that right is not guaranteed in so many words by the first eight amendments to the Constitution is to ignore the Ninth Amendment and to
give it no effect whatsoever. . . .

I do not mean to imply that the Ninth Amendment is applied against
the States by the Fourteenth. Nor do I mean to state that the Ninth
Amendment constitutes an independent source of rights protected from
infringement by either the States or the Federal Government. Rather,
the Ninth Amendment shows a belief of the Constitution's authors that
fundamental rights exist that are not expressly enumerated in the first
eight amendments and an intent that the list of rights included there
not be deemed exhaustive.

In determining which rights are fundamental, judges are not left at
large to decide cases in light of their personal and private notions.
Rather, they must look to the "traditions and [collective] conscience
of our people" to determine whether a principle is "so rooted [there]
. . . as to be ranked as fundamental." . . .

The entire fabric of the Constitution and the purposes that clearly
underlie its specific guarantees demonstrate that the rights to marital
privacy and to marry and raise a family are of similar order and magnitude as the fundamental rights specifically protected.

Although the Constitution does not speak in so many words of the
right of privacy in marriage, I cannot believe that it offers these fundamental rights no protection. The fact that no particular provision of
the Constitution explicitly forbids the State from disrupting the traditional relation of the family—a relation as old and as fundamental as
our entire civilization—surely does not show that the Government was
meant to have the power to do so. Rather, as the Ninth Amendment
expressly recognizes, there are fundamental personal rights such as this
one, which are protected from abridgment by the Government though
not specifically mentioned in the Constitution. . . .

While it may shock some of my Brethren that the Court today holds
that the Constitution protects the right of marital privacy, in my view
it is far more shocking to believe that the personal liberty guaranteed
by the Constitution does not include protection against such totalitarian
limitation of family size, which is at complete variance with our constitutional concepts. Yet, if upon a showing of a slender basis of ra-
tionality, a law outlawing voluntary birth control by married persons is
valid, then, by the same reasoning, a law requiring compulsory birth

control also would seem to be valid. In my view, however, both types of law would unjustifiably intrude upon rights of marital privacy which are constitutionally protected. . . .

Finally, it should be said of the Court's holding today that it in no way interferes with a State's proper regulation of sexual promiscuity or misconduct. As my Brother Harlan so well stated in his dissenting opinion in *Poe v. Ullman* [1961].

"Adultery, homosexuality and the like are sexual intimacies which the State forbids . . . but the intimacy of husband and wife is necessarily an essential and accepted feature of the institution of marriage, an institution which the State not only must allow, but which always and in every age it has fostered and protected. It is one thing when the State exerts its power either to forbid extra-marital sexuality . . . or to say who may marry, but it is quite another when, having acknowledged a marriage and the intimacies inherent in it, it undertakes to regulate by means of the criminal law the details of that intimacy."

MR. JUSTICE HARLAN, CONCURRING IN THE JUDGMENT:

[W]hat I find implicit in the Court's opinion is that the "incorporation" doctrine may be used to *restrict* the reach of Fourteenth Amendment Due Process. For me this is just as unacceptable constitutional doctrine as is the use of the "incorporation" approach to *impose* upon the States all the requirements of the Bill of Rights as found in the provisions of the first eight amendments and in the decisions of this Court interpreting them.

In my view, the proper constitutional inquiry in this case is whether this Connecticut statute infringes the Due Process Clause of the Fourteenth Amendment because the enactment violates basic values "implicit in the concept of ordered liberty," *Palko v. Connecticut* [1937]. For reasons stated at length in my dissenting opinion in *Poe v. Ullman* [1961], I believe that it does. While the relevant inquiry may be aided by resort to one or more of the provisions of the Bill of Rights, it is not dependent on them or any of their radiations. The Due Process Clause of the Fourteenth Amendment stands, in my opinion, on its own bottom.

[Mr. Justice White also wrote an opinion concurring in the judgment.]

MR. JUSTICE BLACK, WITH WHOM MR. JUSTICE STEWART
JOINS, DISSENTING:

In order that there may be no room at all to doubt why I vote as I do, I feel constrained to add that the law is every bit as offensive to me as it is to my Brethren. There is no single one of the graphic and eloquent strictures and criticisms fired at the policy of this Connecticut law either by the Court's opinion or by those of my concurring Brethren to which I cannot subscribe—except their conclusion that the evil qualities they see in the law make it unconstitutional. . . .

The Court talks about a constitutional "right of privacy" as though there is some constitutional provision or provisions forbidding any law ever to be passed which might abridge the "privacy" of individuals. But there is not. There are, of course, guarantees in certain specific constitutional provisions which are designed in part to protect privacy at certain times and places with respect to certain activities. Such, for example, is the Fourth Amendment's guarantee against "unreasonable searches and seizures." But I think it belittles that Amendment to talk about it as though it protects nothing but "privacy." . . .

One of the most effective ways of diluting or expanding a constitutionally guaranteed right is to substitute for the crucial word or words of a constitutional guarantee another word or words, more or less flexible and more or less restricted in meaning. This fact is well illustrated by the use of the term "right of privacy" as a comprehensive substitute for the Fourth Amendment's guarantee against "unreasonable searches and seizures." "Privacy" is a broad, abstract and ambiguous concept which can easily be shrunken in meaning but which can also, on the other hand, easily be interpreted as a constitutional ban against many things other than searches and seizures. . . . I like my privacy as well as the next one, but I am nevertheless compelled to admit that government has a right to invade it unless prohibited by some specific constitutional provision.

I think that if properly construed neither the Due Process Clause nor the Ninth Amendment, nor both together, could under any circumstances be a proper basis for invalidating the Connecticut law. I discuss the due process and Ninth Amendment arguments together because on analysis they turn out to be the same thing—merely using different words to claim for this Court and the federal judiciary power to invalidate any legislative act which the judges find irrational, unreasonable or offensive.

The due process argument which my Brothers Harlan and White adopt here is based, as their opinions indicate, on the premise that this Court is vested with power to invalidate all state laws that it considers to be arbitrary, capricious, unreasonable, or oppressive, or on this Court's belief that a particular state law under scrutiny has no "rational or justifying" purpose, or is offensive to a "sense of fairness and justice." If these formulas based on "natural justice," or others which mean the same thing, are to prevail, they require judges to determine what is or is not constitutional on the basis of their own appraisal of what laws are unwise or unnecessary. . . . I do not believe that we are granted power by the Due Process Clause or any other constitutional provision or provisions to measure constitutionality by our belief that legislation is arbitrary, capricious or unreasonable, or accomplishes no justifiable purpose, or is offensive to our own notions of "civilized standards of conduct." Such an appraisal of the wisdom of legislation is an attribute of the power to make laws, not of the power to interpret them. The use by federal courts of such a formula or doctrine or whatnot to veto federal or state laws simply takes away from Congress and States the power to make laws based on their own judgment of fairness and wisdom and transfers that power to this Court for ultimate determination—a power which was specifically denied to federal courts by the convention that framed the Constitution. . . .

My Brother Goldberg has adopted the recent discovery that the Ninth Amendment as well as the Due Process Clause can be used by this Court as authority to strike down all state legislation which this Court thinks violates "fundamental principles of liberty and justice," or is contrary to the "traditions and [collective] conscience of our people." He also states, without proof satisfactory to me, that in making decisions on this basis judges will not consider "their personal and private notions." One may ask how they can avoid considering them. Our Court certainly has no machinery with which to take a Gallup Poll. And the scientific miracles of this age have not yet produced a gadget which the Court can use to determine what traditions are rooted in the "[collective] conscience of our people." Moreover, one would certainly have to look far beyond the language of the Ninth Amendment to find that the Framers vested in this Court any such awesome veto powers over lawmaking, either by the States or by the Congress. Nor does anything in the history of the Amendment offer any support for such a shocking doctrine. The whole history of the adoption of the Constitution and Bill of Rights points the other way, and the very material quoted by my Brother Goldberg shows that the Ninth Amendment was intended to protect against the idea that "by enumerating particular exceptions to the grant of power" to the Federal Government, "those rights which were not singled out, were intended to be assigned into the hands of the General Government [the United States], and were consequently insecure." That Amendment was passed, not to broaden the powers of this Court or any other department of "the General Government," but, as every student of history knows, to assure the people that the Constitution in all its provisions was intended to limit the Federal Government to the powers granted expressly or by necessary implication. If any broad, unlimited power to hold laws unconstitutional because they offend what this Court conceives to be the "[collective] conscience of our people" is vested in this Court by the Ninth Amendment, the Fourteenth Amendment, or any other provision of the Constitution, it was not given by the Framers, but rather has been bestowed on the Court by the Court. This fact is perhaps responsible for the peculiar phenomenon that for a period of a century and a half no serious suggestion was ever made that the Ninth Amendment, enacted to protect state powers against federal invasion, could be used as a weapon of federal power to prevent state legislatures from passing laws they consider appropriate to govern local affairs. Use of any such broad, unbounded judicial authority would make of this Court's members a day-to-day constitutional convention. . . .

My point is that there is no provision of the Constitution which either expressly or impliedly vests power in this Court to sit as a supervisory agency over acts of duly constituted legislative bodies and set aside their laws because of the Court's belief that the legislative policies adopted are unreasonable, unwise, arbitrary, capricious or irrational. The adoption of such a loose, flexible, uncontrolled standard for holding laws unconstitutional, if ever it is finally achieved, will amount to a great unconstitutional shift of power to the courts which I believe and am constrained to say will be bad for the courts and worse for the country. Subjecting federal and state laws to such an unrestrained and unrestrainable judicial control as to the wisdom of legislative enactments would, I fear, jeopardize the separation of governmental powers that the Framers set up and at the same time threaten to take away much of the power of States to govern themselves which the Constitution plainly intended them to have.

I realize that many good and able men have eloquently spoken and written, sometimes in rhapsodical strains, about the duty of this Court to keep the Constitution in tune with the times. The idea is that the Constitution must be changed from time to time and that this Court is charged with a duty to make those changes. For myself, I must with all deference reject that philosophy. The Constitution makers knew the need for change and provided for it. Amendments suggested by the people's elected representatives can be submitted to the people or their selected agents for ratification. That method of change was good for our Fathers, and being somewhat old-fashioned I must add it is good enough for me. And so, I cannot rely on the Due Process Clause or the Ninth Amendment or any mysterious and uncertain natural law concept as a reason for striking down this state law. The Due Process Clause with an "arbitrary and capricious" or "shocking to the conscience" formula was liberally used by this Court to strike down economic legislation in the early decades of this century, threatening, many people thought, the tranquility and stability of the Nation.

[Mr. Justice Stewart also wrote a dissenting opinion.]

The right to an abortion is guaranteed by the Constitution's "right of privacy."

33. *Roe v. Wade* (1973)

Roe v. Wade marked a bold extension of the *Griswold* doctrine. In one of the most far-reaching decisions in its history, the Court, on grounds of right of privacy, held to be unconstitutional laws restricting abortion and in effect overturned the abortion statutes of nearly all the states as well as the District of Columbia. Few decisions have created as much furor as this one. The controversy saw continuing, and unsuccessful, attempts in Congress to have the decision "overruled" by the adoption of a constitutional amendment, and continues unabated.

Background: Texas law made abortion a crime, except when necessary to save the life of the potential mother. "Jane Roe," a pseudonym for a single woman who wished to terminate her pregnancy through an abortion performed by a physician, sought a declaratory judgment that the Texas criminal abortion statutes were unconstitutional. The Supreme Court agreed with the district court that the Texas abortion statutes violated her right of privacy.

MR. JUSTICE BLACKMUN DELIVERED
THE OPINION OF THE COURT:

The principal thrust of appellant's attack on the Texas statutes is that they improperly invade a right, said to be possessed by the pregnant woman, to choose to terminate her pregnancy. Appellant would discover this right in the concept of personal "liberty" embodied in the Fourteenth Amendment's Due Process Clause; or in personal, marital, familial, and sexual privacy said to be protected by the Bill of Rights or its penumbras or among those rights reserved to the people by the Ninth Amendment. . . . Before addressing this claim, we feel it desirable briefly to survey, in several aspects, the history of abortion, for such insight as that history may afford us, and then to examine the state purposes and interests behind the criminal abortion laws.

It perhaps is not generally appreciated that the restrictive criminal abortion laws in effect in a majority of States today are of relatively recent vintage. Those laws, generally proscribing abortion or its attempt at any time during pregnancy except when necessary to preserve the pregnant woman's life, are not of ancient or even of common-law origin. Instead, they derive from statutory changes effected, for the most part, in the latter half of the 19th century. . . .

Three reasons have been advanced to explain historically the enactment of criminal abortion laws in the 19th century and to justify their continued existence.

It has been argued occasionally that these laws were the product of a Victorian social concern to discourage illicit sexual conduct. Texas, however, does not advance this justification in the present case, and it appears that no court or commentator has taken the argument seriously. . . .

A second reason is concerned with abortion as a medical procedure. When most criminal abortion laws were first enacted, the procedure was a hazardous one for the woman. This was particularly true prior to the development of antisepsis. Antiseptic techniques, of course, were based on discoveries by Lister, Pasteur, and others first announced in 1867, but were not generally accepted and employed until about the turn of the century. Abortion mortality was high. . . .

Modern medical techniques have altered this situation. Appellants and various amici refer to medical data indicating that abortion in early pregnancy, this is, prior to the end of the first trimester, although not without its risk, is now relatively safe. Mortality rates for women undergoing early abortions, where the procedure is legal, appear to be as low as or lower than the rates for normal childbirth. Consequently, any interest of the State in protecting the woman from an inherently hazardous procedure, except when it would be equally dangerous for her to forgo it, has largely disappeared. Of course, important state interests in the area of health and medical standards do remain.

The State has a legitimate interest in seeing to it that abortion, like any other medical procedure, is performed under circumstances that insure maximum safety for the patient. This interest obviously extends at least to the performing physician and his staff, to the facilities involved, to the availability of aftercare, and to adequate provision for any complication or emergency that might arise. The prevalence of high mortality rates at illegal "abortion mills" strengthens, rather than weakens, the State's interest in regulating the conditions under which abortions are performed. Moreover, the risk to the woman increases as her pregnancy continues. Thus, the State retains a definite interest in protecting the woman's own health and safety when an abortion is proposed at a late stage of pregnancy.

The third reason is the State's interest—some phrase it in terms of duty—in protecting prenatal life. Some of the argument for this justification rests on the theory that a new human life is present from the moment of conception. The State's interest and general obligation to protect life then extends, it is argued, to prenatal life. Only when the life of the pregnant mother herself is at stake, balanced against the life she carries within her, should the interest of the embryo or fetus not prevail. Logically, of course, a legitimate state interest in this area need not stand or fall on acceptance of the belief that life begins at conception or at some other point prior to live birth. In assessing the State's interest, recognition may be given to the less rigid claim that as long as at least *potential* life is involved, the State may assert interests beyond the protection of the pregnant woman alone.

Parties challenging state abortion laws have sharply disputed in some courts the contention that a purpose of these laws, when enacted, was to protect prenatal life.

It is with these interests, and the weight to be attached to them, that this case is concerned.

The Constitution does not explicitly mention any right of privacy. In a line of decisions, however, . . . the Court has recognized that a right of personal privacy, or a guarantee of certain areas or zones of privacy, does exist under the Constitution. In varying contexts, the Court or individual Justices have, indeed, found at least the roots of that right in the First Amendment, in the Fourth and Fifth Amendments, in the penumbras of the Bill of Rights, in the Ninth Amendment, or in the concept of liberty guaranteed by the first section of the Fourteenth Amendment. . . . These decisions make it clear that only personal rights that can be deemed "fundamental" or "implicit in the concept of ordered liberty" are included in this guarantee of personal privacy. They also make it clear that the right has some extension to activities relating to marriage, procreation, contraception, family relationships, and child rearing and education.

This right of privacy, whether it be founded in the Fourteenth Amendment's concept of personal liberty and restrictions upon state action, as we feel it is, or, as the District Court determined, in the Ninth Amendment's reservation of rights to the people, is broad enough to encompass a woman's decision whether or not to terminate her pregnancy. The detriment that the State would impose upon the pregnant woman by denying this choice altogether is apparent. Specific and direct harm medically diagnosable even in early pregnancy may be involved. Maternity, or additional offspring, may force upon the woman a distressful life and future. Psychological harm may be imminent. Mental and physical health may be taxed by child care. There is also the distress, for all concerned, associated with the unwanted child, and there is the problem of bringing a child into a family already unable, psychologically and otherwise, to care for it. In other cases, as in this one, the additional difficulties and continuing stigma of unwed motherhood may be involved. All these are factors the woman and her responsible physician necessarily will consider in consultation.

On the basis of elements such as these, appellant and some amici argue that the woman's right is absolute and that she is entitled to terminate her pregnancy at whatever time, in whatever way, and for whatever reason she alone chooses. With this we do not agree. Appellant's arguments that Texas either has no valid interest at all in regulating the abortion decision, or no interest strong enough to support any limitation upon the woman's sole determination, is unpersuasive. The Court's decisions recognizing a right of privacy also acknowledge that some state regulation in areas protected by that right is appropriate. As noted above, a State may properly assert important interests in safeguarding health, in maintaining medical standards, and in protecting potential life. At some point in pregnancy, these respective interests become sufficiently compelling to sustain regulation of the factors that govern the abortion decision. The privacy right involved, therefore, cannot be said to be absolute. In fact, it is not clear to us that the claim asserted by some amici that one has an unlimited right to do with one's body as one pleases bears a close relationship to the right of privacy previously articulated in the Court's decisions. . . .

The appellee and certain amici argue that the fetus is a "person" within the language and meaning of the Fourteenth Amendment. In support of this, they outline at length and in detail the well-known facts of fetal development. If this suggestion of personhood is established, the appellant's case, of course, collapses, for the fetus' right to life is then guaranteed specifically by the Amendment. . . .

The Constitution does not define "person" in so many words. Section 1 of the Fourteenth Amendment contains three references to "person." The first, in defining "citizens," speaks of "persons born or naturalized in the United States." The word also appears both in the Due Process Clause and in the Equal Protection Clause. "Person" is used in other places in the Constitution. [The Court lists several other references to persons in the Constitution] . . . But in nearly all these instances, the use of the word is such that it has application only postnatally. None indicates, with any assurance, that it has any possible prenatal application. . . .

The pregnant woman cannot be isolated in her privacy. She carries an embryo and, later, a fetus, if one accepts the medical definitions of the developing young in the human uterus. . . . As we have intimated above, it is reasonable and appropriate for a State to decide that at some point in time another interest, that of health of the mother or that of potential human life, becomes significantly involved. The woman's privacy is no longer sole and any right of privacy she possesses must be measured accordingly.

Texas urges that, apart from the Fourteenth Amendment, life begins at conception and is present throughout pregnancy, and that, therefore, the State has a compelling interest in protecting that life from and after conception. We need not resolve the difficult question of when life begins. When those trained in the respective disciplines of medicine, philosophy, and theology are unable to arrive at any consensus, the judiciary, at this point in the development of man's knowledge, is not in a position to speculate as to the answer. . . .

[W]e do not agree that, by adopting one theory of life, Texas may override the rights of the pregnant woman that are at stake. We repeat, however, that the State does have an important and legitimate interest in preserving and protecting the health of the pregnant woman, whether she be a resident of the State or a nonresident who seeks medical consultation and treatment there; and that it has still *another* important and legitimate interest in protecting the potentiality of human life. These interests are separate and distinct. Each grows in substantiality as the woman approaches term and, at a point during pregnancy, each becomes ''compelling.''

With respect to the State's important and legitimate interest in the health of the mother, the ''compelling'' point, in the light of present medical knowledge, is at approximately the end of the first trimester. This is so because of the now-established medical fact that until the end of the first trimester mortality in abortion may be less than mortality in normal childbirth. It follows that, from and after this point, a State may regulate the abortion procedure to the extent that the regulation reasonably relates to the preservation and protection of maternal health. Examples of permissible state regulation in this area are requirements as to the qualifications of the person who is to perform the abortion; as to the licensure of that person; as to the facility in which the procedure is to be performed, that is, whether it must be a hospital or may be a clinic or some other place of less-than-hospital status; as to the licensing of the facility; and the like.

This means, on the other hand, that, for the period of pregnancy prior to this ''compelling'' point, the attending physician, in consultation with his patient, is free to determine, without regulation by the State, that, in his medical judgment, the patient's pregnancy should be terminated. If that decision is reached, the judgment may be effectuated by an abortion free of interference by the State.

With respect to the State's important and legitimate interest in potential life, the "compelling" point is at viability. This is so because the fetus then presumably has the capability of meaningful life outside the mother's womb. State regulation protective of fetal life after viability thus has both logical and biological justifications. If the State is interested in protecting fetal life after viability, it may go so far as to proscribe abortion during that period, except when it is necessary to preserve the life or health of the mother.

Measured against these standards, . . . the Texas Penal Code in restricting legal abortions to those "procured or attempted by medical advice for the purpose of saving the life of the mother," sweeps too broadly. The statute makes no distinction between abortions performed early in pregnancy and those performed later, and it limits to a single reason, "saving" the mother's life, the legal justification for the procedure. The statute, therefore, cannot survive the constitutional attack made upon it here.

[Chief Justice Burger and Mr. Justice Douglas wrote concurring opinions.]

MR. JUSTICE WHITE, WITH WHOM MR. JUSTICE REHNQUIST JOINS, DISSENTING:

With all due respect, I dissent. I find nothing in the language or history of the Constitution to support the Court's judgment. The Court simply fashions and announces a new constitutional right for pregnant mothers and, with scarcely any reason or authority for its action, invests that right with sufficient substance to override most existing state abortion statutes. The upshot is that the people and the legislatures of the 50 States are constitutionally disentitled to weigh the relative importance of the continued existence and development of the fetus, on the one hand, against a spectrum of possible impacts on the mother, on the other hand. As an exercise of raw judicial power, the Court perhaps has authority to do what it does today; but in my view its judgment is an improvident and extravagant exercise of the power of judicial review that the Constitution extends to this Court.

MR. JUSTICE REHNQUIST, DISSENTING:

I have difficulty in concluding, as the Court does, that the right of "privacy" is involved in this case. Texas, by the statute here challenged, bars the performance of a medical abortion by a licensed physician on a plaintiff such as Roe. A transaction resulting in an operation such as this is not "private" in the ordinary usage of that word. Nor is the "privacy" that the Court finds here even a distant relative of the freedom from searches and seizures protected by the Fourth Amendment to the Constitution, which the Court has referred to as embodying a right to privacy. . . .

I agree . . . that the "liberty," against deprivation of which without due process the Fourteenth Amendment protects, embraces more than the rights found in the Bill of Rights. But that liberty is not guaranteed absolutely against deprivation, only against deprivation without due process of law. The test traditionally applied in the area of social and economic legislation is whether or not a law such as that challenged has a rational relation to a valid state objective. . . . But the Court's sweeping invalidation of any restrictions on abortion during the first trimester is impossible to justify under that standard, and the conscious weighing of competing factors that the Court's opinion apparently substitutes for the established test is far more appropriate to a legislative judgment than to a judicial one. . . .

While the Court's opinion quotes from the dissent of Mr. Justice Holmes in *Lochner v. New York* (1905), the result it reaches is more closely attuned to the majority opinion of Mr. Justice Peckham in that case. As in *Lochner* and similar cases applying substantive due process standards to economic and social welfare legislation, the adoption of the compelling state interest standard will inevitably require this Court to examine the legislative policies and pass on the wisdom of these policies in the very process of deciding whether a particular state interest put forward may or may not be "compelling." The decision here to break pregnancy into three distinct terms and to outline the permissible restrictions the State may impose in each one, for example, partakes more of judicial legislation than it does of a determination of the intent of the drafters of the Fourteenth Amendment.

The fact that a majority of the States reflecting, after all, the majority sentiment in those States, have had restrictions on abortions for at least a century is a strong indication, it seems to me, that the asserted right to an abortion is not "so rooted in the traditions and conscience of our people as to be ranked as fundamental." . . . Even today, when society's views on abortion are changing, the very existence of the debate is evidence that the "right" to an abortion is not so universally accepted as the appellants would have us believe.

To reach its result the Court necessarily has had to find within the scope of the Fourteenth Amendment a right that was apparently completely unknown to the drafters of the Amendment. As early as 1821, the first state law dealing directly with abortion was enacted by the Connecticut Legislature. By the time of the adoption of the Fourteenth Amendment in 1868, there were at least 36 laws enacted by state or territorial legislatures limiting abortion. While many States have amended or updated their laws, 21 of the laws on the books in 1868 remain in effect today. Indeed, the Texas statute struck down today was, as the majority notes, first enacted in 1857. . . . The only conclusion possible from this history is that the drafters did not intend to have the Fourteenth Amendment withdraw from the States the power to legislate with respect to this matter.

The Constitution does not require government to finance abortions for indigent women.

34. *Harris v. McRae* (1980)

Congress has, through the so-called Hyde Amendment, consistently barred the use of federal funds to finance abortions, except for victims of rape or incest, or where the life of the woman is endangered by her pregnancy. The Hyde Amendment was challenged as an impingement on the constitutional right to privacy recognized in *Roe v. Wade*, but was validated in the Supreme Court.

Background: Cora McRae, a Medicaid recipient in New York, sought an abortion on grounds of medical necessity, and won her case on the constitutional issue in the district court. Patricia Harris, the secretary of health and human services, carried an appeal to the Supreme Court.

MR. JUSTICE STEWART DELIVERED
THE OPINION OF THE COURT:

Since September 1976, Congress has prohibited—either by an amendment to the annual appropriations bill for the Department of Health, Education, and Welfare or by a joint resolution—the use of any federal funds to reimburse the cost of abortions under the Medicaid program except under certain specified circumstances. This funding restriction is commonly known as the "Hyde Amendment," after its original congressional sponsor, Representative Hyde. . . .

It is well settled that . . . if a law "impinges upon a fundamental right explicitly or implicitly secured by the Constitution [it] is presumptively unconstitutional." . . .

We address . . . the appellees' argument that the Hyde Amendment, by restricting the availability of certain medically necessary abortions under Medicaid, impinges on the "liberty" protected by the Due Process Clause as recognized in *Roe v. Wade* [1973] and its progeny. . . .

But, . . . it simply does not follow that a woman's freedom of choice carries with it a constitutional entitlement to the financial resources to avail herself of the full range of protected choices. . . . [A]lthough government may not place obstacles in the path of a woman's exercise of her freedom of choice, it need not remove those not of its own creation. Indigency falls in the latter category. The financial constraints that restrict an indigent woman's ability to enjoy the full range of constitutionally protected freedom of choice are the product not of governmental restrictions on access to abortions, but rather of her indigency. Although Congress has opted to subsidize medically necessary services generally, but not certain medically necessary abortions, the fact remains that the Hyde Amendment leaves an indigent woman with at least the same range of choice in deciding whether to obtain a medically necessary abortion as she would have had if Congress had chosen to subsidize no health care costs at all. We are thus not persuaded that the Hyde Amendment impinges on the constitutionally protected freedom of choice recognized in *Wade*.

Although the liberty protected by the Due Process Clause affords protection against unwarranted government interference with freedom of choice in the context of certain personal decisions, it does not confer an entitlement to such funds as may be necessary to realize all the advantages of that freedom. To hold otherwise would mark a drastic change in our understanding of the Constitution. It cannot be that because government may not prohibit the use of contraceptives, *Griswold v. Connecticut* [1965], or prevent parents from sending their child to a private school, *Pierce v. Society of Sisters* [1925], government, therefore, has an affirmative constitutional obligation to ensure that all persons have the financial resources to obtain contraceptives or send their children to private schools. To translate the limitation on governmental power implicit in the Due Process Clause into an affirmative funding obligation would require Congress to subsidize the medically necessary abortion of an indigent woman even if Congress had not enacted a Medicaid program to subsidize other medically necessary services. Nothing in the Due Process Clause supports such an extraordinary result. Whether freedom of choice that is constitutionally protected warrants federal subsidization is a question for Congress to answer, not a matter of constitutional entitlement.

[Mr. Justice White wrote a concurring opinion.]

MR. JUSTICE BRENNAN, WITH WHOM MR. JUSTICE MARSHALL AND MR. JUSTICE BLACKMUN JOIN, DISSENTING:

[T]he Hyde Amendment is a transparent attempt by the Legislative Branch to impose the political majority's judgment of the morally acceptable and socially desirable preference on a sensitive and intimate decision that the Constitution entrusts to the individual. . . .

A poor woman in the early stages of pregnancy confronts two alternatives: she may elect either to carry the fetus to term or to have an abortion. In the abstract, of course, this choice is hers alone, and the Court rightly observes that the Hyde Amendment "places no governmental obstacle in the path of a woman who chooses to terminate her pregnancy." But the reality of the situation is that the Hyde Amendment has effectively removed this choice from the indigent woman's hands. By funding all of the expenses associated with childbirth and none of the expenses incurred in terminating pregnancy, the Government literally makes an offer that the indigent woman cannot afford to refuse. It matters not that in this instance the Government has used the carrot rather than the stick. What is critical is the realization that as a practical matter, many poverty-stricken women will choose to carry their pregnancy to term simply because the Government provides funds for the associated medical services, even though these same women would have chosen to have an abortion if the Government had also paid for that option, or indeed if the Government had stayed out of the picture altogether and had defrayed the costs of neither procedure.

[Mr. Justice Marshall, Mr. Justice Blackmun and Mr. Justice Stevens also wrote dissenting opinions.]

Restrictions on abortion that do not "unduly burden" the right are constitutional.

35. *Planned Parenthood v. Casey* (1992)

Opposition to *Roe* manifested itself with great intensity in the following two decades. Public opinion, as measured in the polls, was deeply divided. In addition to nation-wide agitation for an overriding constitutional amendment, Congress forbade federal financing of abortions for the indigent (see *McRae*, p. 248); several states passed laws regulating abortions in various ways; and the Reagan administration urged the Court to overrule *Roe* on a half dozen occasions in *amici* briefs. Above all, opposition on the Court itself was mounting. The two dissenters in *Roe* (Rehnquist and White) remained on the Court, and three later appointees (O'Connor, Kennedy, and Scalia) had expressed serious reservations about *Roe*'s continued viability. To some observers, *Roe*'s demise seemed a mere matter of time.

Planned Parenthood v. Casey confounded these predictions. The decision reaffirmed *Roe*'s "central holding" of a right to abortion, even as it decisively limited the scope of the right by substituting a more lenient standard of "undue burden" in place of *Roe*'s "compelling state interest" for testing legislation affecting abortion.

The Court's fragmentation—as evidenced in a set of opinions ranging from unflinching support of *Roe*'s undiluted holding, on the one hand, to a call for complete reversal, on the other—should not obscure the fact that the rulings on all five challenged provisions were supported by a majority of justices. Informed consent, the twenty-four-hour waiting period, and parental consent were upheld by seven Court members (O'Connor, Kennedy, Souter, Rehnquist, White, Scalia, and Thomas), the record-keeping requirement by eight members (the above plus Stevens), while five (O'Connor, Kennedy, Souter, Stevens, and Blackmun) voted to strike the spousal-consent notice. The joint opinion of Justices O'Connor, Kennedy, and Souter captured, in effect, the consensus of the Court.

Background: A Pennsylvania law, suggestively named the Abortion Control Act, contained provisions requiring informed consent, a twenty-four-hour waiting period, parental consent for minors, record-keeping, and spousal consent. (The law is summarized in the opening paragraphs of the main opinion.) Each one of the challenged provisions was struck down in the district court. The court of appeals upheld all except the spousal-consent requirement, a judgment affirmed by the Court.

JOINT OPINION BY JUSTICE O'CONNOR, JUSTICE KENNEDY AND JUSTICE SOUTER:

I

Liberty finds no refuge in a jurisprudence of doubt. Yet 19 years after our holding that the Constitution protects a woman's right to terminate her pregnancy in its early stages, *Roe v. Wade* (1973), that definition of liberty is still questioned. Joining the respondents as amicus curiae, the United States, as it has done in five other cases in the last decade, again asks us to overrule *Roe*.

At issue in these cases are five provisions of the Pennsylvania Abortion Control Act of 1982 as amended in 1988 and 1989. The Act requires that a woman seeking an abortion give her informed consent prior to the abortion procedure, and specifies that she be provided with certain information at least 24 hours before the abortion is performed. For a minor to obtain an abortion, the Act requires the informed consent of one of her parents, but provides for a judicial bypass option if the minor does not wish to or cannot obtain a parent's consent. Another provision of the Act requires that, unless certain exceptions apply, a married woman seeking an abortion must sign a statement indicating that she has notified her husband of her intended abortion. The Act exempts compliance with these three requirements in the event of a ''medical emergency,'' which is defined in the Act. In addition to the above provisions regulating the performance of abortions, the Act imposes certain reporting requirements on facilities that provide abortion services. . . .

State and federal courts as well as legislatures throughout the Union must have guidance as they seek to address this subject in conformance with the Constitution. Given these premises, we find it imperative to review once more the principles that define the rights of the woman and the legitimate authority of the State respecting the termination of pregnancies by abortion procedures.

After considering the fundamental constitutional questions resolved by *Roe*, principles of institutional integrity, and the rule of stare decisis, we are led to conclude this: the essential holding of *Roe v. Wade* should be retained and once again reaffirmed. . . .

II

It is a promise of the Constitution that there is a realm of personal liberty which the government may not enter. We have vindicated this principle before. Marriage is mentioned nowhere in the Bill of Rights and interracial marriage was illegal in most States in the 19th century, but the Court was no doubt correct in finding it to be an aspect of liberty protected against state interference by the substantive component of the Due Process Clause in *Loving v. Virginia* (1967). . . .

Neither the Bill of Rights nor the specific practices of States at the time of the adoption of the Fourteenth Amendment marks the outer limits of the substantive sphere of liberty which the Fourteenth Amendment protects. See US Const, Amend 9. . . .

In *Griswold*, we held that the Constitution does not permit a State to forbid a married couple to use contraceptives. That same freedom was later guaranteed, under the Equal Protection Clause, for unmarried couples. See *Eisenstadt v. Baird* (1972). . . . It is settled now, that the Constitution places limits on a State's right to interfere with a person's most basic decisions about family and parenthood, as well as bodily integrity. . . .

Men and women of good conscience can disagree, and we suppose some always shall disagree, about the profound moral and spiritual implications of terminating a pregnancy, even in its earliest stage. Some of us as individuals find abortion offensive to our most basic principles of morality, but that cannot control our decision. Our obligation is to define the liberty of all, not to mandate our own moral code. . . .

Our law affords constitutional protection to personal decisions relating to marriage, procreation, contraception, family relationships, child rearing, and education. . . . These matters, involving the most intimate and personal choices a person may make in a lifetime, choices central to personal dignity and autonomy, are central to the liberty protected by the Fourteenth Amendment. At the heart of liberty is the right to define one's own concept of existence, of meaning, of the universe, and of the mystery of human life. . . .

The mother who carries a child to full term is subject to anxieties, to physical constraints, to pain that only she must bear. That these sacrifices have from the beginning of the human race been endured by woman with a pride that ennobles her in the eyes of others and gives to the infant a bond of love cannot alone be grounds for the State to insist she make the sacrifice. Her suffering is too intimate and personal for the State to insist, without more, upon its own vision of the woman's role, however dominant that vision has been in the course of our history and our culture. The destiny of the woman must be shaped to a large extent on her own conception of her spiritual imperatives and her place in society. . . .

While we appreciate the weight of the arguments made on behalf of the State in the case before us, arguments which in their ultimate formulation conclude that *Roe* should be overruled, the reservations any of us may have in reaffirming the central holding of *Roe* are outweighed by the explication of individual liberty we have given combined with the force of stare decisis. We turn now to that doctrine.

III
A

[The first portion of the Court's discussion of precedent is excerpted on p. 63, above.]

[I]n this case we may inquire whether *Roe*'s central rule has been found unworkable; whether the rule's limitation on state power could be removed without serious inequity to those who have relied upon it or significant damage to the stability of the society governed by the rule in question; whether the law's growth in the intervening years has left *Roe*'s central rule a doctrinal anachronism discounted by society; and whether *Roe*'s premises of fact have so far changed in the ensuing two decades as to render its central holding somehow irrelevant or unjustifiable in dealing with the issue it addressed.

1

Although *Roe* has engendered opposition, it has in no sense proven "unworkable," representing as it does a simple limitation beyond which a state law is unenforceable. . . .

2

The inquiry into reliance counts the cost of a rule's repudiation as it would fall on those who have relied reasonably on the rule's continued application. . . .

[F]or two decades of economic and social developments, people have organized intimate relationships and made choices that define their views of themselves and their places in society, in reliance on the availability of abortion in the event that contraception should fail. The ability of women to participate equally in the economic and social life of the Nation has been facilitated by their ability to control their reproductive lives. The Constitution serves human values, and while the effect of reliance on Roe cannot be exactly measured, neither can the certain cost of overruling *Roe* for people who have ordered their thinking and living around that case be dismissed.

3

No evolution of legal principle has left *Roe*'s doctrinal footings weaker than they were in 1973. No development of constitutional law since the case was decided has implicitly or explicitly left Roe behind as a mere survivor of obsolete constitutional thinking. . . .

Roe may be seen not only as an exemplar of *Griswold* liberty but as a rule (whether or not mistaken) of personal autonomy and bodily integrity, with doctrinal affinity to cases recognizing limits on governmental power to mandate medical treatment or to bar its rejection. . . .

Finally, one could classify *Roe* as sui generis. If the case is so viewed, then there clearly has been no erosion of its central determination. The original holding resting on the concurrence of seven Members of the Court in 1973 was expressly affirmed by a majority of six in 1983, expressing adherence to the constitutional ruling despite legislative efforts in some States to test its limits. More recently, in *Webster v. Reproductive Health Services* (1989), although two of the present authors questioned the trimester framework in a way consistent with our judgment today, a majority of the Court either decided to reaffirm or declined to address the constitutional validity of the central holding of *Roe*.

Nor will courts building upon *Roe* be likely to hand down erroneous decisions as a consequence. Even on the assumption that the central holding of *Roe* was in error, that error would go only to the strength of the state interest in fetal protection, not to the recognition afforded by the Constitution to the woman's liberty. . . .

4

[T]ime has overtaken some of *Roe*'s factual assumptions: advances in maternal health care allow for abortions safe to the mother later in pregnancy than was true in 1973, and advances in neonatal care have advanced viability to a point somewhat earlier.

But these facts go only to the scheme of time limits on the realization of competing interests, and the divergences from the factual premises of 1973 have no bearing on the validity of *Roe*'s central holding, that viability marks the earliest point at which the State's interest in fetal life is constitutionally adequate to justify a legislative ban on nontherapeutic abortions. The soundness or unsoundness of that constitutional judgment in no sense turns on whether viability occurs at approximately 28 weeks, as was usual at the time of *Roe*, at 23 to 24 weeks, as it sometimes does today. . . . Whenever it may occur, the attainment of viability may continue to serve as the critical fact, just as it has done since *Roe* was decided; which is to say that no change in *Roe*'s factual underpinning has left its central holding obsolete, and none supports an argument for overruling it.

5

The sum of the precedential inquiry to this point shows *Roe*'s underpinnings unweakened in any way affecting its central holding. . . . Within the bounds of normal stare decisis analysis, then, and subject to the considerations on which it customarily turns, the stronger argument is for affirming *Roe*'s central holding, with whatever degree of personal reluctance any of us may have, not for overruling it. . . .

C

[O]verruling *Roe*'s central holding would not only reach an unjustifiable result under principles of stare decisis, but would seriously weaken the Court's capacity to exercise the judicial power and to function as the Supreme Court of a Nation dedicated to the rule of law. . . .

As Americans of each succeeding generation are rightly told, the Court cannot buy support for its decisions by spending money and, except to a minor degree, it cannot independently coerce obedience to its decrees. The Court's power lies, rather, in its legitimacy, a product of substance and perception that shows itself in the people's acceptance of the Judiciary as fit to determine what the Nation's law means and to declare what it demands. . . .

The Court must take care to speak and act in ways that allow people to accept its decisions on the terms the Court claims for them, as grounded truly in principle, not as compromises with social and political pressures having, as such, no bearing on the principled choices that the Court is obliged to make. . . .

People understand that some of the Constitution's language is hard to fathom and that the Court's Justices are sometimes able to perceive significant facts or to understand principles of law that eluded their predecessors and that justify departures from existing decisions. However upsetting it may be to those most directly affected when one judicially derived rule replaces another, the country can accept some correction of error without necessarily questioning the legitimacy of the Court.

In two circumstances, however, the Court would almost certainly fail to receive the benefit of the doubt in overruling prior cases. There is, first, a point beyond which frequent overruling would overtax the country's belief in the Court's good faith. Despite the variety of reasons that may inform and justify a decision to overrule, we cannot forget that such a decision is usually perceived (and perceived correctly) as, at the least, a statement that a prior decision was wrong. There is a limit to the amount of error that can plausibly be imputed to prior courts. If that limit should be exceeded, disturbance of prior rulings would be taken as evidence that justifiable reexamination of principle had given way to drives for particular results in the short term. The legitimacy of the Court would fade with the frequency of its vacillation.

That first circumstance can be described as hypothetical; the second is to the point here and now. Where, in the performance of its judicial duties, the Court decides a case in such a way as to resolve the sort of intensely divisive controversy reflected in *Roe* and those rare, comparable cases, its decision has a dimension that the resolution of the normal case does not carry. It is the dimension present whenever the Court's interpretation of the Constitution calls the contending sides of a national controversy to end their national division by accepting a common mandate rooted in the Constitution.

The Court is not asked to do this very often, having thus addressed the Nation only twice in our lifetime, in the decisions of *Brown* [*v. Board of Education* (1954)] and *Roe*. But when the Court does act in this way, its decision requires an equally rare precedential force to counter the inevitable efforts to overturn it and to thwart its implementation. . . .

Like the character of an individual, the legitimacy of the Court must be earned over time. So, indeed, must be the character of a Nation of people who aspire to live according to the rule of law. Their belief in themselves as such a people is not readily separable from their understanding of the Court invested with the authority to decide their constitutional cases and speak before all others for their constitutional ideals. If the Court's legitimacy should be undermined, then, so would the country be in its very ability to see itself through its constitutional ideals. The Court's concern with legitimacy is not for the sake of the Court but for the sake of the Nation to which it is responsible.

The Court's duty in the present case is clear. In 1973, it confronted the already-divisive issue of governmental power to limit personal choice to undergo abortion, for which it provided a new resolution based on the due process guaranteed by the Fourteenth Amendment. Whether or not a new social consensus is developing on that issue, its divisiveness is no less today than in 1973, and pressure to overrule the decision, like pressure to retain it, has grown only more intense. A decision to overrule *Roe*'s essential holding under the existing circumstances would address error, if error there was, at the cost of both profound and unnecessary damage to the Court's legitimacy, and to the Nation's commitment to the rule of law. It is therefore imperative to adhere to the essence of *Roe*'s original decision, and we do so today. . . .

IV

Liberty must not be extinguished for want of a line that is clear. And it falls to us to give some real substance to the woman's liberty to determine whether to carry her pregnancy to full term.

We conclude the line should be drawn at viability, so that before that time the woman has a right to choose to terminate her pregnancy. We adhere to this principle for two reasons. First, as we have said, is the doctrine of stare decisis. Any judicial act of line-drawing may seem somewhat arbitrary, but *Roe* was a reasoned statement, elaborated with great care. We have twice reaffirmed it in the face of great opposition. See *Thornburgh v. American College of Obstetricians & Gynecologists* [1986]; *Akron [Center for Reproductive Health] I* [1983]. Although we must overrule those parts of *Thornburgh* and *Akron I* which, in our view, are inconsistent with *Roe*'s statement that the State has a legitimate interest in promoting the life or potential life of the unborn the central premise of those cases represents an unbroken commitment by this Court to the essential holding of *Roe*. It is that premise which we reaffirm today.

The second reason is that the concept of viability, as we noted in *Roe*, is the time at which there is a realistic possibility of maintaining and nourishing a life outside the womb, so that the independent existence of the second life can in reason and all fairness be the object of state protection that now overrides the rights of the woman. . . . We must justify the lines we draw. And there is no line other than viability which is more workable. . . .

Yet it must be remembered that *Roe v. Wade* speaks with clarity in establishing not only the woman's liberty but also the State's ''important and legitimate interest in potential life.'' That portion of the decision in *Roe* has been given too little acknowledgement and implementation by the Court in its subsequent cases. Those cases decided that any regulation touching upon the abortion decision must survive strict scrutiny, to be sustained only if drawn in narrow terms to further a compelling state interest. . . .

The trimester framework no doubt was erected to ensure that the woman's right to choose not become so subordinate to the State's interest in promoting fetal life that her choice exists in theory but not in fact. We do not agree, however, that the trimester approach is necessary to accomplish this objective. A framework of this rigidity was unnecessary and in its later interpretation sometimes contradicted the State's permissible exercise of its powers.

Though the woman has a right to choose to terminate or continue her pregnancy before viability, it does not at all follow that the State is prohibited from taking steps to ensure that this choice is thoughtful and informed. Even in the earliest stages of pregnancy, the State may enact rules and regulations designed to encourage her to know that there are philosophic and social arguments of great weight that can be brought to bear in favor of continuing the pregnancy to full term and that there are procedures and institutions to allow adoption of unwanted children as well as a certain degree of state assistance if the mother chooses to raise the child herself. . . .

We reject the trimester framework, which we do not consider to be part of the essential holding of *Roe*. . . .

[T]he Court's experience applying the trimester framework has led to the striking down of some abortion regulations which in no real sense deprived women of the ultimate decision. . . .

The very notion that the State has a substantial interest in potential life leads to the conclusion that not all regulations must be deemed unwarranted. Not all burdens on the right to decide whether to terminate a pregnancy will be undue. In our view, the undue burden standard is the appropriate means of reconciling the State's interest with the woman's constitutionally protected liberty. . . .

A finding of an undue burden is a shorthand for the conclusion that a state regulation has the purpose or effect of placing a substantial obstacle in the path of a woman seeking an abortion of a nonviable fetus. A statute with this purpose is invalid because the means chosen by the State to further the interest in potential life must be calculated to inform the woman's free choice, not hinder it. . . .

Regulations which do no more than create a structural mechanism by which the State, or the parent or guardian of a minor, may express profound respect for the life of the unborn are permitted, if they are not a substantial obstacle to the woman's exercise of the right to choose. Unless it has that effect on her right of choice, a state measure designed to persuade her to choose childbirth over abortion will be upheld if reasonably related to that goal. Regulations designed to foster the health of a woman seeking an abortion are valid if they do not constitute an undue burden. . . .

V

We now consider the separate statutory sections at issue.

A

Because it is central to the operation of various other requirements, we begin with the statute's definition of medical emergency. . . .

[T]he Court of Appeals stated: "we read the medical emergency exception as intended by the Pennsylvania legislature to assure that compliance with its abortion regulations would not in any way pose a significant threat to the life or health of a woman." . . . We conclude that, as construed by the Court of Appeals, the medical emergency definition imposes no undue burden on a woman's abortion right.

B

We next consider the informed consent requirement. Except in a medical emergency, the statute requires that at least 24 hours before performing an abortion a physician inform the woman of the nature of the procedure, the health risks of the abortion and of childbirth, and the "probable gestational age of the unborn child." The physician or a qualified nonphysician must inform the woman of the availability of printed materials published by the State describing the fetus and providing information about medical assistance for childbirth, information about child support from the father, and a list of agencies which provide adoption and other services as alternatives to abortion. An abortion may not be performed unless the woman certifies in writing that she has been informed of the availability of these printed materials and has been provided them if she chooses to view them.

Our prior decisions establish that as with any medical procedure, the State may require a woman to give her written informed consent to an abortion. In this respect, the statute is unexceptional. Petitioners challenge the statute's definition of informed consent because it includes the provision of specific information by the doctor and the mandatory

24-hour waiting period. The conclusions reached by a majority of the Justices in the separate opinions filed today and the undue burden standard adopted in this opinion require us to overrule in part some of the Court's past decisions, decisions driven by the trimester framework's prohibition of all previability regulations designed to further the State's interest in fetal life. . . .

To the extent *Akron I* and *Thornburgh* find a constitutional violation when the government requires, as it does here, the giving of truthful, nonmisleading information about the nature of the procedure, the attendant health risks and those of childbirth, and the "probable gestational age" of the fetus, those cases go too far, are inconsistent with *Roe*'s acknowledgment of an important interest in potential life, and are overruled. . . .

This requirement cannot be considered a substantial obstacle to obtaining an abortion, and, it follows, there is no undue burden. . . .

Our analysis of Pennsylvania's 24-hour waiting period between the provision of the information deemed necessary to informed consent and the performance of an abortion under the undue burden standard requires us to reconsider the premise behind the decision in *Akron I* invalidating a parallel requirement. We consider that conclusion to be wrong. The idea that important decisions will be more informed and deliberate if they follow some period of reflection does not strike us as unreasonable. . . .

C

Section 3209 of Pennsylvania's abortion law provides, except in cases of medical emergency, that no physician shall perform an abortion on a married woman without receiving a signed statement from the woman that she has notified her spouse that she is about to undergo an abortion. . . .

In well-functioning marriages, spouses discuss important intimate decisions such as whether to bear a child. But there are millions of women in this country who are the victims of regular physical and psychological abuse at the hands of their husbands. Should these women become pregnant, they may have very good reasons for not wishing to inform their husbands of their decision to obtain an abortion. . . .

The spousal notification requirement is thus likely to prevent a significant number of women from obtaining an abortion. It does not merely make abortions a little more difficult or expensive to obtain; for many women, it will impose a substantial obstacle. We must not blind ourselves to the fact that the significant number of women who fear for their safety and the safety of their children are likely to be deterred from procuring an abortion as surely as if the Commonwealth had outlawed abortion in all cases. . . .

This conclusion is in no way inconsistent with our decisions upholding parental notification or consent requirements. Those enactments, and our judgment that they are constitutional, are based on the quite reasonable assumption that minors will benefit from consultation with their parents and that children will often not realize that their parents have their best interests at heart. We cannot adopt a parallel assumption about adult women. . . .

D

We next consider the parental consent provision. Except in a medical emergency, an unemancipated young woman under 18 may not obtain an abortion unless she and one of her parents (or guardian) provides informed consent as defined above. If neither a parent nor a guardian provides consent, a court may authorize the performance of an abortion upon a determination that the young woman is mature and capable of giving informed consent and has in fact given her informed consent, or that an abortion would be in her best interests.

We have been over most of this ground before. Our cases establish, and we reaffirm today, that a State may require a minor seeking an abortion to obtain the consent of a parent or guardian, provided that there is an adequate judicial bypass procedure. . . .

E

Under the recordkeeping and reporting requirements of the statute, every facility which performs abortions is required to file a report. . . . [The Court here details the information required in the report.] In all events, the identity of each woman who has had an abortion remains confidential.

The collection of information with respect to actual patients is a vital element of medical research, and so it cannot be said that the requirements serve no purpose other than to make abortions more difficult.

Nor do we find that the requirements impose a substantial obstacle to a woman's choice. At most they might increase the cost of some abortions by a slight amount. . . .

VI

Our Constitution is a covenant running from the first generation of Americans to us and then to future generations. It is a coherent succession. Each generation must learn anew that the Constitution's written terms embody ideas and aspirations that must survive more ages than one. We accept our responsibility not to retreat from interpreting the full meaning of the covenant in light of all of our precedents. We invoke it once again to define the freedom guaranteed by the Constitution's own promise, the promise of liberty.

[Justice Stevens wrote an opinion concurring in part and dissenting in part.]

JUSTICE BLACKMUN, CONCURRING IN PART, CONCURRING IN THE JUDGMENT IN PART, AND DISSENTING IN PART:

I do not underestimate the significance of today's joint opinion. Yet I remain steadfast in my belief that the right to reproductive choice is entitled to the full protection afforded by this Court before *Webster*. And I fear for the darkness as four Justices anxiously await the single vote necessary to extinguish the light.

I

Make no mistake, the joint opinion of Justices O'Connor, Kennedy, and Souter is an act of personal courage and constitutional principle. . . .

II

Today, no less than yesterday, the Constitution and decisions of this Court require that a State's abortion restrictions be subjected to the strictest judicial scrutiny. Our precedents and the joint opinion's principles require us to subject all non-de minimis abortion regulations to strict scrutiny. Under this standard, the Pennsylvania statute's provisions requiring content-based counseling, a 24-hour delay, informed parental consent, and reporting of abortion-related information must be invalidated. . . .

B

The Court has held that limitations on the right of privacy are permissible only if they survive "strict" constitutional scrutiny—that is, only if the governmental entity imposing the restriction can demonstrate that the limitation is both necessary and narrowly tailored to serve a compelling governmental interest. . . .

In my view, application of this analytical framework is no less warranted than when it was approved by seven Members of this Court in *Roe*. Strict scrutiny of state limitations on reproductive choice still offers the most secure protection of the woman's right to make her own reproductive decisions, free from state coercion. No majority of this Court has ever agreed upon an alternative approach. The factual premises of the trimester framework have not been undermined, and the *Roe* framework is far more administrable, and far less manipulable, than the "undue burden" standard adopted by the joint opinion. . . .

C

Measured against these principles, some aspects of the Pennsylvania informed-consent scheme are unconstitutional. While it is unobjectionable for the Commonwealth to require that the patient be informed of the nature of the procedure, the health risks of the abortion and of childbirth, and the probable gestational age of the unborn child, I remain unconvinced that there is a vital state need for insisting that the information be provided by a physician rather than a counselor. . . .

The 24-hour waiting period following the provision of the foregoing information is also clearly unconstitutional. . . .

Except in the case of a medical emergency, [the Pennsylvania law] requires a physician to obtain the informed consent of a parent or guardian before performing an abortion on an unemancipated minor or an incompetent woman. . . . While the State has an interest in encouraging parental involvement in the minor's abortion decision, [this law] is not narrowly drawn to serve that interest.

Finally, the Pennsylvania statute requires every facility performing abortions to report its activities to the Commonwealth. The Commonwealth attempts to justify its required reports on the ground that the public has a right to know how its tax dollars are spent. A regulation designed to inform the public about public expenditures does not further the Commonwealth's interest in protecting maternal health. Accordingly, such a regulation cannot justify a legally significant burden on a woman's right to obtain an abortion. . . .

III

The Chief Justice's criticism of *Roe* follows from his stunted conception of individual liberty. While recognizing that the Due Process Clause protects more than simple physical liberty, he then goes on to construe this Court's personal-liberty cases as establishing only a laundry list of particular rights, rather than a principled account of how these particular rights are grounded in a more general right of privacy. This constricted view is reinforced by The Chief Justice's exclusive reliance on tradition as a source of fundamental rights. . . .

Even more shocking than The Chief Justice's cramped notion of individual liberty is his complete omission of any discussion of the effects that compelled childbirth and motherhood have on women's lives. . . . In short, The Chief Justice's view of the State's compelling interest in maternal health has less to do with health than it does with compelling women to be maternal. . . .

But, we are reassured, there is always the protection of the democratic process. While there is much to be praised about our democracy, our country since its founding has recognized that there are certain fundamental liberties that are not to be left to the whims of an election. A woman's right to reproductive choice is one of those fundamental liberties. Accordingly, that liberty need not seek refuge at the ballot box.

IV

In one sense, the Court's approach is worlds apart from that of The Chief Justice and Justice Scalia. And yet, in another sense, the distance between the two approaches is short—the distance is but a single vote.

I am 83 years old. I cannot remain on this Court forever, and when

I do step down, the confirmation process for my successor well may focus on the issue before us today. That, I regret, may be exactly where the choice between the two worlds will be made.

CHIEF JUSTICE REHNQUIST, WITH WHOM JUSTICE WHITE, JUSTICE SCALIA, AND JUSTICE THOMAS JOIN, CONCURRING IN THE JUDGMENT IN PART AND DISSENTING IN PART:

The joint opinion, following its newly-minted variation on stare decisis, retains the outer shell of *Roe v Wade*, but beats a wholesale retreat from the substance of that case. We believe that *Roe* was wrongly decided, and that it can and should be overruled consistently with our traditional approach to stare decisis in constitutional cases. . . .

I

Unfortunately for those who must apply this Court's decisions, the reexamination undertaken today leaves the Court no less divided than beforehand. Although they reject the trimester framework that formed the underpinning of *Roe*, Justices O'Connor, Kennedy, and Souter adopt a revised undue burden standard to analyze the challenged regulations. We conclude, however, that such an outcome is an unjustified constitutional compromise, one which leaves the Court in a position to closely scrutinize all types of abortion regulations despite the fact that it lacks the power to do so under the Constitution. . . .

In *Roe v. Wade*, the Court recognized a "guarantee of personal privacy" which "is broad enough to encompass a woman's decision whether or not to terminate her pregnancy." We are now of the view that, in terming this right fundamental, the Court in *Roe* read the earlier opinions upon which it based its decision much too broadly. Unlike marriage, procreation and contraception, abortion "involves the purposeful termination of potential life." The abortion decision must therefore "be recognized as sui generis, different in kind from the others that the Court has protected under the rubric of personal or family privacy and autonomy." One cannot ignore the fact that a woman is not isolated in her pregnancy, and that the decision to abort necessarily involves the destruction of a fetus.

Nor do the historical traditions of the American people support the view that the right to terminate one's pregnancy is "fundamental." The common law which we inherited from England made abortion after "quickening" an offense. At the time of the adoption of the Fourteenth Amendment, statutory prohibitions or restrictions on abortion were commonplace; in 1868, at least 28 of the then-37 States and 8 Territories had statutes banning or limiting abortion. By the turn of the century virtually every State had a law prohibiting or restricting abortion on its books. By the middle of the present century, a liberalization trend had set in. But 21 of the restrictive abortion laws in effect in 1868 were still in effect in 1973 when *Roe* was decided, and an overwhelming majority of the States prohibited abortion unless necessary to preserve the life or health of the mother. On this record, it can scarcely be said that any deeply rooted tradition of relatively unrestricted abortion in our history supported the classification of the right to abortion as "fundamental" under the Due Process Clause of the Fourteenth Amendment. . . .

II

The joint opinion of Justices O'Connor, Kennedy, and Souter cannot bring itself to say that *Roe* was correct as an original matter. . . . Instead, . . . the opinion . . . contains an elaborate discussion of stare decisis. This discussion of the principle of stare decisis appears to be almost entirely dicta, because the joint opinion does not apply that principle in dealing with *Roe*. *Roe* decided that a woman had a fundamental right to an abortion. The joint opinion rejects that view. *Roe* decided that abortion regulations were to be subjected to "strict scrutiny" and could be justified only in the light of "compelling state interests." The joint opinion rejects that view. *Roe* analyzed abortion regulation under a rigid trimester framework, a framework which has guided this Court's decisionmaking for 19 years. The joint opinion rejects that framework.

While purporting to adhere to precedent, the joint opinion instead revises it. *Roe* continues to exist, but only in the way a storefront on a western movie set exists: a mere facade to give the illusion of reality. . . .

In our view, authentic principles of stare decisis do not require that any portion of the reasoning in *Roe* be kept intact. "Stare decisis is not . . . a universal, inexorable command," especially in cases involving the interpretation of the Federal Constitution. Erroneous decisions in such constitutional cases are uniquely durable, because correction through legislative action, save for constitutional amendment, is impossible. It is therefore our duty to reconsider constitutional interpretations that "depar[t] from a proper understanding" of the Constitution. Our constitutional watch does not cease merely because we have spoken before on an issue; when it becomes clear that a prior constitutional interpretation is unsound we are obliged to reexamine the question. . . .

The joint opinion . . . turns to what can only be described as an unconventional—and unconvincing—notion of reliance, a view based on the surmise that the availability of abortion since *Roe* has led to "two decades of economic and social developments" that would be undercut if the error of *Roe* were recognized. The joint opinion's assertion of this fact is undeveloped and totally conclusory. In fact, one can not be sure to what economic and social developments the opinion is referring. Surely it is dubious to suggest that women have reached their "places in society" in reliance upon *Roe*, rather than as a result of their determination to obtain higher education and compete with men in the job market, and of society's increasing recognition of their ability to fill positions that were previously thought to be reserved only for men. . . .

In the end, having failed to put forth any evidence to prove any true reliance, the joint opinion's argument is based solely on generalized assertions about the national psyche on a belief that the people of this country have grown accustomed to the *Roe* decision over the last 19 years and have "ordered their thinking and living around" it. . . .

Apparently realizing that conventional stare decisis principles do not support its position, the joint opinion advances a belief that retaining a portion of *Roe* is necessary to protect the "legitimacy" of this Court. Because the Court must take care to render decisions "grounded truly in principle," and not simply as political and social compromises, the joint opinion properly declares it to be this Court's duty to ignore the public criticism and protest that may arise as a result of a decision. Few would quarrel with this statement, although it may be doubted that Members of this Court, holding their tenure as they do during constitutional "good behavior," are at all likely to be intimidated by such public protests.

But the joint opinion goes on to state that when the Court "resolve[s] the sort of intensely divisive controversy reflected in *Roe* and those rare, comparable cases," its decision is exempt from reconsideration under established principles of stare decisis in constitutional cases. This is a truly novel principle, one which is contrary to both the Court's historical practice and to the Court's traditional willingness to tolerate criticism of its opinions. Under this principle, when the Court has ruled on a divisive issue, it is apparently prevented from overruling that decision for the sole reason that it was incorrect, *unless opposition to the original decision has died away.* . . .

The Judicial Branch derives its legitimacy, not from following public opinion, but from deciding by its best lights whether legislative enactments of the popular branches of Government comport with the Constitution. The doctrine of stare decisis is an adjunct of this duty, and should be no more subject to the vagaries of public opinion than is the basic judicial task. . . .

The joint opinion asserts that, in order to protect its legitimacy, the Court must refrain from overruling a controversial decision lest it be viewed as favoring those who oppose the decision. But a decision to *adhere* to prior precedent is subject to the same criticism, for in such a case one can easily argue that the Court is responding to those who have demonstrated in favor of the original decision. The decision in *Roe* has engendered large demonstrations, including repeated marches on this Court and on Congress, both in opposition to and in support of that opinion. A decision either way on *Roe* can therefore be perceived as favoring one group or the other. . . .

The end result of the joint opinion's paeans of praise for legitimacy is the enunciation of a brand new standard for evaluating state regulation of a woman's right to abortion—the "undue burden" standard. As indicated above, *Roe v. Wade* adopted a "fundamental right" standard under which state regulations could survive only if they met the requirement of "strict scrutiny." While we disagree with that standard, it at least had a recognized basis in constitutional law at the time *Roe* was decided. The same cannot be said for the "undue burden" standard, which is created largely out of whole cloth by the authors of the joint opinion. It is a standard which even today does not command the support of a majority of this Court. . . .

The sum of the joint opinion's labors in the name of stare decisis and "legitimacy" is this: *Roe v. Wade* stands as a sort of judicial Potemkin Village, which may be pointed out to passers by as a monument to the importance of adhering to precedent. But behind the facade, an entirely new method of analysis, without any roots in constitutional law, is imported to decide the constitutionality of state laws regulating abortion. Neither stare decisis nor "legitimacy" are truly served by such an effort. . . .

IV

[We] would hold that each of the challenged provisions of the Pennsylvania statute is consistent with the Constitution.

JUSTICE SCALIA, WITH WHOM THE CHIEF JUSTICE, JUSTICE WHITE, AND JUSTICE THOMAS JOIN, CONCURRING IN THE JUDGMENT IN PART AND DISSENTING IN PART:

The permissibility of abortion, and the limitations upon it, are to be resolved like most important questions in our democracy: by citizens trying to persuade one another and then voting. . . . A State's choice between two positions on which reasonable people can disagree is constitutional even when (as is often the case) it intrudes upon a "liberty" in the absolute sense. Laws against bigamy, for example— which entire societies of reasonable people disagree with—intrude upon men and women's liberty to marry and live with one another. But bigamy happens not to be a liberty specially "protected" by the Constitution.

That is, quite simply, the issue in this case: not whether the power of a woman to abort her unborn child is a "liberty" in the absolute sense; or even whether it is a liberty of great importance to many women. Of course it is both. The issue is whether it is a liberty protected by the Constitution of the United States. I am sure it is not. I reach that conclusion . . . for the same reason I reach the conclusion that bigamy is not constitutionally protected—because of two simple facts: (1) the Constitution says absolutely nothing about it, and (2) the longstanding traditions of American society have permitted it to be legally proscribed.

The emptiness of the "reasoned judgment" that produced *Roe* is displayed in plain view by the fact that, after more than 19 years of effort by some of the brightest (and most determined) legal minds in the country, after more than 10 cases upholding abortion rights in this Court, and after dozens upon dozens of amicus briefs submitted in this and other cases, the best the Court can do to explain how it is that the word "liberty" *must* be thought to include the right to destroy human fetuses is to rattle off a collection of adjectives that simply decorate a value judgment and conceal a political choice. Those adjectives might be applied, for example, to homosexual sodomy, polygamy, adult incest, and suicide, all of which are equally "intimate" and "deep[ly] personal" decisions involving "personal autonomy and bodily integrity," and all of which can constitutionally be proscribed because it is our unquestionable constitutional tradition that they are proscribable. It is not reasoned judgment that supports the Court's decision; only personal predilection. . . .

The Court's reliance upon stare decisis can best be described as contrived. It insists upon the necessity of adhering not to all of *Roe*, but only to what it calls the "central holding." It seems to me that stare decisis ought to be applied even to the doctrine of stare decisis, and I confess never to have heard of this new, keep-what-you-want-and-throw-away-the-rest version. . . .

I am certainly not in a good position to dispute that the Court *has saved* the "central holding" of *Roe*, since to do that effectively I would have to know what the Court has saved, which in turn would require me to understand (as I do not) what the "undue burden" test means. I must confess, however, that I have always thought, and I think a lot of other people have always thought, that the arbitrary trimester framework, which the Court today discards, was quite as central to *Roe* as the arbitrary viability test, which the Court today retains. . . .

The Court's description of the place of *Roe* in the social history of the United States is unrecognizable. Not only did *Roe* not, as the Court suggests, *resolve* the deeply divisive issue of abortion; it did more than anything else to nourish it, by elevating it to the national level where it is infinitely more difficult to resolve. National politics were not plagued by abortion protests, national abortion lobbying, or abortion marches on Congress, before *Roe v. Wade* was decided. Profound disagreement existed among our citizens over the issue—as it does over other issues, such as the death penalty—but that disagreement was being worked out at the state level. . . .

Roe's mandate for abortion-on-demand destroyed the compromises of the past, rendered compromise impossible for the future, and required the entire issue to be resolved uniformly, at the national level. At the same time, *Roe* created a vast new class of abortion consumers and abortion proponents by eliminating the moral opprobrium that had attached to the act. . . . [T]o portray *Roe* as the statesmanlike "settlement" of a divisive issue, a jurisprudential Peace of Westphalia that is worth preserving, is nothing less than Orwellian. *Roe* fanned into life an issue that has inflamed our national politics in general, and has obscured with its smoke the selection of Justices to this Court in particular, ever since. . . .

The Imperial Judiciary lives. It is instructive to compare this Nietzschean vision of us unelected, life-tenured judges—leading a Volk who will be "tested by following," and whose very "belief in themselves" is mystically bound up in their "understanding" of a Court that "speak[s] before all others for their constitutional ideals"—with the somewhat more modest role envisioned for these lawyers by the Founders. . . .

[T]he notion that we would decide a case differently from the way we otherwise would have in order to show that we can stand firm against public disapproval is frightening. It is a bad enough idea, even in the head of someone like me, who believes that the text of the Constitution, and our traditions, say what they say and there is no fiddling with them. . . . [T]he notion that the Court must adhere to a decision for as long as the decision faces "great opposition" and the Court is "under fire" acquires a character of almost czarist arrogance. We are offended by these marchers who descend upon us, every year on the anniversary of *Roe*, to protest our saying that the Constitution requires what our society has never thought the Constitution requires. These people who refuse to be "tested by following" must be taught a lesson. We have no Cossacks, but at least we can stubbornly refuse to abandon an erroneous opinion that we might otherwise change—to show how little they intimidate us. . . .

What makes all this relevant to the bothersome application of "political pressure" against the Court are the twin facts that the American people love democracy and the American people are not fools. As long as this Court thought (and the people thought) that we Justices were doing essentially lawyers' work up here—reading text and discerning our society's traditional understanding of that text—the public pretty much left us alone. Texts and traditions are facts to study, not convictions to demonstrate about. But if in reality our process of constitutional adjudication consists primarily of making *value judgments* . . . then a free and intelligent people's attitude towards us can be expected to be (*ought* to be) quite different. The people know that their value judgments are quite as good as those taught in any law school—maybe better. If, indeed, the "liberties" protected by the Constitution are, as the Court says, undefined and unbounded, then the people *should* demonstrate, to protest that we do not implement *their* values instead of *ours*. Not only that, but confirmation hearings for new Justices *should* deteriorate into question-and-answer sessions in which Senators go through a list of their constituents' most favored and most disfavored alleged constitutional rights, and seek the nominee's commitment to support or oppose them. Value judgments, after all, should be voted on, not dictated; and if our Constitution has somehow accidently committed them to the Supreme Court, at least we can have a sort of plebiscite each time a new nominee to that body is put forward. Justice Blackmun not only regards this prospect with equanimity, he solicits it.

* * *

There is a poignant aspect to today's opinion. Its length, and what might be called its epic tone, suggest that its authors believe they are bringing to an end a troublesome era in the history of our Nation and of our Court. . . .

There comes vividly to mind a portrait by Emanuel Leutze that hangs in the Harvard Law School: Roger Brooke Taney, painted in 1859, the 82d year of his life, the 24th of his Chief Justiceship, the second after his opinion in *Dred Scott* [*v. Sandford* (1857)]. He is all in black, sitting in a shadowed red armchair, left hand resting upon a pad of paper in his lap, right hand hanging limply, almost lifelessly, beside the inner arm of the chair. He sits facing the viewer, and staring straight out. There seems to be on his face, and in his deep-set eyes, an expression of profound sadness and disillusionment. Perhaps he always looked that way, even when dwelling upon the happiest of thoughts. But those of us who know how the lustre of his great Chief Justiceship came to be eclipsed by *Dred Scott* cannot help believing that he had that case— its already apparent consequences for the Court, and its soon-to-be-played-out consequences for the Nation—burning on his mind. I expect that two years earlier he, too, had thought himself "call[ing] the contending sides of national controversy to end their national division by accepting a common mandate rooted in the Constitution."

It is no more realistic for us in this case, than it was for him in that, to think that an issue of the sort they both involved—an issue involving life and death, freedom and subjugation—can be "speedily and finally settled'' by the Supreme Court, as President James Buchanan in his inaugural address said the issue of slavery in the territories would be. Quite to the contrary, by foreclosing all democratic outlet for the deep passions this issue arouses, by banishing the issue from the political forum that gives all participants, even the losers, the satisfaction of a fair hearing and an honest fight, by continuing the imposition of a rigid national rule instead of allowing for regional differences, the Court merely prolongs and intensifies the anguish.

We should get out of this area where we have no right to be, and where we do neither ourselves nor the country any good by remaining.

Equal Protection

"Neither slavery nor involuntary servitude, except as a punishment for crime whereof the party shall have been duly convicted, shall exist within the United States, or any place subject to their jurisdiction."—Thirteenth Amendment

"No state shall . . . deny to any person within its jurisdiction the equal protection of the laws."—Fourteenth Amendment, Sec. 1

"The right of citizens of the United States to vote shall not be denied or abridged by the United States or by any state on account of race, color, or any previous condition of servitude."—Fifteenth Amendment, Sec. 1

Congress cannot protect against discrimination unless "state action" is involved.

36. *Civil Rights Cases* (1883)

This decision is important in that it illustrates the difficulty and complexity involved in the prolonged struggle for minority rights. In the *Civil Rights Cases*, by a vote of eight to one, the Court refused to sanction congressional legislation designed to grant equality in privately owned public accommodations.

Background: Congress, determined to implement the Thirteenth and Fourteenth Amendments, passed the Civil Rights Act of 1875. The act made it a crime for one person to deprive another of the "full and equal enjoyment of the accommodations, advantages, facilities, and privileges of inns, public conveyances on land or water, theatres, and other places of public amusement,'' regardless of color or previous conditions of servitude. Thereafter, several blacks, each having been separately denied some accommodations on account of color, appealed to the Supreme Court. The Court ruled that the Fourteenth Amendment only authorized Congress to legislate against discrimination by ''state action,'' not by private individuals. Thus, the crucial sections of the Civil Rights Act did not come under the purview of the Fourteenth Amendment and were invalid. This decision ended, for all intents and purposes, federal legislative efforts to protect blacks against discrimination to the contemporary period. (See *Heart of Atlanta Motel v. United States*, p. 209.)

MR. JUSTICE BRADLEY DELIVERED
THE OPINION OF THE COURT:

Has Congress constitutional power to make such a law? Of course, no one will contend that the power to pass it was contained in the Constitution before the adoption of the last three Amendments. The power is sought, first, in the Fourteenth Amendment, and the views and arguments of distinguished Senators, advanced while the law was under consideration, claiming authority to pass it by virtue of that Amendment, are the principal arguments adduced in favor of the power. . . .

The first section of the Fourteenth Amendment (which is the one relied on), after declaring who shall be citizens of the United States, and of the several States, is prohibitory in its character, and prohibitory upon the States. It declares that:

''No state shall make or enforce any law which shall abridge the privileges or immunities of citizens of the United States; nor shall any state deprive any person of life, liberty, or property without due process of law; nor deny to any person within its jurisdiction the equal protection of the laws.''

It is state action of a particular character that is prohibited. Individual invasion of individual rights is not the subject-matter of the Amendment. It has a deeper and broader scope. It nullifies and makes void all state legislation, and state action of every kind, which impairs the privileges and immunities of citizens of the United States, or which injures them in life, liberty or property without due process of law, or which denies to any of them the equal protection of the laws. It not only does this, but . . . the last section of the Amendment invests Congress with power to enforce it by appropriate legislation. . . . It does not authorize Congress to create a code of municipal law for the regulation of private rights; but to provide modes of redress against the operation of state laws, and the action of state officers executive or judicial, when these are subversive of the fundamental rights specified in the Amendment. Positive rights and privileges are undoubtedly secured by the Fourteenth Amendment; but they are secured by way of prohibition against state laws and state proceedings affecting those rights and privileges, and by power given to Congress to legislate for the purpose of carrying such prohibition into effect: and such legislation must necessarily be predicted upon such supposed state laws or state proceedings, and be directed to the correction of their operation and effect. . . .

Until some state law has been passed, or some state action through its officers or agents has been taken, adverse to the rights of citizens sought to be protected by the Fourteenth Amendment, no legislation of the United States under said Amendment nor any proceeding under such legislation, can be called into activity: for the prohibitions of the Amendment are against state laws and acts done under state authority. Of course, legislation may, and should be, provided in advance to meet the exigency when it arises; but it should be adapted to the mischief and wrong which the Amendment was intended to provide against; and that is, state laws, or state action of some kind, adverse to the rights of the citizen secured by the Amendment. Such legislation cannot properly cover the whole domain of rights appertaining to life, liberty and property, defining them and providing for their vindication. That would be to establish a code of municipal law regulative of all private rights between man and man in society. It would be to make Congress take the place of the state legislatures and to supersede them. It is absurd to affirm that, because the rights of life, liberty and property (which include all civil rights that men have), are by the Amendment sought to be protected against invasion on the part of the State without due process of law, Congress may therefore provide due process of law for their vindication in every case; and that, because the denial by a State to any persons, of the equal protection of the laws, is prohibited by the Amendment, therefore Congress may establish laws for their equal protection. . . .

An inspection of the law shows that it makes no reference whatever to any supposed or apprehended violation of the Fourteenth Amendment on the part of the States. It is not predicated on any such view. It proceeds *ex directo* to declare that certain acts committed by individuals shall be deemed offenses, and shall be prosecuted and punished by proceedings in the courts of the United States. It does not profess to be corrective of any constitutional wrong committed by the States; it does not make its operation to depend upon any such wrong committed. . . .

If this legislation is appropriate for enforcing the prohibitions of the Amendment, it is difficult to see where it is to stop. Why may not Congress with equal show of authority enact a code of laws for the enforcement and vindication of all rights of life, liberty, and property? . . .

In this connection it is proper to state that civil rights, such as are guaranteed by the Constitution against state aggression, cannot be impaired by the wrongful acts of individuals, unsupported by state authority in the shape of laws, customs, or judicial or executive proceedings. . . . [I]n all those cases where the Constitution seeks to protect the rights of the citizen against discriminative and unjust laws of the State by prohibiting such laws, it is not individual offenses, but abrogation and denial of rights, which it denounces, and for which it clothes the Congress with power to provide a remedy. This abrogation and denial of rights, for which the States alone were or could be responsible, was the great seminal and fundamental wrong which was intended to be remedied. And the remedy to be provided must necessarily be predicated upon that wrong. It must assume that in the cases provided for, the evil or wrong actually committed rests upon some state law or state authority for its excuse and perpetration. . . .

But the power of Congress to adopt direct and primary, as distinguished from corrective legislation, on the subject in hand, is sought, in the second place, from the Thirteenth Amendment, which abolishes slavery. This Amendment declares "that neither slavery, nor involuntary servitude, except as a punishment for crime, whereof the party shall have been duly convicted, shall exist within the United States, or any place subject to their jurisdiction"; and it gives Congress power to enforce the Amendment by appropriate legislation. . . .

When a man has emerged from slavery, and by the aid of beneficent legislation has shaken off the inseparable concomitants of that state, there must be some stage in the progress of his elevation when he takes the rank of a mere citizen, and ceases to be the special favorite of the laws, and when his rights as a citizen, or a man, are to be protected in the ordinary modes by which other men's rights are protected. There were thousands of free colored people in this country before the abolition of slavery, enjoying all the essential rights of life, liberty and property the same as white citizens; yet no one, at that time, thought that it was any invasion of his personal status as a freeman because he was not admitted to all the privileges enjoyed by white citizens, or because he was subjected to discriminations in the enjoyment of accommodations in inns, public conveyances and places of amusement. Mere discriminations on account of race or color were not regarded as badges of slavery. If, since that time, the enjoyment of equal rights in all these respects has become established by constitutional enactment, it is not by force of the Thirteenth Amendment (which merely abolishes slavery), but by force of the Fourteenth and Fifteenth Amendments.

MR. JUSTICE HARLAN, DISSENTING:

Congress has not, in these matters, entered the domain of state control and supervision. . . . It simply declares, in effect, that since the nation has established universal freedom in this country, for all time, there shall be no discrimination, based merely upon race or color, in respect of the accommodations and advantages of public conveyances, inns, and places of public amusement.

I am of the opinion that such discrimination practiced by corporations and individuals in the exercise of their public or quasi-public functions is a badge of servitude, the imposition of which Congress may prevent under its power, by appropriate legislation, to enforce the Thirteenth Amendment; and, consequently, without reference to its enlarged power under the Fourteenth Amendment, the Act of March 1, 1875, is not, in my judgment, repugnant to the Constitution. . . . The assumption that this Amendment [the Fourteenth] consists wholly of prohibitions upon state laws and state proceedings in hostility to its provisions is unauthorized by its language. The first clause of the first section—"All persons born or naturalized in the United States, and subject to the jurisdiction thereof, are citizens of the United States, and of the state wherein they reside"—is of a distinctly affirmative character. In its application to the colored race, previously liberated, it created and granted, as well citizenship of the United States, as citizenship of the State in which they respectively resided. It introduced all of that race, whose ancestors had been imported and sold as slaves, at once, into the political community known as the "People of the United States." . . .

The citizenship thus acquired by that race, in virtue of an affirmative grant from the Nation, may be protected, not alone by the judicial branch of the Government, but by congressional legislation of a primary direct character; this, because the power of Congress is not restricted to the enforcement of prohibitions upon state laws or state action. It is, in terms distinct and positive, to enforce "the *provisions of this article*" of amendment; not simply those of a prohibitive character, but the provisions—*all* of the provisions—affirmative and prohibitive, of the Amendment. It is, therefore, a grave misconception to suppose that the fifth section of the Amendment has reference exclusively to express prohibitions upon state laws or state action. . . .

I agree that government has nothing to do with social, as distinguished from technically legal, rights of individuals. No government ever has brought, or ever can bring, its people into social intercourse against their wishes. Whether one person will permit or maintain social relations with another is a matter with which government has no concern. I agree that if one citizen chooses not to hold social intercourse with another, he is not and cannot be made amenable to the law for his conduct in that regard; for even upon grounds of race, no legal right of a citizen is violated by the refusal of others to maintain merely social relations with him. What I affirm is that no State, nor the officers of any State, nor any corporation or individual wielding power under state authority for the public benefit or the public convenience, can, consistently either with the freedom established by the fundamental law, or with that equality of civil rights which now belongs to every citizen, discriminate against freemen or citizens, in those rights, because of their race, or because they once labored under the disabilities of slavery imposed upon them as a race. The rights which Congress, by the Act of 1875, endeavored to secure and protect are legal, not social rights. The right, for instance, of a colored citizen to use the accommodations of a public highway, upon the same terms as are permitted to white citizens, is no more a social right than his right, under the law, to use the public streets of a city or a town, or a turnpike road, or a public market, or a post office, or his right to sit in a public building with others, of whatever race, for the purpose of hearing the political questions of the day discussed.

The Court sanctions "separate but equal" accommodations for the races.

37. *Plessy v. Ferguson* (1896)

The history-making decision in *Dred Scott v. Sandford* (1857) was one of the most denounced of the United States Supreme Court. In that decision, written by Chief Justice Taney, the Court, by a vote of seven to two, denied that a Negro was a citizen of the United States even though he happened to live in a "free" state. The Court also declared the Missouri Compromise (1820), forbidding slavery in certain federal territories, unconstitutional. The decision helped to crystallize public opinion on the slavery issue, which ultimately led to the Civil War.

The Fourteenth Amendment, adopted in 1868, in effect "overruled" the *Dred Scott* case by declaring, in its first section, that "All persons born or naturalized in the United States . . . are citizens of the United States and of the states wherein they reside." More significantly, the amendment's Equal Protection Clause was intended to guarantee equality of treatment for blacks and whites. But hopes for a resolution of the race problem were shattered for decades on the reefs of the "separate but equal" doctrine announced in *Plessy v. Ferguson*. (This decision was subsequently overruled in *Brown v. Board of Education*, p. 287.)

Background: A Louisiana law of 1890, one of the first "Jim Crow" laws enacted in the South, required railroads within the state to provide and enforce "equal but separate accommodations for the white and colored races." Plessy, a black man (he was actually "seven-eighths Caucasian and one-eighth African blood," according to his own description), was arrested when he refused to leave a coach reserved for whites. After the Louisiana Supreme Court upheld the law, Plessy appealed on equal-protection grounds to the United States Supreme Court, where he again lost. Only Justice Harlan, the "great dissenter" of his era, disagreed, in his most memorable dissenting opinion.

MR. JUSTICE BROWN DELIVERED
THE OPINION OF THE COURT:

This case turns upon the constitutionality of an act of the general assembly of the state of Louisiana, passed in 1890, providing for separate railway carriages for the white and colored races. . . .

By the 14th Amendment, all persons born or naturalized in the United States, and subject to the jurisdiction thereof, are made citizens of the United States and of the state wherein they reside; and the states are forbidden from making or enforcing any law which shall . . . deny to any person within their jurisdiction the equal protection of the laws. . . .

The object of the amendment was undoubtedly to enforce the absolute equality of the two races before the law, but in the nature of things it could not have been intended to abolish distinctions based upon color, or to enforce social, as distinguished from political, equality, or a commingling of the two races upon terms unsatisfactory to either. Laws permitting, and even requiring their separation in places where they are liable to be brought into contact do not necessarily imply the inferiority of either race to the other, and have been generally, if not universally, recognized as within the competency of the state legislatures in the exercise of their police power. The most common instance of this is connected with the establishment of separate schools for white and colored children, which have been held to be a valid exercise of the legislative power even by courts of states where the political rights of the colored race have been longest and most earnestly enforced.

One of the earliest of these cases is that of *Roberts v. Boston* [1849], in which the supreme judicial court of Massachusetts held that the general school committee of Boston had power to make provision for the instruction of colored children in separate schools established exclusively for them, and to prohibit their attendance upon the other schools. . . .

It was held that the powers of the committee extended to the establishment of separate schools for children of different ages, sexes, and colors, and that they might also establish special schools for poor and neglected children, who have become too old to attend the primary school, and yet have not acquired the rudiments of learning, to enable them to enter the ordinary schools. Similar laws have been enacted by

Congress under its general power of legislation over the District of Columbia as well as by the legislatures of many of the states, and have been generally, if not uniformly, sustained by the courts. . . .

The distinction between laws interfering with the political equality of the negro and those requiring the separation of the two races in schools, theaters, and railway carriages, has been frequently drawn by this court. . . .

So far, then, as a conflict with the 14th Amendment is concerned, the case reduces itself to the question whether the statute of Louisiana is a reasonable regulation, and with respect to this there must necessarily be a large discretion on the part of the legislature. In determining the question of reasonableness it is at liberty to act with reference to the established usages, customs, and traditions of the people, and with a view to the promotion of their comfort, and the preservation of the public peace and good order. Gauged by this standard, we cannot say that a law which authorizes or even requires the separation of the two races in public conveyances is unreasonable or more obnoxious to the 14th Amendment than the acts of Congress requiring separate schools for colored children in the District of Columbia, the constitutionality of which does not seem to have been questioned, or the corresponding acts of state legislatures.

We consider the underlying fallacy of the plaintiff's argument to consist in the assumption that the enforced separation of the two races stamps the colored race with a badge of inferiority. If this be so, it is not by reason of anything found in the act, but solely because the colored race chooses to put that construction upon it. The argument necessarily assumes that if, as has been more than once the case, and is not unlikely to be so again, the colored race should become the dominant power in the state legislature, and should enact a law in precisely similar terms, it would thereby relegate the white race to an inferior position. We imagine that the white race, at least, would not acquiesce in this assumption. The argument also assumes that social prejudices may be overcome by legislation, and that equal rights cannot be secured to the negro except by an enforced commingling of the two races. We cannot accept this proposition. If the two races are to meet on terms of social equality, it must be the result of natural affinities, a mutual appreciation of each other's merits and a voluntary consent of individuals.

Legislation is powerless to eradicate racial instincts or to abolish distinctions based upon physical differences, and the attempt to do so can only result in accentuating the difficulties of the present situation. If the civil and political rights of both races be equal, one cannot be inferior to the other civilly or politically. If one race be inferior to the other socially, the Constitution of the United States cannot put them upon the same plane.

MR. JUSTICE HARLAN, DISSENTING:

In respect of civil rights, common to all citizens, the Constitution of the United States does not, I think, permit any public authority to know the race of those entitled to be protected in the enjoyment of such rights. Every true man has pride of race, and under appropriate circumstances, when the rights of others, his equals before the law, are not to be affected, it is his privilege to express such pride and to take such action based upon it as to him seems proper. But I deny that any legislative body or judicial tribunal may have regard to the race of citizens when the civil rights of those citizens are involved. Indeed such legislation as that here in question is inconsistent, not only with that equality of rights which pertains to citizenship, national and state, but with the personal liberty enjoyed by every one within the United States. . . .

The white race deems itself to be the dominant race in this country. And so it is, in prestige, in achievements, in education, in wealth, and in power. So, I doubt not that it will continue to be for all time, if it remains true to its great heritage and holds fast to the principles of constitutional liberty. But in view of the Constitution, in the eye of the law, there is in this country no superior, dominant, ruling class of citizens. There is no caste here. Our Constitution is color-blind, and neither knows nor tolerates classes among citizens. In respect of civil rights, all citizens are equal before the law. The humblest is the peer of the most powerful. The law regards man as man, and takes no account of his surroundings or of his color when his civil rights as guaranteed by the supreme law of the land are involved. It is therefore to be regretted that this high tribunal, the final expositor of the fundamental law of the land, has reached the conclusion that it is competent for a state to regulate the enjoyment by citizens of their civil rights solely upon the basis of race.

In my opinion, the judgment this day rendered will, in time, prove to be quite as pernicious as the decision made by this tribunal in the *Dred Scott Case* [1857]. . . .

The sure guaranty of the peace and security of each race is the clear, distinct, unconditional recognition by our governments, national and state, of every right that inheres in civil freedom, and of the equality before the law of all citizens of the United States without regard to race. State enactments, regulating the enjoyment of civil rights, upon the basis of race, and cunningly devised to defeat legitimate results of the war, under the pretense of recognizing equality of rights, can have no other result than to render permanent peace impossible and to keep alive a conflict of races, the continuance of which must do harm to all concerned.

The arbitrary separation of citizens, on the basis of race, while they are on a public highway, is a badge of servitude wholly inconsistent with the civil freedom and the equality before the law established by the Constitution. It cannot be justified upon any legal grounds.

If evils will result from the commingling of the two races upon public highways established for the benefit of all, they will be infinitely less than those that will surely come from state legislation regulating the enjoyment of civil rights upon the basis of race. We boast of the freedom enjoyed by our people above all other peoples. But it is difficult to reconcile that boast with a state of the law which, practically, puts the brand of servitude and degradation upon a large class of our fellow citizens, our equals before the law. The thin disguise of "equal" accommodations for passengers in railroad coaches will not mislead anyone, or atone for the wrong this day done. . . .

I am of opinion that the statute of Louisiana is inconsistent with the personal liberty of citizens, white and black, in that state, and hostile to both the spirit and letter of the Constitution of the United States. If laws of like character should be enacted in the several states of the Union, the effect would be in the highest degree mischievous. Slavery as an institution tolerated by law would, it is true, have disappeared from our country, but there would remain a power in the states, by sinister legislation, to interfere with the full enjoyment of the blessings of freedom; to regulate civil rights, common to all citizens, upon the basis of race; and to place in a condition of legal inferiority a large body of American citizens, now constituting a part of the political community, called the people of the United States, for whom and by whom, through representatives, our government is administered. Such a system is inconsistent with the guarantee given by the Constitution to each state of a republican form of government, and may be stricken down by congressional action, or by the courts in the discharge of their solemn duty to maintain the supreme law of the land, anything in the Constitution or laws of any state to the contrary notwithstanding.

Segregation on the basis of race is a denial of equal protection in violation of the Constitution.

38a. *Brown v. Board of Education of Topeka* (1954)
38b. *Bolling v. Sharpe* (1954)

These are epochal decisions of the United States Supreme Court. Racial segregation in employment, housing, recreation, education, and other fields had long been widely practiced in the United States, despite the Fourteenth Amendment's command of "equal protection of the laws." The famous judicial doctrine of "separate but equal," announced in *Plessy v. Ferguson* (1896), actually provided more separation than equality. Furthermore, the concept of separation in itself seemed to violate the principle of equality articulated in the Constitution. Over the years, particularly between the 1930s and the early 1950s, the Supreme Court moved gradually to strike down various state provisions that did not meet the "equal" requirements of *Plessy v. Ferguson*. In *Brown v. Board of Education*, which dealt specifically with elementary education, the Court took the final logical step. In a unanimous decision, it outlawed segregation altogether. The consequences of the decision, stimulating the Negro drive for full equality in all fields, have been nothing short of revolutionary.

Brown v. Board of Education contains a condemnation, based to some extent on sociological literature, of the evils of segregation. The decision affected state-mandated segregation in seventeen states and the District of Columbia (*Bolling v. Sharpe*) and four states where public school segregation was permitted as a local option.

Background: The facts of the *Brown* case are given by Chief Justice Warren in the opening paragraphs of the opinion.

Brown v. Board of Education of Topeka

MR. CHIEF JUSTICE WARREN DELIVERED
THE OPINION OF THE COURT:

These cases come to us from the States of Kansas, South Carolina, Virginia, and Delaware. They are premised on different facts and different local conditions, but a common legal question justifies their consideration together in this consolidated opinion.

In each of the cases, minors of the Negro race, through their legal representatives, seek the aid of the courts in obtaining admission to the public schools of their community on a nonsegregated basis. In each instance, they had been denied admission to schools attended by white children under laws requiring or permitting segregation according to race. This segregation was alleged to deprive the plaintiffs of the equal protection of the laws under the Fourteenth Amendment. In each of the cases other than the Delaware case, a three-judge federal district court denied relief to the plaintiffs on the so-called "separate but equal" doctrine announced by this Court in *Plessy v. Ferguson* [1896]. Under that doctrine, equality of treatment is accorded when the races are provided substantially equal facilities, even though these facilities be separate. In the Delaware case, the Supreme Court of Delaware adhered to that doctrine, but ordered that the plaintiffs be admitted to the white schools because of their superiority to the Negro schools.

The plaintiffs contend that segregated public schools are not "equal" and cannot be made "equal," and that hence they are deprived of the equal protection of the laws. Because of the obvious importance of the question presented, the Court took jurisdiction. Argument was heard in the 1952 Term, and reargument was heard this Term on certain questions propounded by the Court.

Reargument was largely devoted to the circumstances surrounding the adoption of the Fourteenth Amendment in 1868. It covered exhaustively consideration of the Amendment in Congress, ratification by the states, then existing practices in racial segregation, and the views of proponents and opponents of the Amendment. This discussion and our own investigation convince us that, although these sources cast some light, it is not enough to resolve the problem with which we are faced. At best, they are inconclusive. The most avid proponents of the post-War Amendments undoubtedly intended them to remove all legal distinctions among "all persons born or naturalized in the United States." Their opponents, just as certainly, were antagonistic to both the letter and the spirit of the Amendments and wished them to have the most limited effect. What others in Congress and the state legislatures had in mind cannot be determined with any degree of certainty.

An additional reason for the inconclusive nature of the Amendment's history, with respect to segregated schools, is the status of public education at that time. In the South, the movement toward free common schools, supported by general taxation, had not yet taken hold. Education of white children was largely in the hands of private groups. Education of Negroes was almost nonexistent, and practically all of the race were illiterate. In fact, any education of Negroes was forbidden by law in some states. Today, in contrast, many Negroes have achieved outstanding success in the arts and sciences as well as in the business and professional world. It is true that public school education at the time of the Amendment had advanced further in the North, but the effect of the Amendment on Northern States was generally ignored in the congressional debates. Even in the North, the conditions of public education did not approximate those existing today. The curriculum was usually rudimentary; ungraded schools were common in rural areas; the school term was but three months a year in many states; and compulsory school attendance was virtually unknown. As a consequence, it is not surprising that there should be so little in the history of the Fourteenth Amendment relating to its intended effect on public education. . . .

Here, . . . there are findings below that the Negro and white schools involved have been equalized, or are being equalized, with respect to buildings, curricula, qualifications and salaries of teachers, and other "tangible" factors. Our decision, therefore, cannot turn on merely a comparison of these tangible factors in the Negro and white schools involved in each of the cases. We must look instead to the effect of segregation itself on public education.

In approaching this problem, we cannot turn the clock back to 1868 when the Amendment was adopted, or even to 1896 when *Plessy v. Ferguson* was written. We must consider public education in the light of its full development and its present place in American life throughout the Nation. Only in this way can it be determined if segregation in public schools deprives these plaintiffs of the equal protection of the laws.

Today, education is perhaps the most important function of state and local governments. Compulsory school attendance laws and the great expenditures for education both demonstrate our recognition of the importance of education to our democratic society. It is required in the performance of our most basic public responsibilities, even service in the armed forces. It is the very foundation of good citizenship. Today it is a principal instrument in awakening the child to cultural values, in preparing him for later professional training, and in helping him to adjust normally to his environment. In these days, it is doubtful that any child may reasonably be expected to succeed in life if he is denied the opportunity of an education. Such an opportunity, where the state has undertaken to provide it, is a right which must be made available to all on equal terms.

We come then to the question presented: Does segregation of children in public schools solely on the basis of race, even though the physical facilities and other "tangible" factors may be equal, deprive the children of the minority group of equal educational opportunities? We believe that it does.

In *Sweatt v. Painter* [1950], in finding that a segregated law school for Negroes could not provide them equal educational opportunities, this Court relied in large part on "those qualities which are incapable of objective measurement but which make for greatness in a law school." In *McLaurin v. Oklahoma State Regents*, the Court [1950], in requiring that a Negro admitted to a white graduate school be treated like all other students, again resorted to intangible considerations: ". . . his ability to study, to engage in discussions and exchange views with other students, and, in general, to learn his profession." Such considerations apply with added force to children in grade and high schools. To separate them from others of similar age and qualifications solely because of their race generates a feeling of inferiority as to their status in the community that may affect their hearts and minds in a way unlikely ever to be undone. The effect of this separation on their educational opportunities was well stated by a finding in the Kansas case by a court which nevertheless felt compelled to rule against the Negro plaintiffs:

"Segregation of white and colored children in public schools has a detrimental effect upon the colored children. The impact is greater when it has the sanction of the law; for the policy of separating the races is usually interpreted as denoting the inferiority of the negro group. A sense of inferiority affects the motivation of a child to learn. Segregation with the sanction of law, therefore, has a tendency to [retard] the educational and mental development of Negro children and to deprive them of some of the benefits they would receive in a racial[ly] integrated school system.''

Whatever may have been the extent of psychological knowledge at the time of *Plessy v. Ferguson*, this finding is amply supported by modern authority. [In a now famous footnote the court cites a number of sociological and psychological studies on the adverse effects of segregation.] Any language in *Plessy v. Ferguson* contrary to this finding is rejected.

We conclude that in the field of public education the doctrine of ''separate but equal'' has no place. Separate educational facilities are inherently unequal. Therefore, we hold that the plaintiffs and others similarly situated for whom the actions have been brought are, by reason of the segregation complained of, deprived of the equal protection of the laws guaranteed by the Fourteenth Amendment.

Bolling v. Sharpe

MR. CHIEF JUSTICE WARREN DELIVERED
THE OPINION OF THE COURT:

This case challenges the validity of segregation in the public schools of the District of Columbia. The petitioners, minors of the Negro race, allege that such segregation deprives them of due process of law under the Fifth Amendment. They were refused admission to a public school attended by white children solely because of their race. . . .

We have this day held that the Equal Protection Clause of the Fourteenth Amendment prohibits the states from maintaining racially segregated public schools. The legal problem in the District of Columbia is somewhat different, however. The Fifth Amendment, which is applicable in the District of Columbia, does not contain an equal protection clause as does the Fourteenth Amendment which applies only to the states. But the concepts of equal protection and due process, both stemming from our American ideal of fairness, are not mutually exclusive. The "equal protection of the laws" is a more explicit safeguard of prohibited unfairness than "due process of law," and, therefore, we do not imply that the two are always interchangeable phrases. But, as this Court has recognized, discrimination may be so unjustifiable as to be violative of due process.

Classifications based solely upon race must be scrutinized with particular care, since they are contrary to our traditions and hence constitutionally suspect. As long ago as 1896, this Court declared the principle "that the Constitution of the United States, in its present form, forbids, so far as civil and political rights are concerned, discrimination by the General Government, or by the States, against any citizen because of his race." And in *Buchanan v. Warley* [1917], the Court held that a statute which limited the right of a property owner to convey his property to a person of another race was, as an unreasonable discrimination, a denial of due process of law.

Although the Court has not assumed to define "liberty" with any great precision, that term is not confined to mere freedom from bodily restraint. Liberty under law extends to the full range of conduct which the individual is free to pursue, and it cannot be restricted except for a proper governmental objective. Segregation in public education is not reasonably related to any proper governmental objective, and thus it imposes on Negro children of the District of Columbia a burden that constitutes an arbitrary deprivation of their liberty in violation of the Due Process Clause.

In view of our decision that the Constitution prohibits the states from maintaining racially segregated public schools, it would be unthinkable that the same Constitution would impose a lesser duty on the Federal Government. We hold that racial segregation in the public schools of the District of Columbia is a denial of the due process of law guaranteed by the Fifth Amendment to the Constitution.

Preferential racial quotas in education violate the Civil Rights Act of 1964.

39. *Regents of the University of California v. Bakke* (1978)

The issue of favored treatment for racial minorities to compensate for past discrimination—or "reverse discrimination," as it is sometimes called—has come to the fore in recent years. The sharp division on this issue in the *Bakke* case reflects, as is so often true of important constitutional cases, a division in the country at large.

Background: The University of California Medical School at Davis set up a two-tier admission system for minority applicants. For eighty-four of the one hundred annual openings, minority applicants competed on the same basis as others. The remaining sixteen openings were reserved exclusively for minority students. Bakke, a white, was rejected for admission in 1973 and 1974 even though his Medical College Admission Test Scores were higher than the scores of most of the minority applicants admitted in those years under the special program. Bakke's claim that the Davis system violated both the Equal Protection Clause and Title VI of the Civil Rights Act of 1964 was sustained by the California Supreme Court. The United States Supreme Court agreed that Bakke had unlawfully been denied admission to the medical school, but the justices were unusually fragmented in arriving at this decision.

Justice Powell's opinion announcing the judgment of the Court drew a distinction between the Davis racial quota, as forbidden by the Equal Protection Clause, and the nonquota racial preference practiced in some other universities, as constitutionally permitted. (Some of his brethren professed to see little difference in his distinction.) Ironically, Powell's opinion conformed *in toto* only to Powell's own views. It essentially mediated between the sharply contrasting views of the other eight justices, who divided equally on the issue of quotas. Four members of the Court (Justices Brennan, White, Marshall, and Blackmun, in a joint opinion) would have upheld even the quota system on constitutional as well as statutory grounds. Four others (Chief Justice Burger, and Justices Stewart, Rehnquist, and Stevens, in an opinion by Stevens) agreed with Powell that the Davis racial quota was unlawful, but they refused to rule on favored racial treatment that did not include quotas, since this issue was not, properly speaking, before the Court; to complicate matters further, these justices would have rested the decision solely on Title VI grounds and avoided a constitutional ruling. Following the Court's ruling, Bakke was admitted to the medical school.

MR. JUSTICE POWELL ANNOUNCED
THE JUDGMENT OF THE COURT:

The language of § 601 [of Title VI], like that of the Equal Protection Clause, is majestic in its sweep:

"No person in the United States shall, on the ground of race, color, or national origin, be excluded from participation in, be denied the benefits of, or be subjected to discrimination under any program or activity receiving Federal financial assistance."

Examination of the voluminous legislative history of Title VI reveals a congressional intent to halt federal funding of entities that violate a prohibition of racial discrimination similar to that of the Constitution. Although isolated statements of various legislators, taken out of context, can be marshaled in support of the proposition that § 601 enacted a purely colorblind scheme, without regard to the reach of the Equal Protection Clause, these comments must be read against the background of both the problem that Congress was addressing and the broader view of the statute that emerges from a full examination of the legislative debates. . . .

In view of the clear legislative intent, Title VI must be held to proscribe only those racial classifications that would violate the Equal Protection Clause or the Fifth Amendment. . . .

[T]he parties fight a sharp preliminary action over the proper characterization of the special admissions program. Petitioner prefers to view it as establishing a "goal" of minority representation in the Medical School. Respondent, echoing the courts below, labels it a racial quota.

This semantic distinction is beside the point; the special admissions program is undeniably a classification based on race and ethnic background. To the extent that there existed a pool of at least minimally qualified minority applicants to fill the 16 special admissions seats, white applicants could compete only for 84 seats in the entering class, rather than the 100 open to minority applicants. Whether this limitation is described as a quota or a goal, it is a line drawn on the basis of race and ethnic status.

The guarantees of the Fourteenth Amendment extend to all persons. . . . The guarantee of equal protection cannot mean one thing when applied to one individual and something else when applied to a person of another color. If both are not accorded the same protection, then it is not equal.

Nevertheless, petitioner argues that the court below erred in applying strict scrutiny to the special admissions program because white males . . . are not a "discrete and insular minority" requiring extraordinary protection from the majoritarian political process. . . .

Racial and ethnic distinctions of any sort are inherently suspect and thus call for the most exacting judicial examination.

Although many of the Framers of the Fourteenth Amendment conceived of its primary function as bridging the vast distance between members of the Negro race and the white "majority," the Amendment itself was framed in universal terms, without reference to color, ethnic origin, or condition of prior servitude.

[I]t is not unlikely that among the Framers were many who would have applauded a reading of the Equal Protection Clause that states a principle of universal application and is responsive to the racial, ethnic, and cultural diversity of the Nation. . . .

Petitioner urges us to adopt for the first time a more restrictive view of the Equal Protection Clause and hold that discrimination against members of the white "majority" cannot be suspect if its purpose can be characterized as "benign." The clock of our liberties, however, cannot be turned back to 1868.

It is far too late to argue that the guarantee of equal protection to *all* persons permits the recognition of special wards entitled to a degree of protection greater than that accorded others. . . . The concepts of "majority" and "minority" necessarily reflect temporary arrangements and political judgments. As observed above, the white "majority" itself is composed of various minority groups, most of which can lay claim to a history of prior discrimination at the hands of the State and private individuals. Not all of these groups can receive preferential treatment and corresponding judicial tolerance of distinctions drawn in terms of race and nationality, for then the only "majority" left would be a new minority of white Anglo-Saxon Protestants. There is no principled basis

for deciding which groups would merit "heightened judicial solici-
tude" and which would not. Courts would be asked to evaluate the
extent of the prejudice and consequent harm suffered by various minority groups. Those whose societal injury is thought to exceed some
arbitrary level of tolerability then would be entitled to preferential classifications at the expense of individuals belonging to other groups.
Those classifications would be free from exacting judicial scrutiny. As
these preferences began to have their desired effect, and the consequences of past discrimination were undone, new judicial rankings
would be necessary. The kind of variable sociological and political
analysis necessary to produce such rankings simply does not lie within
the judicial competence—even if they otherwise were politically feasible and socially desirable. . . .

We have held that in "order to justify the use of a suspect classification, a State must show that its purpose or interest is both constitutionally permissible and substantial, and that its use of the classification
is 'necessary . . . to the accomplishment' of its purpose or the safeguarding of its interest." . . .

The State certainly has a legitimate and substantial interest in ame-
liorating, or eliminating where feasible, the disabling effects of identified discrimination. . . . In the school cases, the States were required
by court order to redress the wrongs worked by specific instances of
racial discrimination. That goal was far more focused than the remedying of the effects of "societal discrimination," an amorphous concept of injury that may be ageless in its reach into the past.

We have never approved a classification that aids persons perceived
as members of relatively victimized groups at the expense of other
innocent individuals in the absence of judicial, legislative, or administrative findings of constitutional or statutory violations. . . . After such
findings have been made, the governmental interest in preferring members of the injured groups at the expense of others is substantial, since
the legal rights of the victims must be vindicated. In such a case, the
extent of the injury and the consequent remedy will have been judicially, legislatively, or administratively defined. Also, the remedial action usually remains subject to continuing oversight to assure that it
will work the least harm possible to other innocent persons competing
for the benefit. Without such findings of constitutional or statutory violations, it cannot be said that the government has any greater interest
in helping one individual than in refraining from harming another.

Thus, the government has no compelling justification for inflicting such harm.

Petitioner does not purport to have made, and is in no position to make, such findings. Its broad mission is education, not the formulation of any legislative policy or the adjudication of particular claims of illegality. . . .

[I]solated segments of our vast governmental structures are not competent to make those decisions, at least in the absence of legislative mandates and legislatively determined criteria. . . .

Petitioner identifies, as another purpose of its program, improving the delivery of health-care services to communities currently underserved. . . . It may be assumed that in some situations a State's interest in facilitating the health care of its citizens is sufficiently compelling to support the use of a suspect classification. But there is virtually no evidence in the record indicating that petitioner's special admissions program is either needed or geared to promote that goal. . . .

[An additional] goal asserted by petitioner is the attainment of a diverse student body. This clearly is a constitutionally permissible goal for an institution of higher education. Academic freedom, though not a specifically enumerated constitutional right, long has been viewed as a special concern of the First Amendment. The freedom of a university to make its own judgment as to education includes the selection of its student body. . . .

Thus, in arguing that its universities must be accorded the right to select those students who will contribute the most to the "robust exchange of ideas," petitioner invokes a countervailing constitutional interest, that of the First Amendment. In this light, petitioner must be viewed as seeking to achieve a goal that is of paramount importance in the fulfillment of its mission.

It may be argued that there is greater force to these views at the undergraduate level than in a medical school where the training is centered primarily on professional competency. But even at the graduate level, our tradition and experience lend support to the view that the contribution of diversity is substantial. . . .

It may be assumed that the reservation of a specified number of seats in each class for individuals from the preferred ethnic groups would contribute to the attainment of considerable ethnic diversity in the student body. But petitioner's argument that this is the only effective means of serving the interest of diversity is seriously flawed. . . . The diversity that furthers a compelling state interest encompasses a far broader array of qualifications and characteristics of which racial or ethnic origin is but a single though important element. Petitioner's special admissions program, focused *solely* on ethnic diversity, would hinder rather than further attainment of genuine diversity.. . . .

The experience of other university admissions programs, which take race into account in achieving the educational diversity valued by the First Amendment, demonstrates that the assignment of a fixed number of places to a minority group is not a necessary means toward that end. An illuminating example is found in the Harvard College program. . . .

In such an admissions program, race or ethnic background may be deemed a "plus" in a particular applicant's file, yet it does not insulate the individual from comparison with all other candidates for the available seats. The file of a particular black applicant may be examined for his potential contribution to diversity without the factor of race being decisive when compared, for example, with that of an applicant identified as an Italian-American if the latter is thought to exhibit qualities more likely to promote beneficial educational pluralism. Such qualities could include exceptional personal talents, unique work or service experience, leadership potential, maturity, demonstrated compassion, a history of overcoming disadvantage, ability to communicate with the poor, or other qualifications deemed important. In short, an admissions program operated in this way is flexible enough to consider all pertinent elements of diversity in light of the particular qualifications of each applicant, and to place them on the same footing for consideration, although not necessarily according them the same weight. . . .

This kind of program treats each applicant as an individual in the admissions process. The applicant who loses out on the last available seat to another candidate receiving a "plus" on the basis of ethnic background will not have been foreclosed from all consideration for that seat simply because he was not the right color or had the wrong surname. It would mean only that his combined qualifications, which may have included similar nonobjective factors, did not outweigh those of the other applicant. His qualifications would have been weighed fairly and competitively, and he would have no basis to complain of unequal treatment under the Fourteenth Amendment.

It has been suggested that an admissions program which considers race only as one factor is simply a subtle and more sophisticated—but no less effective—means of according racial preference than the Davis program. A facial intent to discriminate, however, is evident in petitioner's preference program and not denied in this case. No such facial infirmity exists in an admissions program where race or ethnic background is simply one element—to be weighed fairly against other elements—in the selection process. "A boundary line," as Mr. Justice Frankfurter remarked in another connection, "is none the worse for being narrow."

In summary, it is evident that the Davis special admissions program involves the use of an explicit racial classification never before countenanced by this Court. It tells applicants who are not Negro, Asian, or Chicano that they are totally excluded from a specific percentage of the seats in an entering class. No matter how strong their qualifications, quantitative and extracurricular, including their own potential for contribution to educational diversity, they are never afforded the chance to compete with applicants from the preferred groups for the special admissions seats. At the same time, the preferred applicants have the opportunity to compete for every seat in the class. . . .

In enjoining petitioner from ever considering the race of any applicant, however, the courts below failed to recognize that the State has a substantial interest that legitimately may be served by a properly devised admissions program involving the competitive consideration of race and ethnic origin. For this reason, so much of the California court's judgment as enjoins petitioner from any consideration of the race of any applicant must be reversed.

With respect to respondent's entitlement to an injunction directing his admission to the Medical School, petitioner has conceded that it could not carry its burden of proving that, but for the existence of its unlawful special admissions program, respondent still would not have been admitted. Hence, respondent is entitled to the injunction, and that portion of the judgment must be affirmed.

OPINION OF MR. JUSTICE BRENNAN, MR. JUSTICE WHITE, MR. JUSTICE MARSHALL, AND MR. JUSTICE BLACKMUN, CONCURRING IN THE JUDGMENT IN PART AND DISSENTING IN PART:

Since we conclude that the affirmative admissions program at the Davis Medical School is constitutional, we would reverse the judgment below in all respects. Mr. Justice Powell agrees that some uses of race in university admissions are permissible and, therefore, he joins with us to make five votes reversing the judgment below insofar as it prohibits the University from establishing race-conscious programs in the future. . . .

[C]laims that law must be "colorblind" or that the datum of race is no longer relevant to public policy must be seen as aspiration rather than as description of reality. This is not to denigrate aspiration; for reality rebukes us that race has too often been used by those who would stigmatize and oppress minorities. Yet we cannot . . . let color blindness become myopia which makes the reality that many "created equal" have been treated within our lifetimes as inferior both by the law and by their fellow citizens.

The threshold question we must decide is whether Title VI of the Civil Rights Act of 1964 bars recipients of federal funds from giving preferential consideration to disadvantaged members of racial minorities as part of a program designed to enable such individuals to surmount the obstacles imposed by racial discrimination. . . . Title VI prohibits only those uses of racial criteria that would violate the Fourteenth Amendment if employed by a State or its agencies; it does not bar the preferential treatment of racial minorities as a means of remedying past societal discrimination to the extent that such action is consistent with the Fourteenth Amendment. The legislative history of Title VI, administrative regulations interpreting the statute, subsequent congressional and executive action, and the prior decisions of this Court compel this conclusion. . . .

[T]he legislative history shows that Congress specifically eschewed any static definition of discrimination in favor of broad language that could be shaped by experience, administrative necessity, and evolving judicial doctrine. . . .

Unquestionably we have held that a government practice or statute which restricts "fundamental rights" or which contains "suspect classifications" is to be subjected to "strict scrutiny" and can be justified only if it furthers a compelling government purpose and, even then, only if no less restrictive alternative is available. But no fundamental right is involved here. Nor do whites as a class have any of the "traditional indicia of suspectness: the class is not saddled with such disabilities, or subjected to such a history of purposeful unequal treatment, or relegated to such a position of political powerlessness as to command extraordinary protection from the majoritarian political process.'' . . .

On the other hand, the fact that this case does not fit neatly into our prior analytic framework for race cases does not mean that it should be analyzed by applying the very loose rational-basis standard of review that is the very least that is always applied in equal protection cases. Instead, a number of considerations—developed in gender-discrimination cases but which carry even more force when applied to racial classifications—lead us to conclude that racial classifications designed to further remedial purposes '' 'must serve important governmental objectives and must be substantially related to achievement of those objectives.' ''

First, race, like ''gender-based classifications[,] too often [has] been inexcusably utilized to stereotype and stigmatize politically powerless segments of society.'' . . .

Second, race, like gender and illegitimacy, is an immutable characteristic which its possessors are powerless to escape or set aside. . . . Thus, our review under the Fourteenth Amendment should be strict—not '' 'strict' in theory and fatal in fact,'' because it is stigma that causes fatality—but strict and searching nonetheless.

Davis' articulated purpose of remedying the effects of past societal discrimination is, under our cases, sufficiently important to justify the use of race-conscious admissions programs where there is a sound basis for concluding that minority underrepresentation is substantial and chronic, and that the handicap of past discrimination is impeding access of minorities to the Medical School. . . .

[O]ur cases under Title VII of the Civil Rights Act have held that, in order to achieve minority participation in previously segregated areas of public life, Congress may require or authorize preferential treatment for those likely disadvantaged by societal racial discrimination. . . . These decisions compel the conclusion that States also may adopt race-conscious programs designed to overcome substantial, chronic minority underrepresentation where there is reason to believe that the evil addressed is a product of past racial discrimination. . . .

Davis had very good reason to believe that the national pattern of underrepresentation of minorities in medicine would be perpetuated if it retained a single admissions standard. For example, the entering classes in 1968 and 1969, the years in which such a standard was used, included only 1 Chicano and 2 Negroes out of the 50 admittees for each year. Nor is there any relief from this pattern of underrepresentation in the statistics for the regular admissions program in later years.

Davis clearly could conclude that the serious and persistent underrepresentation of minorities in medicine depicted by these statistics is the result of handicaps under which minority applicants labor as a consequence of a background of deliberate, purposeful discrimination against minorities in education and in society generally, as well as in the medical profession. . . .

Nor was Bakke in any sense stamped as inferior by the Medical School's rejection of him. Indeed, it is conceded by all that he satisfied those criteria regarded by the school as generally relevant to academic performance better than most of the minority members who were admitted. Moreover, there is absolutely no basis for concluding that Bakke's rejection as a result of Davis' use of racial preference will affect him throughout his life in the same way as the segregation of the Negro school children in *Brown I* would have affected them. Unlike discrimination against racial minorities, the use of racial preferences for remedial purposes does not inflict a pervasive injury upon individual whites in the sense that wherever they go or whatever they do there is a significant likelihood that they will be treated as second-class citizens because of their color. This distinction does not mean that the exclusion of a white resulting from the preferential use of race is not sufficiently serious to require justification; but it does mean that the injury inflicted by such a policy is not distinguishable from disadvantages caused by a wide range of government actions, none of which has ever been thought impermissible for that reason alone. . . .

The Davis program does not simply advance less qualified applicants; rather, it compensates applicants, who it is uncontested are fully qualified to study medicine, for educational disadvantages which it was reasonable to conclude were a product of state-fostered discrimination. Once admitted, these students must satisfy the same degree requirements as regularly admitted students.

MR. JUSTICE MARSHALL:

I agree with the judgment of the Court only insofar as it permits a university to consider the race of an applicant in making admissions decisions. I do not agree that petitioner's admissions program violates the Constitution. For it must be remembered that, during most of the past 200 years, the Constitution as interpreted by this Court did not prohibit the most ingenious and pervasive forms of discrimination against the Negro. Now, when a State acts to remedy the effects of that legacy of discrimination, I cannot believe that this same Constitution stands as a barrier. . . .

It is because of a legacy of unequal treatment that we now must permit the institutions of this society to give consideration to race in making decisions about who will hold the positions of influence, affluence, and prestige in America. For far too long, the doors to those positions have been shut to Negroes. If we are ever to become a fully integrated society, one in which the color of a person's skin will not determine the opportunities available to him or her, we must be willing to take steps to open those doors. I do not believe that anyone can truly look into America's past and still find that a remedy for the effects of that past is impermissible.

MR. JUSTICE BLACKMUN:

[D]espite its two-track aspect, the Davis program, for me, is within constitutional bounds, though perhaps barely so. . . .

I suspect that it would be impossible to arrange an affirmative action program in a racially neutral way and have it successful. To ask that this be so is to demand the impossible. In order to get beyond racism, we must first take account of race. There is no other way. And in order to treat some persons equally, we must treat them differently.

MR. JUSTICE STEVENS, WITH WHOM THE CHIEF JUSTICE, MR. JUSTICE STEWART, AND MR. JUSTICE REHNQUIST JOIN, CONCURRING IN THE JUDGMENT IN PART AND DISSENTING IN PART:

[T]he question whether race can ever be used as a factor in an admissions decision is not an issue in this case, and that discussion of that issue is inappropriate.

Both petitioner and respondent have asked us to determine the legality of the University's special admissions program by reference to the Constitution. Our settled practice, however, is to avoid the decision of a constitutional issue if a case can be fairly decided on a statutory ground. "If there is one doctrine more deeply rooted than any other in the process of constitutional adjudication, it is that we ought not to pass on questions of constitutionality . . . unless such adjudication is unavoidable.'' . . . Only if petitioner should prevail on the statutory issue would it be necessary to decide whether the University's admissions program violated the Equal Protection Clause of the Fourteenth Amendment. . . .

The University, through its special admissions policy, excluded Bakke from participation in its program of medical education because of his race. . . . The plain language of the statute therefore requires affirmance of the judgment below. . . .

[I]t seems clear that the proponents of Title VI assumed that the Constitution itself required a colorblind standard on the part of government. . . . [They] plainly considered Title VI consistent with their view of the Constitution and they sought to provide an effective weapon to implement that view. . . .

In short, nothing in the legislative history justifies the conclusion that the broad language of § 601 should not be given its natural meaning. We are dealing with a distinct statutory prohibition, enacted at a particular time with particular concerns in mind; neither its language nor any prior interpretation suggests that its place in the Civil Rights Act, won after long debate, is simply that of a constitutional appendage. In unmistakable terms the Act prohibits the exclusion of individuals from federally funded programs because of their race. As succinctly phrased during the Senate debate, under Title VI it is not ''permissible to say 'yes' to one person; but to say 'no' to another person, only because of the color of his skin.'' . . .

The University's special admissions program violated Title VI of the Civil Rights Act of 1964 by excluding Bakke from the Medical School because of his race. It is therefore our duty to affirm the judgment ordering Bakke admitted to the University.

Accordingly, I concur in the Court's judgment insofar as it affirms the judgment of the Supreme Court of California. To the extent that it purports to do anything else, I respectfully dissent.

Local "affirmative action" plans may not require minority "set-asides" in public-works contracts.

40. *Richmond v. Croson Co.* (1989)

This case writes another chapter in the unfolding affirmative action drama. Since *Bakke*, the Court has continued to be deeply fragmented on this divisive issue. The continuing, and heated, judicial debate on racial preference indicates that the ultimate outcome of this controversy remains in doubt.

Background: In *Fullilove v. Klutznick* (1980), the Court had upheld an act of Congress mandating that minority contractors be awarded 10 percent of certain federal construction contracts. In *Croson*, however, a plan drafted by the Richmond, Virginia, city council which required companies awarded city construction contracts to subcontract 30 percent of the contract's dollar value to minority firms was struck down. The district court upheld the plan but was reversed by the court of appeals.

JUSTICE O'CONNOR DELIVERED THE OPINION OF THE COURT, IN WHICH CHIEF JUSTICE REHNQUIST, AND JUSTICES WHITE AND KENNEDY, JOINED IN SUBSTANTIAL PART:

In this case, we confront once again the tension between the Fourteenth Amendment's guarantee of equal treatment to all citizens, and the use of race-based measures to ameliorate the effects of past discrimination on the opportunities enjoyed by members of minority groups in our society. In *Fullilove v. Klutznick* (1980), we held that a congressional program requiring that 10% of certain federal construction grants be awarded to minority contractors did not violate the equal protection principles embodied in the Due Process Clause of the Fifth Amendment.

I

On April 11, 1983, the Richmond City Council adopted the Minority Business Utilization Plan (the Plan). The Plan required prime contractors to whom the city awarded construction contracts to subcontract at least 30% of the dollar amount of the contract to one or more Minority

Business Enterprises (MBE's). The 30% set-aside did not apply to city contracts awarded to minority-owned prime contractors.

The Plan defined an MBE as "[a] business at least fifty-one (51) percent of which is owned and controlled . . . by minority group members." "Minority group members" were defined as "[c]itizens of the United States who are Blacks, Spanish-speaking, Orientals, Indians, Eskimos, or Aleuts." There was no geographic limit to the Plan; an otherwise qualified MBE from anywhere in the United States could avail itself of the 30% set-aside. The Plan declared that it was "remedial" in nature, and enacted "for the purpose of promoting wider participation by minority business enterprises in the construction of public projects." The Plan expired on June 30, 1988, and was in effect for approximately five years. . . .

Proponents of the set-aside provision relied on a study which indicated that, while the general population of Richmond was 50% black, only 0.67% of the city's prime construction contracts had been awarded to minority businesses in the 5-year period from 1978 to 1983. It was also established that a variety of contractors' associations, whose representatives appeared in opposition to the ordinance, had virtually no minority businesses within their membership. The city's legal counsel indicated his view that the ordinance was constitutional under this Court's decision in *Fullilove*. . . .

There was no direct evidence of race discrimination on the part of the city in letting contracts or any evidence that the city's prime contractors had discriminated against minority-owned subcontractors. . . .

II

The parties and their supporting amici fight an initial battle over the scope of the city's power to adopt legislation designed to address the effects of past discrimination. . . . [A]ppellee argues that the city must limit any race-based remedial efforts to eradicating the effects of its own prior discrimination. Appellant argues that our decision in *Fullilove* is controlling, and that as a result the city of Richmond enjoys sweeping legislative power to define and attack the effects of prior discrimination in its local construction industry. We find that neither of these two rather stark alternatives can withstand analysis. . . .

Appellant and its supporting amici rely heavily on *Fullilove* for the proposition that a city council, like Congress, need not make specific findings of discrimination to engage in race-conscious relief. . . .

What appellant ignores is that Congress, unlike any State or political subdivision, has a specific constitutional mandate to enforce the dictates of the Fourteenth Amendment. The power to "enforce" may at times also include the power to define situations which *Congress* determines threaten principles of equality and to adopt prophylactic rules to deal with those situations. . . .

That Congress may identify and redress the effects of society-wide discrimination does not mean that, a fortiori, the States and their political subdivisions are free to decide that such remedies are appropriate. Section 1 of the Fourteenth Amendment is an explicit *constraint* on state power, and the States must undertake any remedial efforts in accordance with that provision. To hold otherwise would be to cede control over the content of the Equal Protection Clause to the 50 state legislatures and their myriad political subdivisions. The mere recitation of a benign or compensatory purpose for the use of a racial classification would essentially entitle the States to exercise the full power of Congress under § 5 of the Fourteenth Amendment and insulate any racial classification from judicial scrutiny under § 1. We believe that such a result would be contrary to the intentions of the Framers of the Fourteenth Amendment, who desired to place clear limits on the States' use of race as a criterion for legislative action, and to have the federal courts enforce those limitations. . . .

It would seem equally clear, however, that a state or local subdivision (if delegated the authority from the State) has the authority to eradicate the effects of private discrimination within its own legislative jurisdiction. This authority must, of course, be exercised within the constraints of § 1 of the Fourteenth Amendment.

Thus, if the city could show that it had essentially become a "passive participant" in a system of racial exclusion practiced by elements of the local construction industry, we think it clear that the city could take affirmative steps to dismantle such a system. It is beyond dispute that any public entity, state or federal, has a compelling interest in assuring that public dollars, drawn from the tax contributions of all citizens, do not serve to finance the evil of private prejudice. . . .

III

The Equal Protection Clause of the Fourteenth Amendment provides that "[n]o State shall . . . deny to *any person* within its jurisdiction the equal protection of the laws." (Emphasis added.) As this Court has noted in the past, the "rights created by the first section of the Fourteenth Amendment are, by its terms, guaranteed to the individual. The rights established are personal rights." The Richmond Plan denies certain citizens the opportunity to compete for a fixed percentage of public contracts based solely upon their race. To whatever racial group these citizens belong, their "personal rights" to be treated with equal dignity and respect are implicated by a rigid rule erecting race as the sole criterion in an aspect of public decisionmaking.

Absent searching judicial inquiry into the justification for such race-based measures, there is simply no way of determining what classifications are "benign" or "remedial" and what classifications are in fact motivated by illegitimate notions of racial inferiority or simple racial politics. Indeed, the purpose of strict scrutiny is to "smoke out" illegitimate uses of race by assuring that the legislative body is pursuing a goal important enough to warrant use of a highly suspect tool. The test also ensures that the means chosen "fit" this compelling goal so closely that there is little or no possibility that the motive for the classification was illegitimate racial prejudice or stereotype.

Classifications based on race carry a danger of stigmatic harm. Unless they are strictly reserved for remedial settings, they may in fact promote notions of racial inferiority and lead to a politics of racial hostility. . . .

Even were we to accept a reading of the guarantee of equal protection under which the level of scrutiny varies according to the ability of different groups to defend their interests in the representative process, heightened scrutiny would still be appropriate in the circumstances of this case. One of the central arguments for applying a less exacting standard to "benign" racial classifications is that such measures essentially involve a choice made by dominant racial groups to disadvantage themselves. If one aspect of the judiciary's role under the Equal Protection Clause is to protect "discrete and insular minorities" from majoritarian prejudice or indifference, see *United States v. Carolene Products Co.* [note 4] (1938), some maintain that these concerns are not implicated when the "white majority" places burdens upon itself.

In this case, blacks constitute approximately 50% of the population of the city of Richmond. Five of the nine seats on the city council are held by blacks. The concern that a political majority will more easily act to the disadvantage of a minority based on unwarranted assumptions or incomplete facts would seem to militate for, not against, the application of heightened judicial scrutiny in this case. . . .

Appellant argues that it is attempting to remedy various forms of past discrimination that are alleged to be responsible for the small number of minority businesses in the local contracting industry. Among these the city cites the exclusion of blacks from skilled construction trade unions and training programs. This past discrimination has prevented them "from following the traditional path from laborer to entrepreneur." The city also lists a host of nonracial factors which would seem to face a member of any racial group attempting to establish a new business enterprise, such as deficiencies in working capital, inability to meet bonding requirements, unfamiliarity with bidding procedures, and disability caused by an inadequate track record.

While there is no doubt that the sorry history of both private and public discrimination in this country has contributed to a lack of opportunities for black entrepreneurs, this observation, standing alone, cannot justify a rigid racial quota in the awarding of public contracts in Richmond, Virginia. Like the claim that discrimination in primary and secondary schooling justifies a rigid racial preference in medical school admissions, an amorphous claim that there has been past discrimination in a particular industry cannot justify the use of an unyielding racial quota.

It is sheer speculation how many minority firms there would be in Richmond absent past societal discrimination, just as it was sheer speculation how many minority medical students would have been admitted to the medical school at Davis absent past discrimination in educational opportunities. Defining these sorts of injuries as "identified discrimination" would give local governments license to create a patchwork of racial preferences based on statistical generalizations about any particular field of endeavor.

These defects are readily apparent in this case. The 30% quota cannot in any realistic sense be tied to any injury suffered by anyone. . . .

[T]he city council designated the Plan as "remedial." But the mere recitation of a "benign" or legitimate purpose for a racial classification is entitled to little or no weight. Racial classifications are suspect, and that means that simple legislative assurances of good intention cannot suffice.

Reliance on the disparity between the number of prime contracts awarded to minority firms and the minority population of the city of Richmond is similarly misplaced. . . .

[W]here special qualifications are necessary, the relevant statistical pool for purposes of demonstrating discriminatory exclusion must be the number of minorities qualified to undertake the particular task.

In this case, the city does not even know how many MBE's in the relevant market are qualified to undertake prime or subcontracting work in public construction projects. Nor does the city know what percentage of total city construction dollars minority firms now receive as subcontractors on prime contracts let by the city. . . .

Without any information on minority participation in subcontracting, it is quite simply impossible to evaluate overall minority representation in the city's construction expenditures.

The city and the District Court also relied on evidence that MBE membership in local contractors' associations was extremely low. Again, standing alone this evidence is not probative of any discrimination in the local construction industry. . . .

For low minority membership in these associations to be relevant, the city would have to link it to the number of local MBE's eligible for membership. . . .

Finally, the city and the District Court relied on Congress' finding in connection with the set-aside approved in *Fullilove* that there had been nationwide discrimination in the construction industry. The probative value of these findings for demonstrating the existence of discrimination in Richmond is extremely limited. . . .

While the States and their subdivisions may take remedial action when they possess evidence that their own spending practices are exacerbating a pattern of prior discrimination, they must identify that discrimination, public or private, with some specificity before they may use race-conscious relief. Congress has made national findings that there has been societal discrimination in a host of fields. If all a state or local government need do is find a congressional report on the subject to enact a set-aside program, the constraints of the Equal Protection Clause will, in effect, have been rendered a nullity. . . .

In sum, none of the evidence presented by the city points to any identified discrimination in the Richmond construction industry. We, therefore, hold that the city has failed to demonstrate a compelling interest in apportioning public contracting opportunities on the basis of race. To accept Richmond's claim that past societal discrimination alone can serve as the basis for rigid racial preferences would be to open the door to competing claims for "remedial relief" for every disadvantaged group. The dream of a Nation of equal citizens in a society where race is irrelevant to personal opportunity and achievement would be lost in a mosaic of shifting preferences based on inherently unmeasurable claims of past wrongs. We think such a result would be contrary to both the letter and spirit of a constitutional provision whose central command is equality.

The foregoing analysis applies only to the inclusion of blacks within the Richmond set-aside program. There is *absolutely no evidence* of past discrimination against Spanish-speaking, Oriental, Indian, Eskimo, or Aleut persons in any aspect of the Richmond construction industry. It may well be that Richmond has never had an Aleut or Eskimo citizen. The random inclusion of racial groups that, as a practical matter, may never have suffered from discrimination in the construction industry in Richmond suggests that perhaps the city's purpose was not in fact to remedy past discrimination.

If a 30% set-aside was "narrowly tailored" to compensate black contractors for past discrimination, one may legitimately ask why they are forced to share this "remedial relief" with an Aleut citizen who moves to Richmond tomorrow? The gross overinclusiveness of Richmond's racial preference strongly impugns the city's claim of remedial motivation.

IV

As noted by the court below, it is almost impossible to assess whether the Richmond Plan is narrowly tailored to remedy prior discrimination since it is not linked to identified discrimination in any way. We limit ourselves to two observations in this regard.

First, there does not appear to have been any consideration of the use of race-neutral means to increase minority business participation in city contracting. Many of the barriers to minority participation in the construction industry relied upon by the city to justify a racial classification appear to be race neutral. If MBE's disproportionately lack capital or cannot meet bonding requirements, a race-neutral program of city financing for small firms would, a fortiori, lead to greater minority participation. The principal opinion in *Fullilove* found that Congress had carefully examined and rejected race-neutral alternatives before enacting the MBE set-aside. There is no evidence in this record that the Richmond City Council has considered any alternatives to a race-based quota.

Second, the 30% quota cannot be said to be narrowly tailored to any goal, except perhaps outright racial balancing. It rests upon the "completely unrealistic" assumption that minorities will choose a particular trade in lockstep proportion to their representation in the local population. . . .

[T]he city's only interest in maintaining a quota system rather than investigating the need for remedial action in particular cases would seem to be simple administrative convenience. But the interest in avoiding the bureaucratic effort necessary to tailor remedial relief to those who truly have suffered the effects of prior discrimination cannot justify a rigid line drawn on the basis of a suspect classification. Under Richmond's scheme, a successful black, Hispanic, or Oriental entrepreneur from anywhere in the country enjoys an absolute preference over other citizens based solely on their race. We think it obvious that such a program is not narrowly tailored to remedy the effects of prior discrimination.

Nothing we say today precludes a state or local entity from taking action to rectify the effects of identified discrimination within its jurisdiction. . . . In the extreme case, some form of narrowly tailored racial preference might be necessary to break down patterns of deliberate exclusion. . . .

Even in the absence of evidence of discrimination, the city has at its disposal a whole array of race-neutral devices to increase the accessibility of city contracting opportunities to small entrepreneurs of all races. Simplification of bidding procedures, relaxation of bonding requirements, and training and financial aid for disadvantaged entrepreneurs of all races would open the public contracting market to all those who have suffered the effects of past societal discrimination or neglect. The city may also act to prohibit discrimination in the provision of credit or bonding by local suppliers and banks. . . .

In the case at hand, the city has not ascertained how many minority enterprises are present in the local construction market nor the level of their participation in city construction projects. . . .

Proper findings in this regard are necessary to define both the scope of the injury and the extent of the remedy necessary to cure its effects. Such findings also serve to assure all citizens that the deviation from the norm of equal treatment of all racial and ethnic groups is a temporary matter, a measure taken in the service of the goal of equality itself. Absent such findings, there is a danger that a racial classification is merely the product of unthinking stereotypes or a form of racial politics. . . .

Because the city of Richmond has failed to identify the need for remedial action in the awarding of its public construction contracts, its treatment of its citizens on a racial basis violates the dictates of the Equal Protection Clause.

JUSTICE STEVENS, CONCURRING IN PART
AND CONCURRING IN THE JUDGMENT:

The justification for the ordinance is the fact that in the past white contractors—and presumably other white citizens in Richmond—have discriminated against black contractors. The class of persons benefited by the ordinance is not, however, limited to victims of such discrimination—it encompasses persons who have never been in business in Richmond as well as minority contractors who may have been guilty of discriminating against members of other minority groups. Indeed, for all the record shows, all of the minority-business enterprises that have benefited from the ordinance may be firms that have prospered notwithstanding the discriminatory conduct that may have harmed other minority firms years ago. Ironically, minority firms that have survived in the competitive struggle, rather than those that have perished, are most likely to benefit from an ordinance of this kind.

The ordinance is equally vulnerable because of its failure to identify the characteristics of the disadvantaged class of white contractors that justify the disparate treatment. That class unquestionably includes some white contractors who are guilty of past discrimination against blacks, but it is only habit, rather than evidence or analysis, that makes it seem acceptable to assume that every white contractor covered by the ordinance shares in that guilt. Indeed, even among those who have discriminated in the past, it must be assumed that at least some of them have complied with the city ordinance that has made such discrimination unlawful since 1975. Thus, the composition of the disadvantaged class of white contractors presumably includes some who have been guilty of unlawful discrimination, some who practiced discrimination before it was forbidden by law, and some who have never discriminated against anyone on the basis of race. Imposing a common burden on such a disparate class merely because each member of the class is of the same race stems from reliance on a stereotype rather than fact or reason.

[Justice Kennedy concurred in the judgment.]

JUSTICE SCALIA, CONCURRING IN THE JUDGMENT:

I do not agree . . . with . . . Justice O'Connor's dictum suggesting that, despite the Fourteenth Amendment, state and local governments may in some circumstances discriminate on the basis of race in order (in a broad sense) ''to ameliorate the effects of past discrimination.'' The benign purpose of compensating for social disadvantages, whether they have been acquired by reason of prior discrimination or otherwise, can no more be pursued by the illegitimate means of racial discrimination than can other assertedly benign purposes we have repeatedly rejected. The difficulty of overcoming the effects of past discrimination is as nothing compared with the difficulty of eradicating from our society the source of those effects, which is the tendency— fatal to a Nation such as ours—to classify and judge men and women on the basis of their country of origin or the color of their skin. . . .

In my view there is only one circumstance in which the States may act *by race* to ''undo the effects of past discrimination'': where that is necessary to eliminate their own maintenance of a system of unlawful racial classification. If, for example, a state agency has a discriminatory pay scale compensating black employees in all positions at 20% less than their nonblack counterparts, it may assuredly promulgate an order raising the salaries of ''all black employees'' to eliminate the differential. This distinction explains our school desegregation cases, in which we have made plain that States and localities sometimes have an obligation to adopt race-conscious remedies. . . .

While thus permitting the use of race to *de*classify racially classified students, teachers, and educational resources, however, we have also made it clear that the remedial power extends no further than the scope of the continuing constitutional violation. And it is implicit in our cases that after the dual school system has been completely disestablished, the States may no longer assign students by race. . . .

A State can, of course, act "to undo the effects of past discrimination" in many permissible ways that do not involve classification by race. In the particular field of state contracting, for example, it may adopt a preference for small businesses, or even for new businesses—which would make it easier for those previously excluded by discrimination to enter the field. Such programs may well have racially disproportionate impact, but they are not based on race. And, of course, a State may "undo the effects of past discrimination" in the sense of giving the identified victim of state discrimination that which it wrongfully denied him—for example, giving to a previously rejected black applicant the job that, by reason of discrimination, had been awarded to a white applicant, even if this means terminating the latter's employment. In such a context, the white jobholder is not being selected for disadvantageous treatment because of his race, but because he was wrongfully awarded a job to which another is entitled. That is worlds apart from the system here, in which those to be disadvantaged are identified solely by race. . . .

It is plainly true that in our society blacks have suffered discrimination immeasurably greater than any directed at other racial groups. But those who believe that racial preferences can help to "even the score" display, and reinforce, a manner of thinking by race that was the source of the injustice and that will, if it endures within our society, be the source of more injustice still. Racial preferences appear to "even the score" (in some small degree) only if one embraces the proposition that our society is appropriately viewed as divided into races, making it right that an injustice rendered in the past to a black man should be compensated for by discriminating against a white. Nothing is worth that embrace.

JUSTICE MARSHALL, WITH WHOM JUSTICE BRENNAN AND JUSTICE BLACKMUN JOIN, DISSENTING:

It is a welcome symbol of racial progress when the former capital of the Confederacy acts forthrightly to confront the effects of racial discrimination in its midst. In my view, nothing in the Constitution can be construed to prevent Richmond, Virginia, from allocating a portion of its contracting dollars for businesses owned or controlled by members of minority groups. . . .

The essence of the majority's position is that Richmond has failed to catalog adequate findings to prove that past discrimination has impeded minorities from joining or participating fully in Richmond's construction contracting industry. I find deep irony in second-guessing Richmond's judgment on this point. As much as any municipality in the United States, Richmond knows what racial discrimination is. In any event, the Richmond City Council *has* supported its determination that minorities have been wrongly excluded from local construction contracting. Its proof includes statistics showing that minority-owned businesses have received virtually no city contracting dollars and rarely if ever belonged to area trade associations; testimony by municipal officials that discrimination has been widespread in the local construction industry; and the same exhaustive and widely publicized federal studies relied on in *Fullilove*, studies which showed that pervasive discrimination in the Nation's tight-knit construction industry had operated to exclude minorities from public contracting. These are precisely the types of statistical and testimonial evidence which, until today, this Court had credited in cases approving of race-conscious measures designed to remedy past discrimination.

More fundamentally, today's decision marks a deliberate and giant step backward in this Court's affirmative-action jurisprudence. Cynical of one municipality's attempt to redress the effects of past racial discrimination in a particular industry, the majority launches a grapeshot attack on race-conscious remedies in general. The majority's unnecessary pronouncements will inevitably discourage or prevent governmental entities, particularly States and localities, from acting to rectify the scourge of past discrimination. This is the harsh reality of the majority's decision, but it is not the Constitution's command.

JUSTICE BLACKMUN, WITH WHOM JUSTICE BRENNAN JOINS, DISSENTING:

I never thought that I would live to see the day when the city of Richmond, Virginia, the cradle of the Old Confederacy, sought on its own, within a narrow confine, to lessen the stark impact of persistent discrimination. But Richmond, to its great credit, acted. Yet this Court, the supposed bastion of equality, strikes down Richmond's efforts as though discrimination had never existed or was not demonstrated in this particular litigation. . . .

So the Court today regresses. I am confident, however, that, given time, it one day again will do its best to fulfill the great promises of the Constitution's Preamble and of the guarantees embodied in the Bill of Rights—a fulfillment that would make this Nation very special.

Gender discrimination violates the Constitution.

41. *Reed v. Reed* (1971)

Legal classifications based on gender, like those based on race, have come under increasing judicial assault. Concern about gender discrimination is, however, a relatively recent development; it almost certainly was not part of the original understanding of those who drafted the Fourteenth Amendment. It must be remembered that the Nineteenth Amendment was adopted in 1920 to give women a constitutional right to vote.

Background: An Idaho law gave preference to males over equally qualified females for appointment to administer the estate of a relative who dies intestate. The Idaho Supreme Court upheld the preference as based on legal convenience but was reversed by the Supreme Court.

MR. CHIEF JUSTICE BURGER DELIVERED
THE OPINION OF THE COURT:

Richard Lynn Reed, a minor, died intestate in Ada County, Idaho, on March 29, 1967. . . . [H]is mother, appellant Sally Reed, filed a petition . . . seeking appointment as administratrix of her son's estate. . . . [A]ppellee Cecil Reed, the father of the decedent, filed a competing petition seeking to have himself appointed administrator of the son's estate. The probate court held a joint hearing on the two petitions and thereafter ordered that letters of administration be issued to appellee Cecil Reed upon his taking the oath and filing the bond required by law. The court treated the Idaho Code . . . as compelling a preference for Cecil Reed because he was a male.

[Idaho law] . . . designates the persons who are entitled to administer the estate of one who dies intestate. . . . [It] lists 11 classes of persons who are so entitled and provides, in substance, that the order in which those classes are listed in the section shall be determinative of the relative rights of competing applicants for letters of administration. One of the 11 classes so enumerated is "[t]he father or mother" of the person dying intestate. Under this section, then, appellant and appellee, being members of the same entitlement class, would seem to have been equally entitled to administer their son's estate. [However, the law also provides] that "[o]f several persons claiming and equally entitled to administer, males must be preferred to females. . . ."

In issuing its order, the probate court implicitly recognized the equality of entitlement of the two applicants . . . and noted that neither of the applicants was under any legal disability; the court ruled, however, that appellee, being a male, was to be preferred to the female appellant "by reason of . . . the Idaho Code." In stating this conclusion, the probate judge gave no indication that he had attempted to determine the relative capabilities of the competing applicants to perform the functions incident to the administration of an estate. It seems clear the probate judge considered himself bound by statute to give preference to the male candidate over the female, each being otherwise "equally entitled." . . .

Sally Reed thereupon appealed for review by this Court. . . . [W]e have concluded that the arbitrary preference established in favor of males by . . . the Idaho Code cannot stand in the face of the Fourteenth Amendment's command that no State deny the equal protection of the laws to any person within its jurisdiction. . . .

In applying that clause, this Court has consistently recognized that the Fourteenth Amendment does not deny to States the power to treat different classes of persons in different ways.

The Equal Protection Clause of that amendment does, however, deny to States the power to legislate that different treatment be accorded to persons placed by a statute into different classes on the basis of criteria wholly unrelated to the objective of that statute. . . . The question presented by this case, then, is whether a difference in the sex of competing applicants for letters of administration bears a rational relationship to a state objective that is sought to be advanced by the operation of [this law].

In upholding the [law], the Idaho Supreme Court concluded that its objective was to eliminate one area of controversy when two or more persons, equally entitled under [Idaho law], seek letters of administration and thereby present the probate court "with the issue of which one should be named." The court also concluded that where such persons are not of the same sex, the elimination of females from consideration "is neither an illogical nor arbitrary method devised by the legislature to resolve an issue that would otherwise require a hearing as to the relative merits . . . of the two or more petitioning relatives. . . ."

Clearly the objective of reducing the workload on probate courts by eliminating one class of contests is not without some legitimacy. The crucial question, however, is whether [this law] advances that objective in a manner consistent with the command of the Equal Protection Clause. We hold that it does not. To give a mandatory preference to members of either sex over members of the other, merely to accomplish the elimination of hearings on the merits, is to make the very kind of arbitrary legislative choice forbidden by the Equal Protection Clause of the Fourteenth Amendment.

Equal protection also forbids discrimination against males.

42. *Mississippi University for Women v. Hogan* (1982)

The ban on governmental policies discriminating against females, which the Court announced in such cases as *Frontiero v. Richardson* (1974) and *Reed v. Reed*, was soon extended to include discrimination against males, as this case demonstrates.

Background: Joe Hogan sought admission to the Mississippi University for Women, a state-supported school of nursing, and was rejected solely on the ground that admission was limited to female students. The district court, pointing to the benefits of single-sex education for women, upheld the university, but the court of appeals was sustained in its reversal by the Supreme Court.

JUSTICE O'CONNOR DELIVERED
THE OPINION OF THE COURT:

This case presents the narrow issue of whether a state statute that excludes males from enrolling in a state-supported professional nursing school violates the Equal Protection Clause of the Fourteenth Amendment. . . .

I

In 1979, [Joe] Hogan applied for admission to the MUW School of Nursing's baccalaureate program. Although he was otherwise qualified, he was denied admission to the School of Nursing solely because of his sex. School officials informed him that he could audit the courses in which he was interested, but could not enroll for credit. . . .

II

We begin our analysis aided by several firmly established principles. Because the challenged policy expressly discriminates among applicants on the basis of gender, it is subject to scrutiny under the Equal Protection Clause of the Fourteenth Amendment. That this statutory policy discriminates against males rather than against females does not exempt it from scrutiny or reduce the standard of review. Our decisions also establish that the party seeking to uphold a statute that classifies individuals on the basis of their gender must carry the burden of showing an "exceedingly persuasive justification" for the classification. The burden is met only by showing at least that the classification serves "important governmental objectives and that the discriminatory means employed" are "substantially related to the achievement of those objectives." . . .

If the State's objective is legitimate and important, we next determine whether the requisite direct, substantial relationship between objective and means is present. The purpose of requiring that close relationship is to assure that the validity of a classification is determined through reasoned analysis rather than through the mechanical application of traditional, often inaccurate, assumptions about the proper roles of men and women. . . .

III

The State's primary justification for maintaining the single-sex admissions policy of MUW's School of Nursing is that it compensates for discrimination against women and, therefore, constitutes educational affirmative action. As applied to the School of Nursing, we find the State's argument unpersuasive. . . .

Mississippi has made no showing that women lacked opportunities to obtain training in the field of nursing or to attain positions of leadership in that field when the MUW School of Nursing opened its door or that women currently are deprived of such opportunities. In fact, in 1970, the year before the School of Nursing's first class enrolled, women earned 94 percent of the nursing baccalaureate degrees conferred in Mississippi and 98.6 percent of the degrees earned nationwide. That year was not an aberration; one decade earlier, women had earned all the nursing degrees conferred in Mississippi and 98.9 percent of the degrees conferred nationwide. As one would expect, the labor force reflects the same predominance of women in nursing. When MUW's School of Nursing began operation, nearly 98 percent of all employed registered nurses were female.

Rather than compensate for discriminatory barriers faced by women, MUW's policy of excluding males from admission to the School of Nursing tends to perpetuate the stereotyped view of nursing as an exclusively woman's job. By assuring that Mississippi allots more openings in its state-supported nursing schools to women than it does to men, MUW's admissions policy lends credibility to the old view that women, not men, should become nurses, and makes the assumption that nursing is a field for women a self-fulfilling prophecy. Thus, we conclude that, although the State recited a "benign, compensatory purpose," it failed to establish that the alleged objective is the actual purpose underlying the discriminatory classification.

The policy is invalid also because it fails the second part of the equal protection test, for the State has made no showing that the gender-based classification is substantially and directly related to its proposed compensatory objective. To the contrary, MUW's policy of permitting men to attend classes as auditors fatally undermines its claim that women, at least those in the School of Nursing, are adversely affected by the presence of men. . . .

Thus, considering both the asserted interest and the relationship between the interest and the methods used by the State, we conclude that the State has fallen far short of establishing the "exceedingly persuasive justification" needed to sustain the gender-based classification. Accordingly, we hold that MUW's policy of denying males the right to enroll for credit in its School of Nursing violates the Equal Protection Clause of the Fourteenth Amendment.

[Chief Justice Burger wrote a dissenting opinion.]

JUSTICE BLACKMUN, DISSENTING:

I have come to suspect that it is easy to go too far with rigid rules in this area of claimed sex discrimination, and to lose—indeed destroy—values that mean much to some people by forbidding the State to offer them a choice while not depriving others of an alternative choice. . . .

[This] ruling, it seems to me, places in constitutional jeopardy any state-supported educational institution that confines its student body in any area to members of one sex, even though the State elsewhere provides an equivalent program to the complaining applicant. The Court's reasoning does not stop with the School of Nursing of the Mississippi University for Women.

JUSTICE POWELL, WITH WHOM JUSTICE REHNQUIST JOINS, DISSENTING:

The Court's opinion bows deeply to conformity. Left without honor—indeed, held unconstitutional—is an element of diversity that has characterized much of American education and enriched much of American life. The Court in effect holds today that no State now may provide even a single institution of higher learning open only to women students. It gives no heed to the efforts of the State of Mississippi to provide abundant opportunities for young men and young women to attend coeducational institutions, and none to the preferences of the more than 40,000 young women who over the years have evidenced their approval of an all-women's college by choosing Mississippi University for Women (MUW) over seven coeducational universities within the State. . . .

Nor is respondent significantly disadvantaged by MUW's all-female tradition. His constitutional complaint is based upon a single asserted harm: that he must *travel* to attend the state-supported nursing schools that concededly are available to him. The Court characterizes this injury as one of "inconvenience." This description is fair and accurate, though somewhat embarrassed by the fact that there is, of course, no constitutional right to attend a state-supported university in one's home town. Thus the Court, to redress respondent's injury of inconvenience, must rest its invalidation of MUW's single-sex program on a mode of "sexual stereotype" reasoning that has no application whatever to the respondent or to the "wrong" of which he complains. . . .

I

Coeducation, historically, is a novel educational theory. From grade school through high school, college, and graduate and professional training, much of the Nation's population during much of our history has been educated in sexually segregated classrooms. At the college level, for instance, until recently some of the most prestigious colleges and universities—including most of the Ivy League—had long histories of single-sex education. As Harvard, Yale, and Princeton remained all-male colleges well into the second half of this century, the "Seven Sister" institutions established a parallel standard of excellence for women's colleges. . . .

The sexual segregation of students has been a reflection of, rather than an imposition upon, the preference of those subject to the policy. It cannot be disputed, for example, that the highly qualified women attending the leading women's colleges could have earned admission to virtually any college of their choice. Women attending such colleges have chosen to be there, usually expressing a preference for the special benefits of single-sex institutions. Similar decisions were made by the colleges that elected to remain open to women only. . . .

II

The issue in this case is whether a State transgresses the Constitution when—within the context of a public system that offers a diverse range of campuses, curricula, and educational alternatives—it seeks to accommodate the legitimate personal preferences of those desiring the advantages of an all-women's college. In my view, the Court errs seriously by assuming—without argument or discussion—that the equal protection standard generally applicable to sex discrimination is appropriate here. . . . In no previous case have we applied it to invalidate state efforts to *expand* women's choices. . . .

By applying heightened equal protection analysis to this case, the

Court frustrates the liberating spirit of the Equal Protection Clause. It prohibits the States from providing women with an opportunity to choose the type of university they prefer. And yet it is these women whom the Court regards as the *victims* of an illegal, stereotyped perception of the role of women in our society. The Court reasons this way in a case in which no woman has complained, and the only complainant is a man who advances no claims on behalf of anyone else. . . .

III

I can accept for present purposes the standard applied by the Court: that there is a gender-based distinction that must serve an important governmental objective by means that are substantially related to its achievement. The record in this case reflects that MUW has a historic position in the State's educational system dating back to 1884. More than 2,000 women presently evidence their preference for MUW by having enrolled there. The choice is one that discriminates invidiously against no one. And the State's purpose in preserving that choice is legitimate and substantial. Generations of our finest minds, both among educators and students, have believed that single-sex, college-level institutions afford distinctive benefits.

IV

A distinctive feature of America's tradition has been respect for diversity. This has been characteristic of the peoples from numerous lands who have built our country. It is the essence of our democratic system. At stake in this case as I see it is the preservation of a small aspect of this diversity. But that aspect is by no means insignificant, given our heritage of available choice between single-sex and coeducational institutions of higher learning. The Court answers that there is discrimination—not just that which may be tolerable, as for example between those candidates for admission able to contribute most to an educational institution and those able to contribute less—but discrimination of constitutional dimension. But, having found "discrimination," the Court finds it difficult to identify the victims. It hardly can claim that women are discriminated against. A constitutional case is held to exist solely because one man found it inconvenient to travel to any of the other institutions made available to him by the State of Mississippi. In essence he insists that he has a right to attend a college in his home community. This simply is not a sex discrimination case. The Equal Protection Clause was never intended to be applied to this kind of case.

State electoral districts must be apportioned according to population.

43. *Reynolds v. Sims* (1964)

In *Baker v. Carr* (1962), a memorable case with far-reaching implications, the Supreme Court entered the area of state reapportionment, hitherto shunned as a "political" and therefore "nonjusticiable" question, that is, one unsuitable for judicial decision.

The Court ruled that the subject of apportionment was constitutionally "justiciable" and that electoral malapportionment was a violation of the equal protection guarantee of the Fourteenth Amendment. However, the guidelines for the implementation of this decision were only spelled out in later cases, particularly *Reynolds v. Sims*, where the Court ordered the states to redraw their electoral districts according to population, on a standard of "one man, one vote." These rulings compelled the reapportionment of the great majority of state legislatures. It should be added that the same principle was also applied to congressional districts (through Art. I, Sec. 2 of the Constitution) in *Wesberry v. Sanders* (1964).

Background: Alabama had last apportioned its legislature in 1900, ignoring the requirement of its own state constitution for a decennial reapportionment. It was alleged that population growth since that time had resulted in serious inequities in the allocation of legislative representatives. Electoral districts varied in population from 6,731 to 104,767 in the lower house of the state legislature, and from 15,147 to 634,864 in the upper house. A three-judge federal district court found this scheme unconstitutional. The Supreme Court agreed.

MR. CHIEF JUSTICE WARREN DELIVERED
THE OPINION OF THE COURT:

Plaintiffs below alleged that the last apportionment of the Alabama Legislature was based on the 1900 federal census, despite the requirement of the State Constitution that the legislature be reapportioned decennially. They asserted that, since the population growth in the State from 1900 to 1960 had been uneven, Jefferson and other counties were now victims of serious discrimination with respect to the allocation of legislative representation. As a result of the failure of the legislature to reapportion itself, plaintiffs asserted, they were denied "equal suffrage in free and equal elections . . . and the equal protection of the laws." . . .

The right to vote freely for the candidate of one's choice is of the essence of a democratic society, and any restrictions on that right strike at the heart of representative government. And the right of suffrage can be denied by a debasement or dilution of the weight of a citizen's vote just as effectively as by wholly prohibiting the free exercise of the franchise. . . .

Legislators represent people, not trees or acres. Legislators are elected by voters, not farms or cities or economic interests. As long as ours is a representative form of government, and our legislatures are those instruments of government elected directly by and directly representative of the people, the right to elect legislators in a free and unimpaired fashion is a bedrock of our political system. It could hardly be gainsaid that a constitutional claim had been asserted by an allegation that certain otherwise qualified voters had been entirely prohibited from voting for members of their state legislature. And, if a State should provide that the votes of citizens in one part of the State should be given two times, or five times, or 10 times the weight of votes of citizens in another part of the State, it could hardly be contended that the right to vote of those residing in the disfavored areas had not been effectively diluted. It would appear extraordinary to suggest that a State could be constitutionally permitted to enact a law providing that certain of the State's voters could vote two, five, or 10 times for their legislative representatives, while voters living elsewhere could vote only once. And it is inconceivable that a state law to the effect that, in counting votes for legislators, the votes of citizens in one part of the

State would be multiplied by two, five, or 10, while the votes of persons in another area would be counted only at face value, could be constitutionally sustainable. Of course, the effect of state legislative districting schemes which give the same number of representatives to unequal numbers of constituents is identical. Overweighting and overvaluation of the votes of those living here has the certain effect of dilution and undervaluation of the votes of those living there. The resulting discrimination against those individual voters living in disfavored areas is easily demonstrable mathematically. Their right to vote is simply not the same right to vote as that of those living in a favored part of the State. Two, five, or 10 of them must vote before the effect of their voting is equivalent to that of their favored neighbor. Weighting the votes of citizens differently, by any method or means, merely because of where they happen to reside, hardly seems justifiable. . . .

Diluting the weight of votes because of place of residence impairs basic constitutional rights under the Fourteenth Amendment just as much as invidious discriminations based upon factors such as race, or economic status. Our constitutional system amply provides for the protection of minorities by means other than giving them majority control of state legislatures. And the democratic ideals of equality and majority rule, which have served this Nation so well in the past, are hardly of any less significance for the present and the future. . . .

To the extent that a citizen's right to vote is debased, he is that much less a citizen. The fact that an individual lives here or there is not a legitimate reason for overweighting or diluting the efficacy of his vote. The complexions of societies and civilizations change, often with amazing rapidity. A nation once primarily rural in character becomes predominantly urban. Representation schemes once fair and equitable become archaic and outdated. But the basic principle of representative government remains, and must remain, unchanged—the weight of a citizen's vote cannot be made to depend on where he lives. Population is, of necessity, the starting point for consideration and the controlling criterion for judgment in legislative apportionment controversies. A citizen, a qualified voter, is no more nor no less so because he lives in the city or on the farm. This is the clear and strong command of our Constitution's Equal Protection Clause. . . .

Much has been written since our decision in *Baker v. Carr* about the applicability of the so-called federal analogy to state legislative apportionment arrangements. . . . We find the federal analogy inapposite and irrelevant to state legislative districting schemes. Attempted reliance on the federal analogy appears often to be little more than an after-the-fact rationalization offered in defense of maladjusted state apportionment arrangements. . . .

The system of representation in the two Houses of the Federal Congress is one ingrained in our Constitution, as part of the law of the land. It is one conceived out of compromise and concession indispensable to the establishment of our federal republic. Arising from unique historical circumstances, it is based on the consideration that in establishing our type of federalism a group of formerly independent States bound themselves together under one national government. Admittedly, the original 13 States surrendered some of their sovereignty in agreeing to join together "to form a more perfect Union." But at the heart of our constitutional system remains the concept of separate and distinct governmental entities which have delegated some, but not all, of their formerly held powers to the single national government. . . .

Political subdivisions of States—counties, cities, or whatever—never were and never have been considered as sovereign entities. Rather, they have been traditionally regarded as subordinate governmental instrumentalities created by the State to assist in the carrying out of state governmental functions. . . .

Since we find the so-called federal analogy inapposite to a consideration of the constitutional validity of state legislative apportionment schemes, we necessarily hold that the Equal Protection Clause requires both houses of a state legislature to be apportioned on a population basis. The right of a citizen to equal representation and to have his vote weighted equally with those of all other citizens in the election of members of one house of a bicameral state legislature would amount to little if States could effectively submerge the equal-population principle in the apportionment of seats in the other house. If such a scheme were permissible, an individual citizen's ability to exercise an effective voice in the only instrument of state government directly representative of the people might be almost as effectively thwarted as if neither house were apportioned on a population basis. Deadlock between the two bodies might result in compromise and concession on some issues. But in all too many cases the more probable result would be frustration of the majority will through minority veto in the house not apportioned on a population basis, stemming directly from the failure to accord adequate overall legislative representation to all of the State's citizens on a nondiscriminatory basis. In summary, we can perceive no constitutional difference, with respect to the geographical distribution of state legislative representation, between the two houses of a bicameral state legislature.

We do not believe that the concept of bicameralism is rendered anachronistic and meaningless when the predominant basis of representation in the two state legislative bodies is required to be the same —population. A prime reason for bicameralism, modernly considered, is to insure mature and deliberate consideration of, and to prevent precipitate action on, proposed legislative measures. Simply because the controlling criterion for apportioning representation is required to be the same in both houses does not mean that there will be no differences in the composition and complexion of the two bodies. Different constituencies can be represented in the two houses. One body could be composed of single-member districts while the other could have at least some multimember districts. The length of terms of the legislators in the separate bodies could differ. The numerical size of the two bodies could be made to differ, even significantly, and the geographical size of districts from which legislators are elected could also be made to differ. And apportionment in one house could be arranged so as to balance off minor inequities in the representation of certain areas in the other house. In summary, these and other factors could be, and are presently in many States, utilized to engender differing complexions and collective attitudes in the two bodies of a state legislature, although both are apportioned substantially on a population basis.

By holding that as a federal constitutional requisite both houses of a state legislature must be apportioned on a population basis, we mean that the Equal Protection Clause requires that a State make an honest and good faith effort to construct districts, in both houses of its legislature, as nearly of equal population as is practicable. We realize that it is a practical impossibility to arrange legislative districts so that each one has an identical number of residents, or citizens, or voters. Mathematical exactness or precision is hardly a workable constitutional requirement.

[Mr. Justice Clark and Mr. Justice Stewart wrote concurring opinions.]

MR. JUSTICE HARLAN, DISSENTING:

[Our reapportionment] decisions . . . cut deeply into the fabric of our federalism. What must follow from them may eventually appear to be the product of state legislatures. Nevertheless, no thinking person can fail to recognize that the aftermath of these cases, however desirable it may be thought in itself, will have been achieved at the cost of a radical alteration in the relationship between the States and the Federal Government, more particularly the Federal Judiciary. Only one who has an overbearing impatience with the federal system and its political processes will believe that that cost was not too high or was inevitable.

Finally, these decisions give support to a current mistaken view of the Constitution and the constitutional function of this Court. This view, in a nutshell, is that every major social ill in this country can find its cure in some constitutional "principle," and that this Court should "take the lead" in promoting reform when other branches of government fail to act. The Constitution is not a panacea for every blot upon the public welfare, nor should this Court, ordained as a judicial body, be thought of as a general haven for reform movements. The Constitution is an instrument of government, fundamental to which is the premise that in a diffusion of governmental authority lies the greatest promise that this Nation will realize liberty for all its citizens. This Court, limited in function in accordance with that premise, does not serve its high purpose when it exceeds its authority, even to satisfy justified impatience with the slow workings of the political process. For when, in the name of constitutional interpretation, the Court *adds* something to the Constitution that was deliberately excluded from it, the Court in reality substitutes its view of what should be so for the amending process.

CHAPTER IX

Civil Liberties:
First Amendment Freedoms

"Congress shall make no law respecting an establishment of religion, or prohibiting the free exercise thereof; or abridging the freedom of speech, or of the press; or the right of the people peaceably to assemble and to petition the government for a redress of grievances."—First Amendment

A. Freedom of Speech and of the Press

The freedoms of speech and press may be abridged when they present "a clear and present danger" to the community.

44. *Schenck v. United States* (1919)

This case is significant because of the Court's formulation of the famous "clear and present danger" test to draw a constitutional line between valid and invalid government restraints on expression.

Background: Schenck, secretary of the Socialist Party, printed and sent through the mails pacifist literature designed to obstruct military recruitment and enlistment. Indicted under the Espionage Act of 1917, he claimed that the act violated the First Amendment. Speaking for a unanimous Court, Justice Holmes upheld the conviction on the ground that when there is a "clear and present danger" that the words used "will bring about the substantive evils that Congress has a right to prevent," restraints on speech may be imposed. In the particular circumstances of this case, Holmes stressed the imperatives of wartime:

"When a nation is at war many things that might be said in time of peace . . . will not be endured so long as men fight."

MR. JUSTICE HOLMES DELIVERED
THE OPINION OF THE COURT:

The defendants were found guilty on all the counts. They set up [as a defense] the 1st Amendment to the Constitution, forbidding Congress to make any law abridging the freedom of speech or of the press. . . .

The document in question, upon its first printed side, recited the 1st section of the 13th Amendment, said that the idea embodied in it was violated by the Conscription Act, and that a conscript is little better than a convict. In impassioned language it intimated that conscription was despotism in its worst form and a monstrous wrong against humanity, in the interest of Wall Street's chosen few. It said: "Do not submit to intimidation;" but in form at least confined itself to peaceful measures, such as a petition for the repeal of the act. The other and later printed side of the sheet was headed, "Assert Your Rights." It stated reasons for alleging that anyone violated the Constitution when he refused to recognize "your right to assert your opposition to the draft," and went on: "If you do not assert and support your rights, you are helping to deny or disparage rights which it is the solemn duty of all citizens and residents of the United States to retain." It described the arguments on the other side as coming from cunning politicians and a mercenary capitalist press, and even silent consent to the Conscription Law as helping to support an infamous conspiracy. It denied the power to send our citizens away to foreign shores to shoot up the people of other lands, and added that words could not express the condemnation such coldblooded ruthlessness deserves, etc., etc., winding up, "You must do your share to maintain, support, and uphold the rights of the people of this country." Of course the document would not have been sent unless it had been intended to have some effect, and we do not see what effect it could be expected to have upon persons subject to the draft except to influence them to obstruct the carrying of it out. The defendants do not deny that the jury might find against them on this point.

But it is said, suppose that that was the tendency of this circular, it is protected by the 1st Amendment to the Constitution. Two of the strongest expressions are said to be quoted respectively from well-known public men. It well may be that the prohibition of laws abridging the freedom of speech is not confined to previous restraints, although to prevent them may have been the main purpose, as intimated in *Paterson v. Colorado* [1907].

We admit that in many places and in ordinary times the defendants, in saying all that was said in the circular, would have been within their constitutional rights. But the character of every act depends upon the circumstances in which it is done. The most stringent protection of free speech would not protect a man in falsely shouting fire in a theater, and causing a panic. It does not even protect a man from an injunction against uttering words that may have all the effect of force. The question in every case is whether the words used are used in such circumstances and are of such a nature as to create a clear and present danger that they will bring about the substantive evils that Congress has a right to prevent. It is a question of proximity and degree. When a nation is at war many things that might be said in time of peace are such a hindrance to its effort that their utterance will not be endured so long as men fight, and that no court could regard them as protected by any constitutional right. It seems to be admitted that if an actual obstruction of the recruiting service were proved, liability for words that produced that effect might be enforced. The Statute of 1917, in § 4, punishes conspiracies to obstruct as well as actual obstruction. If the act (speaking, or circulating a paper), its tendency and the intent with which it is done, are the same, we perceive no ground for saying that success alone warrants making the act a crime.

The First Amendment does not protect conspiracy to advocate the overthrow of the government.

45. *Dennis v. United States* (1951)

The Court held that advocacy of revolution could be made a criminal offense, even where no tangible action toward that end had been taken. Such advocacy is not protected by the First Amendment.

Background: In 1949, Dennis and other Communist leaders were tried under the Smith Act of 1940 for conspiracy to advocate the overthrow of the government. Found guilty, they appealed to the Supreme

Court on the ground that the Smith Act violated the First Amendment. The Court rejected their appeal under a watered-down "clear and present danger" test. The Court's position was subsequently modified in *Yates v. United States* (1957), by making it more difficult for the government to prove "advocacy."

MR. CHIEF JUSTICE VINSON ANNOUNCED THE JUDGMENT OF THE COURT AND AN OPINION IN WHICH MR. JUSTICE REED, MR. JUSTICE BURTON AND MR. JUSTICE MINTON JOIN:

Sections 2 and 3 of the Smith Act provide as follows:
"Sec. 2.

"(a) It shall be unlawful for any person—

"(1) to knowingly or willfully advocate, abet, advise, or teach the duty, necessity, desirability, or propriety of overthrowing or destroying any government in the United States by force or violence, or by the assassination of any officer of such government;

"(2) with the intent to cause the overthrow or destruction of any government in the United States, to print, publish, edit, issue, circulate, sell, distribute, or publicly display any written or printed matter advocating, advising, or teaching the duty, necessity, desirability, or propriety of overthrowing or destroying any government in the United States by force or violence;

"(3) to organize or help to organize any society, group, or assembly of persons who teach, advocate, or encourage the overthrow or destruction of any government in the United States by force or violence; or to be or become a member of, or affiliate with, any such society, group, or assembly of persons, knowing the purposes thereof. . . .

"Sec. 3. It shall be unlawful for any person to attempt to commit, or to conspire to commit, any of the acts prohibited by the provisions of . . . this title." . . .

The obvious purpose of the statute is to protect existing Government, not from change by peaceable, lawful and constitutional means, but from change by violence, revolution and terrorism. That it is within the *power* of the Congress to protect the Government of the United States from armed rebellion is a proposition which requires little discussion. Whatever theoretical merit there may be to the argument that there is a "right" to rebellion against dictatorial governments is without force where the existing structure of the government provides for peaceful and orderly change. We reject any principle of governmental helplessness in the face of preparation for revolution, which principle, carried to its logical conclusion, must lead to anarchy. No one could conceive that it is not within the power of Congress to prohibit acts intended to overthrow the Government by force and violence. The question with which we are concerned here is not whether Congress has such *power*, but whether the *means* which it has employed conflict with the First and Fifth Amendments to the Constitution.

One of the bases for the contention that the means which Congress has employed are invalid takes the form of an attack on the face of the statute on the grounds that by its terms it prohibits academic discussion of the merits of Marxism-Leninism, that it stifles ideas and is contrary to all concepts of a free speech and a free press. . . .

The very language of the Smith Act negates the interpretation which petitioners would have us impose on that Act. It is directed at advocacy, not discussion. Thus, the trial judge properly charged the jury that they could not convict if they found that petitioners did "no more than pursue peaceful studies and discussions or teaching and advocacy in the realm of ideas." He further charged that it was not unlawful "to conduct in an American college and university a course explaining the philosophical theories set forth in the books which have been placed in evidence." Such a charge is in strict accord with the statutory language, and illustrates the meaning to be placed on those words. Congress did not intend to eradicate the free discussion of political theories, to destroy the traditional rights of Americans to discuss and evaluate ideas without fear of governmental sanction. Rather Congress was concerned with the very kind of activity in which the evidence showed these petitioners engaged. . . .

[T]he basis of the First Amendment is the hypothesis that speech can rebut speech, propaganda will answer propaganda, free debate of ideas will result in the wisest governmental policies. It is for this reason that this Court has recognized the inherent value of free discourse. An analysis of the leading cases in this Court which have involved direct limitations on speech, however, will demonstrate that both the majority of the Court and the dissenters in particular cases have recognized that this is not an unlimited, unqualified right, but that the societal value of speech must, on occasion, be subordinated to other values and considerations. . . .

In this case we are squarely presented with the application of the "clear and present danger" test, and must decide what that phrase imports. We first note that many of the cases in which this Court has reversed convictions by use of this or similar tests have been based on the fact that the interest which the State was attempting to protect was itself too insubstantial to warrant restriction of speech. . . . Overthrow of the Government by force and violence is certainly a substantial enough interest for the Government to limit speech. Indeed, this is the ultimate value of any society, for if a society cannot protect its very structure from armed internal attack, it must follow that no subordinate value can be protected. If, then, this interest may be protected, the literal problem which is presented is what has been meant by the use of the phrase "clear and present danger" of the utterances bringing about the evil within the power of Congress to punish.

Obviously, the words cannot mean that before the Government may act, it must wait until the putsch is about to be executed, the plans have been laid and the signal is awaited. If Government is aware that a group aiming at its overthrow is attempting to indoctrinate its members and to commit them to a course whereby they will strike when the leaders feel the circumstances permit, action by the Government is required. The argument that there is no need for Government to concern itself, for Government is strong, it possesses ample powers to put down a rebellion, it may defeat the revolution with ease needs no answer. For that is not the question. Certainly an attempt to overthrow the Government by force, even though doomed from the outset because of inadequate numbers or power of the revolutionists, is a sufficient evil for Congress to prevent. The damage which such attempts create both physically and politically to a nation makes it impossible to measure the validity in terms of the probability of success, or the immediacy of a successful attempt. In the instant case the trial judge charged the jury that they could not convict unless they found that petitioners intended to overthrow the Government "as speedily as circumstances would permit." This does not mean, and could not properly mean, that they would not strike until there was certainty of success. What was meant was that the revolutionists would strike when they thought the time was ripe. We must therefore reject the contention that success or probability of success is the criterion.

[The cases in] which Justices Holmes and Brandeis . . . [applied the "clear and present danger" test involved] comparatively isolated event[s], bearing little relation in their minds to any substantial threat to the safety of the community. . . . They were not confronted with any situation comparable to the instant one—the development of an apparatus designed and dedicated to the overthrow of the Government, in the context of world crisis after crisis.

Chief Judge Learned Hand, writing for the majority below, interpreted the phrase as follows: "In each case [courts] must ask whether the gravity of the 'evil,' discounted by its improbability, justifies such invasion of free speech as is necessary to avoid the danger."

We adopt this statement of the rule. As articulated by Chief Judge Hand, it is as succinct and inclusive as any other we might devise at this time. It takes into consideration those factors which we deem relevant, and relates their significances. More we cannot expect from words.

Likewise, we are in accord with the court below, which affirmed the trial court's finding that the requisite danger existed. The mere fact that from the period 1945 to 1948 petitioners' activities did not result in an attempt to overthrow the Government by force and violence is of course no answer to the fact that there was a group that was ready to make the attempt. The formation by petitioners of such a highly organized conspiracy, with rigidly disciplined members subject to call when the leaders, these petitioners, felt that the time had come for action, coupled with the inflammable nature of world conditions, similar uprisings in other countries, and the touch-and-go nature of our relations with countries with whom petitioners were in the very least ideologically attuned, convince us that their convictions were justified on this score.

And this analysis disposes of the contention that a conspiracy to advocate, as distinguished from the advocacy itself, cannot be constitutionally restrained, because it comprises only the preparation. It is the existence of the conspiracy which creates the danger. If the ingredients of the reaction are present, we cannot bind the Government to wait until the catalyst is added.

The argument that the action of the trial court is erroneous, in declaring as a matter of law that such violation shows sufficient danger to justify the punishment despite the First Amendment, rests on the theory that a jury must decide a question of the application of the First Amendment. We do not agree.

When facts are found that establish the violation of a statute, the protection against conviction afforded by the First Amendment is a matter of law. The doctrine that there must be a clear and present danger of a substantive evil that Congress has a right to prevent is a judicial rule to be applied as a matter of law by the courts. The guilt is established by proof of facts. Whether the First Amendment protects the activity which constitutes the violation of the statute must depend upon a judicial determination of the scope of the First Amendment applied to the circumstances of the case.

Petitioners intended to overthrow the Government of the United States as speedily as the circumstances would permit. Their conspiracy to organize the Communist Party and to teach and advocate the overthrow of the Government of the United States by force and violence created a "clear and present danger" of an attempt to overthrow the Government by force and violence. They were properly and constitutionally convicted for violation of the Smith Act.

MR. JUSTICE FRANKFURTER, CONCURRING
IN AFFIRMANCE OF THE JUDGMENT:

The language of the First Amendment is to be read not as barren words found in a dictionary but as symbols of historic experience illumined by the presuppositions of those who employed them. Not what words did Madison and Hamilton use, but what was it in their minds which they conveyed? Free speech is subject to prohibition of those abuses of expression which a civilized society may forbid. As in the case of every other provision of the Constitution that is not crystallized by the nature of its technical concepts, the fact that the First Amendment is not self-defining and self-enforcing neither impairs its usefulness nor compels its paralysis as a living instrument. . . .

The demands of free speech in a democratic society as well as the interest in national security are better served by candid and informed weighing of the competing interests, within the confines of the judicial process, than by announcing dogmas too inflexible for the non-Euclidian problems to be solved.

But how are competing interests to be assessed? Since they are not subject to quantitative ascertainment, the issue necessarily resolves itself into asking, who is to make the adjustment?—who is to balance the relevant factors and ascertain which interest is in the circumstances to prevail? Full responsibility for the choice cannot be given to the courts. Courts are not representative bodies. They are not designed to be a good reflex of a democratic society. Their judgment is best informed, and therefore most dependable, within narrow limits. Their essential quality is detachment, founded on independence. History teaches that the independence of the judiciary is jeopardized when courts become embroiled in the passions of the day and assume primary responsibility in choosing between competing political, economic and social pressures.

Primary responsibility for adjusting the interests which compete in the situation before us of necessity belongs to the Congress. The nature of the power to be exercised by this Court has been delineated in decisions not charged with the emotional appeal of situations such as that now before us. . . .

[T]here is underlying validity in the distinction between advocacy and the interchange of ideas, and we do not discard a useful tool because it may be misused. That such a distinction could be used unreasonably by those in power against hostile or unorthodox views does not negate the fact that it may be used reasonably against an organization wielding the power of the centrally controlled international Communist movement. The object of the conspiracy before us is clear enough that the chance of error in saying that the defendants conspired to advocate rather than to express ideas is slight. Mr. Justice Douglas quite properly points out that the conspiracy before us is not a conspiracy to overthrow the Government. But it would be equally wrong to treat it as a seminar in political theory. . . .

It is not for us to decide how we would adjust the clash of interests which this case presents were the primary responsibility for reconciling it ours. Congress has determined that the danger created by advocacy of overthrow justifies the ensuing restriction on freedom of speech. The determination was made after due deliberation, and the seriousness of the congressional purpose is attested by the volume of legislation passed to effectuate the same ends.

Can we then say that the judgment Congress exercised was denied it by the Constitution? Can we establish a constitutional doctrine which forbids the elected representatives of the people to make this choice? Can we hold that the First Amendment deprives Congress of what it deemed necessary for the Government's protection?

To make validity of legislation depend on judicial reading of events still in the womb of time—a forecast, that is, of the outcome of forces at best appreciated only with knowledge of the topmost secrets of nations—is to charge the judiciary with duties beyond its equipment.

We do not expect courts to pronounce historic verdicts on bygone events. Even historians have conflicting views to this day on the origin and conduct of the French Revolution. It is as absurd to be confident that we can measure the present clash of forces and their outcome as to ask us to read history still enveloped in clouds of controversy. . . .

Civil liberties draw at best only limited strength from legal guaranties. Preoccupation by our people with the constitutionality, instead of with the wisdom, of legislation or of executive action is preoccupation with a false value. Even those who would most freely use the judicial brake on the democratic process by invalidating legislation that goes deeply against their grain, acknowledge, at least by paying lip service, that constitutionality does not exact a sense of proportion or the sanity of humor or an absence of fear. Focusing attention on constitutionality tends to make constitutionality synonymous with wisdom. When legislation touches freedom of thought and freedom of speech, such a tendency is a formidable enemy of the free spirit. Much that should be rejected as illiberal, because repressive and envenoming, may well be not unconstitutional. The ultimate reliance for the deepest needs of civilization must be found outside their vindication in courts of law.

MR. JUSTICE JACKSON, CONCURRING:

The "clear and present danger" test was an innovation by Mr. Justice Holmes in the *Schenck Case*, reiterated and refined by him and Mr. Justice Brandeis in later cases, all arising before the era of World War II revealed the subtlety and efficacy of modernized revolutionary techniques used by totalitarian parties. In those cases, they were faced with convictions under so-called criminal syndicalism statutes aimed at anarchists but which, loosely construed, had been applied to punish socialism, pacifism, and left-wing ideologies, the charges often resting on far-fetched inferences which, if true, would establish only technical or trivial violations. They proposed "clear and present danger" as a test for the sufficiency of evidence in particular cases.

I would save it, unmodified, for application as a "rule of reason" in the kind of case for which it was devised. When the issue is criminality of a hot-headed speech on a street corner, or circulation of a few incendiary pamphlets, or parading by some zealots behind a red flag, or refusal of a handful of school children to salute our flag, it is not beyond the capacity of the judicial process to gather, comprehend, and weigh the necessary materials for decision whether it is a clear and present danger of substantive evil or a harmless letting off of steam. . . . The formula in such cases favors freedoms that are vital to our society, and, even if sometimes applied too generously, the consequences cannot be grave. But its recent expansion has extended, in particular to Communists, unprecedented immunities. Unless we are to hold our Government captive in a judge-made verbal trap, we must approach the problem of a well-organized, nation-wide conspiracy, such as I have described, as realistically as our predecessors faced the trivialities that were being prosecuted until they were checked with a rule of reason.

MR. JUSTICE BLACK, DISSENTING:

At the outset I want to emphasize what the crime involved in this case is, and what it is not. These petitioners were not charged with an attempt to overthrow the Government. They were not charged with overt acts of any kind designed to overthrow the Government. They were not even charged with saying anything or writing anything designed to overthrow the Government. The charge was that they agreed to assemble and to talk and publish certain ideas at a later date: The indictment is that they conspired to organize the Communist Party and to use speech or newspapers and other publications in the future to teach and advocate the forcible overthrow of the Government. No matter how it is worded, this is a virulent form of prior censorship of speech and press, which I believe the First Amendment forbids. I would hold § 3 of the Smith Act authorizing this prior restraint unconstitutional on its face and as applied. . . .

So long as this Court exercises the power of judicial review of legislation, I cannot agree that the First Amendment permits us to sustain laws suppressing freedom of speech and press on the basis of Congress' or our own notions of mere ''reasonableness.'' Such a doctrine waters down the First Amendment so that it amounts to little more than an admonition to Congress. The Amendment as so construed is not likely to protect any but those ''safe'' or orthodox views which rarely need its protection. . . .

Public opinion being what it now is, few will protest the conviction of these Communist petitioners. There is hope, however, that in calmer times, when present pressures, passions and fears subside, this or some later Court will restore the First Amendment liberties to the high preferred place where they belong in a free society.

MR. JUSTICE DOUGLAS, DISSENTING:

If this were a case where those who claimed protection under the First Amendment were teaching the techniques of sabotage, the assassination of the President, the filching of documents from public files, the planting of bombs, the art of street warfare, and the like, I would have no doubts. The freedom to speak is not absolute; the teaching of methods of terror and other seditious conduct should be beyond the pale along with obscenity and immorality. This case was argued as if those were the facts. The argument imported much seditious conduct into the record. That is easy and it has popular appeal, for the activities of Communists in plotting and scheming against the free world are common knowledge. But the fact is that no such evidence was introduced at the trial. There is a statute which makes a seditious conspiracy unlawful. Petitioners, however, were not charged with a "conspiracy to overthrow" the Government. They were charged with a conspiracy to form a party and groups and assemblies of people who teach and advocate the overthrow of our Government by force or violence and with a conspiracy to advocate and teach its overthrow by force and violence. It may well be that indoctrination in the techniques of terror to destroy the Government would be indictable under either statute. But the teaching which is condemned here is of a different character. . . .

I repeat that we deal here with speech alone, not with speech *plus* acts of sabotage or unlawful conduct. Not a single seditious act is charged in the indictment. To make a lawful speech unlawful because two men conceive it is to raise the law of conspiracy to appalling proportions. That course is to make a radical break with the past and to violate one of the cardinal principles of our constitutional scheme. . . .

There comes a time when even speech loses its constitutional immunity. Speech innocuous one year may at another time fan such destructive flames that it must be halted in the interests of the safety of the Republic. That is the meaning of the clear and present danger test. When conditions are so critical that there will be no time to avoid the evil that the speech threatens, it is time to call a halt. Otherwise, free speech which is the strength of the Nation will be the cause of its destruction.

Yet free speech is the rule, not the exception. The restraint to be constitutional must be based on more than fear, on more than passionate opposition against the speech, on more than a revolted dislike for its contents. There must be some immediate injury to society that is likely if speech is allowed.

Criticism of the public conduct of a government official cannot result in a damage award for libel unless the criticism was made with "actual malice" or "reckless disregard" for the truth.

46. *New York Times Co. v. Sullivan* (1964)

In this decision, the Supreme Court extended the freedom of the press by limiting the application of libel laws where the discussion concerns public affairs. Justice Brennan's opinion pointed to "a profound national commitment to the principle that debate on public issues should be uninhibited, robust, and wide-open, and that it may well include vehement, caustic, and sometimes unpleasantly sharp attacks on government and public officials."

Background: During the civil rights struggle in Montgomery, Alabama, in 1960, *The New York Times* carried an advertisement attacking brutality against blacks. Commissioner Sullivan, in charge of the Montgomery police, considered himself personally libeled, sued the *Times*, and won an award of $500,000 in damages. The Alabama Supreme Court upheld the verdict. *The New York Times* appealed to the United States Supreme Court, which reversed the Alabama decision.

Mr. Justice Brennan delivered
the opinion of the Court:

We are required in this case to determine for the first time the extent to which the constitutional protections for speech and press limit a State's power to award damages in a libel action brought by a public official against critics of his official conduct.

Respondent L. B. Sullivan is one of the three elected Commissioners of the City of Montgomery, Alabama. He brought this civil libel action against the four individual petitioners, who are Negroes and Alabama clergymen, and against petitioner the New York Times Company, a New York corporation which publishes the New York Times, a daily newspaper. A jury in the Circuit Court of Montgomery County awarded him damages of $500,000, the full amount claimed, against all the petitioners, and the Supreme Court of Alabama affirmed.

Respondent's complaint alleged that he had been libeled by statements in a full-page advertisement that was carried in the New York Times on March 29, 1960. Entitled "Heed Their Rising Voices," the advertisement began by stating that "As the whole world knows by now, thousands of Southern Negro students are engaged in widespread non-violent demonstrations in positive affirmation of the right to live in human dignity as guaranteed by the U.S. Constitution and the Bill of Rights." It went on to charge that "in their efforts to uphold these guarantees, they are being met by an unprecedented wave of terror by those who would deny and negate that document which the whole world looks upon as setting the pattern for modern freedom. . . ."

The text appeared over the names of 64 persons, many widely known for their activities in public affairs, religion, trade unions, and the performing arts. . . . The advertisement was signed at the bottom of the page by the "Committee to Defend Martin Luther King and the Struggle for Freedom in the South," and the officers of the Committee were listed.

Of the 10 paragraphs of text in the advertisement, the third and a portion of the sixth were the basis of respondent's claim of libel. They read as follows:

Third paragraph:

"In Montgomery, Alabama, after students sang 'My Country, 'Tis of Thee' on the State Capitol steps, their leaders were expelled from school, and truckloads of police armed with shotguns and tear-gas ringed the Alabama State College Campus. When the entire student body protested to state authorities by refusing to re-register, their dining hall was padlocked in an attempt to starve them into submission."

Sixth paragraph:

"Again and again the Southern violators have answered Dr. King's peaceful protests with intimidation and violence. They have bombed his home almost killing his wife and child. They have assaulted his person. They have arrested him seven times—for 'speeding,' 'loitering' and similar 'offenses.' And now they have charged him with 'perjury'—a *felony* under which they could imprison him for *ten years.* . . .''

Although neither of these statements mentions respondent by name, he contended that the word ''police'' in the third paragraph referred to him as the Montgomery Commissioner who supervised the Police Department, so that he was being accused of ''ringing'' the campus with police. He further claimed that the paragraph would be read as imputing to the police, and hence to him, the padlocking of the dining hall in order to starve the students into submission. As to the sixth paragraph, he contended that since arrests are ordinarily made by the police, the statement ''They have arrested [Dr. King] seven times'' would be read as referring to him; he further contended that the ''They'' who did the arresting would be equated with the ''They'' who committed the other described acts and with the ''Southern violators.'' . . .

We reverse the judgment. We hold that the rule of law applied by the Alabama courts is constitutionally deficient for failure to provide the safeguards for freedom of speech and of the press that are required by the First and Fourteenth Amendments in a libel action brought by a public official against critics of his official conduct. We further hold that under the proper safeguards the evidence presented in this case is constitutionally insufficient to support the judgment for respondent. . . .

The publication here was not a ''commercial'' advertisement in the [usual] sense. . . . It communicated information, expressed opinion, recited grievances, protested claimed abuses, and sought financial support on behalf of a movement whose existence and objectives are matters of the highest public interest and concern. That the Times was paid for publishing the advertisement is as immaterial in this connection as is the fact that newspapers and books are sold. Any other conclusion would discourage newspapers from carrying ''editorial advertisements'' of this type, and so might shut off an important outlet for the promulgation of information and ideas by persons who do not themselves have access to publishing facilities—who wish to exercise their freedom of speech even though they are not members of the press. The effect would be to shackle the First Amendment in its attempt to secure ''the widest possible dissemination of information from diverse and antagonistic sources.'' To avoid placing such a handicap upon the freedoms of expression, we hold that if the allegedly libelous statements would otherwise be constitutionally protected from the present judgment, they do not forfeit that protection because they were published in the form of a paid advertisement. . . .

Respondent relies heavily, as did the Alabama courts, on statements of this Court to the effect that the Constitution does not protect libelous publications. Those statements do not foreclose our inquiry here. None of the cases sustained the use of libel laws to impose sanctions upon expression critical of the official conduct of public officials. . . .

Like insurrection, contempt, advocacy of unlawful acts, breach of the peace, obscenity, solicitation of legal business, and the various other formulae for the repression of expression that have been challenged in this Court, libel can claim no talismanic immunity from constitutional limitations. It must be measured by standards that satisfy the First Amendment. . . .

Thus we consider this case against the background of a profound national commitment to the principle that debate on public issues should be uninhibited, robust, and wide-open, and that it may well include vehement, caustic, and sometimes unpleasantly sharp attacks on government and public officials. The present advertisement, as an expression of grievance and protest on one of the major public issues of our time, would seem clearly to qualify for the constitutional protection. The question is whether it forfeits that protection by the falsity of some of its factual statements and by its alleged defamation of respondent. . . .

Madison said, "Some degree of abuse is inseparable from the proper use of every thing; and in no instance is this more true than in that of the press." 4 Elliot's *Debates on the Federal Constitution* (1876) p. 571. . . . [E]rroneous statement is inevitable in free debate, and . . . it must be protected if the freedoms of expression are to have the "breathing space" that they "need . . . to survive." . . .

Injury to official reputation affords no more warrant for repressing speech that would otherwise be free than does factual error. Where judicial officers are involved, this Court has held that concern for the dignity and reputation of the courts does not justify the punishment as criminal contempt of criticism of the judge or his decision. *Bridges v. California* [1941]. This is true even though the utterance contains "half-truths" and misinformation. Such repression can be justified, if at all, only by a clear and present danger of the obstruction of justice. If judges are to be treated as "men of fortitude, able to thrive in a hardy climate," surely the same must be true of other government officials, such as elected city commissioners. Criticism of their official conduct does not lose its constitutional protection merely because it is effective criticism and hence diminishes their official reputations.

If neither factual error nor defamatory content suffices to remove the constitutional shield from criticism of official conduct, the combination of the two elements is no less inadequate. This is the lesson to be drawn from the great controversy over the Sedition Act of 1798 which first crystallized a national awareness of the central meaning of the First Amendment.

That statute made it a crime, punishable by a $5,000 fine and five years in prison, "if any person shall write, print, utter or publish . . . any false, scandalous and malicious writing or writings against the government of the United States, or either house of the Congress . . . , or the President . . . , with intent to defame . . . or to bring them, or either of them, into contempt or disrepute; or to excite against them, or either or any of them, the hatred of the good people of the United States." The Act allowed the defendant the defense of truth, and provided that the jury were to be judges both of the law and the facts. Despite these qualifications, the Act was vigorously condemned as unconstitutional in an attack joined in by Jefferson and Madison. . . .

Although the Sedition Act was never tested in this Court, the attack upon its validity has carried the day in the court of history. Fines levied in its prosecution were repaid by Act of Congress on the ground that it was unconstitutional. . . . Jefferson, as President, pardoned those who had been convicted and sentenced under the Act and remitted their fines. . . .

A rule compelling the critic of official conduct to guarantee the truth of all his factual assertions—and to do so on pain of libel judgments virtually unlimited in amount—leads to a comparable "self-censorship." Allowance of the defense of truth, with the burden of proving it on the defendant, does not mean that only false speech will be deterred. Even courts accepting this defense as an adequate safeguard have recognized the difficulties of adducing legal proofs that the alleged libel was true in all its factual particulars. Under such a rule, would-be critics of official conduct may be deterred from voicing their criticism, even though it is believed to be true and even though it is in fact true, because of doubt whether it can be proved in court or fear of the expense of having to do so. They tend to make only statements which "steer far wider of the unlawful zone." . . . The rule thus dampens the vigor and limits the variety of public debate. It is inconsistent with the First and Fourteenth Amendments.

The constitutional guarantees require, we think, a federal rule that prohibits a public official from recovering damages for a defamatory falsehood relating to his official conduct unless he proves that the statement was made with "actual malice"—that is, with knowledge that it was false or with reckless disregard of whether it was false or not. . . .

We hold today that the Constitution delimits a State's power to award damages for libel in actions brought by public officials against critics of their official conduct. Since this is such an action, the rule requiring proof of actual malice is applicable. . . .

Applying these standards, we consider that the proof presented to show actual malice lacks the convincing clarity which the constitutional standard demands, and hence that it would not constitutionally sustain the judgment for respondent under the proper rule of law. The case of the individual petitioners requires little discussion. Even assuming that they could constitutionally be found to have authorized the use of their names on the advertisement, there was no evidence whatever that they were aware of any erroneous statements or were in any way reckless in that regard. The judgment against them is thus without constitutional support.

As to the Times, we similarly conclude that the facts do not support a finding of actual malice. . . . We think the evidence against the Times supports at most a finding of negligence in failing to discover the misstatements, and is constitutionally insufficient to show the recklessness that is required for a finding of actual malice.

MR. JUSTICE BLACK, WITH WHOM MR. JUSTICE DOUGLAS JOINS, CONCURRING:

Unlike the Court . . . I vote to reverse exclusively on the ground that the Times and the individual defendants had an absolute, unconditional constitutional right to publish in the Times advertisement their criticisms of the Montgomery agencies and officials. I do not base my vote to reverse on any failure to prove that these individual defendants signed the advertisement or that their criticism of the Police Department was aimed at the plaintiff Sullivan, who was then the Montgomery City Commissioner having supervision of the city's police; for present purposes I assume these things were proved. Nor is my reason for reversal the size of the half-million-dollar-judgment, large as it is. If Alabama has constitutional power to use its civil libel law to impose damages on the press for criticizing the way public officials perform or fail to perform their duties, I know of no provision in the Federal Constitution which either expressly or impliedly bars the State from fixing the amount of damages. . . .

We would, I think, more faithfully interpret the First Amendment by holding that at the very least it leaves the people and the press free to criticize officials and discuss public affairs with impunity. . . . These officials are responsible to the people for the way they perform their duties. While our Court has held that some kinds of speech and writings, such as "obscenity," and "fighting words," are not expression within the protection of the First Amendment, freedom to discuss public affairs and public officials is unquestionably, as the Court today holds, the kind of speech the First Amendment was primarily designed to keep within the area of free discussion. To punish the exercise of this right to discuss public affairs or to penalize it through libel judgments is to abridge or shut off discussion of the very kind most needed.

Mr. Justice Goldberg, with whom Mr. Justice Douglas joins, concurring:

In my view, the First and Fourteenth Amendments to the Constitution afford to the citizen and to the press an absolute, unconditional privilege to criticize official conduct despite the harm which may flow from excesses and abuses. . . . The theory of our Constitution is that every citizen may speak his mind and every newspaper express its view on matters of public concern and may not be barred from speaking or publishing because those in control of government think that what is said or written is unwise, unfair, false, or malicious. In a democratic society, one who assumes to act for the citizens in an executive, legislative, or judicial capacity must expect that his official acts will be commented upon and criticized. Such criticism cannot, in my opinion, be muzzled or deterred by the courts at the instance of public officials under the label of libel. . . .

This is not to say that the Constitution protects defamatory statements directed against the private conduct of a public official or private citizen. . . . Purely private defamation has little to do with the political ends of a self-governing society. The imposition of liability for private defamation does not abridge the freedom of public speech or any other freedom protected by the First Amendment.

Restrictions on hate speech must not be drawn too narrowly.

47. *R.A.V. v. St. Paul* (1992)

First Amendment interpretation is, surprisingly, a relatively new constitutional field for the Supreme Court. Long after the Court had rendered hundreds of decisions involving the Commerce and Due Process Clauses, for example, it decided its first important free speech case in *Schenck* (p. 331). The number and variety of First Amendment cases decided since then is truly astonishing. *R.A.V. v. St. Paul* is one of the most prominent, and timely, recent cases dealing with a city ordinance that banned display of symbols arousing anger in others on the basis of race, gender, or religion.

The Court was unanimous in striking down the law but was badly divided over the reasons. The majority of five justices held the law unconstitutional for being underinclusive—i.e., it improperly singled out certain kinds of unpleasant speech but not others. The four other justices, paradoxically, found the law overbroad—i.e., it prohibited more speech than was necessary to meet its objective.

An essential backdrop to this case is a much earlier decision, *Chaplinsky v. New Hampshire*, decided in 1942. Writing for one of the most distinguished benches in the Court's history (which included Chief Justice Stone and Justices Black, Douglas, Frankfurter, and Jackson), Justice Murphy declared:

> Allowing the broadest scope to the language and purpose of the Fourteenth Amendment, it is well understood that the right of free speech is not absolute at all times and under all circumstances. There are certain well-defined and narrowly limited classes of speech, the prevention and punishment of which have never been thought to raise any Constitutional problem. These include the lewd and obscene, the profane, the libelous, and the insulting or "fighting" words—those which by their very utterance inflict injury or tend to incite an immediate breach of the

peace. It has been well observed that such utterances are no essential part of any exposition of ideas, and are of such slight social value as a step to truth that any benefit that may be derived from them is clearly outweighed by the social interest in order and morality.

This unanimous statement is referred to in the *R.A.V.* opinion and, officially, it remains sound First Amendment doctrine to this day. However, its meaning, scope, and importance are things about which the contemporary justices are quite at odds.

Background: A teenager burned a homemade cross inside the yard of a black family. The trial court granted a motion to dismiss on the ground that the ordinance was "overbroad." The Minnesota Supreme Court upheld the law and was reversed by the Court.

JUSTICE SCALIA DELIVERED THE OPINION OF THE COURT:

In the predawn hours of June 21, 1990, petitioner and several other teenagers allegedly assembled a crudely-made cross by taping together broken chair legs. They then allegedly burned the cross inside the fenced yard of a black family that lived across the street from the house where petitioner was staying. Although this conduct could have been punished under any of a number of laws, one of the two provisions under which respondent city of St. Paul chose to charge petitioner (then a juvenile) was the St. Paul Bias-Motivated Crime Ordinance, which provides:

> "Whoever places on public or private property a symbol, object, appellation, characterization or graffiti, including, but not limited to, a burning cross or Nazi swastika, which one knows or has reasonable grounds to know arouses anger, alarm or resentment in others on the basis of race, color, creed, religion or gender commits disorderly conduct and shall be guilty of a misdemeanor."

Petitioner moved to dismiss this count on the ground that the St. Paul ordinance was substantially overbroad and impermissibly content-base and therefore facially invalid under the First Amendment. . . .

I

The First Amendment generally prevents government from proscribing speech, or even expressive conduct, *Texas v. Johnson* (1989), because of disapproval of the ideas expressed. Content-based regulations are presumptively invalid. From 1791 to the present, however, our society, like other free but civilized societies, has permitted restrictions upon the content of speech in a few limited areas, which are "of such slight social value as a step to truth that any benefit that may be derived from them is clearly outweighed by the social interest in order and morality." [The opinion here lists cases upholding laws banning obscenity, defamation, and "fighting words."] . . .

We have sometimes said that these categories of expression are "not within the area of constitutionally protected speech," or that the "protection of the First Amendment does not extend" to them. Such statements must be taken in context, however. . . . What they mean is that these areas of speech can, consistently with the First Amendment be regulated *because of their constitutionally proscribable content* (obscenity, defamation, etc.)—not that they are categories of speech entirely invisible to the Constitution, so that they may be made the vehicles for content discrimination unrelated to their distinctively proscribable content. Thus, the government may proscribe libel; but it may not make the further content discrimination of proscribing *only* libel critical of the government.

Our cases surely do not establish the proposition that the First Amendment imposes no obstacle whatsoever to regulation of particular instances of such proscribable expression. That would mean that a city council could enact an ordinance prohibiting only those legally obscene works that contain criticism of the city government or, indeed, that do not include endorsement of the city government. Such a simplistic, all-or-nothing-at-all approach to First Amendment protection is at odds with common sense and with our jurisprudence as well. . . .

The proposition that a particular instance of speech can be proscribable on the basis of one feature (e.g., obscenity) but not on the basis of another (e.g., opposition to the city government) is commonplace, and has found application in many contexts. We have long held, for example, that nonverbal expressive activity can be banned because of the action it entails, but not because of the ideas it expresses—so that burning a flag in violation of an ordinance against outdoor fires could be punishable, whereas burning a flag in violation of an ordinance against dishonoring the flag is not. . . .

In other words, the exclusion of "fighting words" from the scope of the First Amendment simply means that, for purposes of that Amendment, the unprotected features of the words are, despite their verbal character, essentially a "non-speech" element of communication. Fighting words are thus analogous to a noisy sound truck: . . . both can be used to convey an idea; but neither has, in and of itself, a claim upon the First Amendment. As with the sound truck, however, so also with fighting words: The government may not regulate use based on hostility—or favoritism—towards the underlying message expressed. . . .

II

Although the phrase in the ordinance, "arouses anger, alarm or resentment in others," has been limited by the Minnesota Supreme Court's construction to reach only those symbols or displays that amount to "fighting words," the remaining, unmodified terms make clear that the ordinance applies only to "fighting words" that insult, or provoke violence, "on the basis of race, color, creed, religion or gender." Displays containing abusive invective, no matter how vicious or severe, are permissible unless they are addressed to one of the specified disfavored topics. Those who wish to use "fighting words" in connection with other ideas . . . are not covered. The First Amendment does not permit St. Paul to impose special prohibitions on those speakers who express views on disfavored subjects. . . .

St. Paul and its amici defend the conclusion of the Minnesota Supreme Court that, even if the ordinance regulates expression based on hostility towards its protected ideological content, this discrimination is nonetheless justified because it is narrowly tailored to serve compelling state interests. Specifically, they assert that the ordinance helps to ensure the basic human rights of members of groups that have historically been subjected to discrimination, including the right of such group members to live in peace where they wish. We do not doubt that these interests are compelling, and that the ordinance can be said to promote them. But the "danger of censorship" presented by a facially content-based statute, requires that that weapon be employed only where it is "*necessary* to serve the asserted [compelling] interest." The dispositive question in this case, therefore, is whether content discrimination is reasonably necessary to achieve St. Paul's compelling interests; it plainly is not. An ordinance not limited to the favored topics, for example, would have precisely the same beneficial effect. In fact the only interest distinctively served by the content limitation is that of displaying the city council's special hostility towards the particular biases thus singled out. That is precisely what the First Amendment forbids. . . .

* * *

Let there be no mistake about our belief that burning a cross in someone's front yard is reprehensible. But St. Paul has sufficient means at its disposal to prevent such behavior without adding the First Amendment to the fire.

JUSTICE WHITE, WITH WHOM JUSTICE BLACKMUN AND JUSTICE O'CONNOR JOIN, AND WITH WHOM JUSTICE STEVENS JOINS [IN SUBSTANTIAL PART] CONCURRING IN THE JUDGMENT:

I agree with the majority that the judgment of the Minnesota Supreme Court should be reversed. However, our agreement ends there.

This case could easily be decided within the contours of established First Amendment law by holding, as petitioner argues, that the St. Paul ordinance is fatally overbroad because it criminalizes not only unprotected expression but expression protected by the First Amendment. Instead . . . the Court holds the ordinance facially unconstitutional on a ground that was never presented to the Minnesota Supreme Court, a ground that has not been briefed by the parties before this Court, a ground that requires serious departures from the teaching of prior cases. . . .

I

A

This Court's decisions have plainly stated that expression falling within certain limited categories so lacks the values the First Amendment was designed to protect that the Constitution affords no protection to that expression. *Chaplinsky v. New Hampshire* (1942). . . .

Thus . . . this Court has long held certain discrete categories of expression to be proscribable on the basis of their content. For instance, the Court has held that the individual who falsely shouts ''fire'' in a crowded theatre may not claim the protection of the First Amendment. The Court has concluded that neither child pornography, nor obscenity, is protected by the First Amendment. And the Court has observed that, ''[l]eaving aside the special considerations when public officials [and public figures] are the target, a libelous publication is not protected by the Constitution.''

All of these categories are content based. But the Court has held that the First Amendment does not apply to them because their expressive content is worthless or of de minimis value to society. . . . This categorical approach has provided a principled and narrowly focused means for distinguishing between expression that the government may regulate freely and that which it may regulate on the basis of content only upon a showing of compelling need. . . .

[T]he majority holds that the First Amendment protects those narrow categories of expression long held to be undeserving of First Amendment protection—at least to the extent that lawmakers may not regulate some fighting words more strictly than others because of their content. Should the government want to criminalize certain fighting words, the Court now requires it to criminalize all fighting words. . . .

[T]he Court's insistence on inventing its brand of First Amendment underinclusiveness puzzles me. The overbreadth doctrine has the redeeming virtue of attempting to avoid the chilling of protected expression, but the Court's new ''underbreadth'' creation serves no desirable function. Instead, it permits, indeed invites, the continuation of expressive conduct that in this case is evil and worthless in First Amendment terms, until the city of St. Paul cures the underbreadth by adding to its ordinance a catch-all phrase such as ''and all other fighting words that may constitutionally be subject to this ordinance.'' . . .

Furthermore, the Court obscures the line between speech that could be regulated freely on the basis of content (i. e., the narrow categories of expression falling outside the First Amendment) and that which could be regulated on the basis of content only upon a showing of a compelling state interest (i. e., all remaining expression). By placing fighting words, which the Court has long held to be valueless, on at least equal constitutional footing with political discourse and other forms of speech that we have deemed to have the greatest social value, the majority devalues the latter category.

B

In a second break with precedent, the Court refuses to sustain the ordinance even though it would survive under the strict scrutiny applicable to other protected expression. Assuming, arguendo, that the St. Paul ordinance is a content-based regulation of protected expression, it nevertheless would pass First Amendment review under settled law upon a showing that the regulation " 'is necessary to serve a compelling state interest and is narrowly drawn to achieve that end.' " . . . The Court expressly concedes that this interest is compelling and is promoted by the ordinance. Nevertheless . . . a narrowly drawn, content-based ordinance could never pass constitutional muster if the object of that legislation could be accomplished by banning a wider category of speech.

The ordinance proscribes a subset of "fighting words," those that injure "on the basis of race, color, creed, religion or gender." This selective regulation reflects the City's judgment that harms based on race, color, creed, religion, or gender are more pressing public concerns than the harms caused by other fighting words. In light of our Nation's long and painful experience with discrimination, this determination is plainly reasonable. Indeed, as the majority concedes, the interest is compelling. . . .

II

Although I disagree with the Court's analysis, I do agree with its conclusion: The St. Paul ordinance is unconstitutional. However, I would decide the case on overbreadth grounds. . . .

A defendant being prosecuted for speech or expressive conduct may challenge the law on its face if it reaches protected expression, even when that person's activities are not protected by the First Amendment. This is because "the possible harm to society in permitting some unprotected speech to go unpunished is outweighed by the possibility that protected speech of others may be muted." . . .

I agree with petitioner that the ordinance is invalid on its face. Although the ordinance as construed reaches categories of speech that are constitutionally unprotected, it also criminalizes a substantial amount of expression that—however repugnant—is shielded by the First Amendment. . . .

I . . . understand the [Minnesota Supreme C]ourt to have ruled that St. Paul may constitutionally prohibit expression that "by its very utterance" causes "anger, alarm or resentment."

Our fighting words cases have made clear, however, that such generalized reactions are not sufficient to strip expression of its constitutional protection. The mere fact that expressive activity causes hurt feelings, offense, or resentment does not render the expression unprotected. . . .

Although the ordinance reaches conduct that is unprotected, it also makes criminal expressive conduct that causes only hurt feelings, offense, or resentment, and is protected by the First Amendment. The ordinance is therefore fatally overbroad and invalid on its face.

III

Today, the Court has disregarded two established principles of First Amendment law without providing a coherent replacement theory. Its decision is an arid, doctrinaire interpretation, driven by the frequently irresistible impulse of judges to tinker with the First Amendment. The decision is mischievous at best and will surely confuse the lower courts. I join the judgment, but not the folly of the opinion.

[Justice Blackmun and Justice Stevens wrote separate opinions concurring in the judgment.]

B. Establishment of Religion, Free Exercise

Government cannot compel individuals to participate in ceremonies that violate their religious beliefs.

48a. *Minersville School District v. Gobitis* (1940)
48b. *West Virginia State Board of Education v. Barnette* (1943)

Both of these cases deal with the same problem: whether the law can compel school children to salute the flag despite their religious convictions. In the Minersville decision, the Supreme Court ruled that children could be forced to salute the flag; three years later, in the West Virginia decision, it ruled the opposite.

Background: The two children of Walter Gobitis were expelled from the Minersville, Pennsylvania, public schools for refusing to salute the flag as required by the board of education. Gobitis brought suit against the board of education and won his case in the Pennsylvania courts. The Minersville School Board appealed to the United States Supreme Court, which, by a vote of eight to one, ruled against Gobitis. The argument of the Court, as formulated by Justice Frankfurter, was that the "flag is the symbol of our national unity" and that it was, therefore, legitimate for the state to train children in "patriotic impulses."

In the case of West Virginia, the situation was practically identical, but the judicial decision was different. This time, by a vote of six to three, the Court ruled that the flag-saluting ceremony was in violation of the First Amendment.

The dramatic reversal of the Court between 1940 and 1943 was due in part to the addition of two new members—Justices Jackson and Rutledge—and in part to a change of view by Justices Black, Douglas, and Murphy, who had been with the majority in the *Gobitis* case.

Minersville School District v. *Gobitis*

MR. JUSTICE FRANKFURTER DELIVERED
THE OPINION OF THE COURT:

A grave responsibility confronts this Court whenever in course of litigation it must reconcile the conflicting claims of liberty and authority. But when the liberty invoked is liberty of conscience, and the authority is authority to safeguard the nation's fellowship, judicial conscience is put to its severest test. Of such a nature is the present controversy.

Lillian Gobitis, aged twelve, and her brother William, aged ten, were expelled from the public schools of Minersville, Pennsylvania, for refusing to salute the national flag as part of a daily school exercise. . . .

The Gobitis children were of an age for which Pennsylvania makes school attendance compulsory. Thus they were denied a free education, and their parents had to put them into private schools. To be relieved of the financial burden thereby entailed, their father, on behalf of the children and in his own behalf, brought this suit. He sought to enjoin the authorities from continuing to exact participation in the flag-salute ceremony as a condition of his children's attendance at the Minersville school. . . .

We must decide whether the requirement of participation in such a ceremony, exacted from a child who refuses upon sincere religious grounds, infringes without due process of law the liberty guaranteed by the Fourteenth Amendment. . . .

Certainly the affirmative pursuit of one's convictions about the ultimate mystery of the universe and man's relation to it is placed beyond the reach of law. . . .

But the manifold character of man's relations may bring his conception of religious duty into conflict with the secular interests of his fellow-men. When does the constitutional guarantee compel exemption from doing what society thinks necessary for the promotion of some great common end, or from a penalty for conduct which appears dangerous to the general good? To state the problem is to recall the truth that no single principle can answer all of life's complexities. The right to freedom of religious belief, however dissident and however obnoxious to the cherished beliefs of others—even of a majority—is itself the denial of an absolute. But to affirm that the freedom to follow conscience has itself no limits in the life of a society would deny that very plurality of principles which, as a matter of history, underlies protection of religious toleration. Our present task then, as so often the case with courts, is to reconcile two rights in order to prevent either from destroying the other. But, because in safeguarding conscience we are dealing with interests so subtle and so dear, every possible leeway should be given to the claims of religious faith. . . .

The religious liberty which the Constitution protects has never excluded legislation of general scope not directed against doctrinal loyalties of particular sects. . . . Conscientious scruples have not, in the course of the long struggle for religious toleration, relieved the individual from obedience to a general law not aimed at the promotion or restriction of religious beliefs. The mere possession of religious convictions which contradict the relevant concerns of a political society does not relieve the citizen from the discharge of political responsibilities. . . . [T]he question remains whether school children, like the Gobitis children, must be excused from conduct required of all the other children in the promotion of national cohesion. We are dealing with an interest inferior to none in the hierarchy of legal values. National unity is the basis of national security. To deny the legislature the right to select appropriate means for its attainment presents a totally different order of problem from that of the propriety of subordinating the possible ugliness of littered streets to the free expression of opinion through distribution of handbills.

Situations like the present are phases of the profoundest problem confronting a democracy—the problem which Lincoln cast in memorable dilemma: "Must a government of necessity be too *strong* for the liberties of its people, or too *weak* to maintain its own existence?" No mere textual reading or logical talisman can solve the dilemma. And when the issue demands judicial determination, it is not the personal notion of judges of what wise adjustment requires which must prevail. . . .

[T]he case before us is not concerned with an exertion of legislative power for the promotion of some specific need or interest of secular society—the protection of the family, the promotion of health, the common defense, the raising of public revenues to defray the cost of government. But all these specific activities of government presuppose the existence of an organized political society. The ultimate foundation of a free society is the binding tie of cohesive sentiment. Such a sentiment is fostered by all those agencies of the mind and spirit which may serve to gather up the traditions of a people, transmit them from generation to generation, and thereby create that continuity of a treasured common life which constitutes a civilization. "We live by symbols." The flag is the symbol of our national unity, transcending all internal differences, however large, within the framework of the Constitution. . . .

The precise issue, then, for us to decide is whether the legislatures of the various states and the authorities in a thousand counties and school districts of this country are barred from determining the appropriateness of various means to evoke that unifying sentiment without which there can ultimately be no liberties, civil or religious. To stigmatize legislative judgment in providing for this universal gesture of respect for the symbol of our national life in the setting of the common school as a lawless inroad on that freedom of conscience which the Constitution protects, would amount to no less than the pronouncement of pedagogical and psychological dogma in a field where courts possess no marked and certainly no controlling competence. The influences

which help toward a common feeling for the common country are manifold. Some may seem harsh and others no doubt are foolish. Surely,
however, the end is legitimate. And the effective means for its attainment are still so uncertain and so unauthenticated by science as to
preclude us from putting the widely prevalent belief in flag-saluting
beyond the pale of legislative power. . . .

The wisdom of training children in patriotic impulses by those compulsions which necessarily pervade so much of the educational process
is not for our independent judgment. Even were we convinced of the
folly of such a measure, such belief would be no proof of its unconstitutionality. For ourselves, we might be tempted to say that the deepest patriotism is best engendered by giving unfettered scope to the most
crochety beliefs. . . . But the courtroom is not the arena for debating
issues of educational policy. It is not our province to choose among
competing considerations in the subtle process of securing effective
loyalty to the traditional ideals of democracy, while respecting at the
same time individual idiosyncracies among a people so diversified in
racial origins and religious allegiances. So to hold would in effect make
us the school board for the country. That authority has not been given
to this Court, nor should we assume it.

[Mr. Justice McReynolds concurred in the result.]

MR. JUSTICE STONE, DISSENTING:

Concededly the constitutional guaranties of personal liberty are not
always absolutes. Government has a right to survive and powers
conferred upon it are not necessarily set at naught by the express prohibitions of the Bill of Rights. . . . But it is a long step, and one which
I am unable to take, to the position that government may, as a supposed
educational measure and as a means of disciplining the young, compel
public affirmations which violate their religious conscience. . . .

History teaches us that there have been but few infringements of
personal liberty by the state which have not been justified, as they are
here, in the name of righteousness and the public good, and few which
have not been directed, as they are now, at politically helpless minorities. The framers were not unaware that under the system which they
created most governmental curtailments of personal liberty would have
the support of a legislative judgment that the public interest would be

better served by its curtailment than by its constitutional protection. I cannot conceive that in prescribing, as limitations upon the powers of government, the freedom of the mind and spirit secured by the explicit guaranties of freedom of speech and religion, they intended or rightly could have left any latitude for a legislative judgment that the compulsory expression of belief which violates religious convictions would better serve the public interest than their protection. The Constitution may well elicit expressions of loyalty to it and to the government which it created, but it does not command such expressions or otherwise give any indication that compulsory expressions of loyalty play any such part in our scheme of government as to override the constitutional protection of freedom of speech and religion. And while such expressions of loyalty, when voluntarily given, may promote national unity, it is quite another matter to say that their compulsory expression by children in violation of their own and their parents' religious convictions can be regarded as playing so important a part in our national unity as to leave school boards free to exact it despite the constitutional guaranty of freedom of religion. The very terms of the Bill of Rights preclude, it seems to me, any reconciliation of such compulsions with the constitutional guaranties by a legislative declaration that they are more important to the public welfare than the Bill of Rights.

But even if this view be rejected and it is considered that there is some scope for the determination by legislatures whether the citizen shall be compelled to give public expression of such sentiments contrary to his religion, I am not persuaded that we should refrain from passing upon the legislative judgment "as long as the remedial channels of the democratic process remain open and unobstructed." This seems to me no more than the surrender of the constitutional protection of the liberty of small minorities to the popular will. We have previously pointed to the importance of a searching judicial inquiry into the legislative judgment in situations where prejudice against discrete and insular minorities may tend to curtail the operation of those political processes ordinarily to be relied on to protect minorities. See *United States v. Carolene Products Co.*, note 4 [1937]. . . . Here we have such a small minority entertaining in good faith a religious belief, which is such a departure from the usual course of human conduct, that most persons are disposed to regard it with little toleration or concern. In such circumstances careful scrutiny of legislative efforts to secure conformity of belief and opinion by a compulsory affirmation of the desired belief, is especially needful if civil rights are to receive any protection. Tested by this standard, I am not prepared to say that the right of this small and helpless minority, including children having a strong religious conviction, whether they understand its nature or not, to refrain from an expression obnoxious to their religion, is to be overborne by the interest of the state in maintaining discipline in the schools.

West Virginia State Board of Education v. Barnette

MR. JUSTICE JACKSON DELIVERED
THE OPINION OF THE COURT:

The Board of Education on January 9, 1942, adopted a resolution containing recitals taken largely from the Court's *Gobitis* opinion and ordering that the salute to the flag become "a regular part of the program of activities in the public schools," that all teachers and pupils "shall be required to participate in the salute honoring the Nation represented by the Flag; provided, however, that refusal to salute the Flag be regarded as an Act of insubordination, and shall be dealt with accordingly." . . .

This case calls upon us to reconsider a precedent decision, as the Court throughout its history often has been required to do. Before turning to the *Gobitis Case*, however, it is desirable to notice certain characteristics by which this controversy is distinguished.

The freedom asserted by these appellees does not bring them into collision with rights asserted by any other individual. It is such conflicts which most frequently require intervention of the State to determine where the rights of one end and those of another begin. But the refusal of these persons to participate in the ceremony does not interfere with or deny rights of others to do so. Nor is there any question in this case that their behavior is peaceable and orderly. The sole conflict is between authority and rights of the individual. The State asserts power to condition access to public education on making a prescribed sign and profession and at the same time to coerce attendance by punishing both parent and child. The latter stand on a right of self-determination in matters that touch individual opinion and personal attitude. . . .

Here, . . . we are dealing with a compulsion of students to declare a belief. They are not merely made acquainted with the flag salute so that they may be informed as to what it is or even what it means. The issue here is whether this slow and easily neglected route to aroused loyalties constitutionally may be short-cut by substituting a compulsory salute and slogan. . . .

There is no doubt that, in connection with the pledges, the flag salute is a form of utterance. Symbolism is a primitive but effective way of communicating ideas.

Here it is the State that employs a flag as a symbol of adherence to government as presently organized. It requires the individual to communicate by word and sign his acceptance of the political ideas it thus bespeaks. Objection to this form of communication when coerced is an old one, well known to the framers of the Bill of Rights.

It is also to be noted that the compulsory flag salute and pledge requires affirmation of a belief and an attitude of mind. It is not clear whether the regulation contemplates that pupils forego any contrary convictions of their own and become unwilling converts to the prescribed ceremony or whether it will be acceptable if they simulate assent by words without belief and by a gesture barren of meaning. It is now a commonplace that censorship or suppression of expression of opinion is tolerated by our Constitution only when the expression presents a clear and present danger of action of a kind the State is empowered to prevent and punish. It would seem that involuntary affirmation could be commanded only on even more immediate and urgent grounds than silence. But here the power of compulsion is invoked without any allegation that remaining passive during a flag salute ritual creates a clear and present danger that would justify an effort even to muffle expression. To sustain the compulsory flag salute we are required to say that a Bill of Rights which guards the individual's right to speak his own mind, left it open to public authorities to compel him to utter what is not in his mind. . . .

The *Gobitis* decision, however, *assumed*, as did the argument in that case and in this, that power exists in the State to impose the flag salute discipline upon school children in general. The Court only examined and rejected a claim based on religious beliefs of immunity from an unquestioned general rule. The question which underlies the flag salute controversy is whether such a ceremony so touching matters of opinion and political attitude may be imposed upon the individual by official authority under powers committed to any political organization under our Constitution. . . .

In weighing arguments of the parties it is important to distinguish between the due process clause of the Fourteenth Amendment as an instrument for transmitting the principles of the First Amendment and those cases in which it is applied for its own sake. The test of legislation which collides with the Fourteenth Amendment, because it also collides with the principles of the First, is much more definite than the test when only the Fourteenth is involved. Much of the vagueness of the due process clause disappears when the specific prohibitions of the First become its standard. The right of a State to regulate, for example, a public utility may well include, so far as the due process test is concerned, power to impose all of the restrictions which a legislature may have a "rational basis" for adopting. But freedoms of speech and of press, of assembly, and of worship may not be infringed on such slender grounds. They are susceptible of restriction only to prevent grave and immediate danger to interests which the state may lawfully protect. It is important to note that while it is the Fourteenth Amendment which bears directly upon the State it is the more specific limiting principles of the First Amendment that finally govern this case.

Nor does our duty to apply the Bill of Rights to assertions of official authority depend upon our possession of marked competence in the field where the invasion of rights occurs. True, the task of translating the majestic generalities of the Bill of Rights, conceived as part of the pattern of liberal government in the eighteenth century, into concrete restraints on officials dealing with the problems of the twentieth century, is one to disturb self-confidence. . . . But we act in these matters not by authority of our competence but by force of our commissions. We cannot, because of modest estimates of our competence in such specialties as public education, withhold the judgment that history authenticates as the function of this Court when liberty is infringed. . . .

The case is made difficult not because the principles of its decision are obscure but because the flag involved is our own. Nevertheless, we apply the limitations of the Constitution with no fear that freedom to be intellectually and spiritually diverse or even contrary will disintegrate the social organization. To believe that patriotism will not flourish if patriotic ceremonies are voluntary and spontaneous instead of a compulsory routine is to make an unflattering estimate of the appeal of our institutions to free minds. We can have intellectual individualism and the rich cultural diversities that we owe to exceptional minds only at the price of occasional eccentricity and abnormal attitudes. When they are so harmless to others or the State as those we deal with here, the price is not too great. But freedom to differ is not limited to things that do not matter much. That would be a mere shadow of freedom. The test of its substance is the right to differ as to things that touch the heart of the existing order.

If there is any fixed star in our constitutional constellation, it is that no official, high or petty, can prescribe what shall be orthodox in politics, nationalism, religion, or other matters of opinion or force citizens to confess by word or act their faith therein. If there are any circumstances which permit an exception, they do not now occur to us.

We think the action of the local authorities in compelling the flag salute and pledge transcends constitutional limitations on their power and invades the sphere of intellect and spirit which it is the purpose of the First Amendment to our Constitution to reserve from all official control.

[Mr. Justice Black and Mr. Justice Douglas jointly, and Mr. Justice Murphy, wrote concurring opinions.]

Mr. Justice Roberts and Mr. Justice Reed adhere to the views expressed by the court in *Minersville School District v. Gobitis* and are of the opinion that the judgment below should be reversed.

MR. JUSTICE FRANKFURTER, DISSENTING:

One who belongs to the most vilified and persecuted minority in history is not likely to be insensible to the freedoms guaranteed by our Constitution. Were my purely personal attitude relevant I should wholeheartedly associate myself with the general libertarian views in the Court's opinion, representing as they do the thought and action of a lifetime. . . . As a member of this Court I am not justified in writing my private notions of policy into the Constitution, no matter how deeply I may cherish them or how mischievous I may deem their disregard. . . . It can never be emphasized too much that one's own opinion about the wisdom or evil of a law should be excluded altogether when one is doing one's duty on the bench. The only opinion of our own even looking in that direction that is material is our opinion whether legislators could in reason have enacted such a law. . . . I cannot bring my mind to believe that the "liberty" secured by the Due Process Clause gives this Court authority to deny to the State of West Virginia the attainment of that which we all recognize as a legitimate legislative end, namely, the promotion of good citizenship, by employment of the means here chosen.

Parents may keep children out of high school on grounds of religious conviction.

49. *Wisconsin v. Yoder* (1972)

This case raises a perennial question: how to reconcile the First Amendment's guarantee of free exercise of religion with a law of general application that is facially "neutral" toward religion yet burdens the right by requiring individuals to act contrary to their religious beliefs. In *Yoder*, the Court adopted a standard which requires the state to demonstrate a "compelling interest" in the legislation; otherwise it cannot prevail.

Yoder is also noteworthy for another reason. In *Employment Division v. Smith* (1990), the Court discarded the compelling interest standard, holding that the government need not justify burdens on religion imposed by "neutral" laws.

In an extraordinary rebuke to the Court (though one that went largely unnoticed in the country at large), Congress in 1993 passed the Religious Freedom Restoration Act, aimed at restoring *Yoder*'s requirement of a "compelling interest" in legislation. The law declared that "Government shall not substantially burden a person's exercise of religion even if the law results from a rule of general applicability . . . [unless] it demonstrates that application of the burden to the person is in furtherance of a compelling government interest and is the least restrictive means of furthering that compelling government interest." Furthermore, the law "applies to all Federal and State law . . . whether adopted before or after" its enactment. Of course, the Court's position as ultimate interpreter of the Constitution permits it to reject the view of

Congress. Nevertheless, it is highly probable that the Court will bow to the will of the national legislature, which was expressed with near unanimity.

Background: Yoder and other members of a religious group known as the Old Order Amish refused to allow their children to attend school after completion of the eighth grade despite Wisconsin's compulsory attendance law. Their objections, based on religious grounds, are discussed at length in the opinion. The Wisconsin Supreme Court upheld Yoder and the Supreme Court affirmed.

MR. CHIEF JUSTICE BURGER DELIVERED
THE OPINION OF THE COURT:

[W]e granted the writ of certiorari in this case to review a decision of the Wisconsin Supreme Court holding that respondents' convictions for violating the State's compulsory school-attendance law were invalid under the Free Exercise Clause of the First Amendment to the United States Constitution made applicable to the States by the Fourteenth Amendment. . . .

Respondents Jonas Yoder and Wallace Miller are members of the Old Order Amish religion, and respondent Adin Yutzy is a member of the Conservative Amish Mennonite Church. They and their families are residents of Green County, Wisconsin. Wisconsin's compulsory school-attendance law required them to cause their children to attend public or private school until reaching age 16 but the respondents declined to send their children, ages 14 and 15, to public school after they completed the eighth grade. . . .

On complaint of the school district administrator for the public schools, respondents were charged, tried, and convicted of violating the compulsory-attendance law in Green County Court and were fined the sum of $5 each. Respondents defended on the ground that the application of the compulsory-attendance law violated their rights under the First and Fourteenth Amendments. The trial testimony showed that respondents believed, in accordance with the tenets of Old Order Amish communities generally, that their children's attendance at high school, public or private, was contrary to the Amish religion and way of life. They believed that by sending their children to high school, they would not only expose themselves to the danger of the censure of the church community, but, as found by the county court, also endanger their own salvation and that of their children. The State stipulated that respondents' religious beliefs were sincere. . . .

As a result of their common heritage, Old Order Amish communities today are characterized by a fundamental belief that salvation requires life in a church community separate and apart from the world and worldly influence. This concept of life aloof from the world and its values is central to their faith. . . .

They object to the high school, and higher education generally, because the values they teach are in marked variance with Amish values and the Amish way of life; they view secondary school education as an impermissible exposure of their children to a "worldly" influence in conflict with their beliefs. The high school tends to emphasize intellectual and scientific accomplishments, self-distinction, competitiveness, worldly success, and social life with other students. Amish society emphasizes informal learning-through-doing; a life of "goodness," rather than a life of intellect; wisdom, rather than technical knowledge; community welfare, rather than competition; and separation from, rather than integration with, contemporary worldly society.

Formal high school education beyond the eighth grade is contrary to Amish beliefs, not only because it places Amish children in an environment hostile to Amish beliefs with increasing emphasis on competition in class work and sports and with pressure to conform to the styles, manners, and ways of the peer group, but also because it takes them away from their community, physically and emotionally, during the crucial and formative adolescent period of life. During this period, the children must acquire Amish attitudes favoring manual work and self-reliance and the specific skills needed to perform the adult role of an Amish farmer or housewife. They must learn to enjoy physical labor. Once a child has learned basic reading, writing, and elementary mathematics, these traits, skills, and attitudes admittedly fall within the category of those best learned through example and "doing" rather than in a classroom. . . .

The Amish do not object to elementary education through the first eight grades as a general proposition because they agree that their children must have basic skills in the "three R's" in order to read the Bible, to be good farmers and citizens, and to be able to deal with non-Amish people when necessary in the course of daily affairs. They view such a basic education as acceptable because it does not significantly expose their children to worldly values or interfere with their development in the Amish community during the crucial adolescent period. . . . In the Amish belief higher learning tends to develop values they reject as influences that alienate man from God.

On the basis of such considerations, Dr. [John] Hostetler [an expert on Amish society] testified that compulsory high school attendance could not only result in great psychological harm to Amish children, because of the conflicts it would produce, but would also, in his opinion, ultimately result in the destruction of the Old Order Amish church community as it exists in the United States today. The testimony of Dr. Donald A. Erickson, an expert witness on education, also showed that the Amish succeed in preparing their high school age children to be productive members of the Amish community. He described their system of learning through doing the skills directly relevant to their adult roles in the Amish community as "ideal" and perhaps superior to ordinary high school education. The evidence also showed that the Amish have an excellent record as law-abiding and generally self-sufficient members of society. . . .

I

There is no doubt as to the power of a State, having a high responsibility for education of its citizens, to impose reasonable regulations for the control and duration of basic education. Providing public schools ranks at the very apex of the function of a State. Yet even this paramount responsibility was, in *Pierce* [v. *Society of Sisters* (1925)], made to yield to the right of parents to provide an equivalent education in a privately operated system. There the Court held that Oregon's statute compelling attendance in a public school from age eight to age 16 unreasonably interfered with the interest of parents in directing the rearing of their offspring, including their education in church-operated schools. As that case suggests, the values of parental direction of the religious upbringing and education of their children in their early and formative years have a high place in our society. Thus, a State's interest in universal education, however highly we rank it, is not totally free from a balancing process when it impinges on fundamental rights and interests, such as those specifically protected by the Free Exercise Clause of the First Amendment, and the traditional interest of parents with respect to the religious upbringing of their children. . . .

It follows that in order for Wisconsin to compel school attendance beyond the eighth grade against a claim that such attendance interferes with the practice of a legitimate religious belief, it must appear either that the State does not deny the free exercise of religious belief by its requirement, or that there is a state interest of sufficient magnitude to override the interest claiming protection under the Free Exercise Clause. . . .

The essence of all that has been said and written on the subject is that only those interests of the highest order and those not otherwise served can overbalance legitimate claims to the free exercise of religion. We can accept it as settled, therefore, that, however strong the State's interest in universal compulsory education, it is by no means absolute to the exclusion or subordination of all other interests. . . .

II

The record shows that the respondents' religious beliefs and attitude toward life, family, and home have remained constant—perhaps some would say static—in a period of unparalleled progress in human knowledge generally and great changes in education. The respondents freely concede, and indeed assert as an article of faith, that their religious beliefs and what we would today call ''life style'' have not altered in fundamentals for centuries. . . . Their rejection of telephones, automobiles, radios, and television, their mode of dress, of speech, their habits of manual work do indeed set them apart from much of contemporary society; these customs are both symbolic and practical. . . .

The conclusion is inescapable that secondary schooling, by exposing Amish children to worldly influences in terms of attitudes, goals, and values contrary to beliefs, and by substantially interfering with the religious development of the Amish child and his integration into the way of life of the Amish faith community at the crucial adolescent stage of development, contravenes the basic religious tenets and practice of the Amish faith, both as to the parent and the child. . . .

In sum, the unchallenged testimony of acknowledged experts in education and religious history, almost 300 years of consistent practice, and strong evidence of a sustained faith pervading and regulating respondents' entire mode of life support the claim that enforcement of the State's requirement of compulsory formal education after the eighth grade would gravely endanger if not destroy the free exercise of respondents' religious beliefs.

III

We turn, then, to the State's . . . contention that its interest in its system of compulsory education is so compelling that even the established religious practices of the Amish must give way. . . .

The State advances two primary arguments in support of its system of compulsory education. It notes, as Thomas Jefferson pointed out early in our history, that some degree of education is necessary to prepare citizens to participate effectively and intelligently in our open political system if we are to preserve freedom and independence. Further, education prepares individuals to be self-reliant and self-sufficient participants in society. We accept these propositions.

However, the evidence adduced by the Amish in this case is persuasively to the effect that an additional one or two years of formal high school for Amish children in place of their long-established program of informal vocational education would do little to serve those interests. . . . It is one thing to say that compulsory education for a year or two beyond the eighth grade may be necessary when its goal is the preparation of the child for life in modern society as the majority live, but it is quite another if the goal of education be viewed as the preparation of the child for life in the separated agrarian community that is the keystone of the Amish faith. . . .

Whatever their idiosyncrasies as seen by the majority, this record strongly shows that the Amish community has been a highly successful social unit within our society, even if apart from the conventional "mainstream." Its members are productive and very law-abiding members of society; they reject public welfare in any of its usual modern forms. The Congress itself recognized their self-sufficiency by authorizing exemption of such groups as the Amish from the obligation to pay social security taxes. . . .

We must not forget that in the Middle Ages important values of the civilization of the Western World were preserved by members of religious orders who isolated themselves from all worldly influences against great obstacles. There can be no assumption that today's majority is "right" and the Amish and others like them are "wrong." A way of life that is odd or even erratic but interferes with no rights or interests of others is not to be condemned because it is different. . . .

When Thomas Jefferson emphasized the need for education as a bulwark of a free people against tyranny, there is nothing to indicate he had in mind compulsory education through any fixed age beyond a basic education. Indeed, the Amish communities singularly parallel and reflect many of the virtues of Jefferson's ideal of the "sturdy yeoman" who would form the basis of what he considered as the ideal of a democratic society. Even their idiosyncratic separateness exemplifies the diversity we profess to admire and encourage. . . .

[C]ourts must move with great circumspection in performing the sensitive and delicate task of weighing a State's legitimate social concern when faced with religious claims for exemption from generally applicable educational requirements. It cannot be overemphasized that we are not dealing with a way of life and mode of education by a group claiming to have recently discovered some "progressive" or more enlightened process for rearing children for modern life.

Aided by a history of three centuries as an identifiable religious sect and a long history as a successful and self-sufficient segment of American society, the Amish in this case have convincingly demonstrated the sincerity of their religious beliefs, the interrelationship of belief with their mode of life, the vital role that belief and daily conduct play in the continued survival of Old Order Amish communities and their religious organization, and the hazards presented by the State's enforcement of a statute generally valid as to others. Beyond this, they have carried the even more difficult burden of demonstrating the adequacy of their alternative mode of continuing informal vocational education in terms of precisely those overall interests that the State advances in support of its program of compulsory high school education.

[Mr. Justice Powell and Mr. Justice Rehnquist did not participate. Mr. Justice Stewart and Mr. Justice White wrote separate concurring opinions. Mr. Justice Douglas dissented in part.]

State and local rules requiring prayers or other religious exercises in public schools violate the First Amendment.

50. *Abington School District v. Schempp* (1963)

This is actually a consolidated decision for two cases in which the Supreme Court considered the meaning and intent of the First Amendment's Establishment Clause. Reviewing the cases, one in Pennsylvania and one in Maryland, involving religious exercises in public schools, the Court ruled that such practices were unconstitutional. Only Justice Stewart dissented.

Background: In Pennsylvania, parents whose children attended Abington Senior High School brought suit enjoining enforcement of a state statute that required a daily Bible reading in the classroom. A federal district court ruled in their favor. In Maryland, a mother brought suit against Baltimore, whose schools (one of which her son attended) opened with a Bible reading or prayer, as required by Maryland law. The Maryland Court of Appeals upheld the state law. (In both jurisdictions, children could be exempted from participation at parental request.) The Supreme Court affirmed the decision of the district court in Pennsylvania, and reversed the decision of the Maryland Court of Appeals.

MR. JUSTICE CLARK DELIVERED
THE OPINION OF THE COURT:

Once again we are called upon to consider the scope of the provision of the First Amendment to the United States Constitution which declares that "Congress shall make no law respecting an establishment of religion, or prohibiting the free exercise thereof. . . ." These companion cases present the issues in the context of state action requiring that schools begin each day with readings from the Bible. While raising the basic questions under slightly different factual situations, the cases permit of joint treatment. In light of the history of the First Amendment and of our cases interpreting and applying its requirements, we hold that the practices at issue and the laws requiring them are unconstitutional under the Establishment Clause, as applied to the States through the Fourteenth Amendment. . . .

It is true that religion has been closely identified with our history and government. . . .

In *Zorach v. Clauson* (1952), we gave specific recognition to the proposition that "[w]e are a religious people whose institutions presuppose a Supreme Being." The fact that the Founding Fathers believed devotedly that there was a God and that the unalienable rights of man were rooted in Him is clearly evidenced in their writings, from the Mayflower Compact to the Constitution itself. This background is evidenced today in our public life through the continuance in our oaths of office from the Presidency to the Alderman of the final supplication, "So help me God." Likewise each House of the Congress provides through its Chaplain an opening prayer, and the sessions of this Court are declared open by the crier in a short ceremony, the final phrase of which invokes the grace of God. . . .

The wholesome [governmental] "neutrality" [toward religion] of which this Court's cases speak thus stems from a recognition of the teachings of history that powerful sects or groups might bring about a fusion of governmental and religious functions or a concert or dependency of one upon the other to the end that official support of the State or Federal Government would be placed behind the tenets of one or of all orthodoxies. This the Establishment Clause prohibits. And a further reason for neutrality is found in the Free Exercise Clause, which recognizes the value of religious training, teaching and observance and, more particularly, the right of every person to freely choose his own course with reference thereto, free of any compulsion from the state. This the Free Exercise Clause guarantees. Thus, as we have seen, the two clauses may overlap. As we have indicated, the Establishment Clause has been directly considered by this Court eight times in the past score of years and, with only one Justice [Stewart] dissenting on the point, it has consistently held that the clause withdrew all legislative power respecting religious belief or the expression thereof. The test may be stated as follows: what are the purpose and the primary effect of the enactment? If either is the advancement or inhibition of religion then the enactment exceeds the scope of legislative power as circumscribed by the Constitution. That is to say that to withstand the strictures of the Establishment Clause there must be a secular legislative purpose and a primary effect that neither advances nor inhibits religion. The Free Exercise Clause, likewise considered many times here, withdraws from legislative power, state and federal, the exertion of any restraint on the free exercise of religion. Its purpose is to secure religious liberty in the individual by prohibiting any invasions thereof by civil authority. Hence it is necessary in a free exercise case for one to show the coercive effect of the enactment as it operates against him in the practice of his religion. The distinction between the two clauses is apparent—a violation of the Free Exercise Clause is predicated on coercion while the Establishment Clause violation need not be so attended.

Applying the Establishment Clause principles to the cases at bar we find that the States are requiring the selection and reading at the opening of the school day of verses from the Holy Bible and the recitation of the Lord's Prayer by the students in unison. These exercises are prescribed as part of the curricular activities of students who are required by law to attend school. They are held in the school buildings under the supervision and with the participation of teachers employed in those schools. . . . The trial court . . . has found that such an opening exercise is a religious ceremony and was intended by the State to be so. We agree with the trial court's finding as to the religious character of the exercises. Given that finding, the exercises and the law requiring them are in violation of the Establishment Clause. . . .

The conclusion follows that in both cases the laws require religious exercises and such exercises are being conducted in direct violation of the rights of the appellees and petitioners. Nor are these required exercises mitigated by the fact that individual students may absent themselves upon parental request, for that fact furnishes no defense to a claim of unconstitutionality under the Establishment Clause. Further, it is no defense to urge that the religious practices here may be relatively minor encroachments on the First Amendment. The breach of neutrality that is today a trickling stream may all too soon became a raging torrent and, in the words of Madison, "it is proper to take alarm at the first experiment on our liberties." . . .

It is insisted that unless these religious exercises are permitted a "religion of secularism" is established in the schools. We agree of course that the State may not establish a "religion of secularism" in the sense of affirmatively opposing or showing hostility to religion, thus "preferring those who believe in no religion over those who do believe." We do not agree, however, that this decision in any sense has that effect. . . .

Finally, we cannot accept that the concept of neutrality, which does not permit a State to require a religious exercise even with the consent of the majority of those affected, collides with the majority's right to free exercise of religion. While the Free Exercise Clause clearly prohibits the use of state action to deny the rights of free exercise to *anyone*, it has never meant that a majority could use the machinery of the State to practice its beliefs. . . .

The place of religion in our society is an exalted one, achieved through a long tradition of reliance on the home, the church and the inviolable citadel of the individual heart and mind. We have come to recognize through bitter experience that it is not within the power of government to invade that citadel, whether its purpose or effect be to aid or oppose, to advance or retard. In the relationship between man and religion, the State is firmly committed to a position of neutrality.

MR. JUSTICE BRENNAN, CONCURRING:

The First Amendment forbids both the abridgement of the free exercise of religion and the enactment of laws "respecting an establishment of religion." The two clauses, although distinct in their objectives and their applicability, emerged together from a common panorama of history. The inclusion of both restraints upon the power of Congress to legislate concerning religious matters shows unmistakably that the Framers of the First Amendment were not content to rest the protection of religious liberty exclusively upon either clause. . . .

It is true that the Framers' immediate concern was to prevent the setting up of an official federal church of the kind which England and some of the Colonies had long supported. But nothing in the text of the Establishment Clause supports the view that the prevention of the setting up of an official church was meant to be the full extent of the prohibitions against official involvements in religion. . . .

But an awareness of history and an appreciation of the aims of the Founding Fathers do not always resolve concrete problems. The specific question before us has, for example, aroused vigorous dispute whether the architects of the First Amendment—James Madison and Thomas Jefferson particularly—understood the prohibition against any "law respecting an establishment of religion" to reach devotional exercises in the public schools. . . . I doubt that their view, even if perfectly clear one way or the other, would supply a dispositive answer to the question presented by these cases. A more fruitful inquiry, it seems to me, is whether the practices here challenged threaten those consequences which the Framers deeply feared; whether, in short, they tend to promote that type of interdependence between religion and state which the First Amendment was designed to prevent. . . .

A too literal quest for the advice of the Founding Fathers upon the issues of these cases seems to me futile and misdirected for several reasons: First, on our precise problem the historical record is at best ambiguous, and statements can readily be found to support either side of the proposition. The ambiguity of history is understandable if we recall the nature of the problems uppermost in the thinking of the statesmen who fashioned the religious guarantees; they were concerned with far more flagrant intrusions of government into the realm of religion than any that our century has witnessed. While it is clear to me that the Framers meant the Establishment Clause to prohibit more than the creation of an established federal church such as existed in England, I have no doubt that, in their preoccupation with the imminent question of established churches, they gave no distinct consideration to the particular question whether the clause also forbade devotional exercises in public institutions.

Second, the structure of American education has greatly changed since the First Amendment was adopted. In the context of our modern emphasis upon public education available to all citizens, any views of the eighteenth century as to whether the exercises at bar are an "establishment" offer little aid to decision. Education, as the Framers knew it, was in the main confined to private schools more often than not under strictly sectarian supervision. Only gradually did control of education pass largely to public officials. It would, therefore, hardly be significant if the fact was that the nearly universal devotional exercises in the schools of the young Republic did not provoke criticism; even today religious ceremonies in church-supported private schools are constitutionally unobjectionable.

Third, our religious composition makes us a vastly more diverse people than were our forefathers. They knew differences chiefly among Protestant sects. Today the Nation is far more heterogeneous religiously. . . .

Whatever Jefferson or Madison would have thought of Bible reading or the recital of the Lord's Prayer in what few public schools existed in their day, our use of the history of their time must limit itself to broad purposes, not specific practices. By such a standard, I am persuaded, as is the Court, that the devotional exercises carried on in the Baltimore and Abington schools offend the First Amendment because they sufficiently threaten in our day those substantive evils the fear of which called forth the Establishment Clause of the First Amendment. It is "*a constitution* we are expounding," and our interpretation of the First Amendment must necessarily be responsive to the much more highly charged nature of religious questions in contemporary society.

MR. JUSTICE GOLDBERG, WITH WHOM
MR. JUSTICE HARLAN JOINS, CONCURRING:

It is said, and I agree, that the attitude of government toward religion must be one of neutrality. But untutored devotion to the concept of neutrality can lead to invocation or approval of results which partake not simply of that noninterference and noninvolvement with the religious which the Constitution commands, but of a brooding and pervasive devotion to the secular and a passive, or even active, hostility to the religious. Such results are not only not compelled by the Constitution, but, it seems to me, are prohibited by it.

Neither government nor this Court can or should ignore the significance of the fact that a vast portion of our people believe in and worship God and that many of our legal, political and personal values derive historically from religious teachings. Government must inevitably take cognizance of the existence of religion and, indeed, under certain circumstances the First Amendment may require that it do so. And it seems clear to me from the opinions in the present and past cases that the Court would recognize the propriety of providing military chaplains and of the teaching *about* religion, as distinguished from the teaching of religion, in the public schools. . . .

The practices here involved do not fall within any sensible or acceptable concept of compelled or permitted accommodation and involve the state so significantly and directly in the realm of the sectarian as to give rise to those very divisive influences and inhibitions of freedom which both religion clauses of the First Amendment preclude.

[Mr. Justice Douglas also wrote a concurring opinion.]

MR. JUSTICE STEWART, DISSENTING:

The First Amendment declares that "Congress shall make no law respecting an establishment of religion, or prohibiting the free exercise thereof. . . ." It is, I think, a fallacious oversimplification to regard these two provisions as establishing a single constitutional standard of "separation of church and state," which can be mechanically applied in every case to delineate the required boundaries between government and religion. We err in the first place if we do not recognize, as a matter of history and as a matter of the imperatives of our free society, that religion and government must necessarily interact in countless ways. Secondly, the fact is that while in many contexts the Establishment Clause and the Free Exercise Clause fully complement each other, there are areas in which a doctrinaire reading of the Establishment Clause leads to irreconcilable conflict with the Free Exercise Clause.

A single obvious example should suffice to make the point. Spending federal funds to employ chaplains for the armed forces might be said to violate the Establishment Clause. Yet a lonely soldier stationed at some faraway outpost could surely complain that a government which did *not* provide him the opportunity for pastoral guidance was affirmatively prohibiting the free exercise of his religion. And such examples could readily be multiplied. The short of the matter is simply that the two relevant clauses of the First Amendment cannot accurately be reflected in a sterile metaphor which by its very nature may distort rather than illumine the problems involved in a particular case. . . .

It is this concept of constitutional protection embodied in our decisions which makes the cases before us such difficult ones for me. For there is involved in these cases a substantial free exercise claim on the part of those who affirmatively desire to have their children's school day open with the reading of passages from the Bible. . . .

What seems to me to be of paramount importance, then, is recognition of the fact that the claim advanced here in favor of Bible reading is sufficiently substantial to make simple reference to the constitutional phrase "establishment of religion" as inadequate an analysis of the cases before us as the ritualistic invocation of the nonconstitutional phrase "separation of church and state." . . .

To be specific, it seems to me clear that certain types of exercises would present situations in which no possibility of coercion on the part of secular officials could be claimed to exist. Thus, if such exercises were held either before or after the official school day, or if the school schedule were such that participation were merely one among a number of desirable alternatives, it could hardly be contended that the exercises did anything more than to provide an opportunity for the voluntary expression of religious belief. On the other hand, a law which provided for religious exercises during the school day and which contained no excusal provision would obviously be unconstitutionally coercive upon those who did not wish to participate.

Civil Liberties: Criminal Procedures

"The right of the people to be secure in their persons, houses, papers, and effects, against unreasonable searches and seizures, shall not be violated, and no warrants shall issue but upon probable cause, supported by oath or affirmation, and particularly describing the place to be searched, and the persons or things to be seized."

—Fourth Amendment

"No person shall be held to answer for a capital or other infamous crime unless on a presentment or indictment of a grand jury . . . nor shall any person be subject for the same offence to be twice put in jeopardy of life or limb; nor shall be compelled in any criminal case to be a witness against himself, nor be deprived of life, liberty, or property, without due process of law; nor shall private property be taken for public use, without just compensation."

—Fifth Amendment

"In all criminal prosecutions, the accused shall enjoy the right to a speedy and public trial, by an impartial jury of the state and district wherein the crime shall have been committed, which district shall have been previously ascertained by law, and to be informed of the nature and cause of the accusation; to be confronted with the witnesses against him; to have the compulsory process for obtaining witnesses in his favor, and to have the assistance of counsel for his defense."

—Sixth Amendment

"Excessive bail shall not be required, nor excessive fines imposed, nor cruel and unusual punishments inflicted."

—Eighth Amendment

The Due Process Clause of the Fourteenth Amendment protects those rights that are "of the very essence of a scheme of ordered liberty."

51. *Palko v. Connecticut* (1937)

The Bill of Rights was intended as a protection only against the actions of the federal government; it was not meant to apply to the states, as Chief Justice Marshall made clear in *Barron v. Baltimore* (1833). Marshall's position is correct as a historical matter, and is also borne out by the language of the Bill of Rights, which begins with the words "*Congress* shall make no law. . . ." In 1868, the adoption of the Fourteenth Amendment made it possible for the Court to require the states to obey at least some of the provisions of the Bill (and even certain unenumerated rights designated as "fundamental" by the Court). The process of "absorbing" or "incorporating" Bill of Rights provisions, one by one, into the Fourteenth Amendment did not, however, begin until *Gitlow v. New York* (1925), which dealt with freedom of speech and press. This process was brought to near completion by the Warren Court in a series of cases through the 1960s.

The rule of the Palko case, that the "double jeopardy" immunity of the Fifth Amendment is not applicable to the states, was overturned in *Benton v. Maryland* (1969), and Justice Cardozo's views concerning the dispensability, at the state level, of such Bill of Rights guarantees as jury trial and the privilege against self-incrimination, were subsequently rejected by the Court, particularly during the Warren era. Nonetheless, Cardozo's opinion has proved of enduring significance because of the still valid standards he established for the Court to use in determining whether or not a claimed right is accorded the imprimatur of due process.

Background: Palko's conviction in Connecticut for second-degree murder was successfully appealed by the state. Retried, he was convicted of first-degree murder and sentenced to death. Palko appealed to the United States Supreme Court on the ground that he had been placed in double jeopardy, in violation of the Fifth Amendment. The Supreme Court rejected his appeal.

MR. JUSTICE CARDOZO DELIVERED
THE OPINION OF THE COURT:

The argument for appellant is that whatever is forbidden by the Fifth Amendment is forbidden by the Fourteenth also. The Fifth Amendment, which is not directed to the states, but solely to the federal government, creates immunity from double jeopardy. No person shall be "subject for the same offense to be twice put in jeopardy of life or limb." The Fourteenth Amendment ordains, "nor shall any state deprive any person of life, liberty, or property, without due process of law." To retry a defendant, though under one indictment and only one, subjects him, it is said, to double jeopardy in violation of the Fifth Amendment, if the prosecution is one on behalf of the United States. From this the consequence is said to follow that there is a denial of life or liberty without due process of law, if the prosecution is one on behalf of the People of a State. . . .

We have said that in appellant's view the Fourteenth Amendment is to be taken as embodying the prohibitions of the Fifth. His thesis is even broader. Whatever would be a violation of the original bill of rights (Amendments 1 to 8) if done by the federal government is now equally unlawful by force of the Fourteenth Amendment if done by a state. There is no such general rule.

The Fifth Amendment provides, among other things, that no person shall be held to answer for a capital or otherwise infamous crime unless on presentment or indictment of a grand jury. This court has held that, in prosecutions by a state, presentment or indictment by a grand jury may give way to informations at the instance of a public officer. The Fifth Amendment provides also that no person shall be compelled in any criminal case to be a witness against himself. This court has said that, in prosecutions by a state, the exemption will fail if the state elects to end it. The Sixth Amendment calls for a jury trial in criminal cases and the Seventh for a jury trial in civil cases at common law where the value in controversy shall exceed twenty dollars. This court has ruled that consistently with those amendments trial by jury may be modified by a state or abolished altogether.

On the other hand, the due process clause of the Fourteenth Amendment may make it unlawful for a state to abridge by its statutes the freedom of speech which the First Amendment safeguards against encroachment by the Congress, or the like freedom of the press, or the free exercise of religion, or the right of peaceable assembly, without which speech would be unduly trammeled, or the right of one accused of crime to the benefit of counsel. In these and other situations immunities that are valid as against the federal government by force of the specific pledges of particular amendments have been found to be implicit in the concept of ordered liberty, and thus, through the Fourteenth Amendment, become valid as against the states.

The line of division may seem to be wavering and broken if there is a hasty catalogue of the cases on the one side and the other. Reflection and analysis will induce a different view. There emerges the perception of a rationalizing principle which gives to discrete instances a proper order and coherence. The right to trial by jury and the immunity from prosecution except as the result of an indictment may have value and importance. Even so, they are not of the very essence of a scheme of ordered liberty. To abolish them is not to violate a "principle of justice so rooted in the traditions and conscience of our people as to be ranked as fundamental." Few would be so narrow or provincial as to maintain that a fair and enlightened system of justice would be impossible without them. What is true of jury trials and indictments is true also, as the cases show, of the immunity from compulsory self-incrimination. This too might be lost, and justice still be done. Indeed, today as in the past there are students of our penal system who look upon the immunity as a mischief rather than a benefit, and who would limit its scope or destroy it altogether. No doubt there would remain the need to give protection against torture, physical or mental. Justice, however, would not perish if the accused were subject to a duty to respond to orderly inquiry. The exclusion of these immunities and privileges from the privileges and immunities protected against the action of the states has not been arbitrary or casual. It has been dictated by a study and appreciation of the meaning, the essential implications, of liberty itself.

We reach a different plane of social and moral values when we pass to the privileges and immunities that have been taken over from the earlier articles of the federal bill of rights and brought within the Fourteenth Amendment by a process of absorption. These in their origin were effective against the federal government alone. If the Fourteenth Amendment has absorbed them, the process of absorption has had its source in the belief that neither liberty nor justice would exist if they were sacrificed. This is true, for illustration, of freedom of thought and speech. Of that freedom one may say that it is the matrix, the indispensable condition, of nearly every other form of freedom. With rare aberrations a pervasive recognition of that truth can be traced in our history, political and legal. So it has come about that the domain of liberty, withdrawn by the Fourteenth Amendment from encroachment by the states, has been enlarged by latter-day judgments to include liberty of the mind as well as liberty of action. The extension became, indeed, a logical imperative when once it was recognized, as long ago it was, that liberty is something more than exemption from physical restraint, and that even in the field of substantive rights and duties the legislative judgment, if oppressive and arbitrary, may be overridden by the courts. . . .

Our survey of the cases serves, we think, to justify the statement that the dividing line between them, if not unfaltering throughout its course, has been true for the most part to a unifying principle. On which side of the line the case made out by the appellant has appropriate location must be the next inquiry and the final one. Is that kind of double jeopardy to which the statute has subjected him a hardship so acute and shocking that our polity will not endure it? Does it violate those "fundamental principles of liberty and justice which lie at the base of all our civil and political institutions"?

The answer surely must be "no." What the answer would have to be if the state were permitted after a trial free from error to try the accused over again or to bring another case against him, we have no occasion to consider. We deal with the statute before us and no other. The state is not attempting to wear the accused out by a multitude of cases with accumulated trials. It asks no more than this, that the case against him shall go on until there shall be a trial free from the corrosion of substantial legal error. This is not cruelty at all, nor even vexation in any immoderate degree. If the trial had been infected with error adverse to the accused, there might have been review at his instance, and as often as necessary to purge the vicious taint. A reciprocal privilege, subject at all times to the discretion of the presiding judge, . . . has now been granted to the state. There is here no seismic innovation. The edifice of justice stands, in its symmetry, to many, greater than before.

[Mr. Justice Butler dissented.]

Judicial error in issuing a warrant does not require exclusion of the evidence.

52. *United States v. Leon* (1984)

Under the Fourth Amendment, which prohibits "unreasonable" searches and seizures, the so-called "exclusionary rule" was formulated by the Supreme Court in *Weeks v. United States* (1914) to forbid the use of unconstitutionally seized evidence in the federal courts. Does this prohibition also apply to state courts? In the case of *Wolf v. Colorado* (1949), the Court ruled in the negative. *Mapp v. Ohio* (1961), however, overturned that decision and extended the exclusionary rule to the state courts.

In formulating the rule, the Court did not distinguish between deliberate unlawful conduct on the part of the police and honest mistake, or between illegal police action and a defective search warrant issued by a judicial officer. If the search did not meet Fourth Amendment standards, it appeared, the evidence must always be excluded. In 1976, however, the Court began a trend, continued in *Leon*, of modifying the rule so as to bring it into harmony with its rationale. Since the purpose of the exclusionary rule is to discourage police misconduct by removing the incentive to violate the Fourth Amendment—unlawful searches will not take place, so the reasoning goes, if the evidence they uncover is unusable in court—exclusion should not be applied where the deterrent effect of the rule is marginal or nonexistent. In *Leon*, the Court held that the exclusionary rule should not be enforced where officers had complied in good faith with the Fourth Amendment's requirement, even though a judge had issued the warrant improperly.

Background: A warrant issued by a California state judge resulted in the seizure of drugs, and led to a federal indictment of Leon and others. The district court granted a motion to suppress the evidence on the ground that the warrant had been issued on evidence amounting to less than probable cause. The court of appeals agreed with the district court but was reversed by the Supreme Court.

Justice White delivered
the opinion of the Court:

The Fourth Amendment contains no provision expressly precluding the use of evidence obtained in violation of its commands, and an examination of its origin and purposes makes clear that the use of fruits of a past unlawful search or seizure "work[s] no new Fourth Amendment wrong." The wrong condemned by the Amendment is "fully accomplished" by the unlawful search or seizure itself, and the exclusionary rule is neither intended nor able to "cure the invasion of the defendant's rights which he has already suffered." The rule thus operates as "a judicially created remedy designed to safeguard Fourth Amendment rights generally through its deterrent effect, rather than a personal constitutional right of the party aggrieved."

Whether the exclusionary sanction is appropriately imposed in a particular case, our decisions make clear, is "an issue separate from the question whether the Fourth Amendment rights of the party seeking to invoke the rule were violated by police conduct." Only the former question is currently before us, and it must be resolved by weighing the costs and benefits of preventing the use in the prosecution's case in chief of inherently trustworthy tangible evidence obtained in reliance on a search warrant issued by a detached and neutral magistrate that ultimately is found to be defective.

The substantial social costs exacted by the exclusionary rule for the vindication of Fourth Amendment rights have long been a source of concern. . . . Particularly when law enforcement officers have acted in objective good faith or their transgressions have been minor, the magnitude of the benefit conferred on . . . guilty defendants offends basic concepts of the criminal justice system. Indiscriminate application of the exclusionary rule, therefore, may well "generat[e] disrespect for the law and administration of justice." Accordingly, "[a]s with any remedial device, the application of the rule has been restricted to those areas where its remedial objectives are thought most efficaciously served."

Close attention to those remedial objectives has characterized our recent decisions concerning the scope of the Fourth Amendment exclusionary rule. The Court has, to be sure, not seriously questioned, "in the absence of a more efficacious sanction, the continued application of the rule to suppress evidence from the [prosecution's] case where a

Fourth Amendment violation has been substantial and deliberate. . . .'' Nevertheless, the balancing approach that has evolved in various contexts—including criminal trials—''forcefully suggest[s] that the exclusionary rule be more generally modified to permit the introduction of evidence obtained in the reasonable good-faith belief that a search or seizure was in accord with the Fourth Amendment.''

In *Stone v. Powell* [1976], the Court emphasized the costs of the exclusionary rule, expressed its view that limiting the circumstances under which Fourth Amendment claims could be raised in federal habeas corpus proceedings would not reduce the rule's deterrent effect, and held that a state prisoner who has been afforded a full and fair opportunity to litigate a Fourth Amendment claim may not obtain federal habeas relief on the ground that unlawfully obtained evidence had been introduced at his trial. Proposed extensions of the exclusionary rule to proceedings other than the criminal trial itself have been evaluated and rejected under the same analytic approach. In *United States v. Calandra* [1974], for example, we declined to allow grand jury witnesses to refuse to answer questions based on evidence obtained from an unlawful search or seizure since ''[a]ny incremental deterrent effect which might be achieved by extending the rule to grand jury proceedings is uncertain at best.''

As cases considering the use of unlawfully obtained evidence in criminal trials themselves make clear, it does not follow from the emphasis on the exclusionary rule's deterrent value that ''anything which deters illegal searches is thereby commanded by the Fourth Amendment.'' In determining whether persons aggrieved solely by the introduction of damaging evidence unlawfully obtained from their co-conspirators or co-defendants could seek suppression, for example, we found that the additional benefits of such an extension of the exclusionary rule would not outweigh its costs. Standing to invoke the rule has thus been limited to cases in which the prosecution seeks to use the fruits of an illegal search or seizure against the victim of police misconduct. . . .

Reasonable minds frequently may differ on the question whether a particular affidavit establishes probable cause, and we have thus concluded that the preference for warrants is most appropriately effectuated by according ''great deference'' to a magistrate's determination.

Deference to the magistrate, however, is not boundless. It is clear, first, that the deference accorded to a magistrate's finding of probable cause does not preclude inquiry into the knowing or reckless falsity of the affidavit on which that determination was based. Second, the courts must also insist that the magistrate purport to ''perform his 'neutral and detached' function and not serve merely as a rubber stamp for the police.''

Third, reviewing courts will not defer to a warrant based on an affidavit that does not ''provide the magistrate with a substantial basis for determining the existence of probable cause.'' . . .

Only in the first of these three situations, however, has the Court set forth a rationale for suppressing evidence obtained pursuant to a search warrant; in the other areas, it has simply excluded such evidence without considering whether Fourth Amendment interests will be advanced. To the extent that proponents of exclusion rely on its behavioral effects on judges and magistrates in these areas, their reliance is misplaced. First, the exclusionary rule is designed to deter police misconduct rather than to punish the errors of judges and magistrates. Second, there exists no evidence suggesting that judges and magistrates are inclined to ignore or subvert the Fourth Amendment or that lawlessness among these actors requires application of the extreme sanction of exclusion.

Third, and most important, we discern no basis, and are offered none, for believing that exclusion of evidence seized pursuant to a warrant will have a significant deterrent effect on the issuing judge or magistrate. . . . Judges and magistrates are not adjuncts to the law enforcement team; as neutral judicial officers, they have no stake in the outcome of particular criminal prosecutions. The threat of exclusion thus cannot be expected significantly to deter them. Imposition of the exclusionary sanction is not necessary meaningfully to inform judicial officers of their errors, and we cannot conclude that admitting evidence obtained pursuant to a warrant while at the same time declaring that the warrant was somehow defective will in any way reduce judicial officers' professional incentives to comply with the Fourth Amendment, encourage them to repeat their mistakes, or lead to the granting of all colorable warrant requests. . . .

[W]hen an officer acting with objective good faith has obtained a search warrant from a judge or magistrate and acted within its scope . . . there is no police illegality and thus nothing to deter. It is the magistrate's responsibility to determine whether the officer's allegations establish probable cause and, if so, to issue a warrant comporting in form with the requirements of the Fourth Amendment. In the ordinary case, an officer cannot be expected to question the magistrate's probable-cause determination or his judgment that the form of the warrant is technically sufficient. Penalizing the officer for the magistrate's error, rather than his own, cannot logically contribute to the deterrence of Fourth Amendment violations. . . .

We conclude that the marginal or nonexistent benefits produced by suppressing evidence obtained in objectively reasonable reliance on a subsequently invalidated search warrant cannot justify the substantial costs of exclusion. . . .

Suppression . . . remains an appropriate remedy if the magistrate or judge in issuing a warrant was misled by information in an affidavit that the affiant knew was false or would have known was false except for his reckless disregard of the truth. . . . Nor would an officer manifest objective good faith in relying on a warrant based on an affidavit "so lacking in indicia of probable cause as to render official belief in its existence entirely unreasonable." Finally, depending on the circumstances of the particular case, a warrant may be so facially deficient— i.e., in failing to particularize the place to be searched or the things to be seized—that the executing officers cannot reasonably presume it to be valid.

JUSTICE BLACKMUN, CONCURRING:

As the Court's opinion in this case makes clear, the Court has narrowed the scope of the exclusionary rule because of an empirical judgment that the rule has little appreciable effect in cases where officers act in objectively reasonable reliance on search warrants. Because I share the view that the exclusionary rule is not a constitutionally compelled corollary of the Fourth Amendment itself, I see no way to avoid making an empirical judgment of this sort, and I am satisfied that the Court has made the correct one on the information before it. . . .

If it should emerge from experience that, contrary to our expectations, the good-faith exception to the exclusionary rule results in a material change in police compliance with the Fourth Amendment, we shall have to reconsider what we have undertaken here.

[Justice Stevens wrote an opinion concurring in the judgment.]

Justice Brennan, with whom
Justice Marshall joins, dissenting:

[I]n case after case, I have witnessed the Court's gradual but determined strangulation of the [exclusionary] rule. It now appears that the Court's victory over the Fourth Amendment is complete. That today's decisions represent the pièce de résistance of the Court's past efforts cannot be doubted, for today the Court sanctions the use in the prosecution's case in chief of illegally obtained evidence against the individual whose rights have been violated—a result that had previously been thought to be foreclosed.

The Court seeks to justify this result on the ground that the "costs" of adhering to the exclusionary rule in cases like those before us exceed the "benefits." But the language of deterrence and of cost/benefit analysis, if used indiscriminately, can have a narcotic effect. It creates an illusion of technical precision and ineluctability. It suggests that not only constitutional principle but also empirical data support the majority's result. When the Court's analysis is examined carefully, however, it is clear that we have not been treated to an honest assessment of the merits of the exclusionary rule, but have instead been drawn into a curious world where the "costs" of excluding illegally obtained evidence loom to exaggerated heights and where the "benefits" of such exclusion are made to disappear with a mere wave of the hand.

[T]he task of combating crime and convicting the guilty will in every era seem of such critical and pressing concern that we may be lured by the temptations of expediency into forsaking our commitment to protecting individual liberty and privacy. It was for that very reason that the Framers of the Bill of Rights insisted that law enforcement efforts be permanently and unambiguously restricted in order to preserve personal freedoms. In the constitutional scheme they ordained, the sometimes unpopular task of ensuring that the government's enforcement efforts remain within the strict boundaries fixed by the Fourth Amendment was entrusted to the courts.

If [courts] lose their resolve, however, as the Court has done today, and give way to the seductive call of expediency, the vital guarantees of the Fourth Amendment are reduced to nothing more than a "form of words." . . .

A

[T]he Amendment, like other provisions of the Bill of Rights, restrains the power of the government as a whole; it does not specify only a particular agency and exempt all others. The judiciary is responsible, no less than the executive, for ensuring that constitutional rights are respected.

When that fact is kept in mind, the role of the courts and their possible involvement in the concerns of the Fourth Amendment comes into sharper focus. Because seizures are executed principally to secure evidence, and because such evidence generally has utility in our legal system only in the context of a trial supervised by a judge, it is apparent that the admission of illegally obtained evidence implicates the same constitutional concerns as the initial seizure of that evidence. Indeed, by admitting unlawfully seized evidence, the judiciary becomes a part of what is in fact a single governmental action prohibited by the terms of the Amendment. . . .

For my part, "[t]he right of the people to be secure in their persons, houses, papers, and effects, against unreasonable searches and seizures" comprises a personal right to exclude all evidence secured by means of unreasonable searches and seizures. The right to be free from the initial invasion of privacy and the right of exclusion are coordinate components of the central embracing right to be free from unreasonable searches and seizures. . . .

[I]f the Amendment is to have any meaning, police and the courts cannot be regarded as constitutional strangers to each other; because the evidence-gathering role of the police is directly linked to the evidence-admitting function of the courts, an individual's Fourth Amendment rights may be undermined as completely as by one as by the other.

B

[T]he Court's "reasonable mistake" exception to the exclusionary rule will tend to put a premium on police ignorance of the law. Armed with the assurance provided by today's decisions that evidence will always be admissible whenever an officer has "reasonably" relied upon a warrant, police departments will be encouraged to train officers that if a warrant has simply been signed, it is reasonable, without more, to rely on it. . . .

A chief consequence of today's decisions will be to convey a clear and unambiguous message to magistrates that their decisions to issue warrants are now insulated from subsequent judicial review. . . . If their decision to issue a warrant was correct, the evidence will be admitted; if their decision was incorrect but the police relied in good faith on the warrant, the evidence will also be admitted. Inevitably, the care and attention devoted to such an inconsequential chore will dwindle. . . .

When the public, as it quite properly has done in the past as well as in the present, demands that those in government increase their efforts to combat crime, it is all too easy for those government officials to seek expedient solutions. In contrast to such costly and difficult measures as building more prisons, improving law enforcement methods, or hiring more prosecutors and judges to relieve the overburdened court systems in the country's metropolitan areas, the relaxation of Fourth Amendment standards seems a tempting, costless means of meeting the public's demand for better law enforcement. In the long run, however, we as a society pay a heavy price for such expediency, because as Justice Jackson observed, the rights guaranteed in the Fourth Amendment "are not mere second-class rights but belong in the catalog of indispensable freedoms." *Brinegar v. United States* (1949) (dissenting opinion).

The Fourth Amendment's restrictions on searches apply also to electronic eavesdropping.

53a. *Olmstead v. United States* (1928)
53b. *Katz v. United States* (1967)

The searches familiar to the framers of the Bill of Rights, from their bitter experience with the detested British "writs of assistance" in the pre-Revolutionary period, involved physical entry into places. The framers addressed this problem in the Fourth Amendment through restrictions on searches. Today, however, electronic eavesdropping (which includes wiretapping) poses an even greater threat to personal security than physical searches. Electronic surveillance can be conducted in secret, from locations outside the dwelling; it may last for lengthy periods of time and intercept the conversations of many people besides the suspect. When the constitutional issue was presented to the Court for the first time in *Olmstead v. United States*, Chief Justice Taft's majority opinion took a narrow view of the Fourth Amendment, declaring that it protected only against search and seizures of "material things," not conversations, which are intangible. But Justice Brandeis's eloquent dissent, protesting the Court's failure to take a realistic view of the danger posed to security and privacy by this new type of search, eventually became the law of the land. *Katz v. United States* brought to an end forty years of constitutional controversy by overruling the *Olmstead* case. Justice Stewart's majority opinion declared that "the Fourth Amendment protects people, not places." Only Justice Black dissented, in a vehement opinion.

Background: Olmstead was engaged, during the Prohibition era, in large-scale smuggling of whiskey from Canada to the United States. With a group of confederates, he was convicted on evidence obtained by tapping their telephones from locations outside their homes and business office.

Katz was convicted of violating a federal statute by transmitting gambling information on the telephone from Los Angeles to Miami and Boston. His conversations were monitored by agents, who had attached an electronic device to the outside of the public telephone booth from which he placed his calls.

Olmstead v. United States

MR. CHIEF JUSTICE TAFT DELIVERED
THE OPINION OF THE COURT:

The information which led to the discovery of the conspiracy and its nature and extent was largely obtained by intercepting messages on the telephones of the conspirators by four Federal prohibition officers. Small wires were inserted along the ordinary telephone wires from the residences of four of the petitioners and those leading from the chief office. The insertions were made without trespass upon any property of the defendants. They were made in the basement of the large office building. The taps from house lines were made in the streets near the houses. . . .

The well-known historical purpose of the 4th Amendment, directed against general warrants and writs of assistance, was to prevent the use of governmental force to search a man's house, his person, his papers, and his effects, and to prevent their seizure against his will. . . .

The Amendment itself shows that the search is to be of material things—the person, the house, his papers or his effects. The description of the warrant necessary to make the proceeding lawful is that it must specify the place to be searched and the person or *things* to be seized. . . .

The language of the Amendment can not be extended and expanded to include telephone wires reaching to the whole world from the defendant's house or office. The intervening wires are not part of his house or office, any more than are the highways along which they are stretched. . . .

Congress may, of course, protect the secrecy of telephone messages by making them, when intercepted, inadmissible in evidence in Federal criminal trials, by direct legislation, and thus depart from the common law of evidence. But the courts may not adopt such a policy by attributing an enlarged and unusual meaning to the 4th Amendment. The reasonable view is that one who installs in his house a telephone instrument with connecting wires intends to project his voice to those quite outside, and that the wires beyond his house and messages while passing over them are not within the protection of the 4th Amendment. Here those who intercepted the projected voices were not in the house of either party to the conversation. . . .

We think, therefore, that the wire tapping here disclosed did not amount to a search or seizure within the meaning of the 4th Amendment.

MR. JUSTICE BRANDEIS, DISSENTING:

"We must never forget," said Mr. Chief Justice Marshall in *M'Culloch v. Maryland* [1819], "that it is *a Constitution* we are expounding." Since then, this court has repeatedly sustained the exercise of power by Congress, under various clauses of that instrument, over objects of which the Fathers could not have dreamed. We have likewise held that general limitations on the powers of government, like those embodied in the due process clauses of the 5th and 14th Amendments, do not forbid the United States or the states from meeting modern conditions by regulations which "a century ago, or even half a century ago, probably would have been rejected as arbitrary and oppressive." . . .

When the 4th and 5th Amendments were adopted, "the form that evil had theretofore taken" had been necessarily simple. Force and violence were then the only means known to man by which a government could directly effect self-incrimination. It could compel the individual to testify—a compulsion effected, if need be, by torture. It could secure possession of his papers and other articles incident to his private life—a seizure effected, if need be, by breaking and entry. Protection against such invasion of "the sanctities of a man's home and the privacies of life" was provided in the 4th and 5th Amendments, by specific language.

The protection guaranteed by the Amendments is much broader in scope. The makers of our Constitution undertook to secure conditions favorable to the pursuit of happiness. They recognized the significance of man's spiritual nature, of his feelings and of his intellect. They knew that only a part of the pain, pleasure and satisfactions of life are to be found in material things. They sought to protect Americans in their beliefs, their thoughts, their emotions and their sensations. They conferred, as against the government, the right to be let alone—the most comprehensive of rights and the right most valued by civilized men. To protect that right, every unjustifiable intrusion by the government upon the privacy of the individual, whatever the means employed, must be deemed a violation of the 4th Amendment.

[Mr. Justice Holmes, Mr. Justice Butler, and Mr. Justice Stone also wrote dissenting opinions.]

Katz v. United States

MR. JUSTICE STEWART DELIVERED
THE OPINION OF THE COURT:

Because of the misleading way the issues have been formulated, the parties have attached great significance to the characterization of the telephone booth from which the petitioner placed his calls. The petitioner has strenuously argued that the booth was a "constitutionally protected area.'' The Government has maintained with equal vigor that it was not. But this effort to decide whether or not a given "area," viewed in the abstract, is "constitutionally protected" deflects attention from the problem presented by this case. For the Fourth Amendment protects people, not places. What a person knowingly exposes to the public, even in his own home or office, is not a subject of Fourth Amendment protection. But what he seeks to preserve as private, even in an area accessible to the public, may be constitutionally protected.

The Government stresses the fact that the telephone booth from which the petitioner made his calls was constructed partly of glass, so that he was as visible after he entered it as he would have been if he had remained outside. But what he sought to exclude when he entered the booth was not the intruding eye—it was the uninvited ear. He did not shed his right to do so simply because he made his calls from a place where he might be seen. No less than an individual in a business office, in a friend's apartment, or in a taxicab, a person in a telephone booth may rely upon the protection of the Fourth Amendment. One who occupies it, shuts the door behind him, and pays the toll that permits him to place a call is surely entitled to assume that the words he utters into the mouthpiece will not be broadcast to the world. To read the Constitution more narrowly is to ignore the vital role that the public telephone has come to play in private communication.

The Government contends, however, that the activities of its agents in this case should not be tested by Fourth Amendment requirements, for the surveillance technique they employed involved no physical penetration of the telephone booth from which the petitioner placed his calls. It is true that the absence of such penetration was at one time thought to foreclose further Fourth Amendment inquiry, *Olmstead v. United States* [1928], for that Amendment was thought to limit only searches and seizures of tangible property. But "[t]he premise that property interests control the right of the Government to search and seize has been discredited." . . . Once this much is acknowledged, and once it is recognized that the Fourth Amendment protects people— and not simply "areas"—against unreasonable searches and seizures, it becomes clear that the reach of that Amendment cannot turn upon the presence or absence of a physical intrusion into any given enclosure.

We conclude that the underpinnings of *Olmstead* . . . have been so eroded by our subsequent decisions that the "tresspass" doctrine there enunciated can no longer be regarded as controlling. The Government's activities in electronically listening to and recording the petitioner's words violated the privacy upon which he justifiably relied while using the telephone booth and thus constituted a "search and seizure" within the meaning of the Fourth Amendment. The fact that the electronic device employed to achieve that end did not happen to penetrate the wall of the booth can have no constitutional significance.

The question remaining for decision, then, is whether the search and seizure conducted in this case complied with constitutional standards. In that regard, the Government's position is that its agents acted in an entirely defensible manner: They did not begin their electronic surveillance until investigation of the petitioner's activities had established a strong probability that he was using the telephone in question to transmit gambling information to persons in other States, in violation of federal law. Moreover, the surveillance was limited, both in scope and in duration, to the specific purpose of establishing the contents of the petitioner's unlawful telephonic communications. The agents confined their surveillance to the brief periods during which he used the telephone booth, and they took great care to overhear only the conversations of the petitioner himself.

Accepting this account of the Government's actions as accurate, it is clear that this surveillance was so narrowly circumscribed that a duly authorized magistrate, properly notified of the need for such investigation, specifically informed of the basis on which it was to proceed, and clearly apprised of the precise intrusion it would entail, could constitutionally have authorized, with appropriate safeguards, the very limited search and seizure that the Government asserts in fact took place. . . .

"Over and again this Court has emphasized that the mandate of the [Fourth] Amendment requires adherence to judicial processes," and that searches conducted outside the judicial process, without prior approval by judge or magistrate, are *per se* unreasonable under the Fourth Amendment—subject only to a few specifically established and well-delineated exceptions. . . .

These considerations do not vanish when the search in question is transferred from the setting of a home, an office, or a hotel room to that of a telephone booth. Wherever a man may be, he is entitled to know that he will remain free from unreasonable searches and seizures. The government agents here ignored "the procedure of antecedent justification . . . that is central to the Fourth Amendment,'' a procedure that we hold to be a constitutional precondition of the kind of electronic surveillance involved in this case. Because the surveillance here failed to meet that condition, and because it led to the petitioner's conviction, the judgment must be reversed.

MR. JUSTICE HARLAN, CONCURRING:

As the Court's opinion states, ''the Fourth Amendment protects people, not places.'' The question, however, is what protection it affords to those people. Generally, as here, the answer to that question requires reference to a ''place.'' My understanding of the rule that has emerged from prior decisions is that there is a twofold requirement, first that a person have exhibited an actual (subjective) expectation of privacy and, second, that the expectation be one that society is prepared to recognize as ''reasonable.'' Thus a man's home is, for most purposes, a place where he expects privacy, but objects, activities, or statements that he exposes to the ''plain view'' of outsiders are not ''protected'' because no intention to keep them to himself has been exhibited. On the other hand, conversations in the open would not be protected against being overheard, for the expectation of privacy under the circumstances would be unreasonable.

[Mr. Justice Douglas and Mr. Justice White also concurred in separate opinions.]

MR. JUSTICE BLACK, DISSENTING:

If I could agree with the Court that eavesdropping carried on by electronic means (equivalent to wiretapping) constitutes a ''search'' or ''seizure,'' I would be happy to join the Court's opinion. . . .

My basic objection is twofold: (1) I do not believe that the words of the Amendment will bear the meaning given them by today's decision, and (2) I do not believe that it is the proper role of this Court to rewrite the Amendment in order ''to bring it into harmony with the times'' and thus reach a result that many people believe to be desirable.

While I realize that an argument based on the meaning of words lacks the scope, and no doubt the appeal, of broad policy discussions and philosophical discourses on such nebulous subjects as privacy, for me the language of the Amendment is the crucial place to look in construing a written document such as our Constitution. . . .

The first clause [of the Fourth Amendment] protects "persons, houses, papers, and effects, against unreasonable searches and seizures. . . ." These words connote the idea of tangible things with size, form, and weight, things capable of being searched, seized, or both. The second clause of the Amendment still further establishes its Framers' purpose to limit its protection to tangible things by providing that no warrants shall issue but those "particularly describing the place to be searched, and the persons or things to be seized." A conversation overheard by eavesdropping whether by plain snooping or wiretapping, is not tangible and, under the normally accepted meanings of the words, can neither be searched nor seized. In addition the language of the second clause indicates that the Amendment refers not only to something tangible so it can be seized but to something already in existence so it can be described. Yet the Court's interpretation would have the Amendment apply to overhearing future conversations which by their very nature are nonexistent until they take place. How can one "describe" a future conversation, and, if one cannot, how can a magistrate issue a warrant to eavesdrop one in the future? It is argued that information showing what is expected to be said is sufficient to limit the boundaries of what later can be admitted into evidence; but does such general information really meet the specific language of the Amendment which says "particularly describing"? Rather than using language in a completely artificial way, I must conclude that the Fourth Amendment simply does not apply to eavesdropping.

Tapping telephone wires, of course, was an unknown possibility at the time the Fourth Amendment was adopted. But eavesdropping (and wiretapping is nothing more than eavesdropping by telephone) was . . . "an ancient practice which at common law was condemned as a nuisance. 4 Blackstone, *Commentaries* 168. In those days the eavesdropper listened by naked ear under the eaves of houses or their windows, or beyond their walls seeking out private discourse." There can be no doubt that the Framers were aware of this practice, and if they had desired to outlaw or restrict the use of evidence obtained by eavesdropping, I believe that they would have used the appropriate language to do so in the Fourth Amendment. They certainly would not have left such a task to the ingenuity of language-stretching judges. No one, it seems to me, can read the debates on the Bill of Rights without reaching the conclusion that its Framers and critics well knew the meaning of the words they used, what they would be understood to mean by others, their scope and their limitations. Under these circumstances it strikes me as a charge against their scholarship, their common sense and their candor to give the Fourth Amendment's language the eavesdropping meaning the Court imputes to it today. . . .

By clever word juggling the Court finds it plausible to argue that language aimed specifically at searches and seizures of things that can be searched and seized may, to protect privacy, be applied to eavesdropped evidence of conversations that can neither be searched nor seized. Few things happen to an individual that do not affect his privacy in one way or another. Thus, by arbitrarily substituting the Court's language, designed to protect privacy, for the Constitution's language, designed to protect against unreasonable searches and seizures, the Court has made the Fourth Amendment its vehicle for holding all laws violative of the Constitution which offend the Court's broadest concept of privacy. . . .

No general right is created by the Amendment so as to give this Court the unlimited power to hold unconstitutional everything which affects privacy. Certainly the Framers, well acquainted as they were with the excesses of governmental power, did not intend to grant this Court such omnipotent lawmaking authority as that. The history of governments proves that it is dangerous to freedom to repose such powers in courts.

Where danger threatens, police may "stop and frisk" a suspect on a standard of "reasonable suspicion."

54. *Terry v. Ohio* (1968)

It has been customary for police to conduct a "stop and frisk" (i.e., a pat down) of suspicious persons in situations where danger is apprehended. In *Terry*, the Court for the first time addressed this gray area of police activity, rejecting the polar opposite views that the Fourth Amendment does not apply at all to a "mere" stop and frisk (as opposed to a "full-blown" arrest and search) or, conversely, that the amendment applies in its full rigor. The Court chose instead a standard of "reasonable suspicion" that falls short of the "probable cause" required by the Amendment. The *Terry* rationale has spawned a large progeny, including airport searches based on drug courier "profiles."

Background: McFadden, a veteran Cleveland police officer, observed unusual conduct on the part of Terry and two other men which suggested to him that they were casing a store in order to rob it. He stopped the men, patted them down, and discovered guns, which were admitted into evidence. The Ohio Supreme Court rejected Terry's appeal of his conviction, a judgment sustained by the Supreme Court.

MR. CHIEF JUSTICE WARREN DELIVERED
THE OPINION OF THE COURT:

I

[T]his question thrusts to the fore difficult and troublesome issues regarding a sensitive area of police activity—issues which have never before been squarely presented to this Court. Reflective of the tensions involved are the practical and constitutional arguments pressed with great vigor on both sides of the public debate over the power of the police to "stop and frisk"—as it is sometimes euphemistically termed—suspicious persons.

On the one hand, it is frequently argued that in dealing with the rapidly unfolding and often dangerous situations on city streets the police are in need of an escalating set of flexible responses, graduated in relation to the amount of information they possess. For this purpose it is urged that distinctions should be made between a "stop" and an "arrest" (or a "seizure" of a person), and between a "frisk" and a "search." Thus, it is argued, the police should be allowed to "stop" a person and detain him briefly for questioning upon suspicion that he may be connected with criminal activity. Upon suspicion that the person may be armed, the police should have the power to "frisk" him for weapons. If the "stop" and the "frisk" give rise to probable cause to believe that the suspect has committed a crime, then the police should be empowered to make a formal "arrest," and a full incident "search" of the person. This scheme is justified in part upon the notion that a "stop" and a "frisk" amount to a mere "minor inconvenience and petty indignity," which can properly be imposed upon the citizen in the interest of effective law enforcement on the basis of a police officer's suspicion.

On the other side the argument is made that the authority of the police must be strictly circumscribed by the law of arrest and search as it has developed to date in the traditional jurisprudence of the Fourth Amendment. . . . The heart of the Fourth Amendment, the argument runs, is a severe requirement of specific justification for any intrusion upon protected personal security, coupled with a highly developed system of judicial controls to enforce upon the agents of the State the commands of the Constitution. Acquiescence by the courts in the compulsion inherent in the field interrogation practices at issue here, it is urged, would constitute an abdication of judicial control over, and indeed an encouragement of, substantial interference with liberty and personal security by police officers. . . .

The exclusionary rule has its limitations as a tool of judicial control. It cannot properly be invoked to exclude the products of legitimate police investigative techniques on the ground that much conduct which is closely similar involves unwarranted intrusions upon constitutional protections. Moreover, in some contexts the rule is ineffective as a deterrent. Street encounters between citizens and police officers are incredibly rich in diversity. They range from wholly friendly exchanges of pleasantries or mutually useful information to hostile confrontations of armed men involving arrests, or injuries, or loss of life. . . . Encounters are initiated by the police for a wide variety of purposes, some of which are wholly unrelated to a desire to prosecute for crime. Doubtless some police "field interrogation" conduct violates the Fourth Amendment. But a stern refusal by this Court to condone such activity does not necessarily render it responsive to the exclusionary rule. Regardless of how effective the rule may be where obtaining convictions is an important objective of the police, it is powerless to deter invasions of constitutionally guaranteed rights where the police either have no interest in prosecuting or are willing to forgo successful prosecution in the interest of serving some other goal.

Proper adjudication of cases in which the exclusionary rule is invoked demands a constant awareness of these limitations. The wholesale harassment by certain elements of the police community, of which minority groups, particularly Negroes, frequently complain, will not be stopped by the exclusion of any evidence from any criminal trial. Yet a rigid and unthinking application of the exclusionary rule, in futile protest against practices which it can never be used effectively to control, may exact a high toll in human injury and frustration of efforts to prevent crime. Under our decision, courts still retain their traditional responsibility to guard against police conduct which is overbearing or harassing, or which trenches upon personal security without the objective evidentiary justification which the Constitution requires. When such conduct is identified, it must be condemned by the judiciary and its fruits must be excluded from evidence in criminal trials. . . .

[W]e turn our attention to the quite narrow question posed by the facts before us: whether it is always unreasonable for a policeman to seize a person and subject him to a limited search for weapons unless there is probable cause for an arrest.

II

Our first task is to establish at what point in this encounter the Fourth Amendment becomes relevant. That is, we must decide whether and when Officer McFadden "seized" Terry and whether and when he conducted a "search." There is some suggestion in the use of such terms as "stop" and "frisk" that such police conduct is outside the purview of the Fourth Amendment because neither action rises to the level of a "search" or "seizure" within the meaning of the Constitution. We emphatically reject this notion. It is quite plain that the Fourth Amendment governs "seizures" of the person which do not eventuate in a trip to the station house and prosecution for crime— "arrests" in traditional terminology. It must be recognized that whenever a police officer accosts an individual and restrains his freedom to walk away, he has "seized" that person. And it is nothing less than sheer torture of the English language to suggest that a careful exploration of the outer surfaces of a person's clothing all over his or her body in an attempt to find weapons is not a "search." Moreover, it is simply fantastic to urge that such a procedure performed in public by a policeman while the citizen stands helpless, perhaps facing a wall with his hands raised, is a "petty indignity." It is a serious intrusion upon the sanctity of the person, which may inflict great indignity and arouse strong resentment, and it is not to be undertaken lightly. . . .

We therefore reject the notions that the Fourth Amendment does not come into play at all as a limitation upon police conduct if the officers stop short of something called a "technical arrest" or a "full-blown search."

In this case there can be no question, then, that Officer McFadden "seized" petitioner and subjected him to a "search" when he took hold of him and patted down the outer surfaces of his clothing. We must decide whether at that point it was reasonable for Officer Mc-Fadden to have interfered with petitioner's personal security as he did. And in determining whether the seizure and search were "unreasonable" our inquiry is a dual one—whether the officer's action was justified at its inception, and whether it was reasonably related in scope to the circumstances which justified the interference in the first place.

III

If this case involved police conduct subject to the Warrant Clause of the Fourth Amendment, we would have to ascertain whether "probable cause" existed to justify the search and seizure which took place. . . . But we deal here with an entire rubric of police conduct—necessarily swift action predicated upon the on-the-spot observations of the officer on the beat—which historically has not been, and as a practical matter could not be, subjected to the warrant procedure. Instead, the conduct involved in this case must be tested by the Fourth Amendment's general proscription against unreasonable searches and seizures. . . .

[I]n justifying the particular intrusion the police officer must be able to point to specific and articulable facts which, taken together with rational inferences from those facts, reasonably warrant that intrusion. The scheme of the Fourth Amendment becomes meaningful only when it is assured that at some point the conduct of those charged with enforcing the laws can be subjected to the more detached, neutral scrutiny of a judge who must evaluate the reasonableness of a particular search or seizure in light of the particular circumstances. And in making that assessment it is imperative that the facts be judged against an objective standard: would the facts available to the officer at the moment of the seizure or the search "warrant a man of reasonable caution in the belief" that the action taken was appropriate? Anything less would invite intrusions upon constitutionally guaranteed rights based on nothing more substantial than inarticulate hunches, a result this Court has consistently refused to sanction. And simple " 'good faith on the part of the arresting officer is not enough.' " . . .

The crux of this case, . . . is not the propriety of Officer McFadden's taking steps to investigate petitioner's suspicious behavior, but rather, whether there was justification for McFadden's invasion of Terry's personal security by searching him for weapons in the course of that investigation. We are now concerned with more than the governmental interest in investigating crime; in addition, there is the more immediate interest of the police officer in taking steps to assure himself that the person with whom he is dealing is not armed with a weapon that could unexpectedly and fatally be used against him. Certainly it would be unreasonable to require that police officers take unnecessary risks in the performance of their duties. American criminals have a long tradition of armed violence, and every year in this country many law enforcement officers are killed in the line of duty, and thousands more are wounded. . . .

In view of these facts, we cannot blind ourselves to the need for law enforcement officers to protect themselves and other prospective victims of violence in situations where they may lack probable cause for an arrest. When an officer is justified in believing that the individual whose suspicious behavior he is investigating at close range is armed and presently dangerous to the officer or to others, it would appear to be clearly unreasonable to deny the officer the power to take necessary measures to determine whether the person is in fact carrying a weapon and to neutralize the threat of physical harm.

It does not follow that because an officer may lawfully arrest a person only when he is apprised of facts sufficient to warrant a belief that the person has committed or is committing a crime, the officer is equally unjustified, absent that kind of evidence, in making any intrusions short of an arrest. Moreover, a perfectly reasonable apprehension of danger may arise long before the officer is possessed of adequate information to justify taking a person into custody for the purpose of prosecuting him for a crime.

Our evaluation of the proper balance that has to be struck in this type of case leads us to conclude that there must be a narrowly drawn authority to permit a reasonable search for weapons for the protection of the police officer, where he has reason to believe that he is dealing with an armed and dangerous individual, regardless of whether he has probable cause to arrest the individual for a crime. The officer need not be absolutely certain that the individual is armed; the issue is whether a reasonably prudent man in the circumstances would be warranted in the belief that his safety or that of others was in danger. And in determining whether the officer acted reasonably in such circumstances, due weight must be given, not to his inchoate and unparticularized suspicion or "hunch," but to the specific reasonable inferences which he is entitled to draw from the facts in light of his experience.

IV

We must now examine the conduct of Officer McFadden in this case to determine whether his search and seizure of petitioner were reasonable, both at their inception and as conducted. He had observed Terry, together with Chilton and another man, acting in a manner he took to be preface to a "stick-up." We think on the facts and circumstances Officer McFadden detailed before the trial judge a reasonably prudent man would have been warranted in believing petitioner was armed and thus presented a threat to the officer's safety while he was investigating his suspicious behavior. . . . We cannot say his decision at that point to seize Terry and pat his clothing for weapons was the product of a volatile or inventive imagination, or was undertaken simply as an act of harassment; the record evidences the tempered act of a policeman who in the course of an investigation had to make a quick decision as to how to protect himself and others from possible danger, and took limited steps to do so.

We need not develop at length in this case the limitations which the Fourth Amendment places upon a protective seizure and search for weapons. These limitations will have to be developed in the concrete factual circumstances of individual cases. Suffice it to note that such a search, unlike a search without a warrant incident to a lawful arrest, is not justified by any need to prevent the disappearance or destruction of evidence of crime. The sole justification of the search in the present situation is the protection of the police officer and others nearby, and it must therefore be confined in scope to an intrusion reasonably designed to discover guns, knives, clubs, or other hidden instruments for the assault of the police officer.

The scope of the search in this case presents no serious problem in light of these standards. Officer McFadden patted down the outer clothing of petitioner and his two companions. He did not place his hands in their pockets or under the outer surface of their garments until he had felt weapons, and then he merely reached for and removed the guns. . . . Officer McFadden confined his search strictly to what was minimally necessary to learn whether the men were armed and to disarm them once he discovered the weapons. He did not conduct a general exploratory search for whatever evidence of criminal activity he might find.

V

We conclude that the revolver seized from Terry was properly admitted in evidence against him. At the time he seized petitioner and searched him for weapons, Officer McFadden had reasonable grounds to believe that petitioner was armed and dangerous, and it was necessary for the protection of himself and others to take swift measures to discover the true facts and neutralize the threat of harm if it materialized. The policeman carefully restricted his search to what was appropriate to the discovery of the particular items which he sought. Each case of this sort will, of course, have to be decided on its own facts. We merely hold today that where a police officer observes unusual conduct which leads him reasonably to conclude in light of his experience that criminal activity may be afoot and that the persons with whom he is dealing may be armed and presently dangerous, where in the course of investigating this behavior he identifies himself as a policeman and makes reasonable inquiries, and where nothing in the initial stages of the encounter serves to dispel his reasonable fear for his own or others' safety, he is entitled for the protection of himself and others in the area to conduct a carefully limited search of the outer clothing of such persons in an attempt to discover weapons which might be used to assault him. Such a search is a reasonable search under the Fourth Amendment, and any weapons seized may properly be introduced in evidence against the person from whom they were taken.

[Mr. Justice Black, Mr. Justice Harlan, and Mr. Justice White wrote separate concurring opinions. Mr. Justice Douglas wrote a dissenting opinion.]

The right to counsel in criminal cases applies equally to state and federal courts.

55. *Gideon v. Wainwright* (1963)

The sequence of constitutional events culminating in *Gideon v. Wainwright* began in *Powell v. Alabama* (1932), where the Court held for the first time that due process requires states to provide counsel for indigent defendants in criminal cases. However, in *Betts v. Brady* (1942), the *Powell* decision was narrowed to cases where counsel is deemed indispensable to assure a fair trial. (The *Powell* case had involved illiterate defendants charged with a capital crime; the *Betts* case concerned a small-time robber who had acquired some familiarity with trial procedure from earlier charges against him.) In *Gideon v. Wainwright* the Court reversed itself and rejected the *Betts* decision. This case thus marked another step in the "nationalization" of the Bill of Rights.

Background: Gideon, a Florida indigent, was tried for breaking into a poolroom in order to commit a felony. Denied counsel, he acted as his own lawyer and was found guilty. The Supreme Court reversed the Florida court's decision on the ground that the Sixth Amendment's guarantee of right to counsel was applicable, via the Due Process Clause, in all the courts of the land.

Mr. Justice Black delivered
the opinion of the Court:

Since 1942, when *Betts v. Brady* was decided by a divided Court, the problem of a defendant's federal constitutional right to counsel in a state court has been a continuing source of controversy and litigation in both state and federal courts. To give this problem another review here, we granted certiorari. Since Gideon was proceeding in forma pauperis, we appointed counsel to represent him and requested both sides to discuss in their briefs and oral arguments the following: "Should this Court's holding in *Betts v. Brady* be reconsidered?" . . .

The Sixth Amendment provides, "In all criminal prosecutions, the accused shall enjoy the right . . . to have the Assistance of Counsel for his defence." We have construed this to mean that in federal courts counsel must be provided for defendants unable to employ counsel unless the right is competently and intelligently waived. *Betts* argued that this right is extended to indigent defendants in state courts by the Fourteenth Amendment. In response the Court stated that, while the Sixth Amendment laid down "no rule for the conduct of the States, the question recurs whether the constraint laid by the Amendment upon the national courts expresses a rule so fundamental and essential to a fair trial, and so, to due process of law, that it is made obligatory upon the States by the Fourteenth Amendment." In order to decide whether the Sixth Amendment's guarantee of counsel is of this fundamental nature, the Court in *Betts* set out and considered "[r]elevant data on the subject . . . afforded by constitutional and statutory provisions subsisting in the colonies and the States prior to the inclusion of the Bill of Rights in the national Constitution, and in the constitutional, legislative, and judicial history of the States to the present date." On the basis of this historical data the Court concluded that "appointment of counsel is not a fundamental right, essential to a fair trial." . . .

We accept *Betts v. Brady*'s assumption, based as it was on our prior cases, that a provision of the Bill of Rights which is "fundamental and essential to a fair trial" is made obligatory upon the States by the Fourteenth Amendment. We think the Court in *Betts* was wrong, however, in concluding that the Sixth Amendment's guarantee of counsel is not one of these fundamental rights. Ten years before *Betts v. Brady*, this Court, after full consideration of all the historical data examined in *Betts*, had unequivocally declared that "the right to the aid of counsel is of this fundamental character." *Powell v. Alabama* (1932). While the Court at the close of its *Powell* opinion did by its language, as this Court frequently does, limit its holding to the particular facts and circumstances of that case, its conclusions about the fundamental nature of the right to counsel are unmistakable. . . .

[T]he Court in *Betts v. Brady* made an abrupt break with its own well-considered precedents. In returning to these old precedents, sounder we believe than the new, we but restore constitutional principles established to achieve a fair system of justice. Not only these precedents but also reason and reflection require us to recognize that in our adversary system of criminal justice, any person haled into court, who is too poor to hire a lawyer, cannot be assured a fair trial unless counsel is provided for him. This seems to us to be an obvious truth. Governments, both state and federal, quite properly spend vast sums of money to establish machinery to try defendants accused of crime. Lawyers to prosecute are everywhere deemed essential to protect the public's interest in an orderly society. Similarly, there are few defendants charged with crime, few indeed, who fail to hire the best lawyers they can get to prepare and present their defenses. That government hires lawyers to prosecute and defendants who have the money hire lawyers to defend are the strongest indications of the widespread belief that lawyers in criminal courts are necessities, not luxuries. The right of one charged with crime to counsel may not be deemed fundamental and essential to fair trials in some countries, but it is in ours. From the very beginning, our state and national constitutions and laws have laid great emphasis on procedural and substantive safeguards designed to assure fair trials before impartial tribunals in which every defendant stands equal before the law. This noble ideal cannot be realized if the poor man charged with crime has to face his accusers without a lawyer to assist him. . . .

The Court in *Betts v. Brady* departed from the sound wisdom upon which the Court's holding in *Powell v. Alabama* rested. Florida, supported by two other States, has asked that *Betts v. Brady* be left intact. Twenty-two States, as friends of the Court, argue that *Betts* was "an anachronism when handed down" and that it should now be overruled. We agree.

The judgment is reversed and the case is remanded to the Supreme Court of Florida for further action not inconsistent with this opinion.

MR. JUSTICE HARLAN, CONCURRING:

I agree that *Betts v. Brady* should be overruled, but consider it entitled to a more respectful burial than has been accorded, at least on the part of those of us who were not on the Court when that case was decided.

I cannot subscribe to the view that *Betts v. Brady* represented "an abrupt break with its own well-considered precedents." In 1932, in *Powell v. Alabama*, a capital case, this Court declared that under the particular facts there presented—"the ignorance and illiteracy of the defendants, their youth, the circumstances of public hostility . . . and above all that they stood in deadly peril of their lives"—the state court had a duty to assign counsel for the trial as a necessary requisite of due process of law. It is evident that these limiting facts were not added to the opinion as an afterthought; they were repeatedly emphasized, and were clearly regarded as important to the result.

Thus when this Court, a decade later, decided *Betts v. Brady*, it did no more than to admit of the possible existence of special circumstances in noncapital as well as capital trials, while at the same time insisting that such circumstances be shown in order to establish a denial of due process. The declaration that the right to appointed counsel in state prosecutions, as established in *Powell v. Alabama*, was not limited to capital cases was in truth not a departure from, but an extension of, existing precedent. . . .

I wish to make a further observation. When we hold a right or immunity, valid against the Federal Government, to be "implicit in the concept of ordered liberty" and thus valid against the States, I do not read our past decisions to suggest that by so holding, we automatically carry over an entire body of federal law and apply it in full sweep to the States. Any such concept would disregard the frequently wide disparity between the legitimate interests of the States and of the Federal Government, the divergent problems that they face, and the significantly different consequences of their actions. In what is done today I do not understand the Court to depart from the principles laid down in *Palko v. Connecticut* [1937], or to embrace the concept that the Fourteenth Amendment "incorporates" the Sixth Amendment as such.

[Mr. Justice Douglas and Mr. Justice Clark also wrote concurring opinions.]

Self-incriminating confessions made without the opportunity to consult counsel violate due process.

56. *Miranda v. Arizona* (1966)

This landmark decision of the Warren Court concerns a cluster of cases dealing with self-incriminating confessions made by suspects to the police when no counsel was present. The cases were decided in a consolidated opinion. Prior to the *Miranda* decision the Court had "incorporated" into the Fourteenth Amendment's Due Process Clause, as binding on the states, the Fifth Amendment's privilege against self-incrimination (*Malloy v. Hogan* [1964]) and the Sixth Amendment's right to counsel guarantee (*Gideon v. Wainright* [1963]).

Background: Miranda, arrested for kidnapping and rape, was taken to a special interrogation room where he signed a confession. The document stated that he had confessed voluntarily. He was not, however, advised of his right to remain silent or offered an opportunity to consult with counsel, which he requested. The Arizona Supreme Court upheld the guilty verdict, but the United States Supreme Court reversed the ruling.

Mr. Chief Justice Warren delivered
the opinion of the Court:

The cases before us raise questions which go to the roots of our concepts of American criminal jurisprudence: the restraints society must observe consistent with the Federal Constitution in prosecuting individuals for crime. More specifically, we deal with the admissibility of statements obtained from an individual who is subjected to custodial police interrogation and the necessity for procedures which assure that the individual is accorded his privilege under the Fifth Amendment to the Constitution not to be compelled to incriminate himself.

We start here with the premise that our holding is not an innovation in our jurisprudence, but is an application of principles long recognized and applied in other settings. . . .

[This decision is] but an explication of basic rights that are enshrined in our Constitution—that ''No person . . . shall be compelled in any criminal case to be a witness against himself,'' and that ''the accused shall . . . have the Assistance of Counsel''—rights which were put in jeopardy in that case through official overbearing. These precious rights were fixed in our Constitution only after centuries of persecution and struggle. . . .

Our holding will be spelled out with some specificity in the pages which follow but briefly stated it is this: the prosecution may not use statements, whether exculpatory or inculpatory, stemming from custodial interrogation of the defendant unless it demonstrates the use of procedural safeguards effective to secure the privilege against self-incrimination. By custodial interrogation, we mean questioning initiated by law enforcement officers after a person has been taken into custody or otherwise deprived of his freedom of action in any significant way.

As for the procedural safeguards to be employed, unless other fully effective means are devised to inform accused persons of their right of silence and to assure a continuous opportunity to exercise it, the following measures are required. Prior to any questioning, the person must be warned that he has a right to remain silent, that any statement he does make may be used as evidence against him, and that he has a right to the presence of an attorney, either retained or appointed. The defendant may waive effectuation of these rights, provided the waiver is made voluntarily, knowingly and intelligently. If, however, he indicates in any manner and at any stage of the process that he wishes to consult with an attorney before speaking there can be no questioning. Likewise, if the individual is alone and indicates in any manner that he does not wish to be interrogated, the police may not question him. The mere fact that he may have answered some questions or volunteered some statements on his own does not deprive him of the right to refrain from answering any further inquiries until he has consulted with an attorney and thereafter consents to be questioned.

The constitutional issue we decide in each of these cases is the admissibility of statements obtained from a defendant questioned while in custody or otherwise deprived of his freedom of action in any significant way. In each, the defendant was questioned by police officers, detectives, or a prosecuting attorney in a room in which he was cut off from the outside world. In none of these cases was the defendant given a full and effective warning of his rights at the outset of the interrogation process. In all the cases, the questioning elicited oral admissions, and in three of them, signed statements as well which were admitted at their trials. They all thus share salient features—incommunicado interrogation of individuals in a police-dominated atmosphere, resulting in self-incriminating statements without full warnings of constitutional rights.

An understanding of the nature and setting of this in-custody interrogation is essential to our decisions today. The difficulty in depicting what transpires at such interrogations stems from the fact that in this country they have largely taken place incommunicado. From extensive factual studies undertaken in the early 1930's, including the famous Wickersham Report to Congress by a Presidential Commission, it is clear that police violence and the "third degree" flourished at that time. In a series of cases decided by this Court long after these studies, the police resorted to physical brutality—beating, hanging, whipping—and to sustained and protracted questioning incommunicado in order to extort confessions. The Commission on Civil Rights in 1961 found much evidence to indicate that "some policemen still resort to physical force to obtain confessions." The use of physical brutality and violence is not, unfortunately, relegated to the past or to any part of the country. . . .

The examples given above are undoubtedly the exception now, but they are sufficiently widespread to be the object of concern. Unless a proper limitation upon custodial interrogation is achieved—such as these decisions will advance—there can be no assurance that practices of this nature will be eradicated in the foreseeable future. . . .

Again we stress that the modern practice of in-custody interrogation is psychologically rather than physically oriented. As we have stated before, . . . "coercion can be mental as well as physical, and that the blood of the accused is not the only hallmark of an unconstitutional inquisition." *Blackburn v. Alabama* (1960). Interrogation still takes place in privacy. Privacy results in secrecy and this in turn results in a gap in our knowledge as to what in fact goes on in the interrogation rooms. A valuable source of information about present police practices, however, may be found in various police manuals and texts which document procedures employed with success in the past, and which recommend various other effective tactics. . . .

[T]he setting prescribed by the manuals and observed in practice becomes clear. In essence, it is this: To be alone with the subject is essential to prevent distraction and to deprive him of any outside support. The aura of confidence in his guilt undermines his will to resist. He merely confirms the preconceived story the police seek to have him describe. Patience and persistence, at times relentless questioning, are employed. To obtain a confession, the interrogator must "patiently maneuver himself or his quarry into a position from which the desired objective may be attained." When normal procedures fail to produce the needed result, the police may resort to deceptive stratagems such as giving false legal advice. It is important to keep the subject off balance, for example, by trading on his insecurity about himself or his surroundings. The police then persuade, trick, or cajole him out of exercising his constitutional rights. . . .

It is obvious that such an interrogation environment is created for no purpose other than to subjugate the individual to the will of his examiner. This atmosphere carries its own badge of intimidation. To be sure, this is not physical intimidation, but it is equally destructive of human dignity. The current practice of incommunicado interrogation is at odds with one of our Nation's most cherished principles—that the individual may not be compelled to incriminate himself. Unless adequate protective devices are employed to dispel the compulsion inherent in custodial surroundings, no statement obtained from the defendant can truly be the product of his free choice.

[T]here can be no doubt that the Fifth Amendment privilege is available outside of criminal court proceedings and serves to protect persons in all settings in which their freedom of action is curtailed in any significant way from being compelled to incriminate themselves. We have concluded that without proper safeguards the process of in-custody interrogations of persons suspected or accused of crime contains inherently compelling pressures which work to undermine the individual's will to resist and to compel him to speak where he would not otherwise do so freely. In order to combat these pressures and to permit a full opportunity to exercise the privilege against self-incrimination, the accused must be adequately and effectively apprised of his rights and the exercise of those rights must be fully honored. . . .

The circumstances surrounding in-custody interrogation can operate very quickly to overbear the will of one merely made aware of his privilege by his interrogators. Therefore, the right to have counsel present at the interrogation is indispensable to the protection of the Fifth Amendment privilege under the system we delineate today. Our aim is to assure that the individual's right to choose between silence and speech remains unfettered throughout the interrogation process. . . .

Our decision is not intended to hamper the traditional function of police officers in investigating crime. . . . General on-the-scene questioning as to facts surrounding a crime or other general questioning of citizens in the fact-finding process is not affected by our holding. It is an act of responsible citizenship for individuals to give whatever information they may have to aid in law enforcement. In such situations the compelling atmosphere inherent in the process of in-custody interrogation is not necessarily present.

In dealing with statements obtained through interrogation, we do not purport to find all confessions inadmissible. Confessions remain a proper element in law enforcement. Any statement given freely and voluntarily without any compelling influences is, of course, admissible in evidence. . . .

In announcing these principles, we are not unmindful of the burdens which law enforcement officials must bear, often under trying circumstances. We also fully recognize the obligation of all citizens to aid in enforcing the criminal laws. This Court, while protecting individual rights, has always given ample latitude to law enforcement agencies in the legitimate exercise of their duties. The limits we have placed on the interrogation process should not constitute an undue interference with a proper system of law enforcement. . . .

We have already pointed out that the Constitution does not require any specific code of procedures for protecting the privilege against self-incrimination during custodial interrogation. Congress and the States are free to develop their own safeguards for the privilege, so long as they are fully as effective as those described above in informing accused persons of their right of silence and in affording a continuous opportunity to exercise it. In any event, however, the issues presented are of constitutional dimensions and must be determined by the courts.

MR. JUSTICE HARLAN, WHOM MR. JUSTICE STEWART
AND MR. JUSTICE WHITE JOIN, DISSENTING:

I believe the decision of the Court represents poor constitutional law and entails harmful consequences for the country at large. How serious these consequences may prove to be only time can tell. . . .

The new rules are not designed to guard against police brutality or other unmistakably banned forms of coercion. Those who use third-degree tactics and deny them in court are equally able and destined to lie as skillfully about warnings and waivers. Rather, the thrust of the new rules is to negate all pressures, to reinforce the nervous or ignorant suspect, and ultimately to discourage any confession at all. The aim in short is toward ''voluntariness'' in a utopian sense, or to view it from a different angle, voluntariness with a vengeance. . . .

Without at all subscribing to the generally black picture of police conduct painted by the Court, I think it must be frankly recognized at the onset that police questioning allowable under due process precedents may inherently entail some pressure on the suspect and may seek advantage in his ignorance or weaknesses. The atmosphere and questioning techniques, proper and fair though they be, can in themselves exert a tug on the suspect to confess. . . . Until today, the role of the

Constitution has been only to sift out *undue* pressure, not to assure spontaneous confessions.

[Mr. Justice Clark and Mr. Justice White also wrote dissenting opinions.]

The death penalty does not invariably constitute "cruel and unusual punishment."

57. *Gregg v. Georgia* (1976)

This case must be viewed against the backdrop of the decision in *Furman v. Georgia* (1972), which dealt with the constitutionality of three death sentences, two involving murder and rape in Georgia, and the third, rape in Texas. At the time of that decision, the federal criminal code and the laws of forty states and the District of Columbia authorized capital punishment for a variety of crimes. (Since 1930, murder and rape had accounted for 99 percent of all executions, and murder by itself for around 87 percent. A number of jurisdictions permitted capital punishment also for such crimes as aircraft piracy, espionage, kidnapping, and treason.) But the number of executions had declined steadily, from an average of over 120 annually in the 1940s to 21 in 1963, 15 in 1964, 7 in 1965, 1 in 1966, and 2 in 1967.

The pace has picked up. From the *Gregg* decision in 1976 through December 31, 1993, 226 executions took place—an average of about 13 per year—with two states, Texas (71) and Florida (32), accounting for nearly half the total.

In the *Furman* case, the Court ruled, by a majority of five to four, that the death penalty, as applied in Georgia and Texas—and, in effect, in nearly all other jurisdictions—constituted cruel and unusual punishment, since the sentencing authorities (judges or juries) had been given unfettered discretion to impose or withhold capital punishment. Thereafter, Congress and thirty-five state legislatures revised their capital punishment statutes to bring them into conformity with the *Furman* decision. The Court upheld the new Georgia statute in the *Gregg* case.

Background: Gregg was convicted of murder and sentenced to death in Georgia. The revised Georgia law required that the sentencing jury be properly instructed and guided by the judge as to the factors they were to consider in deciding whether or not to impose a death sentence. The Court upheld the sentence over the dissents of only Justices Brennan and Marshall, who held the death penalty to be unconstitutional under all circumstances.

JUDGMENT OF THE COURT, AND OPINION OF MR. JUSTICE STEWART, MR. JUSTICE POWELL, AND MR. JUSTICE STEVENS, ANNOUNCED BY MR. JUSTICE STEWART:

We address initially the basic contention that the punishment of death for the crime of murder is, under all circumstances, "cruel and unusual" in violation of the Eighth and Fourteenth Amendments of the Constitution. . . .

The Court on a number of occasions has both assumed and asserted the constitutionality of capital punishment. In several cases that assumption provided a necessary foundation for the decision, as the Court was asked to decide whether a particular method of carrying out a capital sentence would be allowed to stand under the Eighth Amendment. But until *Furman v. Georgia* (1972), the Court never confronted squarely the fundamental claim that the punishment of death always, regardless of the enormity of the offense or the procedure followed in imposing the sentence, is cruel and unusual punishment in violation of the Constitution. Although this issue was presented and addressed in *Furman*, it was not resolved by the Court. Four Justices would have held that capital punishment is not unconstitutional *per se*; two Justices would have reached the opposite conclusion; and three Justices, while agreeing that the statutes then before the Court were invalid as applied, left open the question whether such punishment may ever be imposed. We now hold that the punishment of death does not invariably violate the Constitution. . . .

It is clear . . . that the Eighth Amendment has not been regarded as a static concept. As Mr. Chief Justice Warren said, in an oft-quoted phrase, "[t]he Amendment must draw its meaning from the evolving standards of decency that mark the progress of a maturing society." *Trop v. Dulles* [1958]. Thus, an assessment of contemporary values concerning the infliction of a challenged sanction is relevant to the application of the Eighth Amendment. As we develop below more fully, this assessment does not call for a subjective judgment. It requires, rather, that we look to objective indicia that reflect the public attitude toward a given sanction.

But our cases also make clear that public perceptions of standards of decency with respect to criminal sanctions are not conclusive. A penalty also must accord with "the dignity of man," which is the "basic concept underlying the Eighth Amendment." This means, at least, that the punishment not be "excessive." When a form of punishment in the abstract (in this case, whether capital punishment may ever be imposed as a sanction for murder) rather than in the particular (the propriety of death as a penalty to be applied to a specific defendant for a specific crime) is under consideration, the inquiry into "excessiveness" has two aspects. First, the punishment must not involve the unnecessary and wanton infliction of pain. . . . Second, the punishment must not be grossly out of proportion to the severity of the crime. . . .

But, while we have an obligation to insure that constitutional bounds are not overreached, we may not act as judges as we might as legislators.

Therefore, in assessing a punishment selected by a democratically elected legislature against the constitutional measure, we presume its validity. We may not require the legislature to select the least severe penalty possible so long as the penalty selected is not cruelly inhumane or disproportionate to the crime involved. And a heavy burden rests on those who would attack the judgment of the representatives of the people.

This is true in part because the constitutional test is intertwined with an assessment of contemporary standards and the legislative judgment weighs heavily in ascertaining such standards. . . .

We now consider specifically whether the sentence of death for the crime of murder is a *per se* violation of the Eighth and Fourteenth Amendments to the Constitution. We note first that history and precedent strongly support a negative answer to this question.

The imposition of the death penalty for the crime of murder has a long history of acceptance both in the United States and in England. The common-law rule imposed a mandatory death sentence on all convicted murderers. And the penalty continued to be used into the 20th century by most American States, although the breadth of the common-law rule was diminished, initially by narrowing the class of murders to be punished by death and subsequently by widespread adoption of laws expressly granting juries the discretion to recommend mercy.

It is apparent from the text of the Constitution itself that the existence of capital punishment was accepted by the Framers. At the time the Eighth Amendment was ratified, capital punishment was a common sanction in every State. Indeed, the First Congress of the United States enacted legislation providing death as the penalty for specified crimes. The Fifth Amendment, adopted at the same time as the Eighth, contemplated the continued existence of the capital sanction by imposing certain limits on the prosecution of capital cases:

"No person shall be held to answer for a capital, or otherwise infamous crime, unless on a presentment or indictment of a Grand Jury . . . ; nor shall any person be subject for the same offense to be twice put in jeopardy of life or limb; . . . nor be deprived of life, liberty, or property, without due process of law. . . ." And the Fourteenth Amendment adopted over three-quarters of a century later, similarly contemplates the existence of the capital sanction in providing that no State shall deprive any person of "life, liberty, or property" without due process of law.

For nearly two centuries, this Court, repeatedly and often expressly, has recognized that capital punishment is not invalid *per se*. . . .

Four years ago, the petitioners in *Furman* and its companion cases predicated their argument primarily upon the asserted proposition that standards of decency had evolved to the point where capital punishment no longer could be tolerated. The petitioners in those cases said, in effect, that the evolutionary process had come to an end, and that standards of decency required that the Eighth Amendment be construed finally as prohibiting capital punishment for any crime regardless of its depravity and impact on society. This view was accepted by two Justices. Three other Justices were unwilling to go so far; focusing on the procedures by which convicted defendants were selected for the death penalty rather than on the actual punishment inflicted, they joined in the conclusion that the statutes before the Court were constitutionally invalid.

The petitioners in the capital cases before the Court today renew the "standards of decency" argument, but developments during the four years since *Furman* have undercut substantially the assumptions upon which their argument rested. Despite the continuing debate, dating back to the 19th century, over the morality and utility of capital punishment, it is now evident that a large proportion of American society continues to regard it as an appropriate and necessary criminal sanction.

The most marked indication of society's endorsement of the death penalty for murder is the legislative response to *Furman*. The legislatures of at least 35 States have enacted new statutes that provide for the death penalty for at least some crimes that result in the death of another person. And the Congress of the United States, in 1974, enacted a statute providing the death penalty for aircraft piracy that results in death. . . .

As we have seen, however, the Eighth Amendment demands more than that a challenged punishment be acceptable to contemporary society. The Court also must ask whether it comports with the basic concept of human dignity at the core of the Amendment. Although we cannot "invalidate a category of penalties because we deem less severe penalties adequate to serve the ends of penology," the sanction imposed cannot be so totally without penological justification that it results in the gratuitous infliction of suffering.

The death penalty is said to serve two principal social purposes: retribution and deterrence of capital crimes by prospective offenders.

In part, capital punishment is an expression of society's moral outrage at particularly offensive conduct. This function may be unappealing to many, but it is essential in an ordered society that asks its citizens to rely on legal processes rather than self-help to vindicate their wrongs. . . .

Statistical attempts to evaluate the worth of the death penalty as a deterrent to crimes by potential offenders have occasioned a great deal of debate. The results simply have been inconclusive. . . .

Although some of the studies suggest that the death penalty may not function as a significantly greater deterrent than lesser penalties, there is no convincing empirical evidence either supporting or refuting this view. We may nevertheless assume safely that there are murderers, such as those who act in passion, for whom the threat of death has little or no deterrent effect. But for many others, the death penalty undoubtedly is a significant deterrent. There are carefully contemplated murders, such as murder for hire, where the possible penalty of death may well enter into the cold calculus that precedes the decision to act. And there are some categories of murder, such as murder by a life prisoner, where other sanctions may not be adequate.

The value of capital punishment as a deterrent of crime is a complex factual issue the resolution of which properly rests with the legislatures, which can evaluate the results of statistical studies in terms of their own local conditions and with a flexibility of approach that is not available to the courts. . . .

In sum, we cannot say that the judgment of the Georgia legislature that capital punishment may be necessary in some cases is clearly wrong. Considerations of federalism, as well as respect for the ability of a legislature to evaluate, in terms of its particular state the moral consensus concerning the death penalty and its social utility as a sanction, require us to conclude, in the absence of more convincing evidence, that the infliction of death as a punishment for murder is not without justification and thus is not unconstitutionally severe.

Finally, we must consider whether the punishment of death is disproportionate in relation to the crime for which it is imposed. There is no question that death as a punishment is unique in its severity and irrevocability. When a defendant's life is at stake, the Court has been particularly sensitive to insure that every safeguard is observed. But we are concerned here only with the imposition of capital punishment for the crime of murder, and when a life has been taken deliberately by the offender, we cannot say that the punishment is invariably disproportionate to the crime. It is an extreme sanction, suitable to the most extreme of crimes.

We hold that the death penalty is not a form of punishment that may never be imposed, regardless of the circumstances of the offense, regardless of the character of the offender, and regardless of the procedure followed in reaching the decision to impose it.

We now consider whether Georgia may impose the death penalty on the petitioner in this case. . . .

The basic concern of *Furman* centered on those defendants who were being condemned to death capriciously and arbitrarily. Under the procedures before the Court in that case, sentencing authorities were not directed to give attention to the nature or circumstances of the crime committed or to the character or record of the defendant. Left unguided, juries imposed the death sentence in a way that could only be called freakish. The new Georgia sentencing procedures, by contrast, focus the jury's attention on the particularized nature of the crime and the particularized characteristics of the individual defendant. While the jury is permitted to consider any aggravating or mitigating circumstances, it must find and identify at least one statutory aggravating factor before it may impose a penalty of death. In this way the jury's discretion is channeled. No longer can a jury wantonly and freakishly impose the death sentence; it is always circumscribed by the legislative guidelines. . . .

For the reasons expressed in this opinion, we hold that the statutory system under which Gregg was sentenced to death does not violate the Constitution.

[Chief Justice Burger, and Justices White, Blackmun, and Rehnquist concurred in the judgment.]

MR. JUSTICE BRENNAN, DISSENTING:

This Court inescapably has the duty, as the ultimate arbiter of the meaning of our Constitution, to say whether, when individuals condemned to death stand before our Bar, "moral concepts" require us to hold that the law has progressed to the point where we should declare that the punishment of death, like punishments on the rack, the screw, and the wheel, is no longer morally tolerable in our civilized society. My opinion in *Furman v. Georgia* concluded that our civilization and the law had progressed to this point and that therefore the punishment of death, for whatever crime and under all circumstances, is "cruel and unusual" in violation of the Eighth and Fourteenth Amendments of the Constitution. I shall not again canvass the reasons that led to that conclusion. I emphasize only that foremost among the "moral concepts" recognized in our cases and inherent in the Clause is the primary moral principle that the State, even as it punishes, must treat its citizens in a manner consistent with their intrinsic worth as human beings—a punishment must not be so severe as to be degrading to human dignity. . . .

Death is not only an unusually severe punishment, unusual in its pain, in its finality, and in its enormity, but it serves no penal purpose more effectively than a less severe punishment; therefore the principle inherent in the Clause that prohibits pointless infliction of excessive punishment when less severe punishment can adequately achieve the same purposes invalidates the punishment.

Mr. Justice Marshall, dissenting:

In *Furman* I concluded that the death penalty is constitutionally invalid for two reasons. First, the death penalty is excessive. And second, the American people, fully informed as to the purposes of the death penalty and its liabilities, would in my view reject it as morally unacceptable.

Since the decision in *Furman*, the legislatures of 35 States have enacted new statutes authorizing the imposition of the death sentence for certain crimes, and Congress has enacted a law providing the death penalty for air piracy resulting in death. I would be less than candid if I did not acknowledge that these developments have a significant bearing on a realistic assessment of the moral acceptability of the death penalty to the American people. But if the constitutionality of the death penalty turns, as I have urged, on the opinion of an *informed* citizenry, then even the enactment of new death statutes cannot be viewed as conclusive. In *Furman*, I observed that the American people are largely unaware of the information critical to a judgment on the morality of the death penalty, and concluded that if they were better informed they would consider it shocking, unjust, and unacceptable.

Even assuming, however, that the post-*Furman* enactment of statutes authorizing the death penalty renders the prediction of the views of an informed citizenry an uncertain basis for a constitutional decision, the enactment of those statutes has no bearing whatsoever on the conclusion that the death penalty is unconstitutional because it is excessive. An excessive penalty is invalid under the Cruel and Unusual Punishment Clause ''even though popular sentiment may favor'' it.

Appendix A
List of Supreme Court Decisions with Citations

Abington School District v. Schempp, 374 U.S. 203 (1963)

Baldwin v. Fish and Game Commission of Montana, 436 U.S. 371 (1978)

Bolling v. Sharpe, 347 U.S. 497 (1954)

Brown v. Board of Education, 346 U.S. 483 (1954)

Calder v. Bull, 3 U.S. 386 (1798)

Civil Rights Cases, 109 U.S. 3 (1883)

Cohens v. Virginia, 6 Wheaton 264 (1821)

Cooley v. Board of Wardens, 12 Howard 299 (1851)

Dennis v. United States, 341 U.S. 494 (1951)

Garcia v. San Antonio, 469 U.S. 528 (1985)

Gibbons v. Ogden, 9 Wheaton 1 (1824)

Gideon v. Wainwright, 372 U.S. 335 (1963)

Gregg v. Georgia, 428 U.S. 153 (1976)

Griswold v. Connecticut, 381 U.S. 479 (1965)

Hammer v. Dagenhart, 247 U.S. 251 (1918)

Harris v. McRae, 448 U.S. 297 (1980)

Heart of Atlanta Motel v. United States, 379 U.S. 241 (1964)

Humphrey's Executor v. United States, 295 U.S. 602 (1935)

Immigration and Naturalization Service v. Chadha, 462 U.S. 919 (1983)

Katz v. United States, 389 U.S. 347 (1967)

Korematsu v. United States, 323 U.S. 214 (1944)

Lochner v. New York, 198 U.S. 45 (1905)

McCardle, Ex Parte, 7 Wallace 506 (1869)

McCulloch v. Maryland, 4 Wheaton 316 (1819)

Marbury v. Madison, 1 Cranch 137 (1803)

Milligan, Ex Parte, 4 Wallace 2 (1866)

Minersville School District v. Gobitis, 310 U.S. 586 (1940)

Miranda v. Arizona, 384 U.S. 436 (1966)

Mississippi University for Women v. Hogan, 458 U.S. 718 (1982)

Missouri v. Holland, 252 U.S. 416 (1920)

Missouri v. Jenkins, 495 U.S. 33 (1990)

Mistretta v. United States, 488 U.S. 361 (1989)

New York Times Co. v. Sullivan, 376 U.S. 254 (1964)

New York Times Co. v. United States, 403 U.S. 713 (1971)

Olmstead v. United States, 277 U.S. 438 (1928)

Palko v. Connecticut, 302 U.S. 319 (1937)

Philadelphia v. New Jersey, 437 U.S. 617 (1978)

Planned Parenthood v. Casey, 505 U.S. (1992)

Plessy v. Ferguson, 163 U.S. 537 (1896)

Prize Cases, 2 Bl. 67 U.S. 635 (1862)

R.A.V. v. St. Paul, 505 U.S. (1992)

Reed v. Reed, 404 U.S. 71 (1971)

Regents of the University of California v. Bakke, 438 U.S. 265 (1978)

Reynolds v. Sims, 377 U.S. 533 (1964)

Richmond v. Croson, 488 U.S. 469 (1989)

Roe v. Wade, 410 U.S. 113 (1973)

Schenck v. United States, 249 U.S. 47 (1919)

Slaughter-House Cases, 16 Wallace 36 (1873)

South Dakota v. Dole, 483 U.S. 203 (1987)

Southern Pacific Co. v. Arizona, 325 U.S. 761 (1944)

Terry v. Ohio, 392 U.S. 1 (1968)

United States v. Carolene Products Co., 304 U.S. 144 (1938)

United States v. Darby, 312 U.S. 100 (1941)

United States v. Leon, 468 U.S. 897 (1984)

United States v. Nixon, 418 U.S. 683 (1974)

Watkins v. United States, 354 U.S. 178 (1957)

West Coast Hotel Co. v. Parrish, 300 U.S. 379 (1937)

West Virginia State Board of Education v. Barnette, 319 U.S. 624 (1943)

Wickard v. Filburn, 317 U.S. 111 (1942)

Youngstown Sheet and Tube Co. v. Sawyer, 343 U.S. 579 (1952)

Appendix B
Justices of the United States Supreme Court

1. CHIEF JUSTICES
(in alphabetical order)

	Appointed from	Term of Service
Burger, Warren E. (1907–)	Va.	1969–1986
Chase, Salmon P. (1808–1873)	Ohio	1864–1873
Ellsworth, Oliver (1745–1807)	Conn.	1796–1800
Fuller, Melville W. (1833–1910)	Ill.	1888–1910
Hughes, Charles E. (1862–1948)	N.Y.	1930–1941
Jay, John (1745–1829)	N.Y.	1789–1795
Marshall, John (1755–1835)	Va.	1801–1835
Rehnquist, William H. (1924–)	Ariz.	1986–
Rutledge, John (1739–1800)	S.C.	1795
Stone, Harlan F. (1872–1946)	N.Y.	1941–1946
Taft, William H. (1857–1930)	Conn.	1921–1930
Taney, Roger B. (1777–1864)	Md.	1836–1864
Vinson, Fred M. (1890–1953)	Ky.	1946–1953
Waite, Morrison R. (1816–1888)	Ohio	1874–1888
Warren, Earl (1891–1974)	Calif.	1953–1969
White, Edward D. (1845–1921)	La.	1910–1921

2. CHIEF JUSTICES
(in chronological order)

Name	Term of Office	Presidential Administration
John Jay	1789–1795	Washington
John Rutledge	1795	Washington
Oliver Ellsworth	1796–1800	Washington
		Adams, J.
John Marshall	1801–1835	Adams, J.
		Jefferson
		Madison
		Monroe
		Adams, J. Q.
		Jackson
Roger B. Taney	1836–1864	Jackson
		Van Buren
		Harrison, W. H.
		Tyler
		Polk
		Taylor
		Fillmore
		Pierce
		Buchanan
		Lincoln
Salmon P. Chase	1864–1873	Lincoln
		Johnson, A.
		Grant
Morrison R. Waite	1874–1888	Grant
		Hayes
		Garfield
		Arthur
		Cleveland
Melville W. Fuller	1888–1910	Cleveland
		Harrison
		Cleveland
		McKinley
		Roosevelt, T.
		Taft

Edward D. White	1910–1921	Taft
		Wilson
William H. Taft	1921–1930	Harding
		Coolidge
		Hoover
Charles E. Hughes	1930–1940	Hoover
		Roosevelt, F. D.
Harlan F. Stone	1941–1946	Roosevelt, F. D.
		Truman
Frederick M. Vinson	1946–1952	Truman
Earl Warren	1953–1969	Eisenhower
		Kennedy
		Johnson, L.
		Nixon
Warren E. Burger	1969–1986	Nixon
		Ford
		Carter
		Reagan
William H. Rehnquist	1986–	Reagan
		Bush
		Clinton

3. ASSOCIATE JUSTICES
(in alphabetical order)

	Appointed from	Term of Service
Baldwin, Henry (1780–1844)	Pa.	1830–1844
Barbour, Philip P. (1783–1841)	Va.	1836–1841
Black, Hugo L. (1886–1971)	Ala.	1937–1971
Blackmun, Harry A. (1908–)	Minn.	1970–1994
Blair, John (1732–1800)	Va.	1789–1796
Blatchford, Samuel (1820–1893)	N.Y.	1882–1893
Bradley, Joseph P. (1803–1892)	N.J.	1870–1892
Brandeis, Louis D. (1856–1941)	Mass.	1916–1939
Brennan, William J. (1906–)	N.J.	1956–1990
Brewer, David J. (1837–1910)	Kan.	1889–1910
Breyer, Steven G. (1938–)	Mass.	1994–

Brown, Henry B. (1836–1913)	Mich.	1890–1906
Burton, Harold H. (1888–1964)	Ohio	1945–1958
Butler, Pierce (1866–1939)	Minn.	1922–1939
Byrnes, James F. (1879–1972)	S.C.	1941–1942
Campbell, John A. (1811–1889)	Ala.	1853–1861
Cardozo, Benjamin N. (1870–1938)	N.Y.	1932–1938
Catron, John (1778–1865)	Tenn.	1837–1865
Chase, Samuel (1741–1811)	Md.	1796–1811
Clark, Tom C. (1899–1977)	Texas	1949–1967
Clarke, John H. (1857–1945)	Ohio	1916–1922
Clifford, Nathan (1803–1881)	Maine	1858–1881
Curtis, Benjamin R. (1809–1874)	Mass.	1851–1857
Cushing, William (1732–1810)	Mass.	1789–1810
Daniel, Peter V. (1784–1860)	Va.	1841–1860
Davis, David (1815–1886)	Ill.	1862–1877
Day, William R. (1849–1923)	Ohio	1903–1922
Douglas, William O. (1898–1980)	Conn.	1939–1975
Duvall, Gabriel (1752–1844)	Md.	1811–1835
Field, Stephen J. (1816–1899)	Cal.	1863–1897
Fortas, Abe (1910–1982)	Tenn.	1965–1969
Frankfurter, Felix (1882–1965)	Mass.	1939–1962
Ginsburg, Ruth B. (1933–)	D.C.	1993–
Goldberg, Arthur J. (1908–1990)	Ill.	1962–1965
Gray, Horace (1828–1902)	Mass.	1881–1902
Grier, Robert O. (1794–1870)	Pa.	1846–1870
Harlan, John Marshall (1833–1911)	Ky.	1877–1911
Harlan, John Marshall (1899–1971)	N.Y.	1955–1971
Holmes, Oliver W. Jr. (1841–1935)	Mass.	1902–1932
Hughes, Charles E. (1862–1948) (1930–1941, Chief Justice)	N.Y.	1910–1915
Hunt, Ward (1810–1886)	N.Y.	1872–1882
Iredell, James (1751–1799)	N.C.	1790–1799
Jackson, Howell E. (1835–1895)	Tenn.	1893–1895
Jackson, Robert H. (1892–1954)	N.Y.	1941–1954
Johnson, Thomas (1732–1819)	Md.	1791–1793
Johnson, William (1771–1834)	S.C.	1804–1834
Kennedy, Anthony (1936–)	Calif.	1988–
Lamar, Joseph R. (1857–1916)	Ga.	1910–1916
Lamar, Lucius Q. C. (1825–1893)	Miss.	1888–1893

Livingston, Henry B. (1757–1823)	N.Y.	1806–1823
Lurton, Horace H. (1844–1914)	Tenn.	1909–1914
Marshall, Thurgood (1908–1993)	Md.	1967–1991
Matthews, Stanley (1824–1889)	Ohio	1881–1889
McKenna, Joseph (1843–1926)	Calif.	1898–1925
McKinley, John (1780–1852)	Ala.	1837–1852
McLean, John (1785–1861)	Ohio	1829–1861
McReynolds, James C. (1862–1946)	Tenn.	1914–1941
Miller, Samuel F. (1816–1890)	Iowa	1862–1890
Minton, Sherman (1890–1965)	Ind.	1949–1956
Moody, William H. (1853–1917)	Mass.	1906–1910
Moore, Alfred (1755–1809)	N.C.	1799–1804
Murphy, Frank (1893–1949)	Mich.	1940–1949
Nelson, Samuel (1792–1873)	N.Y.	1845–1872
O'Connor, Sandra D. (1930–)	Ariz.	1981–
Paterson, William (1745–1806)	N.J.	1793–1806
Peckham, Rufus W. (1838–1909)	N.Y.	1895–1909
Pitney, Mahlon (1858–1924)	N.J.	1912–1922
Powell, Lewis F. (1907–)	Va.	1972–1987
Reed, Stanley F. (1884–1981)	Ky.	1938–1957
Rehnquist, William H. (1924–) (1986– , Chief Justice)	Ariz.	1972–1986
Roberts, Owen J. (1875–1955)	Pa.	1930–1945
Rutledge, John (1739–1800) (1795, Chief Justice)	S.C.	1789–1791
Rutledge, Wiley B. (1894–1949)	Iowa	1943–1949
Sanford, Edward T. (1865–1930)	Tenn.	1923–1930
Scalia, Antonin (1936–)	Va.	1986–
Shiras, George (1832–1924)	Pa.	1892–1903
Souter, David (1939–)	N.H.	1990–
Stevens, John P. (1920–)	Ill.	1975–
Stewart, Potter (1915–1985)	Ohio	1958–1981
Stone, Harlan F. (1872–1946) (1941–1946, Chief Justice)	N.Y.	1925–1941
Story, Joseph (1779–1845)	Mass.	1811–1845
Strong, William (1808–1895)	Pa.	1870–1880
Sutherland, George (1862–1942)	Utah	1922–1938
Swayne, Noah H. (1804–1884)	Ohio	1862–1881
Thomas, Clarence (1948–)	Va.	1991–

Thompson, Smith (1768–1843)	N.Y.	1823–1843
Todd, Thomas (1765–1826)	Ky.	1807–1826
Trimble, Robert (1777–1828)	Ky.	1826–1828
Van Devanter, Willis (1859–1941)	Wyo.	1910–1937
Washington, Bushrod (1762–1829)	Va.	1798–1829
Wayne, James M. (1790–1867)	Ga.	1835–1867
White, Byron R. (1917–)	Colo.	1962–1993
White, Edward D. (1945–1921) (1910–1921, Chief Justice)	La.	1894–1910
Whittaker, Charles E. (1901–1973)	Mo.	1957–1962
Wilson, James (1724–1798)	Pa.	1789–1798
Woodbury, Levi (1789–1851)	N.H.	1845–1851
Woods, William B. (1824–1887)	Ga.	1880–1887

4. PRESIDENTS AND THEIR
SUPREME COURT APPOINTMENTS

Name of President	Presidential Term	Name of Justice	Appointed
George Washington	1789–1797	John Jay (Chief Justice)	1789
		John Rutledge	1789
		William Cushing	1789
		James Wilson	1789
		John Blair	1789
		James Iredell	1790
		Thomas Johnson	1791
		William Paterson	1793
		John Rutledge (Chief Justice)	1795
		Samuel Chase	1796
		Oliver Ellsworth (Chief Justice)	1796
John Adams	1797–1801	Bushrod Washington	1798
		Alfred Moore	1799
		John Marshall (Chief Justice)	1801

Thomas Jefferson	1801–1809	William Johnson	1804
		Henry Livingston	1806
		Thomas Todd	1807
James Madison	1809–1817	Gabriel Duvall	1811
		Joseph Story	1811
James Monroe	1817–1825	Smith Thompson	1823
John Quincy Adams	1825–1829	Robert Trimble	1826
Andrew Jackson	1829–1837	John McLean	1829
		Henry Baldwin	1830
		James M. Wayne	1835
		Roger B. Taney (Chief Justice)	1836
		Philip P. Barbour	1836
Martin Van Buren	1837–1841	John Catron	1837
		John McKinley	1837
		Peter V. Daniel	1841
John Tyler	1841–1845	Samuel Nelson	1845
James M. Polk	1845–1849	Levi Woodbury	1845
		Robert C. Grier	1846
Millard Fillmore	1850–1853	Benjamin R. Curtis	1851
Franklin Pierce	1853–1857	John A. Campbell	1853
James Buchanan	1857–1861	Nathan Clifford	1858
Abraham Lincoln	1861–1865	Noah H. Swayne	1862
		Samuel F. Miller	1862
		David Davis	1862
		Stephen J. Field	1863
		Salmon P. Chase (Chief Justice)	1864
Ulysses S. Grant	1869–1877	William Strong	1870
		Joseph P. Bradley	1870
		Ward Hunt	1872
		Morrison Waite (Chief Justice)	1874
Rutherford B. Hayes	1877–1881	John Marshall Harlan	1877
		William B. Woods	1880
James A. Garfield	Mar.–Sept. 1881	Stanley Matthews	1881
Chester A. Arthur	1881–1885	Horace Gray	1881
		Samuel Blatchford	1882

Grover Cleveland	1885–1889	Lucius Q. C. Lamar	1888
		Melville W. Fuller (Chief Justice)	1888
Benjamin Harrison	1889–1893	David J. Brewer	1889
		Henry B. Brown	1890
		George Shiras	1892
		Howell E. Jackson	1893
Grover Cleveland	1893–1897	Edward D. White	1894
		Rufus W. Peckham	1895
William McKinley	1897–1901	Joseph McKenna	1898
Theodore Roosevelt	1901–1909	Oliver Wendell Holmes	1902
		William R. Day	1903
		William H. Moody	1906
William H. Taft	1909–1913	Horace H. Lurton	1909
		Charles E. Hughes	1910
		Edward D. White (Chief Justice)	1910
		Willis Van Devanter	1910
		Joseph R. Lamar	1910
		Mahlon Pitney	1912
Woodrow Wilson	1913–1921	James C. McReynolds	1914
		Louis D. Brandeis	1916
		John H. Clarke	1916
Warren G. Harding	1921–1923	William H. Taft (Chief Justice)	1921
		George Sutherland	1922
		Pierce Butler	1922
		Edward T. Sanford	1923
Calvin Coolidge	1923–1929	Harlan F. Stone	1925
Herbert Hoover	1929–1933	Charles E. Hughes (Chief Justice)	1930
		Owen J. Roberts	1930
		Benjamin J. Cardozo	1932
Franklin D. Roosevelt	1933–1945	Hugo L. Black	1937
		Stanley F. Reed	1938
		Felix Frankfurter	1939
		William O. Douglas	1939
		Frank Murphy	1940

		James F. Byrnes	1941
		Harlan F. Stone (Chief Justice)	1941
		Robert H. Jackson	1941
		Wiley B. Rutledge	1943
Harry S. Truman	1945–1953	Harold H. Burton	1945
		Fred M. Vinson (Chief Justice)	1946
		Tom C. Clark	1949
		Sherman Minton	1949
Dwight D. Eisenhower	1953–1961	Earl Warren (Chief Justice)	1953
		John Marshall Harlan	1955
		William J. Brennan, Jr.	1956
		Charles E. Whittaker	1957
		Potter Stewart	1958
John F. Kennedy	1961–1963	Byron R. White	1962
		Arthur J. Goldberg	1962
Lyndon B. Johnson	1963–1969	Abe Fortas	1965
		Thurgood Marshall	1967
Richard M. Nixon	1969–1974	Warren E. Burger (Chief Justice)	1969
		Harry A. Blackmun	1970
		Lewis F. Powell, Jr.	1972
		William H. Rehnquist	1972
Gerald R. Ford	1974–1977	John P. Stevens	1975
Jimmy Carter	1977–1981	(no appointments)	
Ronald Reagan	1981–1989	Sandra D. O'Connor	1981
		Antonin Scalia	1986
		William H. Rehnquist (Chief Justice)	1986
		Anthony Kennedy	1988
George Bush	1989–1993	David M. Souter	1990
		Clarence Thomas	1991
Bill Clinton	1993–	Ruth B. Ginsburg	1993
		Steven G. Breyer	1994

Appendix C
The Declaration
of Independence

Action of Second Continental Congress, July 4, 1776
The unanimous Declaration of the thirteen United States of America

WHEN in the Course of human Events, it becomes necessary for one People to dissolve the Political Bands which have connected them with another, and to assume among the Powers of the Earth, the separate and equal Station to which the Laws of Nature and of Nature's God entitle them, a decent Respect to the Opinions of Mankind requires that they should declare the causes which impel them to the Separation.

WE hold these Truths to be self-evident, that all Men are created equal, that they are endowed by their Creator with certain unalienable Rights, that among these are Life, Liberty, and the Pursuit of Happiness—That to secure these Rights, Governments are instituted among Men, deriving their just Powers from the Consent of the Governed, that whenever any Form of Government becomes destructive of these Ends, it is the Right of the People to alter or to abolish it, and to institute new Government, laying its Foundation on such Principles, and organizing its Powers in such Form, as to them shall seem most likely to effect their Safety and Happiness. Prudence, indeed, will dictate that Governments long established should not be changed for light and transient Causes; and accordingly all Experience hath shewn, that Mankind are more disposed to suffer, while Evils are sufferable, than to right themselves by abolishing the Forms to which they are accustomed. But when a long Train of Abuses and Usurpations, pursuing invariably the same Object, evinces a Design to reduce them under absolute Despotism, it is their Right, it is their Duty, to throw off such Government, and to provide new Guards for their future Security. Such has been the patient Sufferance of these Colonies; and such is now the Necessity which constrains them to alter their former Systems of Government. The History of the present King of Great-Britain is a History of repeated Injuries and Usurpations, all having in direct Object the Establishment of an absolute Tyranny over these States. To prove this, let Facts be submitted to a candid World.

HE has refused his Assent to Laws, the most wholesome and necessary for the public Good.

HE has forbidden his Governors to pass Laws of immediate and pressing Importance, unless suspended in their Operation till his Assent should be obtained; and when so suspended, he has utterly neglected to attend to them.

HE has refused to pass other Laws for the Accommodation of large Districts of People, unless those People would relinquish the Right of Representation in the Legislature, a Right inestimable to them, and formidable to Tyrants only.

HE has called together Legislative Bodies at Places unusual, uncomfortable, and distant from the Depository of their public Records, for the sole Purpose of fatiguing them into Compliance with his Measures.

HE has dissolved Representative Houses repeatedly, for opposing with manly Firmness his Invasions on the Rights of the People.

HE has refused for a long Time, after such Dissolutions, to cause others to be elected; whereby the Legislative Powers, incapable of Annihilation, have returned to the People at large for their exercise; the State remaining in the mean time exposed to all the Dangers of Invasion from without, and Convulsions within.

HE has endeavoured to prevent the Population of these States; for that Purpose obstructing the Laws for Naturalization of Foreigners; refusing to pass others to encourage their Migrations hither, and raising the Conditions of new Appropriations of Lands.

HE has obstructed the Administration of Justice, by refusing his Assent to Laws for establishing Judiciary Powers.

HE has made Judges dependent on his Will alone, for the Tenure of their Offices, and the Amount and Payment of their Salaries.

HE has erected a Multitude of new Offices, and sent hither Swarms of Officers to harrass our People, and eat out their Substance.

HE has kept among us, in Times of Peace, Standing Armies, without the consent of our Legislatures.

HE has affected to render the Military independent of and superior to the Civil Power.

HE has combined with others to subject us to a Jurisdiction foreign to our Constitution, and unacknowledged by our Laws; giving his Assent to their Acts of pretended Legislation:

FOR quartering large Bodies of Armed Troops among us:

FOR protecting them, by a mock Trial, from Punishment for any Murders which they should commit on the Inhabitants of these States:

FOR cutting off our Trade with all Parts of the World:

FOR imposing Taxes on us without our Consent:

FOR depriving us, in many Cases, of the Benefits of Trial by Jury:

FOR transporting us beyond Seas to be tried for pretended Offences:

FOR abolishing the free System of English Laws in a neighbouring Province, establishing therein an arbitrary Government, and enlarging its Boundaries, so as to render it at once an Example and fit Instrument for introducing the same absolute Rule into these Colonies:

FOR taking away our Charters, abolishing our most valuable Laws, and altering fundamentally the Forms of our Governments:

FOR suspending our own Legislatures, and declaring themselves invested with Power to legislate for us in all Cases whatsoever.

HE has abdicated Government here, by declaring us out of his Protection and waging War against us.

HE has plundered our Seas, ravaged our Coasts, burnt our Towns, and destroyed the Lives of our People.

HE is, at this Time, transporting large Armies of foreign Mercenaries to compleat the Works of Death, Desolation, and Tyranny, already begun with circumstances of Cruelty and Perfidy, scarcely paralleled in the most barbarous Ages, and totally unworthy the Head of a civilized Nation.

HE has constrained our fellow Citizens taken Captive on the high Seas to bear Arms against their Country, to become the Executioners of their Friends and Brethren, or to fall themselves by their Hands.

HE has excited domestic Insurrections amongst us, and has endeavoured to bring on the Inhabitants of our Frontiers, the merciless Indian Savages, whose known Rule of Warfare, is an undistinguished Destruction, of all Ages, Sexes and Conditions.

IN every stage of these Oppressions we have Petitioned for Redress in the most humble Terms: Our repeated Petitions have been answered only by repeated Injury. A Prince, whose Character is thus marked by every act which may define a Tyrant, is unfit to be the Ruler of a free People.

NOR have we been wanting in Attentions to our British Brethren. We have warned them from Time to Time of Attempts by their Legislature to extend an unwarrantable Jurisdiction over us. We have reminded them of the Circumstances of our Emigration and Settlement here. We have appealed to their native Justice and Magnanimity, and we have conjured them by the Ties of our common Kindred to disavow these Usurpations, which, would inevitably interrupt our Connections and Correspondence. They too have been deaf to the Voice of Justice and of Consanguinity. We must, therefore, acquiesce in the Necessity, which denounces our Separation, and hold them, as we hold the rest of Mankind, Enemies in War, in Peace, Friends.

WE, therefore, the Representatives of the UNITED STATES OF AMERICA, in GENERAL CONGRESS, Assembled, appealing to the Supreme Judge of the World for the Rectitude of our Intentions, do, in the Name, and by Authority of the good People of these Colonies, solemnly Publish and Declare, That these United Colonies are, and of Right ought to be, FREE AND INDEPENDENT STATES; that they are absolved from all Allegiance to the British Crown, and that all political Connection between them and the State of Great-Britain, is and ought to be totally dissolved; and that as FREE AND INDEPENDENT STATES, they have full Power to levy War, conclude Peace, contract Alliances, establish Commerce, and to do all other Acts and Things which INDEPENDENT STATES may of right do. And for the support of this Declaration, with a firm Reliance on the Protection of divine Providence, we mutually pledge to each other our Lives, our Fortunes, and our sacred Honor.

Appendix D
The Constitution of the United States

We the People of the United States, in order to form a more perfect Union, establish Justice, ensure Domestic Tranquility, provide for the common Defence, promote the general Welfare, and secure the Blessings of Liberty to ourselves and our Posterity, do ordain and establish this CONSTITUTION for the United States of America.

ARTICLE I.

Sec. 1. ALL legislative powers herein granted shall be vested in a Congress of the United States, which shall consist of a Senate and House of Representatives.

Sec. 2. The House of Representatives shall be composed of members chosen every second year by the people of the several states, and the electors in each state shall have the qualifications requisite for electors of the most numerous branch of the state legislature.

No person shall be a representative who shall not have attained to the age of 25 years, and been seven years a citizen of the United States, and who shall not, when elected, be an inhabitant of that state in which he shall be chosen.

Representatives and direct taxes shall be apportioned among the several states which may be included within this union, according to their respective numbers, which shall be determined by adding to the whole number of free persons,[1] including those bound to service for a term of years, and excluding Indians not taxed, three-fifths of all other per-

---

[1] *"which shall be determined . . . free persons"*—modified by the Fourteenth Amendment.

sons.[2] The actual enumeration shall be made within three years after the first meeting of the Congress of the United States, and within every subsequent term of ten years, in such manner as they shall by law direct. The number of representatives shall not exceed one for every 30,000, but each state shall have at least one representative; and until such enumeration shall be made, the state of New-Hampshire shall be entitled to choose three, Massachusetts eight, Rhode-Island and Providence Plantations one, Connecticut five, New-York six, New-Jersey four, Pennsylvania eight, Delaware one, Maryland six, Virginia ten, North-Carolina five, South-Carolina five, and Georgia three.

When vacancies happen in the representation from any state, the executive authority thereof shall issue writs of election to fill such vacancies.

The House of Representatives shall choose their speaker and other officers; and shall have the sole power of impeachment.

Sec. 3. The Senate of the United States shall be composed of two senators from each state, chosen by the legislature thereof, for six years;[3] and each senator shall have one vote.

Immediately after they shall be assembled in consequence of the first election, they shall be divided as equally as may be into three classes. The seats of the senators of the first class shall be vacated at the expiration of the second year, of the second class at the expiration of the fourth year, and of the third class at the expiration of the sixth year, so that one-third may be chosen every second year; and if vacancies happen by resignation, or otherwise, during the recess of the legislature of any state, the executive thereof may make temporary appointments until the next meeting of the legislature, which shall then fill such vacancies.[4]

No person shall be a senator who shall not have attained to the age of 30 years, and been nine years a citizen of the United States, and who shall not, when elected, be an inhabitant of that state for which he shall be chosen.

The vice-president of the United States shall be president of the Senate, but shall have no vote, unless they be equally divided.

The Senate shall choose their other officers, and also a president pro

---

[2] *"Three-fifths . . . persons"*—superseded by the Fourteenth Amendment.
[3] *"The Senate . . . for six years"*—superseded by the Seventeenth Amendment.
[4] *"And if vacancies . . . such vacancies"*—modified by the Seventeenth Amendment.

tempore, in the absence of the vice-president, or when he shall exercise the office of president of the United States.

The Senate shall have the sole power to try all impeachments. When sitting for that purpose, they shall be on oath or affirmation. When the president of the United States is tried, the chief justice shall preside: And no person shall be convicted without the concurrence of two-thirds of the members present.

Judgment in cases of impeachment shall not extend further than to removal from office, and disqualification to hold and enjoy any office of honour, trust or profit under the United States; but the party convicted shall nevertheless be liable and subject to indictment, trial, judgment and punishment, according to law.

Sec. 4. The times, places and manner of holding elections for senators and representatives, shall be prescribed in each state by the legislature thereof: But the Congress may at any time by law make or alter such regulations, except as to the places of choosing senators.

The Congress shall assemble at least once in every year, and such meeting shall be on the first Monday in December, unless they shall by law appoint a different day.[5]

Sec. 5. Each house shall be the judge of the elections, returns and qualifications of its own members, and a majority of each shall constitute a quorum to do business; but a smaller number may adjourn from day to day, and may be authorized to compel the attendance of absent members, in such manner, and under such penalties as each house may provide.

Each house may determine the rules of its proceedings, punish its members for disorderly behaviour, and, with the concurrence of two-thirds, expel a member.

Each house shall keep a journal of its proceedings, and from time to time publish the same, excepting such parts as may, in their judgment, require secrecy; and the yeas and nays of the members of either house on any question, shall, at the desire of one-fifth of those present, be entered on the journal.

Neither house, during the session of Congress, shall, without the consent of the other, adjourn for more than three days, nor to any other place than that in which the two houses shall be sitting.

Sec. 6. The senators and representatives shall receive a compensation

[5] *"The Congress . . . a different day"*—superseded by the Twentieth Amendment.

for their services, to be ascertained by law, and paid out of the treasury of the United States.[6] They shall in all cases, except treason, felony and breach of the peace, be privileged from arrest during their attendance at the session of their respective houses, and in going to and returning from the same; and for any speech or debate in either house, they shall not be questioned in any other place.

No senator or representative shall, during the time for which he was elected, be appointed to any civil office under the authority of the United States, which shall have been created, or the emoluments whereof shall have been increased during such time; and no person holding any office under the United States, shall be a member of either house during his continuance in office.

Sec. 7. All bills for raising revenue shall originate in the House of Representatives; but the Senate may propose or concur with amendments as on other bills.

Every bill which shall have passed the House of Representatives and the Senate, shall, before it become a law, be presented to the president of the United States; if he approve, he shall sign it, but if not, he shall return it, with his objections, to that house in which it shall have originated, who shall enter the objections at large on their journal, and proceed to reconsider it. If after such reconsideration, two thirds of that house shall agree to pass the bill, it shall be sent, together with the objections, to the other house, by which it shall likewise be reconsidered, and if approved by two-thirds of that house, it shall become a law. But in all such cases the votes of both houses shall be determined by yeas and nays, and the names of the persons voting for and against the bill shall be entered on the journal of each house respectively. If any bill shall not be returned by the president within ten days (Sundays excepted) after it shall have been presented to him, the same shall be a law, in like manner as if he had signed it, unless the Congress by their adjournment prevent its return, in which case it shall not be a law.

Every order, resolution, or vote to which the concurrence of the Senate and House of Representatives may be necessary (except on a question of adjournment) shall be presented to the president of the United States; and before the same shall take effect, shall be approved by him, or, being disapproved by him, shall be re-passed by two-thirds

---

[6] *"The Senators . . . the United States"*—modified by the Twenty-seventh Amendment.

of the Senate and House of Representatives, according to the rules and limitations prescribed in the case of a bill.

Sec. 8. The Congress shall have power to lay and collect taxes, duties, imposts and excises, to pay the debts and provide for the common defence and general welfare of the United States; but all duties, imposts and excises shall be uniform throughout the United States:

To borrow money on the credit of the United States:

To regulate commerce with foreign nations, and among the several states, and with the Indian tribes:

To establish an uniform rule of naturalization, and uniform laws on the subject of bankruptcies throughout the United States:

To coin money, regulate the value thereof, and of foreign coin, and fix the standard of weights and measures:

To provide for the punishment of counterfeiting the securities and current coin of the United States:

To establish post-offices and post-roads:

To promote the progress of science and useful arts, by securing for limited times to authors and inventors the exclusive right to their respective writings and discoveries:

To constitute tribunals inferior to the supreme court:

To define and punish piracies and felonies committed on the high seas, and offences against the law of nations:

To declare war, grant letters of marque and reprisal, and make rules concerning captures on land and water:

To raise and support armies, but no appropriation of money to that use shall be for a longer term than two years:

To provide and maintain a navy:

To make rules for the government and regulation of the land and naval forces:

To provide for calling forth the militia to execute the laws of the union, suppress insurrections and repel invasions:

To provide for organizing, arming and disciplining the militia, and for governing such part of them as may be employed in the service of the United States, reserving to the states respectively, the appointment of the officers, and the authority of training the militia according to the discipline prescribed by Congress:

To exercise exclusive legislation in all cases whatsoever, over such district (not exceeding ten miles square) as may, by cession of particular states, and the acceptance of Congress, become the seat of the government of the United States, and to exercise like authority over all places purchased by the consent of the legislature of the state in which the same shall be, for the erection of forts, magazines, arsenals, dock-yards, and other needful buildings: And,

To make all laws which shall be necessary and proper for carrying into execution the foregoing powers, and all other powers vested by this constitution in the government of the United States, or in any department or officer thereof.

Sec. 9. The migration or importation of such persons as any of the states now existing shall think proper to admit, shall not be prohibited by the Congress prior to the year 1808, but a tax or duty may be imposed on such importations, not exceeding 10 dollars for each person.

The privilege of the writ of *habeas corpus* shall not be suspended, unless when in cases of rebellion or invasion the public safety may require it.

No bill of attainder or *ex post facto* law shall be passed.

No capitation, or other direct tax shall be laid unless in proportion to the *census* or enumeration herein before directed to be taken.[7]

No tax or duty shall be laid on articles exported from any state.

No preference shall be given by any regulation of commerce or revenue to the ports of one state over those of another: nor shall vessels bound to, or from one state, be obliged to enter, clear, or pay duties in another.

No money shall be drawn from the treasury but in consequence of appropriations made by law; and a regular statement and account of the receipts and expenditures of all public money shall be published from time to time.

No title of nobility shall be granted by the United States: And no person holding any office or profit or trust under them, shall, without the consent of the Congress, accept of any present, emolument, office, or title, of any kind whatever, from any king, prince or foreign state.

Sec. 10. No state shall enter into any treaty, alliance, or confederation; grant letters of marque and reprisal; coin money; emit bills of credit; make any thing but gold and silver coin a tender in payment of debts; pass any bill of attainder, *ex post facto* law, or law impairing the obligation of contracts, or grant any title of nobility.

---

[7] *"No capitation . . . to be taken"*—modified by the Sixteenth Amendment.

No state shall, without the consent of the Congress, lay any imposts or duties on imports or exports, except what may be absolutely necessary for executing its inspection laws; and the net produce of all duties and imposts, laid by any state on imports or exports, shall be for the use of the treasury of the United States; and all such laws shall be subject to the revision and control of the Congress.

No state shall, without the consent of Congress, lay any duty of tonnage, keep troops, or ships of war in time of peace, enter into any agreement or compact with another state, or with a foreign power, or engage in a war, unless actually invaded, or in such imminent danger as will not admit of delay.

ARTICLE II.

Sec. 1. The executive power shall be vested in a president of the United States of America. He shall hold his office during the term of four years, and, together with the vice-president, chosen for the same term, be elected as follows:

Each state shall appoint, in such manner as the legislature thereof may direct, a number of electors, equal to the whole number of senators and representatives to which the state may be entitled in the Congress; but no senator or representative, or person holding an office of trust or profit under the United States, shall be appointed an elector.

The electors shall meet in their respective states, and vote by ballot for two persons, of whom one at least shall not be an inhabitant of the same state with themselves. And they shall make a list of all the persons voted for, and of the number of votes for each; which list they shall sign and certify, and transmit sealed to the seat of the government of the United States, directed to the president of the Senate. The president of the Senate shall, in the presence of the Senate and House of Representatives, open all the certificates and the votes shall then be counted. The person having the greatest number of votes shall be the president, if such number be a majority of the whole number of electors appointed; and if there be more than one who have such majority, and have an equal number of votes, then the House of Representatives shall immediately choose by ballot one of them for president; and if no person have a majority, then from the five highest on the list, the said House shall, in like manner, choose the president. But in choosing the president, the votes shall be taken by states, the representation from each state having one vote; a quorum for this purpose shall consist of a member or members from two-thirds of the states, and a majority of all the states shall be necessary to a choice. In every case, after the choice of the president, the person having the greatest number of votes of the electors shall be the vice-president. But if there should remain two or more who have equal votes, the Senate shall choose from them by ballot the vice-president.[8]

The Congress may determine the time of choosing the electors, and the day on which they shall give their votes; which day shall be the same throughout the United States.

No person except a natural born citizen, or a citizen of the United States, at the time of the adoption of this constitution, shall be eligible to the office of president; neither shall any person be eligible to that office, who shall not have attained to the age of 35 years, and been 14 years a resident within the United States.

In case of the removal of the president from office, or of his death, resignation, or inability to discharge the powers and duties of the said office, the same shall devolve on the vice-president, and the Congress may by law provide for the case of removal, death, resignation, or inability, both of the president and vice-president, declaring what officer shall then act as president, and such officer shall act accordingly, until the disability be removed, or a president shall be elected.[9]

The president shall, at stated times, receive for his services, a compensation, which shall neither be increased nor diminished during the period for which he shall have been elected, and he shall not receive within that period any other emolument from the United States, or any of them.

Before he enter on the execution of his office, he shall take the following oath or affirmation:

"I do solemnly swear (or affirm) that I will faithfully execute the office of president of the United States, and will to the best of my ability, preserve, protect and defend the constitution of the United States."

Sec. 2. The president shall be commander in chief of the army and navy of the United States, and of the militia of the several states, when

[8] *"The electors shall meet . . . the vice-president"*—superseded by the Twelfth Amendment which is modified by the Twentieth.
[9] *"In case of the removal of the president . . . shall be elected"*—modified by the Twenty-fifth Amendment.

called into the actual service of the United States; he may require the opinion, in writing, of the principal officer in each of the executive departments, upon any subject relating to the duties of their respective offices, and he shall have power to grant reprieves and pardons for offences against the United States, except in cases of impeachment.

He shall have power, by and with the advice and consent of the Senate, to make treaties, provided two-thirds of the senators present concur; and he shall nominate, and by and with the advice and consent of the Senate, shall appoint ambassadors, other public ministers and consuls, judges of the supreme court, and all other officers of the United States, whose appointments are not herein otherwise provided for, and which shall be established by law. But the Congress may by law vest the appointment of such inferior officers, as they think proper in the president alone, in the courts of law, or in the heads of departments.

The president shall have power to fill up all vacancies that may happen during the recess of the Senate, by granting commissions, which shall expire at the end of their next session.

Sec. 3. He shall, from time to time, give to the Congress information of the state of the union, and recommend to their consideration, such measures as he shall judge necessary and expedient; he may, on extraordinary occasions, convene both houses, or either of them, and in case of disagreement between them, with respect to the time of adjournment, he may adjourn them to such time as he shall think proper; he shall receive ambassadors and other public ministers; he shall take care that the laws be faithfully executed, and shall commission all the officers of the United States.

Sec. 4. The president, vice-president, and all civil officers of the United States shall be removed from office on impeachment for, and conviction of, treason, bribery, or other high crimes and misdemeanors.

ARTICLE III.

Sec. 1. The judicial power of the United States, shall be vested in one supreme court, and in such inferior courts as the Congress may, from time to time, ordain and establish. The judges, both of the supreme and inferior courts, shall hold their offices during good behaviour, and shall, at stated times, receive for their services a compensation, which shall not be diminished during their continuance in office.

Sec. 2. The judicial power shall extend to all cases, in law and equity, arising under this constitution, the laws of the United States, and treaties made, or which shall be made under their authority; to all cases affecting ambassadors, other public ministers and consuls; to all cases of admiralty and maritime jurisdiction; to controversies to which the United States shall be a party: to controversies between two or more states, between a state and citizens of another state,[10] between citizens of different states, between citizens of the same state, claiming lands under grants of different states, and between a state, or the citizens thereof, and foreign states, citizens or subjects.[11]

In all cases affecting ambassadors, other public ministers and consuls, and those in which a state shall be a party, the supreme court shall have original jurisdiction. In all the other cases before-mentioned, the supreme court shall have appellate jurisdiction, both as to law and fact, with such exceptions, and under such regulations as the Congress shall make.

The trial of all crimes, except in cases of impeachment, shall be by jury; and such trial shall be held in the state where the said crimes shall have been committed; but when not committed within any state, the trial shall be at such place or places as the Congress may by law have directed.

Sec. 3. Treason against the United States shall consist only in levying war against them, or in adhering to their enemies, giving them aid and comfort. No person shall be convicted of treason unless on the testimony of two witnesses to the same overt act, or on confession in open court.

The Congress shall have power to declare the punishment of treason, but no attainder of treason shall work corruption of blood, or forfeiture, except during the life of the person attainted.

ARTICLE IV.

Sec. 1. Full faith and credit shall be given in each state to the public acts, records and judicial proceedings of every other state. And the Congress may by general laws prescribe the manner in which such acts, records and proceedings shall be proved, and the effect thereof.

---

[10] *"between a state . . . another state"*—limited by the Eleventh Amendment.
[11] *"between a state . . . and foreign states . . ."*—limited by the Eleventh Amendment.

Sec. 2. The citizens of each state shall be entitled to all privileges and immunities of citizens in the several states.

A person charged in any state with treason, felony, or other crime, who shall flee from justice, and be found in another state, shall, on demand of the executive authority of the state from which he fled, be delivered up, to be removed to the state having jurisdiction of the crime.

No person held to service or labour in one state, under the laws thereof, escaping into another, shall, in consequence of any law or regulation therein, be discharged from such service or labour, but shall be delivered up on claim of the party to whom such service or labour may be due.[12]

Sec. 3. New states may be admitted by the Congress into this union; but no new state shall be formed or erected within the jurisdiction of any other state, nor any state be formed by the junction of two or more states, or parts of states, without the consent of the legislatures of the states concerned, as well as of the Congress.

The Congress shall have power to dispose of and make all needful rules and regulations repecting the territory or other property belonging to the United States; and nothing in this constitution shall be so construed as to prejudice any claims of the United States, or of any particular state.

Sec. 4. The United States shall guarantee to every state in this union, a republican form of government, and shall protect each of them against invasion; and on application of the legislature, or of the executive (when the legislature cannot be convened), against domestic violence.

ARTICLE V.

The Congress, whenever two-thirds of both houses shall deem it necessary, shall propose amendments to this constitution, or on the application of the legislatures of two-thirds of the several states, shall call a convention for proposing amendments, which, in either case, shall be valid to all intents and purposes, as part of this constitution, when ratified by the legislatures of three-fourths of the several states, or by conventions in three-fourths thereof, as the one or the other mode of ratification may be proposed by the Congress; Provided, that no amendment which may be made prior to the year 1808, shall in any manner

---

[12] *"No person . . . may be due"*—superseded by the Thirteenth Amendment.

affect the first and fourth clauses in the ninth section of the first article; and that no state, without its consent, shall be deprived of its equal suffrage in the Senate.

ARTICLE VI.

All debts contracted and engagements entered into, before the adoption of this constitution, shall be as valid against the United States under this constitution, as under the confederation.

This constitution, and the laws of the United States which shall be made in pursuance thereof; and all treaties made, or which shall be made, under the authority of the United States, shall be the supreme law of the land; and the judges in every state shall be bound thereby, any thing in the constitution or laws of any state to the contrary notwithstanding.

The senators and representatives before-mentioned, and the members of the several state legislatures, and all executive and judicial officers, both of the United States and of the several states, shall be bound by oath or affirmation, to support this constitution; but no religious test shall ever be required as a qualification to any office or public trust under the United States.

ARTICLE VII.

The ratification of the conventions of nine states, shall be sufficient for the establishment of this constitution between the states so ratifying the same.

DONE in convention, by the unanimous consent of the states present, the 17th day of September, in the year of our Lord 1787, and of the independence of the United States of America the 12th. In witness whereof we have hereunto subscribed our names.

GEORGE WASHINGTON, *President,*
And Deputy from Virginia.

New-Hampshire,   John Langdon,
                          Nicholas Gilman.

Massachusetts,	Nathaniel Gorham, Rufus King.
Connecticut,	William Samuel Johnson, Roger Sherman.
New-York,	Alexander Hamilton.
New-Jersey,	William Livingston, David Brearly, William Paterson, Jonathan Dayton.
Pennsylvania,	Benjamin Franklin, Thomas Mifflin, Robert Morris, George Clymer, Thomas Fitzsimons, Jared Ingersoll, James Wilson, Gouverneur Morris.
Delaware,	George Read, Gunning Bedford, jun., John Dickinson, Richard Bassett, Jacob Broom.
Maryland,	James M'Henry, Daniel of St. Thomas Jenifer, Daniel Carroll.
Virginia,	John Blair, James Madison, jun.
North-Carolina,	William Blount, Richard Dobbs Spaight, Hugh Williamson.
South-Carolina,	John Rutledge, Charles Cotesworth Pinckney, Charles Pinckney, Pierce Butler.

Georgia,
    William Few,
    Abraham Baldwin.

Attest:
    WILLIAM JACKSON, *Secretary.*

AMENDMENTS TO THE CONSTITUTION

AMENDMENT I.

Congress shall make no law respecting an establishment of religion, or prohibiting the free exercise thereof; or abridging the freedom of speech or of the press; or the right of the people peaceably to assemble, and to petition the government for a redress of grievances.

AMENDMENT II.

A well-regulated militia being necessary to the security of a free state, the right of the people to keep and bear arms shall not be infringed.

AMENDMENT III.

No soldier shall, in time of peace, be quartered in any house without the consent of the owner, nor in time of war but in a manner to be prescribed by law.

AMENDMENT IV.

The right of the people to be secure in their persons, houses, papers, and effects, against unreasonable searches and seizures, shall not be violated, and no warrants shall issue but upon probable cause, supported by oath or affirmation, and particularly describing the place to be searched, and the persons or things to be seized.

AMENDMENT V.

No person shall be held to answer for a capital or other infamous crime unless on a presentment or indictment of a grand jury, except in cases arising in the land or naval forces, or in the militia, when in actual service, in time of war or public danger; nor shall any person be subject for the same offence to be twice put in jeopardy of life or limb; nor shall be compelled in any criminal case to be a witness against himself, nor be deprived of life, liberty, or property, without due process of law; nor shall private property be taken for public use without just compensation.

AMENDMENT VI.

In all criminal prosecutions, the accused shall enjoy the right to a speedy and public trial, by an impartial jury of the state and district wherein the crime shall have been committed, which district shall have been previously ascertained by law, and to be informed of the nature and cause of the accusation; to be confronted with the witnesses against him; to have compulsory process of obtaining witnesses in his favor, and to have the assistance of counsel for his defence.

AMENDMENT VII.

In suits at common law, where the value in controversy shall exceed twenty dollars, the right of trial by jury shall be preserved, and no fact tried by a jury shall be otherwise reexamined in any court of the United States than according to the rules of the common law.

AMENDMENT VIII.

Excessive bail shall not be required, nor excessive fines imposed, nor cruel and unusual punishments inflicted.

AMENDMENT IX.

The enumeration in the constitution of certain rights shall not be construed to deny or disparage others retained by the people.

AMENDMENT X.

The powers not delegated to the United States by the constitution, nor prohibited by it to the states, are reserved to the states respectively, or to the people.

[The foregoing ten amendments were adopted at the first session of Congress, and were declared to be in force, December 15, 1791.]

AMENDMENT XI.

The judicial power of the United States shall not be construed to extend to any suit in law or equity, commenced or prosecuted against one of the United States, by citizens of another state, or by citizens or subjects of any foreign state.

[Adopted in 1798.]

AMENDMENT XII.

The electors shall meet in their respective states, and vote by ballot for president and vice-president, one of whom at least shall not be an inhabitant of the same state with themselves; they shall name in their ballots the person voted for as president, and in distinct ballots the person voted for as vice-president; and they shall make distinct lists of all persons voted for as president, and of all persons voted for as vice-president, and of the number of votes for each, which lists they shall sign and certify, and transmit, sealed, to the seat of the government of the United States directed to the president of the Senate; the president of the Senate shall, in the presence of the Senate and House of Representatives, open all the certificates, and the votes shall then be counted; the person having the greatest number of votes for president shall be the president, if such number be a majority of the whole number of electors appointed; and if no person have such majority, then from the persons having the highest numbers not exceeding three, on the list of those voted for as president, the House of Representatives shall choose immediately, by ballot, the president. But in choosing the president, the votes shall be taken by states, the representation from each state having one vote; a quorum for this purpose shall consist of a member or members from two-thirds of the states, and a majority of all the states shall be necessary to a choice. And if the House of Representatives shall not choose a president, whenever the right of choice shall devolve upon them, before the fourth day of March next following, then the vice-president shall act as president, as in the case of the death or other constitutional disability of the president.[1] The person having the greatest number of votes as vice-president shall be the vice-president, if such number be a majority of the whole number of electors appointed, and if no person have a majority, then from the two highest numbers on the list the Senate shall choose the vice-president; a quorum for the purpose shall consist of two-thirds of the whole number of senators, and a majority of the whole number shall be necessary to a choice. But no person constitutionally ineligible to the office of president shall be eligible to that of vice-president of the United States.

[Adopted in 1804.]

AMENDMENT XIII.

Sec. 1. Neither slavery nor involuntary servitude, except as a punishment for crime whereof the party shall have been duly convicted, shall exist within the United States, or any place subject to their jurisdiction.

Sec. 2. Congress shall have power to enforce this article by appropriate legislation.

[Adopted in 1865.]

AMENDMENT XIV.

Sec. 1. All persons born or naturalized in the United States, and subject to the jurisdiction thereof, are citizens of the United States and of the state wherein they reside. No state shall make or enforce any law which shall abridge the privileges or immunities of citizens of the United States; nor shall any state deprive any person of life, liberty, or property without the due process of law; nor deny to any person within its jurisdiction the equal protection of the law.

Sec. 2. Representatives shall be apportioned among the several

---

[1] *And if the house . . . disability of the president''*—superseded by the Twentieth Amendment, section three.

States according to their respective numbers, counting the whole number of persons in each state, excluding Indians not taxed. But when the right to vote at any election for the choice of electors for president and vice-president of the United States, representatives in Congress, the executive and judicial officers of a State, or the members of the legislature thereof, is denied to any of the male members of such state being of twenty-one years of age, and citizens of the United States, or in any way abridged, except for participation in rebellion or other crime, the basis of representation therein shall be reduced in the proportion which the number of such male citizens shall bear to the whole number of male citizens twenty-one years of age in such state.

Sec. 3. No person shall be a senator or representative in Congress, or elector of president and vice-president, or hold any office, civil or military, under the United States, or under any state, who, having previously taken an oath, as a member of Congress, or as an officer of the United States, or as a member of any state legislature, or as an executive or judicial officer of any state, to support the constitution of the United States, shall have engaged in insurrection or rebellion against the same, or given aid and comfort to the enemies thereof. But Congress may, by vote of two-thirds of each House, remove such disability.

Sec. 4. The validity of the public debt of the United States, authorized by law, including debts incurred for payment of pensions and bounties for services in suppressing insurrection or rebellion, shall not be questioned. But neither the United States nor any state shall assume or pay any debt or obligation incurred in aid of insurrection or rebellion against the United States, or any claim for the loss or emancipation of any slave; but all such debts, obligations, and claims shall be held illegal and void.

Sec. 5. The Congress shall have power to enforce, by appropriate legislation, the provisions of this article.

[Adopted in 1868.]

AMENDMENT XV.

Sec. 1. The right of citizens of the United States to vote shall not be denied or abridged by the United States or by any state on account of race, color, or previous condition of servitude.

Sec. 2. The Congress shall have power to enforce this article by appropriate legislation.

[Adopted in 1870.]

AMENDMENT XVI.

The Congress shall have power to lay and collect taxes on incomes, from whatever source derived, without apportionment among the several States, and without regard to any census or enumeration.

[Adopted in 1913.]

AMENDMENT XVII.

The Senate of the United States shall be composed of two senators from each state, elected by the people thereof for six years; and each senator shall have one vote. The electors in each state shall have the qualifications requisite for electors of the most numerous branch of the state legislatures.

When vacancies happen in the representation of any state in the senate, the executive authority of such state shall issue writs of election to fill such vacancies; provided, that the legislature of any state may empower the executive thereof to make temporary apointments until the people fill the vacancies by election as the legislature may direct.

This amendment shall not be so construed as to affect the election or term or any senator chosen before it becomes valid as part of the Constitution.

[Adopted in 1913.]

AMENDMENT XVIII.

Sec. 1. After one year from the ratification of this article the manufacture, sale, or transportation of intoxicating liquors within, the importation thereof into, or exportation thereof from the United States and all territory subject to the jurisdiction thereof, for beverage purposes is hereby prohibited.

Sec. 2. The Congress and the several states shall have concurrent power to enforce this article by appropriate legislation.

Sec. 3. This article shall be inoperative unless it shall have been ratified as an amendment to the Constitution by the legislatures of the several states, as provided in the Constitution, within seven years from the date of submission hereof to the states by the Congress.

[Adopted in 1919; *repealed by Twenty-first Amendment.*]

AMENDMENT XIX.

The right of citizens of the United States to vote shall not be denied or abridged by the United States or by any state on account of sex.

Congress shall have power to enforce this article by appropriate legislation.

[Adopted in 1920.]

AMENDMENT XX.

Sec. 1. The terms of the President and Vice-President shall end at noon on the 20th day of January, and the terms of senators and representatives at noon on the 3rd day of January, of the years in which such terms would have ended if this article had not been ratified; and the terms of their successors shall then begin.

Sec. 2. The Congress shall assemble at least once in every year, and such meeting shall begin at noon on the 3rd day of January, unless they shall by law appoint a different day.

Sec. 3. If, at the time fixed for the beginning of the term of President, the President elect shall have died, the Vice-President elect shall become President. If a President shall not have been chosen before the time fixed for the beginning of his term, or if the President elect shall have failed to qualify, then the Vice-President elect shall act as President until a President shall have qualified; and the Congress may by law provide for the case wherein neither a President elect nor a Vice-President elect shall have qualified, declaring who shall then act as President, or the manner in which one who is to act shall be selected, and such person shall act accordingly until a President or Vice-President shall have qualified.

Sec. 4. The Congress may by law provide for the case of the death of any of the persons from whom the House of Representatives may choose a President, wherever the right of choice shall have devolved upon them, and for the case of the death of any of the persons from whom the Senate may choose a Vice-President, whenever the right of choice shall have devolved upon them.

Sec. 5. Sections 1 and 2 shall take effect on the 15th day of October following the ratification of this article.

Sec. 6. This article shall be inoperative unless it shall have been ratified as an amendment to the Constitution by the legislatures of three-fourths of the several states within seven years from the date of its submission.

[Adopted in 1933.]

AMENDMENT XXI.

Sec. 1. The eighteenth article of amendment to the Constitution of the United States is hereby repealed.

Sec. 2. The transportation or importation into any state, territory, or possession of the United States, for delivery or use therein of intoxicating liquors, in violation of the laws thereof, is hereby prohibited.

Sec. 3. This article shall be inoperative unless it shall have been ratified as an amendment to the Constitution by conventions in the several states, as provided in the Constitution, within seven years from the date of the submission hereof to the states by the Congress.

[Adopted in 1933.]

AMENDMENT XXII.

No person shall be elected to the office of the President more than twice, and no person who has held the office of President, or acted as President, for more than two years of a term to which some other person was elected President shall be elected to the office of the President more than once. But this Article shall not apply to any person holding the office of the President when this Article was proposed by the Congress, and shall not prevent any person who may be holding the office of President, or acting as President, during the term within which this Article becomes operative from holding the office of President or acting as President during the remainder of such term.

[Adopted in 1951.]

AMENDMENT XXIII.

Sec. 1. The District constituting the seat of Government of the United States shall appoint in such manner as the Congress may direct:

A number of electors of President and Vice President equal to the whole number of Senators and Representatives in Congress to which the District would be entitled if it were a State, but in no event more than the least populous State; they shall be in addition to those appointed by the States, but they shall be considered for the purposes of the election of President and Vice President, to be electors appointed by a State; and they shall meet in the District and perform such duties as provided by the twelfth article of amendment.

Sec. 2. The Congress shall have power to enforce this article by appropriate legislation.

[Adopted in 1961.]

AMENDMENT XXIV.

Sec. 1. The right of citizens of the United States to vote in any primary or other election for President or Vice President, for electors for President or Vice-President, or for Senator or Representative in Congress, shall not be denied or abridged by the United States or any State by reason of failure to pay any poll tax or other tax.

Sec. 2. The Congress shall have the power to enforce this article by appropriate legislation.

[Adopted in 1964.]

AMENDMENT XXV.

Sec. 1. In case of the removal of the President from office or his death or resignation, the Vice President shall become President.

Sec. 2. Whenever there is a vacancy in the office of the Vice President, the President shall nominate a Vice President who shall take the office upon confirmation by a majority vote of both houses of Congress.

Sec. 3. Whenever the President transmits to the President pro tempore of the Senate and the Speaker of the House of Representatives has written declaration that he is unable to discharge the powers and duties of his office, and until he transmits to them a written declaration to the contrary, such powers and duties shall be discharged by the Vice President as Acting President.

Sec. 4. Whenever the Vice President and a majority of either the principal officers of the executive departments or of such other body as Congress may by law provide, transmit to the President pro tempore of the Senate and the Speaker of the House of Representatives their written declaration that the President is unable to discharge the powers and duties of his office, the Vice President shall immediately assume the powers and duties of the office as Acting President.

Thereafter, when the President transmits to the President pro tempore of the Senate and the Speaker of the House of Representatives his written declaration that no inability exists, he shall resume the powers and duties of the office unless the Vice President and a majority of either the principal officers of the executive department or of such other body as Congress may by law provide, transmit within four days to the President pro tempore of the Senate and the Speaker of the House of Representatives their written declaration that the President is unable to discharge the powers and duties of his office. Thereupon Congress shall decide the issue, assembling within 48 hours for that purpose if not in session. If the Congress, within 21 days after receipt of the latter written declaration, or, if Congress is not in session, within 21 days after Congress is required to assemble, determine by two-thirds vote of both houses that the President is unable to discharge the powers and duties of his office, the Vice President shall continue to discharge the same as Acting President; otherwise, the President shall resume the powers and duties of his office.

[Adopted in 1967.]

AMENDMENT XXVI.

Sec. 1. The Right of citizens of the United States, who are eighteen years of age or older, to vote shall not be denied or abridged by the United States or by any State on account of age.

Sec. 2. The Congress shall have power to enforce this article by appropriate legislation.

[Adopted in 1972.]

AMENDMENT XXVII.

No law varying the compensation for the services of the Senators and Representatives shall take effect, until an election of Representatives shall have intervened.

[Adopted in 1992.]

Indexed Guide to the Constitution and Supreme Court Decisions